An Activities Handbook
for Teachers
of Young Children

Fourth Edition

An Activities Handbook for Teachers of Young Children

Doreen J. Croft / **Robert D. Hess**

De Anza College   *Stanford University*

HOUGHTON MIFFLIN COMPANY   **BOSTON**

Dallas   Geneva, Illinois   Hopewell, New Jersey   Palo Alto

Cover photograph by Ken O'Donoghue.
Line illustrations of people by Susan Avishai.
Other line drawings by Marcia R. Smith.
Beeware sticker on p. 264 designed by D. Jeff Holland.
© The Central-Coast Counties Regional Poison
Control Center, San Jose, CA.

Part 1 Opener	Michael Hayman / Stock, Boston, Inc.
Part 2 Opener	Robert Overstreet
Part 3 Opener	© Jean-Claude Lejeune / Stock, Boston, Inc.
Part 4 Opener	Robert Overstreet
Part 5 Opener	© Burk Uzzle / Woodfin Camp & Associates
Part 6 Opener	© Elizabeth Crews / Stock, Boston, Inc.
Part 7 Opener	Charles Gatewood / Magnum Photos
Part 8 Opener	© Stanley Rowin / The Picture Cube
Part 9 Opener	© Jean-Claude Lejeune
p. 12	Robert Overstreet
p. 80	© Elizabeth Crews
p. 124	James Scherer
p. 156	Ed Keren
p. 221	James Scherer
p. 262	James Scherer
p. 293	Robert Overstreet
p. 316	© Jean-Claude Lejeune
p. 374	© Richard Frieman / Photo Researchers, Inc.

Printed in the U.S.A.
Library of Congress Catalog Card Number: 84-82414
ISBN: 0-395-35762-4

CDEFGHIJ-SM-89876

Contents

Preface

AUDIENCE AND PURPOSE

This book is suitable for preservice and inservice preschool teachers in a variety of settings. Preservice teachers use this pedagogically sound handbook as a supplement in a first course in Early Childhood Education and in courses specifically on curriculum and methods of teaching the young child. This *Activities Handbook* is an invaluable training tool in lab settings, or in the field experience component of the preprofessional early childhood education program. Inservice preschool teachers, as well as day care center professionals and parents of young children will also find the many activities in the book of great use in everyday learning situations.

This new edition of the handbook is offered with the same recommendations made in the past for its use. The activities are intended to be suggestions, illustrations, and examples designed to make the preschool teacher more aware of the great range of possibilities for enhancing the curriculum. They should be tried, revised, and adapted to suit individual needs. As such, they should help to stimulate the teacher's imagination and to create many "teachable moments" in the preschool classroom.

The activities in the handbook are grouped according to areas or topics for ease of presentation and are not intended to be offered within a rigidly defined format. In the integrated curriculum, a pre-reading activity may be appropriate for use in teaching number concepts, or art might be included with woodworking. How, when, and where the teacher presents specific activities will determine to a great degree how this book will be used.

SPECIAL FEATURES OF THE REVISION

Part Introductions and General Introduction   Completely revised and greatly expanded introductions for each Part present relevant background and discussion material for each subject area. The *Art and Woodworking* introduction, for example, now includes a chart showing the breakdown of skills (physical, social, emotional and cognitive) to be developed by art activities and incorporates a thought-provoking discussion of the differences between emphasizing process and product in woodworking. In addition, a completely new introduction to the book provides theoretical background and discussion of early childhood education principles.

Activity Format   Each activity is still comprised of a comprehensive list of necessary materials and a clear, numbered, step-by-step procedure. However, in addition, each activity now begins with a specific well-defined "Purpose" statement.

Helpful Hints   This well-received feature providing many additional guidelines, tips, and related ideas has been retained and expanded in the fourth edition.

Bibliographies   Each Part (and often each major section of a Part) is followed by an extensive, annotated reference list that includes books for teachers as well as children. For this revision, each list has been overhauled, updated, and greatly expanded.

Art Program   New photographs and completely redrawn illustrations enhance this edition's much larger art program. In addition, each photo and drawing is numbered and directly referenced to an activity step. In this way, the details, directions, purposes, and procedures of many activities are now highlighted and illustrated for greater clarity.

COVERAGE IN THIS EDITION

Part One: Art and Woodworking   The *Arts* section retains many of the standard time-tested recipes for preparation of art materials. *Woodworking* is a new addition designed for the teacher who has little or no experience with tools and materials in that area. Working with wood and related materials is highly satisfying and has many practical applications for young children. We feel this often has been overlooked as a valuable part of a preschool curriculum and hope the teacher will make full use of its possibilities.

Part Two: Music, Drama, and Movement   Old favorites remain within these activity groups. Revisions focusing on use with toddlers are incorporated in the *Movement* and *Sensorimotor* sections.

Part Three: Math Experiences   New material demonstrating the Piagetian principles that apply to many of these activities is incorporated in the expanded Part Introduction. There are many applications, throughout the entire preschool curriculum, for the principles learned through these time-proven math activities.

Part Four: Language Arts   Many well-received activities remain in this Part. New books have been annotated and added to the extensive Bibliography, and although some of the favorites are out of print, we have left them in because most are still available in libraries.

Part Five: The Physical World   *The Physical World* now incorporates science activities, conservation, and ecologically related experiences. It is more crucial than ever to introduce children to the importance of conserving our shrinking resources and to take responsibility for maintaining a healthy environment. The activities contained within this Part should not only help children build these values, but should also — through observation and the testing out of simple theorems — help them to think "scientifically."

Part Six: Health and Safety One of the biggest concerns expressed by parents of young children is that of maintaining health and safety. Because youngsters are placed in the care of teachers for increasingly longer hours, health and self care becomes an important issue in planning and curriculum. This new section addresses these concerns.

Part Seven: Cooking and Nutrition Many attitudes about food are developed at an early age. Children enjoy helping to prepare their snacks and learning about their food — how it is grown, where it comes from and what foods are nutritious. The teacher has a wonderful opportunity during these impressionable years to build attitudes and knowledge that help children to become better informed and wiser consumers. We recommend using recipes that avoid sugar, salt and fats. The teacher can experiment and devise others using herbs for flavoring, and natural sweeteners such as fruit juices instead of sugar. The *Cooking and Nutrition* recipes follow these guidelines and now incorporate more whole grains, fresh fruits, vegetables, and unprocessed foods. New information on nutrition, for both teachers and children, is also included.

Part Eight: Computers for Preschoolers A brand-new section on Computers reflects the interest teachers of young children have expressed in this new technology. As we discuss in the Introduction to Part Eight, we are aware that there are pros and cons on each side of any argument about the value of computers for preschoolers. However, we offer these activities with the realization that computers will ultimately be a part of the children's everyday lives and with the hope that computer familiarity will prove helpful to their futures. We have designed the activities for the beginning teacher and student with detailed examples of a variety of programs the teacher might select to enhance the teaching concepts in other areas of the curriculum. All activities have been extensively field-tested with young children and have proved quite successful.

Part Nine: Themes In this final section of the Handbook, many more Theme suggestions have been added to provide ideas for unifying activities around a central topic. Additions include focus on ethnically-oriented theme units and offer many original plans and ideas.

ACKNOWLEDGMENTS

One of the most exhilarating experiences for an author is reading the last proof sheet, when the book is finally finished. Though this is the fourth edition, the experience is no different from the first except that satisfaction is tempered with the knowledge that a book is never really "finished": a book, especially one such as this, must be reviewed and renewed if it is to remain vital and useful.

Revising a book is not an easy task, and many people contributed long hours. We appreciate working with the efficient and professional editorial staff at Houghton Mifflin, who helped improve the manuscript. Pre-revision reviewers offered helpful suggestions. As new activities were incorporated, old ones deleted or revised, developmental reviewers provided critiques. We thank the following people for their candid criticisms:

Dr. Barbara A. Bieler, Eastern Illinois University; Dr. Judith Bode, San Antonio College; Dr. Elizabeth H. Brady, California State University—Northridge; Dr. Helen Canady, University of North Carolina—Greensboro; Dr. Gerard L. Caracciolo, Montclair State College (New Jersey); Dr. Ted DiRenzo, Ted DiRenzo Montessori School (Pennsylvania); Dr. Sharon F. Harris, University of Cincinnati; Dr. Joan F. Henry, Los Angeles City College; Dr. Marjorie Jobes, College of Lake County (Illinois); Ms. Sim Lesser, Miami-Dade Community College; Dr. Cia McClung, San Jose City College; Dr. Ronald M. Padula, Delaware County Community College; Dr. Toni Phillips, El Camino College (California); Dr. Sandra L. Robinson, University of South Carolina; Dr. Mary Trepanier, University of Michigan—Dearborn; and Dr. Carol Woodward, State University College at Buffalo.

Doreen J. Croft
Robert D. Hess

A Special Note of Thanks

The suggestions received during the revision led to improvement in the book, but invariably required a special kind of mental effort — a willingness to toss out old favorites and use the ideas of others to create something new. The experience, often painful and frustrating, was akin to having someone point out all the faults of a beloved child.

Fortunately I had the support and sympathy of many good friends. Kathy Cameron provided useful information that we incorporated into the section on dental care. Karen Buggé gave generously of her time and materials to enhance the section on health. I could always count on Helen Proctor, Jan Bandich, Paul Chesler, Dottie Hamlin, Barbara Hamilton and Mary Graves to come up with more ideas when I needed them most; Libby Kneeland and Lucy Erman added research and creative ideas.

Many others helped along the way. Tom Whiting, owner of Los Niños Day School in Half Moon Bay, contributed a wealth of helpful suggestions from his excellent carpentry program. Michael Kovach-Long collected woodworking tools and offered additional expertise on the subject of carpentry. Dennis and Linda Ronberg of Linden Tree Children's Records gathered many materials and helped with research on the music section. Sharon Wood improved the sensorimotor and creative movement activities immeasurably.

I'm grateful to my daughter Karen for the time she took to help relieve some of the deadline pressures by researching, editing, and typing parts of the manuscript. I'm very proud of her work as a journalist and editor and glad she could be part of this book's making.

The new section on computers required many hours of classroom testing and revising. Ellie Muhlstein deserves most of the credit for her careful, detailed notes based on her experiences in the classroom using the computer with preschoolers. I relied heavily on her ideas and expert advice. I am also indebted to Jim McCauley for his comments on the LOGO section.

Throughout the whole revision process, one person assumed the responsibility to coordinate the project. She gathered data, made phone calls, pulled together materials, ran the copy machine, organized assignments for me to take home from the office, and rewarded me with praise for meeting deadlines. This edition would not have made it to the publisher without Terry Mullen's help. I am truly in her debt.

Doreen J. Croft

An Activities Handbook
for Teachers
of Young Children

Introduction

Activities are the tools with which the teacher fashions a curriculum and organizes the day at the child-care center or preschool. They are specific processes or procedures that can be selected and planned in advance to meet objectives for a particular child or for a group of children. They promote learning through experience — the aim of all the resources that preschools offer to young children.

All the activities described in this handbook are derived from classroom experience. Some are designed to encourage creativity, as well as to promote general learning. Others are intended primarily to provide practice in specific, school-related skills. And others help keep children creatively occupied with something interesting. Many will combine all of these purposes. Although the activities are presented for use in early education and child-care programs, most of them can also be used at home or in situations outside the classroom.

The child benefits most when teachers share the activities with parents, encouraging them to help reinforce the teaching goals at home. Parents appreciate receiving copies of recipes and information about what is being planned for the classroom. Often they may offer their own suggestions and resources to enhance the curriculum.

In choosing and planning activities, teachers recognize that there are times when children's learning is specific. Children learn to tie shoestrings, for example, by direct instruction. Often they learn names of letters and their home address and telephone number by being taught. However, children also learn in less obvious and specific ways. For instance, they may come to understand what *heavy* means by helping to lift a chair or carry a large block; they experience the concepts of *loud* and *soft* during music and sharing times.

Thus, the teacher uses activities in both direct and indirect ways to enhance the natural curiosity, interest, knowledge, and ability of the children. For much of children's learning, any activity may be a rich source of information, and although any one activity may have a primary purpose, it can also be a rich source of additional kinds of learning and experience.

PLANNING AN EFFECTIVE CURRICULUM

The planned curriculum provides a context in which the needs and characteristics of the children are met. The most effective curriculum is an integrated plan that incorporates long-term goals in all areas of the child's development while recognizing that each child has his or her own internal schedule for learning. Such a curriculum is modified and shaped by each child's level of maturation and ability to perceive and integrate the experiences offered.

Effective curriculum planning implies that the teacher is aware of what children need and how they learn, knows a great deal about each individual child, and chooses activities in order to achieve specified goals. What is offered will not be too difficult for children to manage physically or to comprehend. Nor will the activities be unsuited to the goals the teacher has in mind. Once activities have been selected, their success depends heavily on the teacher's ability to match teaching strategies to the learning styles of individual children.

An effective curriculum is based on the following principles:

1. **Education begins at the level of the child's ability.** What children learn depends largely on what they already know. This is not a new idea. Basing much of her work on this principle, Maria Montessori established procedures for evaluating the ability level of children in her classes so that instruction could focus on individual learning. This same principle underlies many aspects of preschool education today, especially individualized instructional programs and diagnostic testing that is used to assess individual levels of mastery.

2. **Teaching should adapt to the needs of the individual child.** Although children within a group may have similar experiences or abilities, they will differ greatly as individuals. Each child has unique skills, special interests and talents, and particular worries about personal achievement. To be effective, teaching must therefore be geared to the individual characteristics of each child in the group.

3. **A child learns best when motivated.** Exposing children to numerous experiences and providing them with a wide variety of materials does not mean they will absorb what the teacher wants them to learn. No matter how attractive the environment may seem from the teacher's viewpoint, each child has a unique response to various stimuli. Some children respond to concrete rewards such as stars on a chart, a cookie or sweet, or a special privilege. For others, social approval is sufficient. The methods for motivating children may differ, but for the most part, children almost always respond positively to the interest and enthusiasm of the teacher.

4. **A child learns best through firsthand experiences.** Preschoolers are at a level of development in which they learn best through the use of their senses. In teaching the concept of *round*, for example, the teacher should provide many opportunities for children to experience roundness physically: touching and feeling round objects such as balls and hoops; making round shapes out of play

dough; and preparing and eating things that are round, such as cookies and oranges. Woodworking activities using wheels are other opportunities to stress the concept of *round*. In addition, children can form circles and make circular movements with parts of their bodies during music and dance time; and stories, pictures, and computer games can further enhance the child's experiences with the concept. It is through a variety of firsthand experiences involving all the senses that children learn best.

HELPING CHILDREN GAIN COMPETENCE

The teacher plans, prepares, presents, and integrates activities in the curriculum. But that is only one aspect of his or her responsibility. An equally challenging task is implementing techniques to help children solve problems and to use the knowledge they acquire. To the young child, problems come in many forms and at unexpected times. They include a variety of tasks, such as putting puzzles together, building a tower of blocks, learning how to manage the wash basin, or persuading another child to relinquish a swing.

Solving problems takes two types of competence. One is motivational: a child must show interest, a sense of confidence, willingness to attempt new tasks, and the ability to persist if the task is not easily learned. The other type of competence involves specific strategies for solving a problem or accomplishing a task. Although they overlap one another in practice, the distinctions in competence are useful as a way of thinking about children's behavior and recognizing which aspect of problem-solving the child is dealing with at a given time. Here are some things teachers can do to help children acquire both types of competence:

1. **Capture the child's interest.** A child's natural interest and eagerness to approach a task are the teacher's best indications of what the child is ready to learn, and there are many techniques a teacher can use to motivate children. A word or phrase of challenge, enticement with an interesting task, or a well-placed toy or piece of equipment are all strategies that can help arouse the child's curiosity. Whatever the strategy, if it works and is educationally sound, feel free to use it.

2. **Assure that the child will succeed.** During the early stages of learning a new task, or when the child is dealing with an unfamiliar situation, the teacher should try to help the child avoid failure and defeat. This is not to suggest that a child should never experience frustration, but chronic failure is likely to impair the child's self-assurance and sense of adventure. Confidence that a problem can be solved comes from successful attempts made in the past. Rewarding small successes can help a child reach his or her goal more easily: "Maria, today you learned how to make an *M*. That was very good! Tomorrow I'll help you learn how to make an *A*. Before long, you'll be writing your name all by yourself!"

3. **Select problems that are within the child's ability range.** If a child has tackled a problem that is obviously beyond his or her ability and failure is inevitable, the child may need to be diverted or distracted: "This is a hard puzzle, isn't it? Here's an easier one. Let's do this together." In addition, a task can often be simplified by breaking it down into manageable parts: "Let's find all the pieces with straight edges and put them over here. We can work with these first and do the others later."

4. **Keep the level of frustration low.** Once the child has begun a task, help keep the level of frustration low so that emotional responses do not interfere with the child's concentration on the problem. Frustration can be minimized by selecting activities that are appropriate to the child's ability level and by providing support through verbal encouragement, physical contact, and the like: "Sometimes it takes a long time to learn how to skip. Here, hold my hand and we'll try skipping together."

5. **Praise judiciously.** Praise is most effective when it follows a specific accomplishment and is given sincerely. Indiscriminate praise quickly loses its value.

6. **Use a variety of materials and situations.** Children solve problems and learn tasks best through active involvement and by using materials that involve more than one sensory mode. In learning words or letters, for example, children benefit from manipulating letters on a magnetic board, sounding out words, listening to stories, placing words on a flannelboard, playing an alphabet game on the computer, and tracing letters with a felt-tipped pen. All these activities help the child experience words and letters in varied and significant ways.

7. **Observe the child's strategy and give useful feedback.** Each child attempts to solve problems in his or her own way. Discover which strategies a child is using and make suggestions that will help him or her learn from mistakes: "The pieces won't fit when you force them together. Let's try it another way."

8. **Encourage the child to try alternative methods.** Children are less likely to become discouraged if they know that there is more than one way to solve a problem. The teacher can help by asking, "Can you think of another way to try that?" or by giving encouragement: "That doesn't quite do it, but I know you can get it if you try other ways."

9. **Explain, label, and identify the task.** Talk to children as you watch them work on a task. Describe what is happening; help them see a situation as you see it. Label things, put feelings into words, and use vocabulary that fits what a child is doing.

10. **Provide repeated experiences with similar problems.** Competence in problem-solving comes with practice. A child learns to erect a tall block structure from accumulated experiences in constructing with materials of different kinds and shapes. A child learns to get along with others from repeated interactions with different people. A rich variety of experiences helps children acquire the skills needed to approach problems in different ways.

11. **Encourage the child to use a plan.** Children learn a great deal from trial and error, but they can also be encouraged to use a

plan and think about a task in advance. Encourage children to anticipate what will happen; ask them to recall what happened the last time and help them realize that they may be able to predict an outcome based on past experiences. Help the child verbalize his or her plan and talk about it after it has been carried out. Review and repeat the steps of the plan to encourage the child to remember his or her actions. Eventually, the child will be able to use memory to help develop a plan for another task or problem.

12. **Be a good model.** Showing children how adults solve problems is another way teachers can help children gain competence. You can talk about your frustration and disappointment when you fail to solve a problem; you can show the children how you choose another alternative, explaining what you are doing and why. Children learn a great deal about problem-solving strategies by imitating those they admire.

Competence in problem-solving is closely related to the development of mental processes. During the early years, children develop cognitive operations and store knowledge that will help them handle the tasks of learning math, social studies, science, and other topics later on in school. In planning and implementing the curriculum, you, the teacher, can help children learn to remember, to organize information, to sort it according to personal experience, and to apply knowledge and mental operations to new situations.

DID YOU KNOW THAT . . . ?

Amount of equipment has greater impact on social behavior than amount of space. When there are fewer toys and less playground equipment, children show more social interaction *and* more conflict.

The block area is more frequently inhabited by boys, the art area by girls.

Active social interchange is highest in the doll area, moderately high in the block area, and relatively low in the art area.

Children remain longer at the art area than the block area.

Limiting the number of toys increases sociodramatic play.

Teacher attention to an activity sustains child interest more than mere teacher presence.

Vigorous activities lengthen transition times and increase disruptive behaviors in subsequent activities.

Children sleep as well in large spaces as in closed or partitioned areas.

Large mixed-sex groups are more raucous than small single-sex groups.

Changes in space affect the frequency of running behavior, but running behavior is not affected when space is held constant and group size is changed.

Boys resort to hitting more than girls; girls are more apt to scold and insult.

The peak age for aggression in the preschooler is around five years.

PART ONE

Art and Woodworking

Introduction

Visit any preschool with a curriculum designed to meet the developmental needs of young children and you will see preschoolers involved in a variety of art activities. A typical scene in such a preschool might include a group of young children mixing paints and watching the colors drip on easel paper. Perhaps another small group is busily smearing finger paint on a table or rolling out large pieces of play dough. A youngster in one corner of the room might be struggling to wet down and shape a chunk of clay, while another concentrates on squeezing glue onto construction paper for a collage made with dried beans and peas. Exclamations such as "I need more red ones," "Watch what I can do," and "Look, teacher, look what I made" can be heard from time to time. The apparent ease with which the children participate and the busy but smoothly run classroom belie the amount of planning and expertise underlying such a scene.

Planning an effective art program requires a great deal of knowledge about the way a young child grows and develops and an understanding of what children learn from art activities. For example, the teacher who offers finger paint to the two-year-old knows that toddlers need many opportunities to see, touch, taste, smell, and experience different textures and colors. The three-year-old who shapes and reshapes a piece of clay is learning about conservation of quantity, which is important to understanding basic math concepts later in life. Making a collage of colored beans teaches color, shape, and number; it involves planning and decision making and exercises the small muscles that will later be used in writing.

The versatility of art materials and activities allows them to serve many purposes in the curriculum. Art activities give children an opportunity to express their creativity. When provided with materials they can manipulate in an unstructured way, children are free to explore and experiment without fear that there is a right or wrong way to do things. But the teacher can also use art activities to accomplish specific purposes. For example, the teacher might at one time encourage a child to relieve frustrations by pounding play dough; another time, the teacher might use the same material to teach conservation of quantity or names of colors and differences in shapes. All are constructive ways to use art materials and activities.

The art activities in this section teach essential skills that contribute to the physical, social, emotional and cognitive development of young children. These skills include:

Physical development

— gross and fine motor coordination
— visual perception
— visual discrimination
— perceptual-motor skills

Social development

— sharing
— planning
— cooperation
— verbalizing

Emotional development

— awareness and expression of inner feelings
— developing self-esteem
— developing pride in competence

Cognitive development

— learning concepts of size, shape, color, and texture
— learning to compare different attributes, such as large and small; long and short; same and different
— language skills, such as communicating ideas, following directions, and expressing feelings
— math skills such as classifying, counting, conservation, and matching
— developing aesthetic and artistic judgment

This section includes many of the teacher-tested recipes and art activities from previous editions as well as some new and revised activities that teachers can offer or adapt to suit the needs of their children. In planning activities, keep in mind that youngsters follow a sequence of development beginning with scribbling and exploring (ages two to four), followed by a preschematic stage (between ages four and six) when children create without any predetermined product in mind, and ending with the representational stage (usually age five or older) when the child plans in advance and has a specific goal in mind.

A new section of this handbook on woodworking includes information for the teacher about tools and their proper uses, procedures for successful woodworking experiences, and a series of woodworking activities that progress from simple to more complex. Teachers who are willing to invest the time and effort to include woodworking in the curriculum soon come to appreciate the valuable experience children gain from these activities. Observe the expression of pride in a preschooler's face when she has finally sawed through a piece of wood, or the obvious sense of accomplishment when a youngster proudly displays the airplane he has labored so long to glue together! An ordinarily distractable child can develop concentration as he or she focuses on hammering a nail. Woodworking is a marvelous outlet for the aggressive child who discovers he or she can work out angry feelings *and* create something original at the same time. Through woodworking, children develop eye-hand coordination, learn to measure, and become familiar with various materials and their attributes (hard, soft, long, short, and other similar concepts). A typically quiet child will often discuss in great detail and with obvious pride how he or she used tools to make something. Such language-motivating experiences positively affect the child's development and enhance the total curriculum.

Woodworking also offers the young child an opportunity to relate to the "grown-up" world by using adult tools to create something tangible. The child learns how to take responsibility for independent planning and decision making, to be inventive, and to see that persistence pays off with the pride of accomplishment. Acquiring the skills to use carpentry tools have long-term applications, establishing an appreciation for fine wood and wood products and a greater respect for carpenters and others who work with their hands.

Like any other creative activity, woodworking can be appreciated not only for its educational value, but also for the fun and enjoyment it offers the child. The suggestions to plan carefully and to present activities systematically should not lead you to expect a specific end product. It is not undesirable, for example, to set out materials for a holiday candle only to find that some of the children are content to pound their nails in a random manner. The real value of woodworking for young children is in the process, not the product.

Start your woodworking program with quality equipment, provide a good supply of raw materials, observe the safety suggestions accompanying the activities, and you will soon find that the enthusiastic responses of the children will make woodworking an indispensable part of your program. As with all the activities in this handbook, those offered in this section should be viewed as suggestions that can be experimented with and modified to suit your needs. The annotated lists of resource materials found in each section will help you devise and integrate new activities into your curriculum.

Basic Bentonite Extender

2 cups bentonite (powdered bentonite can be purchased at most ceramic supply stores)

2 quarts water
½ cup soap powder

Gradually add water to bentonite and mix well with beater. (A blender is preferred. If it is used, start by filling the container half full of water and add bentonite gradually. Turn blender off after a few seconds to check the consistency.) Let mixture stand in a crock or plastic container for two or three days; stir well each day. Do NOT use a metal container.

EASEL PAINT RECIPES

HELPFUL HINTS

1. An *extender* like bentonite reduces paint cost and gives the desired consistency. It also can be added to tempera to make finger paint.
2. Soap makes paint easier to wash out and helps it adhere to slick surfaces like glass and cellophane.
3. Detergent keeps paint from cracking when the paint dries.
4. Alum is a preservative; glycerin and oil of wintergreen keep paint mixtures fresh.
5. Condensed milk gives paint a glossy finish.

Easel Paint Recipe #1

6–8 tablespoons extender
1 one-pound can of powdered paint

3 cups liquid starch
2 tablespoons soap flakes
water

Put the extender in a large container, such as a one-quart plastic juice container. Gradually stir in the powdered paint and liquid starch, mixing well. Add soap powder. Add water until mixture reaches desired consistency.

This recipe makes a large enough quantity so that it can be stored and poured out into small juice cans each day as needed. The paint will thicken and will need stirring and possibly more water.

Easel Paint Recipe #2

1 part powdered paint
2 parts powdered detergent

2 parts water

Illustration 1.1 **Among the skills developed through art activities are fine motor coordination, cooperation, and aesthetic judgment.**

Mix powdered paint and powdered detergent together. Slowly mix in 2 parts water, stirring to eliminate any lumps. This basic recipe can be used to mix either small or large amounts as long as you keep the proper proportions.

Easel Paint Recipe #3

⅓ **cup water**
¼ **cup liquid starch**

**1 one-pound can powdered
     paint**
1 tablespoon soap powder

Pour liquids into blender. Gradually blend in the powdered paint, using a rubber spatula to scrape the paint down from the sides of the blender jar. Add soap powder; blend. Paint should be smooth and thick. Add more liquid if necessary.

FINGER PAINT RECIPES

Finger Paint Recipe #1

**1 cup dry laundry starch or 1
     cup cornstarch**
1 cup cold water
4 cups boiling water

1 cup soap flakes (Ivory Flakes
     works well)
¼ **cup talcum powder** (optional)

Put the starch in a large saucepan. Add the cold water gradually, stirring until there are no lumps. Continue to stir while adding the boiling water, and cook over medium heat until clear, stirring constantly. When mixture thickens, add the soap flakes and talcum powder. Remove from heat and beat with an egg beater until smooth. Mixture should be thick. Store in plastic container in refrigerator or use while still warm.

HELPFUL HINTS

1. Roll up sleeves, put on aprons, and show children where to wash up before giving them the finger paints.
2. Be sure to have running water and towels nearby, or provide a large basin where children can rinse off.
3. Provide plenty of elbow room and plenty of time for children to finger-paint.
4. Separate disruptive children and limit the number who can finger-paint at one time.
5. Add food coloring or powdered paint to the mixture before it is used, or have the child choose the color he or she wants sprinkled on top of the paint.

Finger Paint Recipe #2

1 cup cornstarch	glycerin or oil of wintergreen
2 cups cold water	(optional)
½ cup soap powder	liquid food coloring
2 quarts boiling water	

Put 1 cup cornstarch in pitcher or bowl. Gradually add 2 cups cold water, stirring until smooth. Pour this mixture slowly into two quarts of boiling water, stirring constantly. Cook until the mixture is clear and thick. Add the soap powder. Stir until smooth. Remove from heat and add a few drops of glycerin or wintergreen and food coloring.

Finger Paint Recipe #3

1 cup dry laundry starch	1½ cups boiling water
½ cup cold water	¾ cup powdered detergent

Put the dry starch in a saucepan. Gradually add cold water, stirring until smooth. Add the boiling water, stirring rapidly and continually. Add the detergent and stir again until smooth. (There is no need to cook this recipe.)

Finger Paint Recipe #4

1 cup dry laundry starch	3 cups soap flakes
1 cup cold water	

Mix all the ingredients together for a quick, no-cook finger paint. The texture will not be as smooth and thick as the cooked variety.

Finger Paint Recipe #5

1 part liquid soap (do not use de-   **4 parts liquid starch**
    tergent)   **powdered tempera**

Add soap to liquid starch and let children use this mixture on a smooth washable surface. Sprinkle tempera paint on the liquid to provide color.

Finger Paint Recipe #6

1 tablespoon soap powder   **1 one-pound can powdered**
¼ cup liquid starch   **paint**
⅓–½ cup water

Pour soap powder, starch, and water into blender. Gradually add powdered paint while machine is running. Blend until smooth.

   This recipe calls for a great deal of paint and is useful when teachers want a lot of pigment in the finger paints to teach color concepts or to get particularly colorful paintings.

HELPFUL HINTS

1. Offer finger paints frequently, at different times of the day and in different areas of the school, indoors and out.
2. Finger-paint on a smooth table top; scrape paint off with spatulas.
3. Some children prefer to paint with cold cream on a sheet of oilcloth.
4. Try using warm finger paints and pastel shades.
5. Finished products are less important than the experience of finger-painting.
6. Display art work at child's eye level.

Finger Paint Recipe #7

1 cup flour   **powdered tempera or liquid food**
1 cup cold water   **coloring**
3 cups boiling water

Mix the flour and water, stirring until smooth. (This can be done by stirring the water into the flour gradually, or by placing the water in a jar and adding the flour a little at a time. Place a cover on the jar and shake well between each addition.) When the mixture is smooth, pour it gradually into the boiling water and bring to a boil, stirring constantly. Add the coloring. Paintings from this recipe dry flat and do not need to be ironed.

PLASTIC ART RECIPES

Play Dough

4 cups flour
¼ cup powdered tempera paint
¼ cup salt

1½ cups water
1 tablespoon oil

Mix together flour, powdered paint, and salt. Mix water and oil. Gradually stir water and oil mixture into flour mixture. Knead the mixture as you add the liquid. Add more water if too stiff, more flour if too sticky. Let the children help with the measuring and mixing.

Note: If using liquid food coloring, add it to the cold water before mixing with the flour.

HELPFUL HINTS

1. Use art recipes to introduce children to the metric system.
2. Order metric chart (C 13.10; 304) from Superintendent of Documents, U.S. Government Printing Office, Washington, D.C. 20402.
3. Purchase scales and dry and liquid measuring containers, and have children help translate measurements from recipes.
4. Practice use of terms in the metric system.
5. For more information, write to the Metric Information Office, National Bureau of Standards, Washington, D.C. 20234.

Alum Play Dough

2 cups flour
1 cup salt
2 tablespoons alum

1 cup water
2 tablespoons oil
liquid food coloring

Pour dry ingredients into a large pan or baby bathtub. Stir together to mix well. Stir oil and food coloring into the water. (Let children see that oil and water do not mix. Have them watch to see what happens to the food coloring.) Pour liquid into the dry ingredients while mixing, squeezing, and kneading the dough. If too sticky, add more flour. This dough keeps best if it is placed in a covered container in the refrigerator.

HELPFUL HINTS

1. Mix large quantities of play dough so each child can have a big piece to play with.
2. Add liquid food coloring to water *before* mixing with flour; add powdered tempera to flour *before* adding water.
3. Mix two or three different colors, and let the children knead portions together to make new colors.
4. Mix white, brown, or black play dough and listen and observe differences in the kind of talk or play that these colors stimulate.
5. Provide cookie cutters, rolling pins, plastic pie-crust cutters, and other utensils; remove these occasionally to encourage direct contact between the child and the art medium.

Stay-fresh Play Dough

1 cup flour	**1 tablespoon oil**
½ cup salt	**⅞ cup boiling water**
1 tablespoon alum	

Mix together flour, salt, alum, and oil in a bowl. Pour in boiling water. Mix well and knead. After using, wrap in plastic bag and store in refrigerator. The dough will stay fresh for months.

Modeling "Goop"

⅔ cup water	**1 cup cornstarch**
2 cups salt	**beads, colored macaroni, and**
½ cup water	**other small objects**

Add ⅔ cup water to the salt in a pan; stir and cook over medium heat, stirring 4–5 minutes until salt is dissolved. Remove mixture from heat. Gradually mix ½ cup water with cornstarch in a separate container. Stir until smooth. Add the cornstarch mixture to the salt mixture. Return to low heat and stir and cook until smooth. The "goop" will thicken quickly. Remove from the heat and use for modeling objects. Objects made from this "goop" may be hardened outdoors in the sun.

Note: This mixture will not crumble when dry as some unfired clay products tend to do. Objects like beads and colored macaroni may be added to the "goop" models. Store unused portions in a plastic bag or airtight container.

Craft Clay

1 cup cornstarch	**1¼ cups water**
2 cups baking soda (1 pound box)	

Combine cornstarch and baking soda in a pan. Add water gradually, stirring until smooth. Place mixture over medium heat and cook until thickened and doughlike in consistency, stirring constantly. Turn mixture out on pastry board and knead well. Cover with damp cloth or keep in a plastic bag.

This clay is good for plaques and other models that will be painted when dry.

Cooked Play Dough

1 cup flour	**1 cup water**
½ cup salt	**1 tablespoon oil**
2 teaspoons cream of tartar	**1 teaspoon food coloring**

Combine flour, salt, and cream of tartar in a saucepan. Mix liquids and gradually stir them into dry ingredients. When mixture is smooth, cook over medium heat, stirring constantly until a ball forms. Remove from heat and knead until smooth.

This is a very pliable and long-lasting play dough, with a more elastic consistency than uncooked play dough. Student teachers voted this their favorite play dough mixture.

Baked Dough

4 cups flour	**small pebbles, macaroni, buttons**
1 cup salt	
1½–2 cups water	**condensed milk**
	food coloring (optional)

Preheat oven to 250°. Mix together flour, salt, and enough water to make a stiff dough. Provide macaroni, buttons, and similar materials for children to press into their dough shapes. Bake completed dough models for one hour. For an antiqued effect, brush on condensed milk before baking, or use a mixture of condensed milk and food coloring.

Sand and Cornstarch Modeling Dough

3 cups sand	**2¼ cups hot water**
1½ cups cornstarch	**food coloring** (optional)
3 teaspoons alum	

Mix sand, cornstarch, and alum in a saucepan. Add hot water and food coloring. Cook over medium heat until mixture thickens. Remove from heat and knead until smooth. Store in an airtight container.

Colored Salt Paste

2 parts salt	**powdered paint**
1 part flour	**water**

Mix salt and flour. Add powdered paint. Gradually stir in enough water to make a smooth, heavy paste. This mixture can be used like regular paste. Store in airtight container.

VARIATION   Add a small amount of boiling water to regular library paste; stir well. Mix in colored tempera or food coloring. This liquid paste can be brushed over a completed collage for a lacquered finish.

HELPFUL HINTS

1. Paste, glue, and tape are important for beginners because of the way these materials feel and what they do.
2. First, let children explore with paste and paper, applying paste with fingers.
3. After children have had many direct tactile experiences, introduce the use of paste brushes.
4. Gradually add other textured materials (such as glue and tape) and additional equipment (such as scissors, punches, rulers, and staplers).

Thin Paste

¼ cup sugar   1¾ cups water
¼ cup non-selfrising wheat flour   ¼ teaspoon oil of wintergreen
½ teaspoon alum

Combine sugar, flour, and alum in a saucepan. Gradually stir in 1 cup water. Bring to a boil and stir until mixture is clear and smooth. Stir in ¾ cup water and oil of wintergreen. Makes 1 pint. Store in an airtight container.

HELPFUL HINTS

1. Thin paste can be spread with a paintbrush or tongue depressor.
2. This is a good adhesive for scrapbooks, collages, and papier-mâché.

Paper Paste

⅓ cup non-selfrising wheat flour   ¼ teaspoon oil of peppermint or
2 tablespoons sugar   wintergreen
1 cup water

Mix flour and sugar in a saucepan. Gradually stir in water and cook over low heat until mixture is clear. Remove from heat and mix in oil of peppermint or wintergreen. Makes about 1 cup. Store in an airtight container.

HELPFUL HINT

Smooth and thick, paper paste is an excellent paste for young children to use for any project because it is easy to spread and makes a good adhesive.

Classroom Paste

1 cup non-selfrising wheat flour   1 tablespoon alum
1 cup sugar   ½ teaspoon oil of wintergreen
1 cup cold water   (optional)
4 cups boiling water

Mix flour and sugar in a saucepan. Gradually stir in cold water to make a paste. Slowly stir in boiling water. Bring to a boil and stir until mixture is thick and clear. Remove from heat and mix in alum and oil of wintergreen. Makes about 1½ quarts. Store in an airtight container.

HELPFUL HINTS

1. Classroom paste is an all-purpose paste; it is an especially good adhesive for papier-mâché projects.
2. Add hot water to the paste if it becomes too thick to spread easily.
3. This paste has a softer texture than paper paste and can be stored for several weeks.

Crepe Paper Paste

½ tablespoon flour   2 tablespoons crepe paper,
½ tablespoon salt   finely cut
        water

Add dry ingredients to crepe paper. (The finer the paper is cut, the smoother the paste will be.) Add enough water to make a paste. Stir and mash the mixture until it is as smooth as possible. Store in an airtight container.

Squeeze Bottle Glitter

1 part flour   1 part water
1 part salt

Mix equal parts of flour, salt, and water. Pour into plastic squeeze bottles, such as those used for mustard and ketchup. Add liquid coloring for variety. Squeeze onto heavy construction paper or cardboard. The salt gives the designs a glistening quality when dry. Pictures can be mounted and framed.

BUBBLE RECIPES

Colored Bubbles

1 cup granulated soap or soap powder	liquid food coloring
1 quart warm water	plastic straws
	small juice cans

Dissolve soap in warm water; stir in food coloring. Give each child a can about ⅓ full of soap mixture and a plastic straw to blow colored bubbles.

Fancy Bubbles

1 cup water	1 tablespoon glycerin
2 tablespoons liquid detergent	1 teaspoon sugar

Mix all ingredients until sugar dissolves. Bubbles made from this recipe float better and last longer.

PAINTINGS, PICTURES, AND COLLAGES

HELPFUL HINTS

1. *Never* use aerosol spray cans of fixatives, paints, or adhesives. Some sprays may cause lung disorders.
2. Do not let children play with powdered mixtures like grout or bentonite. Inhalation can cause lung problems.
3. Use only nontoxic, nonleaded paints.

▶ PURPOSE   **To paint a mural on cellophane**

MATERIALS   — Large sheets of colored cellophane
— Masking tape
— Different colors of paint from Easel Paint Recipe #3
— Small cans and brushes

PROCEDURE   1. Tape large sheets of colored cellophane to a window.
2. Give the children cans of different-colored paint and brushes.
3. Have them paint a mural on the cellophane. Light shining through the windows makes a lovely translucent mural.

▶ **PURPOSE**   **To use paint to make prints**

MATERIALS   — Pie tins
— Absorbent paper (easel or construction paper)
— Kitchen tools with handles (potato mashers, cookie cutters)
— Vegetables cut into different shapes
— Plastic table toys
— Easel paint

PROCEDURE   1. Provide several pie tins containing different colors of paint.
2. Let children "print" by dipping various objects like cookie cutters, carved vegetables, or plastic toys of different shapes into the paint and making designs on paper.

▶ **PURPOSE**   **To make spatter paintings**

MATERIALS   — Fine wire screen cut into 6″ squares
— Colored tape 1½″ wide
— Toothbrushes
— Leaves and other flat objects like paper cutouts
— Easel paint in flat containers

PROCEDURE   1. Attach and fold colored tape over the edges of wire screen to frame the squares.
2. Put the leaves, paper cutouts, and other flat objects on trays and let children select materials to make a design on a piece of paper.
3. Place the wire screen over the design and have them hold the frame steady with one hand while they use a toothbrush dipped in paint to "scrub" the wire mesh.
4. When the leaves and wire screen are removed, outlines of the leaves will appear on a background of finely spattered paint.

Note: Spatter effect is best when children use a minimal amount of paint on their toothbrushes.

▶ **PURPOSE**   **To make paste paintings**

MATERIALS   — 3 tablespoons paste
— 2 tablespoons powdered tempera
— 2–3 tablespoons hot water
— Tongue depressors
— Heavy cardboard or construction paper

PROCEDURE   1. Mix paste, tempera, and hot water, stirring until the mixture reaches the consistency of smooth, thick paint.
2. Mix several colors and let children use tongue depressors to apply the paste paint to cardboard. The paintings will have a thick, textured look.

▶ **PURPOSE**   **To make string pictures**

MATERIALS   — Easel paint
— White glue
— String and yarn of different lengths and thicknesses
— Heavy construction paper

PROCEDURE   **1.** Mix about two parts paint to one part glue.
2. Stir and pour mixture into pie tins or other flat containers.
3. Let children dip the yarn and string into the paint and glue mixture, then make string designs on paper. When dry, the strings will adhere to the paper.

▶ **PURPOSE**   **To make cornstarch paintings**

MATERIALS   — Powdered cornstarch (allow one box for 2–3 children)
— Water
— Large table with smooth surface or large shallow trays, unbreakable mixing bowls, or plastic buckets

PROCEDURE   **1.** Pour cornstarch into containers or onto table.
2. Add water slowly while children help to spread and mix the cornstarch with their hands. (Food coloring may be added.)
3. Encourage children to talk about the consistency and texture of the cornstarch and water while they mix.

Note: This is a good "messy" activity for toddlers as well as older preschoolers.

▶ **PURPOSE**   **To make blow-out pictures**

MATERIALS   — Easel paint
— 3-ounce juice cans
— Plastic straws or other small tubing
— Paper

PROCEDURE   **1.** Pour paint into juice cans.
2. Let children dip their straws into paint and blow out designs onto paper.
3. Fold the paper in half while the paint is still wet to make Rorschach-like designs.

Note: Have children practice blowing with straws before introducing paint. Do not use this activity with young children who might suck in instead of blow out.

VARIATION   Let the children blow black paint on glossy finger-paint paper. Then let them dip a finger into red paint and make little "blossoms" on the black branch-like figures to make oriental-looking scrolls.

▶ **PURPOSE**   **To make roller paintings**

MATERIALS   — Empty roll-on deodorant bottles
— Easel paint
— Paper

PROCEDURE   1. Fill roll-on deodorant bottles with different colors of paint.
2. Let children use the paint at the art table to make designs on paper.

▶ **PURPOSE**   **To make eyedropper paintings**

MATERIALS   — Small juice cans
— Easel paint (thinned down)
— Paper
— Eyedroppers of different sizes

PROCEDURE   1. Provide the children with small juice cans of paint.
2. Let them select from an assortment of different-sized eyedroppers to squeeze drops of paint onto construction paper. This is a good activity for small muscle development.

VARIATION   Let the children squeeze different colors of paint into plastic containers of water to make new colors. Provide primary colors of red, yellow, and blue so that the children can mix them to make orange, green, purple, and brown. Make a color chart like that shown in Illustration 1.2 for children to see while they are mixing paints.

HELPFUL HINT

To encourage use of all materials, put seeds, scraps of paper, and other collage materials in separate containers on a lazy susan. (Or a tray can be made and inserted on top of a turntable.)

▶ **PURPOSE**   **To make colored collage materials**

MATERIALS   — Rock salt
— Egg shells
— Pasta of different shapes
— Rubbing alcohol
— Food coloring or easel paint
— Plastic bags

PROCEDURE   1. Make a thin mixture of coloring and alcohol to pour over collage materials such as rock salt, pasta, and other porous materials.
2. Shake well in a plastic bag.
3. Pour into a flat tin and let dry. Use for collage.

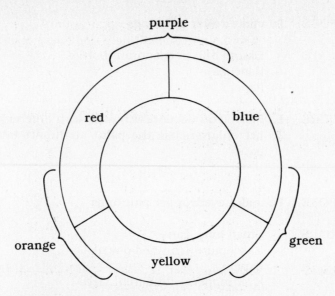

Illustration 1.2   Color chart

▶ **PURPOSE**   **To make tissue collages**

MATERIALS   — Empty juice cans
— Carpet yarn spools
— Small boxes and containers
— Cardboard
— Liquid starch
— White glue
— Paintbrushes
— Colored tissue paper

PROCEDURE   1. Let children use brushes to paint a mixture of liquid starch and glue onto juice cans, spools, small containers, or cardboard.
2. Apply torn-up pieces of colored tissue paper to decorate. Small boxes can be used for gifts; juice cans can be used for pencil holders.

▶ **PURPOSE**   **To make three-dimensional collages**

MATERIALS   — Collection of items such as Styrofoam pieces from packing boxes; small scraps of wood; soft wood (balsa); string, yarn, pipe cleaners; colored macaroni, corks, shells, rice
— Glue and cellophane tape

PROCEDURE   1. Let children attach various objects to pieces of wood to create a three-dimensional sculpture.

2. Let them use their imagination to make an original design. They might want to combine their creations to make one large sculpture.

▶ **PURPOSE**   **To make colored sand paintings**

MATERIALS   — Liquid starch
              — White glue
              — Plastic squeeze bottles
              — Fine-grain white sand
              — Powdered paint
              — Newspapers
              — Construction paper

PROCEDURE   1. Mix equal parts of liquid starch and white glue together and pour into plastic squeeze bottles.
              2. Mix sand and powdered paint together and spread the mixture on large sheets of newspaper.
              3. Let the children squeeze liquid glue designs onto construction paper and then turn the paper, design side down, onto the colored sand. Many lovely sand-painting effects can be made by varying the colors of construction paper and sand.

▶ **PURPOSE**   **To make finger etchings**

MATERIALS   — Masking tape
              — Liquid starch
              — Powdered paint
              — Easel paper or colored newsprint

PROCEDURE   1. Use masking tape to delineate an area on the surface of a smooth table the same size as the easel paper or colored newsprint you plan to use.
              2. Let child finger-paint on the outlined table area, using liquid starch and a choice of powdered paints sprinkled over the starch.
              3. When the child has finished his or her table-top design, take it off by smoothing the newsprint over the design. Vary the colors of paper for different effects. (See Illustration 1.3.)

Note: This technique can be used to make prints of the sun, moon, stars, or other specific designs.

▶ **PURPOSE**   **To make blotter art pictures**

MATERIALS   — Easel paint
              — Water
              — Eyedroppers
              — Straws

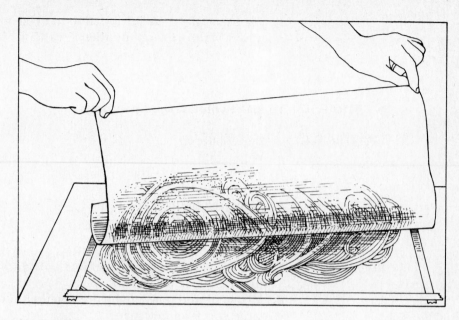

Illustration 1.3   **Finger etching**

— Blotter paper
— Transparent self-sticking shelf paper

PROCEDURE
1. Thin easel paints with water.
2. Give the children small containers of paint and let them use eye-droppers and straws to make designs on white or colored blotter paper.
3. The finished work can be mounted on contrasting colors of construction paper and covered with transparent self-sticking paper to make an effective display.

▶ **PURPOSE**   **To make colored cornmeal paintings**

MATERIALS
— Powdered paint
— Cornmeal
— Small pie tins
— White glue
— Liquid starch or water
— Cotton swabs
— Small brushes
— Plastic spoons
— Colored cornmeal
— Paper

PROCEDURE
1. Mix powdered paint with cornmeal.
2. Give children small pie tins partially filled with a mixture of white glue and liquid starch or water.
3. Let them use cotton swabs, small brushes, and plastic spoons to paint on construction paper.

4. Sprinkle colored cornmeal over the paintings and shake off excess. A variety of colors can be stored in different jars on the shelf for future use.

▶ **PURPOSE** **To make sandpaper paintings**

MATERIALS
— Old crayons of several colors
— Sheets of fine-grained sandpaper
— Oven

PROCEDURE
1. Preheat oven to 250°.
2. Give each child a small sheet of sandpaper and an assortment of old crayons to make designs on the sandpaper. (Have them bear down hard on the crayons, making thick, heavy strokes. Drawings with lots of color provide the best results.)
3. Place each "painting" on a cookie sheet in the oven for 15 seconds. The oven door can be left ajar so children can watch the crayons melt.
4. Use pot holders to remove the cookie sheets from the oven and let the colored sandpaper cool. Finished work can be mounted on contrasting colors of construction paper and framed.

▶ **PURPOSE** **To make texture pictures**

MATERIALS
— Collection of items such as feathers, dry cereals, sequins, textured materials, scrap tiles, pine cones, seed pods, pebbles, shells, buttons, and egg shells
— Glue
— Brushes
— Pieces of smooth scrap lumber about 6″ × 9″

PROCEDURE
1. Let children make texture pictures by gluing items of different textures on wood.
2. When pictures are dry, blindfold the children and have them identify smooth and rough items and describe what they feel.

▶ **PURPOSE** **To make transparent pictures with waxed paper**

MATERIALS
— Scraps of colored tissue paper
— Small leaves and flower petals
— Bits of crayon scrapings
— Scraps of material
— Waxed paper cut into 12″ squares
— Iron

PROCEDURE
1. Let children make a design using the above materials on one sheet of waxed paper.

2. When they have finished, cover it with another piece of waxed paper that is the same size and iron the sheets together.
3. Hang the pictures in a window where the light can shine through.

Note: An adult should do the ironing. Use an old iron that you won't need anymore. Be sure to have a thick padding between the iron and table top or whatever board you use. An ironing pad can be made with old mattress pads and discarded sheets. A small slip of paper with the child's name can be inserted between the sheets of waxed paper before ironing for easier identification.

▶ PURPOSE   **To make patterns on blueprint paper**

MATERIALS   — Blueprint paper
             — 12″-square board
             — 12″-square piece of glass, ¼″ thick
             — Collection of items such as leaves, feathers, flower petals, and other interesting flat shapes
             — 1-gallon glass jar with lid
             — Ammonia

PROCEDURE   1. Place the blueprint paper colored side up on the board.
             2. Have children make patterns with the collected items.
             3. Cover with sheet of glass and place in direct sun for 3 minutes.
             4. Roll paper up and place it in a large jar containing a small amount (about 1 tablespoon) of ammonia.
             5. Place the lid on the jar and wait until the fumes from the ammonia turn the paper blue. Patterns of the art design will be white.

VARIATION   Use cutouts of profiles or handprints for patterns.

▶ PURPOSE   **To make chalk paintings**

MATERIALS   — Pie tins or flat pans
             — Liquid starch
             — Water
             — Large, flat paintbrushes
             — Smooth paper
             — 1″×4″ colored chalk

PROCEDURE   1. Provide pans of liquid starch mixed with a small amount of water for children to paint onto smooth paper (finger-paint paper or butcher wrap is good).
             2. When the paper is painted with starch, have the children make designs on the wet paper with colored chalk. When the design dries, the starch acts as a fixative and the chalk will not rub off the paper.

▶ **PURPOSE**   **To make paintings with buttermilk and chalk**

MATERIALS   — Finger-paint paper
— Buttermilk
— Powdered tempera or colored chalk

PROCEDURE   1. Place about a tablespoonful of buttermilk on paper.
2. Let each child use chalk or powdered paint to make designs. The buttermilk acts as a carrier and the product is similar to finger paint but is more easily controlled by the child.

Note: Be sure to wash chalk or rub it on wire mesh to clean after each use.

▶ **PURPOSE**   **To make Glass Wax art**

MATERIALS   — Glass Wax
— Pieces of dry cloth or sponges

PROCEDURE   1. Let the children rub Glass Wax all over the window and allow to dry.
2. Then let them draw on the window with their fingers.
3. When they are finished, they can use clean cloths to wipe the windows and erase their art work.

▶ **PURPOSE**   **To make footprint paintings**

MATERIALS   — Large sheet of plastic or oilcloth
— Newsprint
— Two small chairs
— Paint
— Large juice cans
— Paintbrushes
— Dishpan of warm, soapy water
— Towels

PROCEDURE   1. Spread plastic sheet or oilcloth on the floor.
2. Place a long sheet of newsprint on top of plastic.
3. Place a chair at each end of the newsprint.
4. At one end of the paper, place cans of paint and brushes.
5. At the other end place pan of soapy water and towels.
6. Have children remove their shoes and socks.
7. Have each child sit on chair while you paint the bottom of his or her feet. Let the child select the color.
8. Instruct the child to walk on the paper, leaving footprints.
9. At the end of the paper, have the child step into pan of soapy water to clean his or her feet.
10. Proceed in the same manner with other children, using the same piece of paper for everyone.

VARIATIONS
1. Select one of each child's footprints and label it with the child's name so that the child can later identify it.
2. Hang the finished product on the wall. Title it "Let's Go Walking" or something similar.
3. The same procedure can be used to make handprints.
4. This project is useful for teaching "right" and "left," counting fingers and toes, and learning the concepts "bigger" and "smaller."

▶ **PURPOSE**   **To make hand-thrown murals**

MATERIALS
— Piece of butcher paper large enough to cover a wall (5′ × 10′)
— Thick paint
— Small sponges, about 2″ square
— Plastic dishes

PROCEDURE
1. Have 2–4 children wear aprons, or preferably remove most of their clothes before engaging in this activity.
2. Give each child a plastic dish filled with paint and 3–4 sponges. Have them stand a few feet away from the papered wall, dip the sponges in paint, and throw the sponges at the wall.
3. Wait until all the children have thrown their sponges before retrieving them. Then let them throw the sponges again.

Note: This is a good activity for toddlers for developing muscle control and eye-hand coordination, learning how to throw, and just for fun when children are restless.

SEWING AND DYEING

▶ **PURPOSE**   **To sew cardboard shapes**

MATERIALS
— Paper punch
— Pieces of cardboard cut into various shapes
— Yarn or old shoelaces
— Melted wax

PROCEDURE
1. Punch holes about an inch apart around the edges of cardboard.
2. Stiffen the ends of yarn by dipping in melted wax.
3. Have children use yarn or shoelaces to sew in and out of the holes in the cardboard. Talk about *up, down, in,* and *out.*

▶ **PURPOSE**   **To sew on burlap**

MATERIALS
— Plastic darning needles
— Yarn
— Pieces of burlap or other loosely woven material
— Embroidery frames or hoops

PROCEDURE
1. Teach children to thread the darning needles with yarn.
2. Help them knot the yarn at one end and show them how to place the material between the embroidery hoops to hold the material taut.
3. Teach them how to insert the needle and how to go in and out, up and down.

Note: Some children will tend to go around the hoop instead of up and down. Many young children who have not had experience will need help initially with the mechanics of sewing. Children also like to weave yarn in and out of plastic berry baskets.

HELPFUL HINTS

Help strengthen small muscles by doing the following:

1. Provide individual hand paper-punches and show children how to hold paper with one hand and squeeze the punch to make holes.
2. Make "train tickets" for the conductor to punch.
3. Provide kitchen tongs for children to pick up articles of varying weights, from cotton balls to nuts and bolts.
4. Space containers at varying distances from one another and ask children to transfer items from one container to another.
5. Sew snaps on separate pieces of material and have children snap them together, first by pushing the snaps together against a table top with just the thumb, then first finger, and so on; do the same with the opposite hand. Then have children hold up the pieces of cloth and snap the snaps together with the thumb and first finger of the right hand, the thumb and last finger of the left hand, and so on.

▶ **PURPOSE**   **To tie dye a piece of cloth**

MATERIALS
— Untreated soft cotton cloth
— String or rubber bands
— Powdered or liquid dye (keep adding dye until desired shade is achieved)
— Container of clear water
— Salt
— Container for dye bath, preferably stainless steel or enamel

PROCEDURE
1. Have the dye bath simmering during the entire dyeing process. (For fastness a few tablespoons of salt can be added.)
2. Have the children tie cloth tightly by bunching it up in a ball and tying with string; or pleating it like a fan (stripes); or picking it up in the center and wrapping string around down to the open

edge (circle); or experimenting any way you choose.[1] You may need to tighten string or rubber bands after the children have tried.

3. Place tied cloth in the clear water until completely soaked.

4. Remove from water and place in the dye. Let simmer in dye for 1–3 minutes, depending on strength of dye and desired shade.

5. Remove from dye (strainer or basket comes in handy) and rinse under faucet until water runs clear.

6. Remove string and repeat the same procedure, omitting step 3 if you want to add another color.

Note: Children should not be involved in steps 4 and 5, for safety's sake.

HELPFUL HINTS

1. Explain that this is the way Latvian children used to color their Easter eggs. Onion skin can also be used in tie dyeing by boiling the material and skins together. The color will vary from yellow to brown. Darker shades result from longer boiling in a larger quantity of onion skins.

2. Discuss how people of different cultures dye their clothing and fabrics with materials made from plants. Explain how Indian rugs are made. Or use the story of "Pelle's New Suit" to discuss the process of making wool, dyeing it, and finally sewing it into clothing. Children can save shaggy dog hair, wash and dye it, and use it for collages. For more information on natural dyes, see "Dye Plants and Dyeing — A Handbook," available through the Brooklyn Botanic Garden, Brooklyn, New York.

3. Other natural dyes are outer leaves of purple cabbage, lupine, silver dollar eucalyptus, and fennel.

▶ **PURPOSE**   **To use onion skin for dyeing a design**

MATERIALS   — Bag of onion skins (available free at produce markets)
— 8″ squares of cloth
— Eggs
— Bits of rice, leaves, and flower petals
— String
— Pot for boiling eggs

PROCEDURE   1. Place 6–8 layers of onion skin on each piece of cloth.
2. Place bits of design material (rice, leaves, or flower petals, etc.) on top of the onion skin.

---

[1] Many beautiful designs are created by accident, and most techniques are acquired through practice, experience, and experimentation.

3. Place an egg on top of the above materials and wrap carefully.
4. Tie the cloth tightly around the egg and onion skin.
5. Put wrapped egg in a pot of water and boil for 30 minutes.
6. Cool and untie egg.

Note: Children should not be involved in step 5.

PROJECTS

▶ **PURPOSE**   **To make Styrofoam art**

MATERIALS — Styrofoam meat trays
— Spackle or glue
— Colored pasta in different shapes
— Natural materials such as leaves, pebbles, and shells

PROCEDURE 1. Give each child a Styrofoam tray.
2. Let them select materials (such as pasta, leaves, and so on) to spackle or glue into a display.

▶ **PURPOSE**   **To make soap snow**

MATERIALS — 2 cups soap powder
— ½ cup water
— Egg beater
— Cardboard
— Cookie press or pastry tube

PROCEDURE 1. Whip soap powder with water to consistency of thick whipped cream.
2. Dip hands in water before molding with this mixture.
3. Use soap snow for "frosting" cardboard by pressing through a cookie press or pastry tube. Soap snow will dry to a porous texture and last for weeks.

▶ **PURPOSE**   **To decorate containers with pasta and paste**

MATERIALS — Variety of pasta shapes
— White glue
— Empty juice cans and other small containers
— Easel paint
— Small brushes

PROCEDURE 1. Give children an assortment of pasta to glue onto the outsides of juice cans.
2. When the designs are dry, let them paint the pasta different colors. The cans may be used for gifts.

HELPFUL HINTS

1. Plan art activities to provide diverse experiences: finger-painting (process oriented); tie dyeing (product oriented); making murals (group oriented).
2. Plan activities so children have to work together to complete a project.
3. Plan some activities that allow children to work independently.
4. Encourage male teachers and volunteers to supervise and participate in all areas of the arts.

▶ **PURPOSE**   **To use paper plates to make a dragon**

MATERIALS — Paper plates of varying sizes
— Paint
— Glitter (optional)[2]
— Glue
— Construction paper

PROCEDURE 1. Have children paint paper plates.
2. When dry, brush with glue and sprinkle with glitter.
3. Make a dragon mural by designing a dragon head and using the plates from large to small for the body and tail of the dragon. (A dramatic-looking dragon can be made by using green paper plates and gold glitter.)

▶ **PURPOSE**   **To make designs on a nail board**

MATERIALS — Nails or furniture tacks
— 6″ x 8″ boards
— Rubber bands of different colors
— Small colored wires

PROCEDURE 1. Hammer small nails or furniture tacks into a rectangular board.
2. Give the children a good supply of rubber bands and flexible colored wires to stretch and bend across and around the nails.

▶ **PURPOSE**   **To use spackle to make imprints**

MATERIALS — Spackling powder (available at paint or hardware stores)
— Water
— Tops of cottage cheese cartons
— Powdered paint

---

[2]Glitter is made of ground aluminum or glass and can be harmful if rubbed into the skin or eyes. The teacher should exercise judgment in determining whether or not such materials are safe for children to use.

PROCEDURE
1. Mix spackling powder with water to the consistency of whipped cream. Be sure mixture is free of lumps.
2. Pour the mixture into cottage cheese carton tops and let each child make an imprint of his or her hand.
3. Powdered paint can be added to the spackle if desired. Or the spackle can be used to make a collage containing bits of twigs, leaves, and other natural materials.

Note: Spackle is superior to plaster of Paris because it dries more slowly, which gives the children time to make their imprints or to change their minds while making designs. The finished product takes 40–60 minutes to dry.

▶ **PURPOSE**   **To make sand castings**

MATERIALS
— Imprint materials, such as shells and juice cans
— Wet sand
— Plaster of Paris
— Candle wax, wicks

PROCEDURE
1. Have children make an imprint in wet sand with their hands or feet or by using juice cans and the like.
2. Pour plaster of Paris or melted candle wax into the imprint. (Insert wick if using candle wax.)
3. Remove wax or plaster of Paris when cool and hard. (See Illustration 1.4.)

▶ **PURPOSE**   **To make a bird feeder from a pine cone**

MATERIALS
— Flour
— Water
— Tongue depressor
— Pine cone
— Bird seed
— Red ribbon or yarn

PROCEDURE
1. Mix flour and water in a bowl to make a thick paste.
2. Have the children spread paste on their pine cone with a tongue depressor.
3. Let them roll their pine cones in a container of bird seed.
4. Tie a piece of red ribbon or yarn around the top of each pine cone and hang them outside on tree limbs.

Note: Attach a name tag to each ribbon. The color red is often used to attract birds.

▶ **PURPOSE**   **To make a kazoo**

MATERIALS
— 1 toilet-tissue tube
— Assorted fabrics cut into different shapes
— ¼ cup white glue
— ½ cup liquid starch

Illustration 1.4 **Making sand castings**

— Paintbrushes
— Wax paper or aluminum foil
— Rubber bands

PROCEDURE
1. Have children dip their brushes into the mixture of glue and starch and paint their tubes.
2. After covering each tube with fabric, apply a light coat of glue and starch mixture and let dry.
3. Punch a hole about an inch and a half from the top of the tube.
4. Cut a circle large enough to cover the bottom of the tube out of wax paper.
5. Attach wax paper to kazoo with a rubber band.

▶ **PURPOSE** **To make melted designs with resin crystals**

MATERIALS
— Resin crystals
— Cookie sheets
— Aluminum foil
— Wire cooling racks
— Plastic containers
— Spoons

PROCEDURE
1. Preheat oven to 450° or 475°.
2. Line cookie sheets with foil and pour crystals into containers.
3. Give each child a spoon and have them make designs by sprinkling the crystals onto the foil with their spoons.
4. Place cookie sheets in oven until crystals melt.
5. Remove and cool on racks.

Note: Use pie tins instead of cookie sheets when there are several children at the art table.

▶ **PURPOSE** **To make *pinata* pigs**

MATERIALS
— Newspaper
— Balloons
— Water
— White glue or classroom paste thinned with water
— Paintbrushes with 1−1½"-wide bristles
— Easel paints or water colors
— 6" pieces of string or curly ribbon for tails

PROCEDURE
1. Have children shred newspapers by tearing into strips 2–3 inches wide.
2. Inflate balloons.
3. Soak some of the paper in water and apply two layers of damp paper to balloons.
4. Coat the paper with glue or paste. Attach two more layers of damp paper.
5. Make pig's legs, snout, and ears out of construction paper and

glue them onto each balloon. Add coiled string or ribbon to form tails.

6. Apply three more layers of shredded paper, using glue or paste instead of water.

7. When dry, let children paint their pigs.

Bibliography of Resources

BOOKS ABOUT ART ACTIVITIES

Carmichael, Viola S. *Curriculum Ideas for Young Children.* Los Angeles: Southern California Association for the Education of Young Children, 1971. Presents ideas for arts and crafts activities under such topics as homes and families, occupations, community helpers, transportation, and seasons.

Cherry, Clare. *Creative Art for the Developing Child.* Belmont, Calif.: Pitman, 1972. Discusses child development, programs, and directions for art activities, including woodworking and printmaking, for children ages two to six.

Croft, Doreen. *Recipes for Busy Little Hands.* Palo Alto, Calif. (585 N. California Ave.), 1973. Booklet compiled for use with student teachers in a college nursery-school training program. The basic recipes for easel paints, finger paints, graphic and plastic art materials were contributed by teachers from other preschool programs and include an unusual dough recipe from the People's Republic of China. A section on most-used finger plays and another on cooking recipes is included.

Frank, Marjorie. *I Can Make a Rainbow.* Nashville, Tenn.: Incentive Publications, 1976. Offers many ideas for arts and crafts activities.

Gregg, Elizabeth. *What to Do When There's Nothing to Do.* New York: Dell Publishing Co., Inc., 1970. Designed by staff members of the Boston Children's Medical Center as a mother's handbook. It includes 601 play ideas for young children with good suggestions and information about the interests of preschoolers at different age levels. Uses simple materials found in the home, such as surprise and comfort bags filled with things like gummed labels and paper, dry cereal, miniature toys, and so forth, to give to the child when mother has to take him or her to the doctor or on a trip when boredom is likely to set in. Other projects call for the use of milk cartons, pots and pans, cereal boxes, old nylons, and the like.

Haskell, Lendall. *Art in the Early Childhood Years.* Columbus, Ohio: Merrill, 1979. How to select and plan art activities by age level, stressing "found" objects. Illustrated with photographs.

Herberholz, Barbara. *Early Childhood Art.* 2nd ed. Dubuque, Iowa: Brown, 1979. Focuses on significant art tasks for children in preschool through third grade. Describes materials and processes with photo illustrations.

Hoover, F. Louis. *Art Activities for the Very Young.* Worcester, Mass.: Davis, 1961. Activities for children ages three to six, including stitchery, puppets, finger painting, and stenciling. Some activities may be too difficult for the very young, but the teacher will find helpful hints and suggestions on involving young children in art activities.

Maxim, George W. *The Sourcebook.* Belmont, Calif.: Wadsworth, 1981. Offers many ideas for activities in all areas of the curriculum that are appropriate for preschoolers and infants.

Mayesky, Mary, et al. *Creative Activities for Young Children.* New York: Delmar, 1980. Activities in arts, crafts, dramatics, play, and other curriculum areas for children ages three to five.

Mergeler, Karen. *Too Good to Eat! The Art of Dough Sculpture.* Santa Ana, Calif.: Folk Art Publications, 1972. Traces the history of dough art in ancient cultures with lovely examples and illustrations. Provides recipes to help the reader explore the magic of the baking art. Includes procedures for baker's clay, bread dough, making sculptures, antiquing, and glazing dough. Interesting for the teacher and adaptable to simpler projects for children.

National Association for the Education of Young Children. *Water, Sand and Mud as Play Materials.* Washington, D.C.: NAEYC Publications, 1959. An excellent little booklet providing a rationale for the use of plastic and fluid materials in a curriculum for young children. Many ideas for promoting outdoor play with water, sand, mud, clay, and so on.

Pile, Naomi F. *Art Experiences for Young Children.* New York: Macmillan, 1973. Classroom anecdotes illustrate ways of interacting with preschoolers to encourage artistic expression. Includes the use of a variety of art materials to increase children's visual awareness.

Pitcher, Evelyn Goodenough, et al. *Helping Young Children Learn.* 3rd ed. Columbus, Ohio: Merrill, 1979. Designed for teachers of young children, this book presents activities and guidelines for the preschool curriculum. Some of the areas include science, art, music, literature, and academic preliminaries with helpful discussions on the teacher's role.

BOOKS ABOUT ART FOR THE TEACHER

Greenberg, Pearl, et al. *Art Education: Elementary.* Washington, D.C.: The National Art Education Association, 1972. A compilation of articles written by a task force of specialists in elementary education. It covers such topics as the child-centered art program, perceptual and behavioral approaches to art, the role of the teacher, and the uses of TV and films.

Hartley, Ruth E., et al. *Understanding Children's Play.* New York: Columbia University Press, 1952. A text based on many observations in the nursery school and on case histories conducted by psychologists exploring the value of play experiences for different types of children. The book covers such topics as dramatic play, music and movement, and water play as well as the art areas such as clay and painting.

Kellogg, Rhoda. *Analyzing Children's Art.* Palo Alto, Calif.: Mayfield Publishing Co., 1970. The author has collected half a million children's drawings and paintings since she began teaching nursery school in 1928. Her book traces the development in art form of the 2–8 age group and classifies the similarities in spontaneous art among children throughout the world.

Kellogg, Rhoda, and Scott O'Dell. *The Psychology of Children's Art.* Del Mar, Calif.: CRM-Random House, 1967. Beautiful color illustrations of children's art showing basic scribbles, designs, and art forms common to all art throughout the world. Scott O'Dell's text helps the reader become aware of the beauty of the "unadulterated vision" of the child.

Lewis, Hilda Present (ed.). *Child Art: The Beginnings of Self-Affirmation.* Berkeley, Calif.: Diablo Press, 1973. A compilation of reports and discussions presented by some of the world's outstanding art educators at a conference at the University of California, Berkeley. The articles include "The Child's Language of Art" by Arno Stern; "Creativity in Children" by Frank X. Barron; and "Questions and Answers About Teaching Art" by Victor D'Amico.

Linderman, Earl W., and Donald W. Herberholz. *Developing Artistic and Perceptual Awareness.* 4th ed. Dubuque, Iowa: Brown, 1979. A comprehensive guide for the teacher interested in fostering creativity in the classroom and developing awareness through experience. Covers ages two to twelve.

Lindstrom, Miriam. *Children's Art: A Study of Normal Development in Children's Modes of Visualization.* Berkeley, Calif.: University of California Press, 1964. Explores the normal development of visualization between ages two and fifteen. Discusses children's art at different levels of the developmental process and helps adults understand what art means to the child.

Mendelowitz, Daniel M. *Children Are Artists.* Stanford, Calif.: Stanford University Press, 1963. The text helps parents and teachers understand the art of children, from the scribbler to the adolescent.

Raboff, Ernest. *Art for Children.* New York: Doubleday. Each book in this series is a short biographical sketch of a famous artist. Includes excellent color reproductions of famous art work. The descriptions and simple discussions of subject matter give teachers and young children an excellent resource for a better understanding and appreciation of great art. Some of the books cover Paul Klee, Rembrandt, Toulouse-Lautrec, Dürer.

Woodworking

WORK AREA

1. Old chairs with the backs cut off make good individual work-benches. Or provide a large, sturdy table cut down to a height of about twenty-four inches (or to the height of a child's knuckles when the arms are held straight down at his or her sides).
2. Place the workbench in an area where the children have plenty of room to walk around the table without disturbing others.
3. Carpentry activities should be situated away from other distractions and out of the pathway of wheel toys.
4. No more than four youngsters (four to five years old) should be allowed in the work area at one time if tools are being used.

TOOLS AND MATERIALS

Quality tools are a *must.* Toy hammers and saws do not hold up and children are frustrated by unsuccessful experiences with inferior equipment. An initial investment in quality tools will be more than compensated by the likelihood of greater success in your program. You'll save money in the long run too, because tools will not need to be replaced as often.

HAMMERS Select some seven-ounce hammers and some weighing between eight and ten ounces. The face of the hammer should be smooth with no pit marks.

Handles should be smooth and small enough for the child's hand to grip, measuring about 11½ inches from handle to head (the Vaughan "Little Pro" and the Estwing E3-12C are good choices). Some teachers like to cut the handles down to accomodate children who prefer holding the handle closer to the head.

Some of the hammers should have claws so nails can be removed. Inexperienced children should use the ball peen hammerheads with rounded ends for safety.

SAWS A *crosscut saw* is used for cutting across the grain of wood. For young children, blades sixteen to twenty inches long are the most comfortable to use. The more teeth or points per inch, the finer the cut. Saws with eight points per inch are used for coarse work; those with ten points are used for finer work; and twelve-point saws are good for finishing if you want to avoid a lot of sanding. It is a good idea to have a child try the handle for comfort before purchasing a saw.

The *ripsaw* is used for cutting with the grain. It has five or six large teeth per inch and is useful for cutting through wood quickly and when the rough finish is not a problem.

A *backsaw* is a crosscut saw, used for cutting wood across the grain. It has a rectangular blade held rigid by a reinforcing piece of metal along the top edge that strengthens the saw and ensures a straight cut.

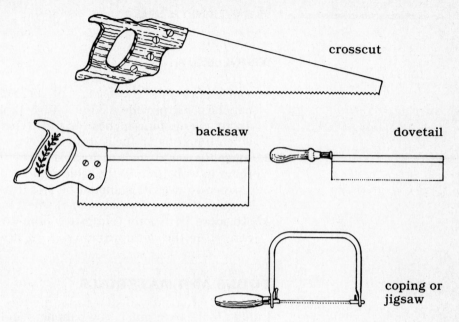

Illustration 1.5 **Four different types of saws**

A *dovetail saw* resembles a backsaw. It has a screwdriver-like handle and a short blade reinforced along the top edge. The blade has fine teeth designed for cabinet work.

The *coping saw* or *jigsaw* consists of a slender, short blade that can be inserted in a U-shaped frame. The advantage of the coping saw is that the direction of the teeth of the blades does not matter. The blade is less likely to bind against the wood if the child uses too much pressure. A supply of replacement blades should be kept on hand. (Use medium or fine blades only; coarse blades will break too easily.)

All of these saws are good choices for young children because they are shorter than the common crosscut saws and easier to handle.

Sawing with a dull blade causes binding and pinching against the wood. Except for the coping saw, all saw blades should be sharpened at least once a year. Store saws so that they do not come in contact with other metal that can dull the blades. (See Illustration 1.5 for drawings of four different saws.)

CLAMPS Clamps are used to hold pieces of wood together while the glue between them dries or to secure a piece of wood to the workbench so it can be drilled, nailed, or sawed. A clamp allows the child to use both hands for working. *C-clamps* come with different size jaws or openings, ranging from one to eight inches. A good size for the preschool is four inches. The *sliding bar clamp* is similar to the C-clamp except that it is more easily adjusted by the child. Be sure to select clamps that will fit the depth of the workbench or table and still leave room for the wood you will be securing.

VISE A *vise*, like a C-clamp, is used to hold pieces of wood. It can be mounted permanently to the workbench so children can secure their own wood.

MITER BOXES *Miter boxes* are made of hardwood and have two sets of grooves in them for sawing straight lines and 45-degree angles. The miter box helps children saw correctly and can be secured to the workbench or table. (See Illustration 1.6.)

HAND DRILL Buy *hand drills* with handles that fit the child's grip comfortably. (A good length is 10¾ inches.) Some drills have removable caps on the handles to store bits of different sizes. The teacher should change the bits for the children.

OTHER TOOLS *Screwdrivers* are good tools for children who have had experience with more basic tools.

A *try square,* or *carpenter's square,* is useful for marking off a right angle.

Rulers and *tape measures* are handy for teaching children to be more exact, but do not hesitate to encourage the use of fingers, hands, and feet for measuring.

Sandpaper of varying grades is useful for calling the children's attention to wood grain. There are several grades or "grits" of sandpaper. The fine grit is 220, medium is 120 grit, and coarse is 80 grit.

Illustration 1.6 **The miter box helps children saw correctly.**

Sanding blocks can be purchased with screws to hold the paper, or you can wrap a piece of sandpaper around a small block of wood.

NAILS The proper kind of nails are important for successful woodworking experiences. Most nails are graded in size by the penny system, abbreviated with the letter *d*. Standard-length nails are identified as follows:

Size	Length in inches
2d	1
3d	1¼
4d	1½
5d	1¾
6d	2

Common nails have large, round, flat heads and come in the sizes listed above. For the preschooler, a selection of 4d and 6d nails is the most practical.

Another kind of nail to consider for the beginner is the *furring nail*, designed for sidings where wire and stucco are used in construction. Inserted in the shank of each nail is a circular washer made of cardboard-like material that prevents the head of the nail from going into the wood.

Roofing nails have large, flat heads. The galvanized kind produce toxic fumes when heated, so do not use them if there is a chance the child's woodwork might end up in the fireplace.

WOOD Use soft wood for nailing. Pine is the best choice for children's carpentry. Other soft woods are fir, cedar, and redwood (the latter tends to be splintery). Ceiling tiles and slats from wooden lettuce crates are also good materials. Lumber is identified by size descriptions, such as 1″ x 4″; 2″ x 4″; 4″ x 4″; and so on, in which the first measurement refers to the thickness of the wood. Wood that is one inch thick works well for children's carpentry because pieces can be easily nailed together. (Finished 1″-thick lumber is actually ¾″ thick.)

Many lumber mills and cabinet shops are glad to donate scrap wood to children's centers. Carpenters, contractors, and workers on building sites are also likely donors. You are more likely to collect materials if you leave a box with the name of your school and phone number on it and labeled "Pick up next week." Occasional samples of the children's work with a thank-you note does wonders for public relations.

Grocery stores can supply wooden crates that can be taken apart. Junior and senior high-school woodworking classes are an excellent source of scrap materials, and their students may be able to give assistance on special projects. For example, students might help drill proper-size holes in wood pieces for such projects as candle holders. One nursery school enlarged action photos of each child, glued them onto plywood, and had the local high-school woodshop class cut the figures out with jigsaws. Individual wooden stands with slots were made so that the children could slide the figures out and play with them or stand them up for display.

Store wood pieces in a sturdy box shallow enough for children to reach in and make their own selections. It is a good idea to have two boxes — one for new and one for used wood. Store boxes near the workbench. From time to time, sort through the boxes and discard wood that is not useful.

OTHER MATERIALS Post or send notices home so parents can contribute materials such as the following:

— coffee cans (to hold nails and other materials)
— cottage cheese cartons
— plastic lids of all sizes
— cardboard
— wire (especially the colored plastic-coated kind)
— baby-food jar lids (for wheels)
— paraffin or bar soap (to rub across the blades of saws)
— spools
— rubber bands
— carpenter's pencils
— Styrofoam
— bottle caps
— linseed oil
— clean rags
— toilet-paper and paper-towel tubes
— yarn
— old drawer pulls
— pieces of leather and plastic
— used tinker toys
— pieces of inner tubes
— end cuts of pegboard
— ceiling tiles
— plastic meat trays
— egg cartons

WHAT TO DO

START SLOWLY Most preschoolers have limited experiences with carpentry, and many do not yet have the coordination to handle some of the tools. Two-year-olds are not ready for complicated projects with hammers and saws. Thus it is important to start slowly, offering simple activities that guarantee success. Give young children (two- and three-year-olds) practice in using vertical wrist movements, such as pounding wooden pegs with mallets. Or let them use their mallets to hammer nails with large heads or golf tees into big pieces of Styrofoam. Pounding large spikes into firm soil offers another opportunity to practice. Wood stumps make excellent spots for hammering nails. Projects such as gluing and sanding give youngsters opportunities to become familiar with some of the characteristics of different kinds of wood and woodworking materials.

ESTABLISH RULES Make rules clear at the beginning of a project. Allow only the number of children you can comfortably supervise. Set limits about proper use of tools before you let the children handle them. Although woodworking often calms a disruptive child, the teacher may have to ask uncooperative children to leave the work area. Many teachers find woodworking activities so popular that they have to maintain a sign-up list to give every child a turn.

SAFETY FIRST   Limit the number of tools available at any one time. Keep them at the work station or in a tool box with a proper place for each tool. A nearby pegboard with an outline showing where each tool is to hang helps maintain orderliness. Have materials such as nails, glue, and wires within easy reach of every child. Keep all tools in good repair.

Maintain constant supervision by monitoring all children even when you are helping one child. Stand where you can see all the children. Encourage everyone to do as much as they can by themselves. You may need to help start hammering a nail or set up a clamp, but do not do the work for the children.

Most injuries consist of hitting a finger with a hammer and getting splinters. Children can generally take primary responsibility for minor injuries by running cold water over the finger or bringing the splinter remover to the teacher. After the splinter has been removed, the child should wash the area thoroughly and apply a bandage if necessary.

Remember:

— Remind children to do carpentry only when an adult is present.
— Teach children to keep looking at the nail while hammering.
— Children who are sawing should be situated at opposite ends of the table with saws pointing away from other children.
— Always look over finished projects and hammer down any sharp nails that may be protruding.

PROCESSES AND PROJECTS

▶ **PURPOSE**   **To glue wood to make original projects**

MATERIALS — Variety of small wood scraps
— Pieces of Styrofoam
— Pieces of corrugated cardboard
— Twigs and sticks
— Styrofoam trays
— Masking tape
— Felt-tip pens
— Fast-drying glue or rubber cement

PROCEDURE 1. Protect the table top with newspapers or plastic cover.
2. Give each child a Styrofoam tray and a small bottle of glue.
3. Let children glue pieces of wood, Styrofoam, cardboard, and twigs together on the tray.
4. Show how a small amount of glue is enough to hold things together.
5. Some children will need to be reminded that their art work will take longer to dry if they use a lot of glue.

6. Label completed work with felt pen and masking tape.

7. Finished products may be painted when dry.

Note: This is a good opportunity to discuss differences in sizes, shapes, and textures.

▶ **PURPOSE**   **To learn to nail different materials**

MATERIALS — Variety of different types of woods, both hard and soft
— Pieces of Styrofoam
— Corrugated cardboard
— Hammers
— Nails

PROCEDURE **1.** Place materials on the carpentry table so they can be reached easily by the children.
2. Have them nail different kinds of materials and talk about qualities of soft and hard.
3. Have children identify which materials are easy to nail and use a felt pen to label the material "soft."
4. Do the same with hard woods.
5. Talk about texture, weight, shape, and thickness of the materials as the children work.

▶ **PURPOSE**   **To learn to nail and remove nails**

MATERIALS — Corrugated cardboard
— Pegboard
— Large pieces of Styrofoam
— Soft wood such as pine
— Ceiling tiles
— Furring nails
— Hammers with claws
— Ball peen hammers
— Nail pullers

PROCEDURE **1.** Let children practice hammering nails into pieces of Styrofoam and cardboard.
2. Then let the children nail pieces of pegboard into Styrofoam.
3. As they become more experienced, let the children nail ceiling tiles and soft wood.
4. Have the children practice removing nails by slipping the claw of the hammer or nail puller under the nail head with the handle pointing away from the child. Pull until the handle is in a vertical position.
5. For longer nails, slip a block of wood under the hammerhead.

Note: Furring nails have washers around each shank so the child can hold on to the nail more easily.

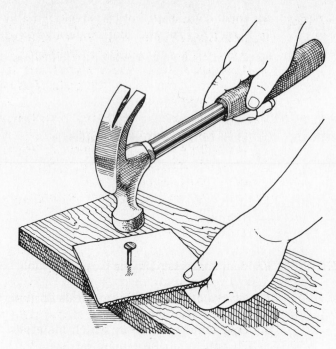

Illustration 1.7   **Protecting fingers while nailing**

HELPFUL HINTS

1. Teach children to get a nail started by holding the nail
   and tapping it gently a few times, making sure to get
   the nail straight. Then they can move their fingers out
   of the way and hammer harder. Getting the nail started
   straight is more important than hitting it hard.
2. Another way to protect fingers is to first push the nail
   through a piece of cardboard or heavy paper. Hold the
   paper by the edge and hit the nail squarely to get it
   straight. (See Illustration 1.7.)

▶ **PURPOSE**   **To learn to sand wood**

MATERIALS   — Variety of wood scraps (cabinet shops are good sources of woods
              with different grains)
            — Sand blocks
            — Sandpaper of varying grades
            — Linseed oil
            — Small plastic squirt bottles
            — Old rags
            — Fast-drying glue
            — Tagboard

PROCEDURE
1. Precut wood into small pieces, about 4″ or 5″ square.
2. Let children smooth the rough edges and surface of each piece of wood with medium-grade sandpaper.
3. Then have them sand the wood with fine sandpaper.
4. Call their attention to the grain of the wood. Discuss concepts of rough and smooth.
5. Have the children wipe the wood clean and squirt a small amount of linseed oil on the surface.
6. Let them work the oil into each piece of wood with a rag.
7. As they work, call their attention to how the oil brings out the grain of the wood.
8. Glue samples of different kinds of wood onto tagboard and label each kind.

▶ **PURPOSE** **To make sanding blocks**

MATERIALS
— Blocks of wood to fit children's hands
— Large pieces of sandpaper of varying grades
— Scissors
— Pencils
— Tacks
— Hammers
— Glue
— Clamps

PROCEDURE
1. Let each child select a block of wood.
2. Show the children a sanding block and explain that they need to cut a piece of sandpaper large enough to wrap around their block of wood.
3. Let them figure out how to measure the sandpaper, making appropriate suggestions to help them (such as how they might use a pencil to mark the width of the block).
4. If children cut the paper too large or too small, encourage them to think about what they did and try again.
5. Sandpaper may be glued or tacked on to the blocks.
6. If using hammers and tacks, secure the wood block with a C-clamp or vise.

▶ **PURPOSE** **To make musical sand blocks**

MATERIALS
— ¼″ or ½″ scrap wood cut into pieces about 4″ inches square (enough for each child to have a matching pair)
— Two wooden spools for each child
— Sandpaper
— Pencils
— Rulers
— Scissors
— Glue

PROCEDURE   1. Have the children place each piece of wood on the smooth side of a large piece of sandpaper.
2. Tell them to hold the wood down firmly and to trace around each piece with a pencil.
3. Have the children cut the sandpaper along the traced lines.
4. Have them glue the sandpaper, rough side out, to each piece of wood.
5. Have children mark the centers of the wood pieces by drawing diagonal lines on the smooth side of the wood.
6. Have them glue a spool in the center of each of the wood blocks.
7. When dry, children can paint and decorate their blocks and use them as rhythm instruments.

▶ **PURPOSE**   **To make a nail board**

MATERIALS   — Precut ¾″ boards about 12″ square
— Nails with heads
— Pencils
— Rulers
— Colored rubber bands
— Felt-tip pens
— Masking tape

PROCEDURE   1. Show the children how to use a ruler to mark dots an inch apart along the width and length of the board.
2. If children do not want to measure and mark the board, let them make random marks.
3. Have the children hammer nails into the wood as marked, but do not let them hammer the nails all the way in or through the wood.
4. Tell the children to start hammering from the center and work out.
5. Let children stretch rubber bands from nail to nail to make designs.
6. Label the boards with felt pens and masking tape.

▶ **PURPOSE**   **To make a hanging scroll**

MATERIALS   — ¼″ dowels about 2′ or 3′ long
— Saws
— Pencils
— Miter boxes
— Heavy string or cord
— Stapler
— Art scrolls (see "To make blow-out pictures," p. 22)

PROCEDURE   1. Have children make scrolls as described on p. 22.
2. Have the children measure dowels to extend beyond the width of the scroll and mark the dowels with a pencil.
3. Have the children place each dowel in a miter box and saw to desired length.

4. Let them measure and staple the ends of the scrolls, leaving enough space for the dowels to be inserted.
5. Tie a cord at the top of each scroll for hanging.

HELPFUL HINTS

1. Children may saw small wedges at either end of the dowel to anchor the cord, or attach rubber bands to each end.
2. Dowels may be painted to match the scroll.
3. As children start to saw, tell them to pull the saw towards themselves several times to make a groove.
4. Use a vise or C-clamp to secure both wood and miter box to the workbench.

▶ **PURPOSE**   **To make a holiday candle**

MATERIALS   — Slices of round wood from a tree branch about 6″ in diameter[3]
— Candles
— Holly berries, nuts, small pine cones, seeds, leaves, and ornaments
— Glue

PROCEDURE   1. Have the children glue a candle in the center of each piece of round wood.
2. Let them arrange decorations around the candle and glue them onto the wood.

▶ **PURPOSE**   **To make a nature hanging**

MATERIALS   — Pieces of ¼″ or ½″ plywood, about 12″ x 14″
— Drill
— Clamps
— Rulers
— Pencils
— Cord or heavy string
— Glue
— Collection of leaves, small sticks, shells, pebbles, or other natural objects suitable for a collage

PROCEDURE   1. Measure and mark two spots about 2″ from the top of the piece of wood and about 2″ in from either side.
2. Use clamps to secure the wood to the table.
3. Have the child drill through the wood.

---

[3] Enlist the help of tree-service workers and someone with a power saw to cut the slices.

4. Turn the wood over and have the child drill through the hole from the other side.
5. Let the children glue objects to the wood to make a collage.
6. Insert a cord through the holes for hanging.

Note: See illustrations for using a drill with a brace and bit. The brace and bit requires complex coordination and is better suited for older children (ages five and up).

▶ **PURPOSE**   **To frame a picture**

MATERIALS   — Colored tagboard about 12″ square
— Lengths of lath or thin, soft wood (1″–2″ wide)
— Saws
— Try square
— Rulers
— Pencils
— Picture hangers

PROCEDURE   1. Help children measure four lengths of lath to fit around the edges of the tagboard.
2. Have the children mark each piece of lath with a pencil, making sure they avoid overlapping at the corners.
3. If the tagboard needs cutting, let children learn how to measure with a try square.
4. Use a mitre box or clamp to hold the wood while children saw the lath to correct lengths.
5. Let the children paint the pieces of lath.
6. When dry, have them glue the pieces around the edges of tagboard.
7. Tape a painting or other piece of art work measured to fit inside the frame.
8. Attach a picture hanger to the back of the frame.

> **HELPFUL HINTS**
>
> Have the children press the handle of the try square firmly against the tagboard while marking with the pencil. This requires coordination and children may need some assistance.

▶ **PURPOSE**   **To use wood scraps to make original projects**

MATERIALS   — Assorted wood scraps of different shapes
— Spools
— Lids from baby-food jars and juice bottles
— ¼″ dowels cut into lengths of 3″ or 4″
— Pencils   — Paper triangles
— Rulers   — Hand drills with ¼″ bits

— Nails	— Yarn
— Hammers	— Hole punch
— Glue	— Saws and clamps

PROCEDURE

1. Children can make all sorts of things with wood scraps. Often the shape of the wood will spark their imagination. A piece of wood with a spool glued on, for example, will become a boat with a smoke stack.
2. An airplane can be made by nailing two long, flat pieces of wood together.
3. Clamp a piece of wood for a child to drill and insert a piece of dowel. Punch two holes in a paper triangle and attach to the wood to make a sailboat.
4. Nailing lids on a block of wood makes a car with wheels.
5. As children become more sophisticated with tools and materials, have them think and talk about what they want to make. Help them plan their projects, using measuring equipment.
6. When children are nailing, turn their work over to check if nails are protruding through the wood. Talk about safety and teach them how to flatten the nails or to select shorter nails by measuring them against the depth of the wood.
7. Be careful not to throw pieces of wood away, thinking children did not "make anything." Often a piece of wood sawed in two or a nail hammered into a block is a treasured project to a child.

Bibliography of Resources

Dawson, Sheila. *Woodshop for Children Ages 3 Through 8.* San Diego, Calif.: Children's Woodshop Publications, 1984. A practical book designed for adults who teach woodworking to young children. Includes description, selection, and proper use of tools. Instructions for projects such as making floating, flying, and rolling objects.

Jackson, Albert, and David Day. *Tools and How to Use Them.* New York: Alfred A. Knopf, 1978. An illustrated encyclopedia of hand and power tools, their history and uses, and how to operate and maintain them.

Skeen, Patsy, et al. *Woodworking for Young Children.* Washington, D.C.: National Association for the Education of Young Children, 1984. Provides information about tools and woodworking. Offers teaching suggestions and ways in which woodworking can be integrated with the development of the whole child.

Thompson, David. *Easy Woodstuff for Kids.* Mt. Rainer, Md.: Gryphon House, Inc., 1981. Simple wood projects for children ages four to ten with accompanying drawings of tools and each project.

Walker, Lester. *Carpentry for Children.* Mt. Vernon, N.Y.: Consumers Union, 1982. Description of tools appropriate for woodworking with children. Detailed sketches accompany photos of each project, such as making a tugboat, block set, lemonade stand. More suited to the older child, but a few activities are adaptable for preschoolers.

Note: Teachers can write to Campus Films, Overhill Road, Scarsdale, New York 10583 for purchase or rental of a filmstrip entitled "Woodworking" (Early Childhood Curriculum No. 802). This filmstrip includes a cassette and guide for developing skills and concepts young children need in woodworking, such as patterning, matching, measuring, eye-hand coordination, and motor skills.

PART TWO

Music, Drama, and Movement

Introduction

In a young child, growth of the body and mind are interdependent. At first, the many impulses received from a baby's sense of touch are processed at a low level of brain function because the higher-level brain structures are not yet fully developed. During the early months, the infant uses his or her mouth for touching and feeling, and then gradually begins using the hands as a major source of information about the environment. Tactile recognition precedes visual recognition, but the environment and everything in it take on new meaning when the child both feels and sees. When the brain organizes sensory information in a meaningful way, cognitive learning takes place. With increasing exposure to sensory-perceptual stimuli, children learn and gain control over themselves and the environment. Learning requires many experiences that stimulate the senses, and young children learn best when they are actively engaged in an environment that provides many appropriate stimuli.

As early as three weeks of age, infants are able to discriminate among small differences in rhythm, speech, and musical sounds. Although the centers controlling music and visual skills are located in different parts of the brain, singing appears to further speech development, and children naturally weave music into their lives. Babies coo and babble and are comforted by humming sounds and lullabies. Early in life, rhythms such as gentle rocking or shaking a rattle engage an infant's attention and interest. And later, at the preschool, music can continue to play a role in development.

Music not only provides pleasure and comfort, but can also improve a child's ability to concentrate and discriminate. The young child's spontaneous movements to music develop body strength and sensorimotor control. Music has helped mentally disturbed children communicate more easily, and can have a calming effect on hyperactive youngsters.

Music need not, and perhaps should not, be set aside as a formal structured activity in the preschool. It is easy to include music, rhythm, and spontaneous movement in other aspects of the curriculum, such as dramatic play and other means of creative self-expression. Music can enhance the informal, unplanned experiences that result spontaneously from a child's curiosity. Teachers can play the guitar, an autoharp, or a recording, or simply sing songs while children are playing. Music also helps make routines and transition times more fun: singing during a field trip or while waiting for a turn makes the time go by more quickly and enjoyably.

The confidence children gain from expressing themselves in musical activities can encourage other forms of self-expression, such as dramatic play. Children who are reluctant to verbalize feelings and talk about themselves when adult attention is focused exclusively on them may readily engage in an extended conversation with a puppet or while wearing a dress-up costume. By assuming another role, children can, in effect, hide behind a facade that protects them from criticism. Children need to be able to play out their fantasies and to express forbidden thoughts without fear of chastisement. Dramatic play provides that outlet, as well as opportunities for language enrichment and emotional development.

Creative expression of all kinds can occur throughout the daily routine when teachers plan activities based on an understanding of how children develop. For example, young children get restless when they have to sit still or listen for extended periods of time. It is natural for children to move — to bend, climb, jump, stretch, lift, run, and dance. Through movement, children develop their muscles, improve coordination, and grow more physically independent. Large muscle movements help to release energy, to develop stronger bodies, and even to express thoughts and feelings.

Creative movement and sensorimotor exercises represent two very different kinds of movement activities. Creative movement is designed to help children become more completely aware of their own bodies and how they express individuality and feelings through movement. Learning to move freely to music may help shy children gain confidence and aggressive children become more peaceful. Activities that help children learn to relax, to stretch, and to relate movement to space are offered so that the teacher can plan a variety of creative movement experiences.

Sensorimotor exercises are concerned primarily with helping children become physically aware of directions (such as right, left, across, over) and other concepts useful in remembering letter forms and achieving a left-right orientation. Guided movement experiences, whether creative or sensorimotor, help young children learn to control their muscles, resulting in better coordination and a sense of satisfaction, accomplishment, and pride in mastering physical skills.

The activities in this section offer young children a variety of creative experiences in the expressive arts of music, dramatic play, and movement. The teacher may find some of the procedures and explanations preceding the exercises helpful in making these activities as useful and effective as possible. One important point to keep in mind is that although a teacher may feel the need to state objectives to justify nonacademic activities such as music and dramatic play, a basic reason for offering them is that they are fun and provide a stimulating and joyful time for children.

Music

RHYTHM

▶ **PURPOSE**   **To move the body in response to rhythm**

MATERIALS   — Piano or recorded instrumental music and record player

PROCEDURE
1. Have children find a place to sit where they can put out their hands and not touch anyone. Play a selection that has the ABA form (starts with theme A, changes to theme B, and ends with theme A). For example, start with a simple melody like "Baa baa, black sheep, have you any wool? Yes sir, yes sir, three bags full" (theme A). "One for my master and one for my dame, and one for the little boy who lives in the lane" (theme B). Then repeat theme A.
2. Ask the children to listen to the song once. Sing or play any bouncy song that is popular with them.[1]
3. Say (while playing music):
   Now as I play the music, I want you to move your body the way the music makes you feel.
4. The next time you play, say:
   This time do something different.
5. When you stop playing, note some of the changes children made.
6. Encourage them to stand up and move as you play.

VARIATION   Use drum to beat a rhythm.

▶ **PURPOSE**   **To make rhythmic sounds with the body**

MATERIALS   — Piano or recorded instrumental music[2] and record player

---

[1] Other suggestions: "Raindrops Are Falling" from the score of *Butch Cassidy and the Sundance Kid* (A&M Records SP4227); "Pop Goes the Weasel" (RCA Victor 45-6180); "The Tartan Ball" (EMI SZLP2118).

[2] Suggestion: "Taos Round Dance" (Canyon ARP142) — a subdued Indian record good for quiet movements as well as rocking, shaking, sliding, shuffling.

PROCEDURE **1.** Have children sit on the floor.
2. Ask:
Who can make a sound using his or her hands? (Possibilities include clapping, slapping various parts of the body, snapping fingers, clapping with cupped hands, and so on.)
If you stand up what new sounds can you make? (Possibilities include stamping, shuffling, tapping toes, sliding feet, heel-toe action.)
What are some of the sounds you can make with your mouth? (Possibilities include tongue-clacking, teeth-clicking, lip-smacking, hissing and sighing.)
3. Play different kinds of music and let the children respond in any way they wish. (See Illustration 2.1.)

HELPFUL HINTS

1. Invite local musicians, perhaps high school students, to perform.
2. Prepare performers from the community by helping them understand that young children are curious, have a short attention span, and want to touch, talk about, and try out instruments for themselves. Try to plan a short presentation that will allow children to satisfy their natural curiosity.
3. Children will often laugh at the sounds of instruments unfamiliar to them.

▶ **PURPOSE**   **To hear rhythm in words**

MATERIALS   None

PROCEDURE   **1.** Sit with children in a circle.
2. Say:
Remember how you clapped time to the music?
Do you know that your names have a rhythm?
I am going to say some of your names.
3. Go around the circle saying the names of the children with one-syllable names: Shawn, Ruth, Ann. Then say some two-syllable names: Mary, Richard, Warren. Ask whether the children hear anything different about the two-syllable names.
4. Ask them to clap when you say "Shawn" or whatever (clap). Then ask them to clap when you say "Richard" (clap, clap).
5. Say the three-syllable names. Ask the children to clap.
6. Either in this session or in a future one, divide the children into groups according to the number of syllables in their names. Have them clap the appropriate pattern according to their names. Ask them how the three groups could work together with their claps to make interesting rhythms. They could try clapping at the same time and hear how three beats take longer than one or two, if rhythm is the same. They could alternate rhythmic patterns.

Illustration 2.1   **Making rhythmic sounds with the body**

VARIATION   Read nonsense rhymes or poems and have children clap to the rhythm of the words they like.

▶ **PURPOSE**   **To play rhythm instruments**

MATERIALS   — Drums and mallets (heads can be covered with lambs wool), tambourines, coconut half-shells, wood blocks, finger cymbals, triangles, sand blocks, rhythm sticks, sleigh bells on leather bracelets, and maracas. (If choice is limited, drums, triangles, and sand blocks provide good contrasts.)

PROCEDURE
1. Use music familiar to the children that has a lively rhythmic pattern.
2. Put the instruments out and allow the children to experiment. If there is one drum per child, drums should be used first.
3. As they play, ask individual children whether they could play another way. Encourage them to hit the drum on various parts of the head and to use different rhythmic patterns.
4. Play loud music, then soft music; slow music, then fast music.
5. The children could play a "call and response" game either in groups or by taking turns being the originator.[3]
6. Use this same procedure to introduce the other rhythm instruments.

▶ PURPOSE **To reproduce rhythmic sounds**[4]

MATERIALS — Empty cardboard cartons, such as those used for oatmeal

PROCEDURE
1. Make up a story based on the children's everyday experiences at home and in school.
2. Tell the story, using the empty carton to produce appropriate sound effects. For example:
   Early in the morning, before it was time to get up for school, Johnny heard shuffle, shuffle. (Rub your hand across top of carton to make a rhythmic shuffling sound.)
   What was that? It was mother shuffling to the kitchen in her slippers. Johnny closed his eyes and listened again. Then he heard. . . .
3. Use simple rhythmic sounds at first, such as click, click, click (scrambling eggs with a fork); clump, clump (Dad's footsteps); tap, tap, tap (the dog). Then increase in difficulty with combinations of sounds — bump, bump, bumpety, bump (brother going down the stairs, dog dragging a slipper or playing with a ball, and so on).
4. After the children have had several opportunities to listen and watch how you do it, select two or three children to help tell a story.
5. Give each of the selected children a carton. Vary the story so they have to listen and watch.
6. Over a period of time, gradually increase the size of the group of storytellers and vary the rhythmic sounds as the children become more skilled. Have them guess occasionally about what the sound represents.
7. Start simply and proceed slowly. The purpose of the activity is to give children practice in listening and reproducing sounds. Keep the story short at first. Handing out too many cartons can cause distraction and confusion. Limit the number until children understand the purpose for which the cartons are intended.

[3] Use Ella Jenkins's "You'll Sing a Song and I'll Sing a Song" (FC 7664) and "Call and Response" (SC 7638) from Folkways.

[4] Some rhythm band records with simple musical concepts are "Rhythm Band Time" (MH-41) and "Rhythm and Rhyme" (MH-87) from Melody House.

▶ **PURPOSE**   **To identify rhythmic sounds**

MATERIALS   — Tape recorder

PROCEDURE   **1.** Identify and tape rhythmic sounds familiar to the children, such as walking, dancing, hammering, sawing, snoring, bouncing a ball, hopping, typing, clapping hands, chewing, clicking the tongue, breathing, using an eggbeater, and brushing teeth.
2. Play each sound and have children guess what it is. Allow plenty of time for guessing, questioning, and discussing. Give clues to help, and encourage children to try to reproduce the human sounds.
3. Have children help decide what kinds of rhythmic sounds the class should tape for other guessing games.
4. Let the children who can identify the sounds be the "teacher." Let them ask questions and give clues to the others.

Note: Use "Adventures in Sound" (MH-55) from Melody House which gives sounds and a three-second pause so that children can identify them.

TONE

▶ **PURPOSE**   **To recognize high and low sounds**

MATERIALS   — Piano or other musical instrument

PROCEDURE   **1.** Have the children sit on the floor and listen while you play a middle C and then follow it with a C an octave higher. Repeat this twice.
2. Ask:
Did both of these notes sound the same?
What can you do to show me when you hear the high note?
What can you do for the low note?
3. Play the notes again and let them respond in the agreed-upon manner.
4. Use another instrument, such as resonator bells, resonator blocks, harmonica, or any bells or whistle.
5. Play a melody that has obvious high and low changes in it. Have the children respond by stretching high for the high notes and crouching low for the low notes.

▶ **PURPOSE**   **To recognize loud and soft sounds**

MATERIALS   — One paper megaphone for each child and for the teacher

PROCEDURE   **1.** Ask the children to make their voices loud when your voice is loud, soft when your voice is soft.
2. Sing a call-response song.
3. Vary the pattern of loud-soft; do not just alternate the two. If you build up to three or four soft versions before you make a loud

sound, you will create a sense of anticipation in the children. Stop and ask them what they felt like while waiting for the loud sound. Explain that composers do the same thing.
4. Play examples from a variety of recordings to demonstrate.[5]

Note: Use "Shout and Whisper" (Tickly Toddle 597) in cassette or record from Educational Activities.

▶ **PURPOSE**   **To learn that different instruments have different sounds**

MATERIALS
— Records with a variety of instrumental solos
— Pictures of people playing those instruments

PROCEDURE
1. Show a picture of someone playing a violin.
2. Play a record with a violin solo, then play another solo with a different style (first a classical piece, then "Hot Canary" or "Pop Goes the Weasel," for example).
3. Then play a trumpet solo for contrast. Show a picture of a person playing a trumpet.
4. Show the children how to pretend they are playing a violin.
5. If possible find a violinist to come and play for the children.
6. Use this same procedure to introduce a woodwind, a brass instrument, and a percussion instrument.

HELPFUL HINTS

1. Call your local music store and inquire about guitar rentals and lessons.
2. If you learn just two simple chords on the guitar (A and E7), you will be able to play all these songs and more: "This Old Man," "My Dreydl," "Hush Little Baby," "Old MacDonald Had a Farm," "Row, Row, Row Your Boat," "Polly Wolly Doodle," "Clementine," "Go Tell Aunt Rhody," "Billy Boy," "On Top of Old Smoky," and "Old Susanna."

3 fingers   2 fingers

3. Refer to the bibliography for books on learning the autoharp.

---

[5] Suggestions: Bowmar Orchestral Library — Bowmar Records: "Classroom Concert" (Bol 68); "Miniatures in Music" (Bol 64); "Fairy Tales in Music" (Bol 57); "Adventures in Music — Grade 1" (RCA Victor LE-1000); "Concert in the Park (RCA Victor LM-2677); "The Light Music of Shostakovich" (Columbia LM-6267); "Gaiete Parisienne" (Offenbach, Columbia ML-5348).

MELODY

▶ **PURPOSE**   **To sing a song from memory**

MATERIALS   — Guitar, piano, or autoharp (optional)

PROCEDURE   1. Choose a simple song that is repetitious.
2. Sing it casually during free play so children become familiar with it.
3. Introduce the song during formal music time. Play it at least once and then ask whether anyone wants to help sing.
4. Ask for requests. If the children choose, they will have more incentive to sing along.

▶ **PURPOSE**   **To recognize identical melodies**

MATERIALS   — Piano, guitar, or records and record player

PROCEDURE   1. Have the children sit on the floor.
2. Play one melody, such as "Baa, Baa, Black Sheep," several times. Play another melody, and then play "Baa, Baa, Black Sheep" again.
3. Ask the children to raise their hands each time they hear the first melody. Then play another new melody. Then play "Baa, Baa, Black Sheep" once again, asking them to raise their hands when the melody is familiar.
4. Go through the sequence again, using two or three more non-matching melodic phrases between the familiar melody.
5. This game can be made more challenging for older children by using songs with similar melodic phrases and rhythmic patterns.

▶ **PURPOSE**   **To create original melodies on an instrument**

MATERIALS   — Piano, resonator blocks, resonator bells, or a xylophone

PROCEDURE   1. If using a piano or xylophone, one child at a time can use the instrument. If using the bells or blocks, children can use the instruments to create three sequential tones at first, building up to four, five, six, and more.
2. Encourage the children to experiment with the sound sequences.
3. Ask if they can play the same melody twice.
4. As children become more knowledgeable, they can play a game of matching one another's melodies.

TEXT

▶ **PURPOSE**   **To listen and respond to words in a song**

MATERIALS   — Piano, guitar, autoharp, or records and record player

PROCEDURE   1. Ask the children to listen very carefully and do what they feel like doing. (You can play songs about animals that the children could imitate, or work songs, or instructive songs — "Put Your Finger in the Air" — or songs that tell a story.)

2. Play at least three different kinds so the children can talk about how songs are used for many different purposes.[6]

MOOD

▶ **PURPOSE**   **To respond to the mood of a song**

MATERIALS   — Piano, guitar, autoharp, or records and record player

PROCEDURE   1. Ask the children to listen carefully to the song and move to the music if they want to do so.
2. Play a series of songs each with a different mood — happy, sad, scary, peaceful.[7]
3. After each song or instrumental, ask the children how the music made them feel. What did it make them think of? Do they know another song that makes them feel the same?

HELPFUL HINTS

1. Tape the children singing some of their favorite songs and play back the tapes.
2. Play music in the art area and let the children paint to music.
3. Turn the lights off or down low and listen to a music box.
4. Play restful music during snack time.
5. Use a special record to signal a transition from one activity to another.

▶ **PURPOSE**   **To learn how music complements text**

MATERIALS   — Record of "Peter and the Wolf" (Leonard Bernstein and N.Y. Philharmonic on Columbia) and record player

PROCEDURE   1. Play the record in one session simply as a listening experience to familiarize the children with the story.
2. During the second session, have them listen several times to the first part, which associates themes with animals. Talk about how the sounds describe the animals.

---

[6] See Bibliography of Resources at the end of this section for helpful resources.
[7] Suggestions: "Suites from Gayne" (Khatchaturian, Capitol P8503); "The Courtly Dances from Gloriana" (Britten, Victor LM 2730); "Zorba, the Greek" (20th Century Fox TFM3167); "Going Places" (Herb Alpert's Tijuana Brass, A&M Records LP112); "Souvenirs From Sweden" (Epic LF18010); "Toshiba Singing Angels" (Capitol T10252); "The Beatles' Yellow Submarine" (Capitol Records SW153).

3. Assign a theme to each child and have them take turns acting out the story.

FORM

▶ **PURPOSE**   **To learn that music has a form — a beginning, a middle, and an end**

MATERIALS   — Piano, guitar, autoharp, or records and record player

PROCEDURE   1. Ask children to stand with space between them.
2. Tell them you are going to play parts of a song and they are to move to the music and stop as soon as the music stops.
3. Play short phrases of a lively tune.[8] Gradually play several phrases together. Then play the whole piece.
4. Contrast the lively piece by playing a slow, flowing song.[9] Have the children lie on the floor and move their arms to the music.

VARIATIONS   1. Set up chairs in a circle, one per child. Ask the children to begin moving around the chairs when the music starts and sit down on chairs as soon as it stops.
2. Give the children rhythm instruments to play with the music.

▶ **PURPOSE**   **To learn that music has patterned forms**

MATERIALS   — Piano, guitar, autoharp, or record and record player
— Set of triangles for half of the children; set of drums for the other half of the children

PROCEDURE   1. Play a selection that has the ABA form (starts with theme A, changes to theme B, and ends with theme A again).
2. Give half the children triangles (or substitutes). Play the first theme again. Tell the children with triangles that is the A theme; that is their part. When they hear that theme they can play along on their triangles.
3. Give the drums to the other half of the class. Play the B theme, identify it as such, and tell the children with drums that is their theme. Ask what they will do when they hear their theme.
4. Ask children to listen while you play the whole ABA pattern again.
5. Ask them to play their instruments when they hear their themes this time.
6. After the children have done this exercise several times, encourage them to find new combinations as they play without music (for example, AABB and ABBA).

---

[8]Bouncy, lively records: "The Tartan Ball" (EMI SZLP2118); "Pop Goes the Weasel" (RCA Victor 45-6180).

[9]Slow, flowing records: "Duets with Spanish Guitar" (Capitol 8406); "Songs in Spanish for Children" (Columbia 91A02029).

Bibliography of Resources

ACTIVITY SONG BOOKS

Chroman, Eleanor. *Songs that Children Sing.* New York: Oak Publications, 1970. Seventy-one international folk songs for children, some with English translations. Charming photographs of the world's children accompany the guitar chords and piano arrangements.

Greenberg, Marvin. *Your Children Need Music.* Englewood Cliffs, N.J.: Prentice-Hall, 1979. A well-written guide for parents and teachers for developing a child's natural capacity to enjoy and respond to music. Activities and songs for the infant to age five.

Jenkins, Ella. *The Ella Jenkins Song Book for Children.* New York: Oak Publications, 1966. Twenty-six of Ella Jenkins's most popular songs used in her rhythm workshops.

Nye, Robert, Vernice Nye, Neva Aubin, and George Kyme. *Singing with Children.* 2nd ed. Belmont, Calif.: Wadsworth, 1970. A collection of songs for the elementary grades, but the teacher of young children will find the sections on action songs and singing games useful. The book also includes a section of songs accompanied by the autoharp and ukelele and by percussion instruments. Teaching objectives are listed at the beginning of each section and suggestions for other uses for songs are given.

Nye, Robert, and Meg Peterson. *Teaching Music with the Autoharp.* Northbrook, Ill.: Music Education Group, 1982. A useful book teaching simple chords and songs for the autoharp. Rhythm, melody, and harmony are some of the concepts that can be taught with the autoharp. Includes thirty-seven songs with strums.

Peterson, Meg. *Autoharp Parade.* Northbrook, Ill.: Oscar Schmidt-International, Inc., 1967. One hundred favorite songs for young people with autoharp chords and strums.

Raffi. *The Raffi Singable Songbook.* Toronto: Chappell. Piano arrangements and guitar and ukelele chords to fifty-one songs for young children. Includes "Five Little Pumpkins," "My Dreydel," "Brush Your Teeth," "Mr. Sun," and "Peanut Butter Sandwich."

Ramsey, Bayless. *Music: A Way of Life for the Young Child.* St. Louis: C. V. Mosby, 1982. Musical concepts appropriate for each age level accompany many of the songs and rhythms in this book. Children's awareness and understanding of these concepts grow out of natural encounters with musical selections. Definitions of musical concepts, glossary, and music fundamentals.

Reynolds, Malvina. *Little Boxes and Other Handmade Songs.* New York: Oak Publications, 1964. Malvina Reynolds is a delightful protester. She says, "This book could be called 'Singin' Mad'. But you can't be meaningfully angry unless you burn because you care truly about people and small children and birds, fishes, ladybugs, and wilderness places, and there are songs here about all that." Includes songs such as "Upside Down," "You Can't Make a Turtle

Come Out," "Morningtown Ride," and "The Faucets Are Dripping." Guitar chords and melody accompany each song.

Seeger, Ruth Crawford. *American Folk Songs for Children in Home, School, and Nursery School.* New York: Doubleday, 1980. The author originally compiled these folk songs for use at a cooperative nursery school. The preface contains an excellent discussion on the rationale for introducing young children to American folk music, with suggestions for the parent and teacher on improvising, accompanying, and using the songs at home and school. The classified index includes such topics as name play, finger play, small dramas, buttons, babies, and days of the week.

Sharon, Lois, and Bram. *Elephant Jam.* New York: McGraw-Hill Ryerson Ltd., 1980. The popular entertainers from Canada offer some of their most popular songs accompanied by suggestions for action rhymes, finger plays, wacky walks, silly sits, and other entertaining activities.

Timmerman, Maureen, and Celeste Griffith. *Guitar in the Classroom.* Dubuque, Iowa: Brown, 1976. Excellent book for teachers who want to use the guitar immediately. One- and two-chord songs.

Wessell, Katherine Tyler. *The Golden Song Book.* New York: Golden Press, 1981. Suggestions for singing games accompany some of the songs for children. Titles with piano chords include old classics such as "The Muffin Man," "Farmer in the Dell," "Three Blind Mice," and "London Bridge."

Winn, Marie (ed.), Allan Miller, and John Alcorn. *The Fireside Book of Children's Songs.* New York: Simon & Schuster, 1966. A good collection of songs including nursery-rhyme songs ("Pop Goes the Weasel," "Eency Weency Spider," "Aiken Drum"); silly songs ("Bill Grogan's Goat," "There Was a Man and He Was Mad," "Horse Named Bill"); and singing games and rounds ("Clap Your Hands," "The Hokey-Pokey," "Kookaburra"). Piano arrangements.

Winn, Marie, Allan Miller, and Karla Kushkin. *What Shall We Do and Allee Galloo!* New York: Harper & Row, 1970. Play songs and singing games all set to music. The book has finger-play songs, follow-the-leader songs, word play, and simple games such as "This Is the Way We Wash Our Hands," "The Little Pony," and "Peek-a-Boo." Attractively illustrated.

Drama and Creative Expression

EXPRESSING FEELINGS

▶ **PURPOSE**   **To learn to imagine and project feelings**

MATERIALS   Pictures from magazines and other sources, mounted on heavy tag-board, showing such situations as:

— mother scolding or spanking a child
— two children fighting
— serious accident
— joyous interactions among people

PROCEDURE   1. Hold pictures up one at a time for children to see.
2. Let the children volunteer their observations. (Most will be descriptive. Give children plenty of time to talk about the pictures.)
3. Then ask:
   What is happening in this picture?
   What do you think happened just before this picture was taken?
4. Later in the discussion, ask:
   What do you think will happen next?
   How do you think the story will end?
5. Repeat some of the stories from beginning to end to help children realize that a picture can stimulate imaginings of the past, present, and future, as well as project their own wishes.

▶ **PURPOSE**   **To recognize and express feelings**

MATERIALS   Pictures from magazines or other sources, mounted on heavy tag-board, showing individuals in emotional states such as:

— man laughing
— person looking sad
— child smiling
— woman looking exasperated
— other dramatic facial expressions (use faces of all ages)

PROCEDURE   1. Hold pictures up one at a time for children to see, or if working with an individual child, let the child hold it and examine it closely.
2. Say:
   Tell me about this picture. (Many first responses will be simple identification. Let all children have plenty of opportunity to comment.)
   Look at this woman's face. How do you think she feels? (Usually the responses will be simple descriptions.)
3. Continue to encourage all the children to look at details of expression. Say:
   Look at her eyes. Do your eyes get that way? Look at her mouth. Can we try to make our mouths look like that? When

do you look like that? (Children will volunteer personal and sometimes seemingly unrelated experiences.)

4. Be aware of, respond to, and encourage the children's individual expressions of feeling.

5. Use a mirror as you do this activity. As the children volunteer facial expressions to illustrate a feeling, let them check themselves in the mirror. Encourage them to make any adjustments they want. Say:

Can you make your eyes look angry too?

Now that you are making a sad face, how can you make it happy again?

HELPFUL HINTS

1. Recreate experiences and have children act them out. For example, pantomime the following:

   — Get out of bed, get dressed, tie your shoes, brush your teeth.
   — Spread mustard, ketchup, relish on a hot dog and eat it.
   — Pour sugar and cream into coffee or tea; stir it, cool it, taste it.

2. Recreate feelings and have children express them. For example, pantomime the following:

   — Pour a glass of milk and spill it.
   — Scoop up some ice cream into a cone and drop it.
   — Pick beautiful flowers and smell them.

Encourage expression of feelings rather than "superficial" acting.

▶ **PURPOSE**   **To express inner feelings through color, line, movement, shape, and form**

MATERIALS   Color pictures and photographs showing scenes such as:

— a colorful day in fall or spring
— a wintry landscape
— a dismal, dreary scene
— a bright, cheerful scene

(Avoid scenes emphasizing people.)

PROCEDURE   1. Hold pictures up one at a time for children to see. Let them comment on what they see.

2. Say:

   Look at the colors! (Children will usually begin to name them.)

   How does this color make you feel?

How do all the colors in the whole picture make you feel? I wonder why? (Young children will have difficulty expressing their inner responses to color. Try to call their attention to the effects colors can have.)

3. Repeat the same procedure with line. Say:
   Look at how the artist made his brush strokes go (up/down). Are these lines straight or crooked? Notice the thick paint and the big hard lines. Do you think these lines help to make you feel happy? sad?
4. Comment on the movement in the pictures. Ask:
   What is happening to the leaves in this picture?
   What is moving?
   Why is the girl's hair back like that? What makes your hair do that?
5. Comment on the other shapes in the pictures. Ask:
   How do you think this feels — round or flat?
   Let's try to think about how the artist made this look round instead of flat.
6. Comment on the textures within the pictures. Ask:
   Do you think this is rough or smooth?
   I wonder why it looks that way.
   Do not expect young children to contribute sophisticated comments at first. They should be given many, many opportunities to learn to look at pictures, people, and nature from the standpoint of the characteristics of color, line, form, and so forth.

ART AND TEXTURE

HELPFUL HINTS

1. Display poster reproductions of famous works of art. These are available in museum shops and art stores.
2. Purchase color slides from museums or art departments of local schools and project them for children to talk about.
3. Read about famous modern art — for example, Jackson Pollock's "Blue Poles" — and have children try some of the same techniques.
4. Whenever possible use art reproductions that have a textured surface. Encourage the children to rub the surface with their fingers to experience the variations in texture.
5. Use children's art works as examples of differing styles and techniques.
6. Read stories from children's picture books illustrated in various art mediums — water colors, oils, drawings, block prints, etc. After the story the books can be appreciated for their pictures as well.

► **PURPOSE**   **To learn that art is a medium of expression**[10]

MATERIALS   Reproductions of paintings, all on the same subject, such as children:

— "A Girl with a Broom" — Rembrandt (Dutch)
— "Portrait of a Boy" — Soutine (Russian)
— "A Girl with a Watering Can" — Renoir (French)
— "Don Emanuel Osorio De Zuniga — Goya (Spanish)
— "Girl with Braids" — Modigliani (Italian)

(Other subjects might be "birds and animals," "flowers," "work," or "places.")

PROCEDURE   **1.** Begin discussion by saying:
When we look at children, we see that they do not always look the same. If you are sad, your face will look a certain way.
(Let one child demonstrate.)
If you are feeling very happy your face might look quite different.
Many things make us see the same children in different ways.
2. Darken the room and have children look at one another.
3. Introduce a light and say:
Light can come into a room and change the way a child looks.
4. Introduce the paintings by placing them on low tables or on the floor.
5. Have each child look at the paintings and tell you which one he or she likes best and why. (You may want to keep a list of the number of children who chose each painting.)
6. Encourage the children to use easel paints to "tell" about the way they feel.
7. Discuss how artists also "tell" the way they feel through their paintings.
8. Discuss how color and light affect the way a person feels.

► **PURPOSE**   **To learn about three-dimensional objects**

MATERIALS   — Paper large enough for a mural
— Three-dimensional objects such as driftwood, sculptures, fruits, vegetables, rocks, flowers, sea shells, and nuts

PROCEDURE   **1.** Select several items that have different textures.
2. Talk to the children about how the objects feel.
3. Have the children close their eyes. Give them an object to pass along, and ask if they can tell what it is by touching and feeling it.
4. Have them turn over each object and look at it another way.
5. Take the children on a nature walk to collect three-dimensional objects.

[10]Adapted from "Elementary Level Pilot Program, Art Appreciation: A Step Toward Aesthetic Awareness," pp. 1–7, prepared by the Palo Alto Unified School District.

6. Have the children cooperate in making a large wall mural with the objects they collect.

7. Hang the mural low enough so children can touch it.

PUPPETS

PAPER BAG PUPPETS   Use a small paper bag with a face drawn on it. Make a hole for the mouth so the child can poke fingers through for a tongue. Two fingers can be the ears.

MITTEN OR SOCK PUPPETS   Use an old mitten or sock with buttons for eyes and nose. A small piece of colored material can be used for the mouth and yarn for the hair.

HAND PUPPETS   A hand can be a puppet. Using a washable marker, draw eyes, nose, and mouth in the creases of the child's palm. By moving the fingers and stretching them, the child can create many amusing expressions.

POTATO OR APPLE PUPPETS   Use a potato or apple to make a puppet. Cut a hole large enough for the child's finger. With toothpicks, stick on some of the features using slices of olives, cloves, or pieces of the potato or apple. A handkerchief wrapped around the hand becomes a body.

SHADOW PUPPETS   Make shadow puppets by tracing figures on construction paper and gluing them onto poster board. Cut out the shapes and attach them to handles made of heavy plastic straws or flat sticks.

Note: When telling stories with puppets, practice in front of a mirror. Remember to tip the face of the puppet toward the children to maintain eye contact. Shy children will often respond more easily to a puppet than to the teacher. (Illustration 2.2 shows a variety of puppets.)

DRAMATIC PLAY KITS

The young child recreates and integrates many personal experiences through fantasy and dramatic play. In this way, the child "makes sense" out of his or her world. You can help provide many opportunities for dramatic play by supplying props and encouraging both boys and girls to assume a variety of roles. Chairs can become trains, cars, boats, or houses. A table covered with a blanket or bedspread becomes a cave or special hiding place. Cardboard cartons that children can decorate convert into houses, forts, or fire stations. Below are some suggested dramatic play kits.

SUPERMARKET   Cash register, play money, paper pads, pencils or crayons, paper punches, paper sacks, empty clean food cartons, wax or plastic models of food, grocery boxes, cans with smooth edges.

Illustration 2.2   **Various kinds of puppets**

BEAUTY PARLOR   Plastic brushes, combs, make-up, cotton balls, scarves, clip-on rollers, colored water in nail polish bottles, empty shampoo and rinse bottles, wigs.

COOKING   Pots, pans, egg beaters, spoons, pitchers, salt and flour shakers, medicine bottles with colored water, tablecloth, aprons.

POST OFFICE   Index card file, stamp pads, stampers, crayons, pencils, holiday or commemorative stamps, old envelopes.

SHOE SHINE   Small cans of clear (natural) polish, sponges, buffers, soft cloths.

CLEANING SET   Small brooms, mops, cake of soap, sponges, toweling, plastic spray bottle.

LAUNDRY   Plastic basin, clothes line, clothes pins, doll clothes to wash.

DOCTOR AND NURSE   Tongue depressers, stethoscope, satchel, adhesive bandages, cotton balls, uniforms.

LETTER CARRIER   Hats, badges, envelopes, mail satchel.

FIRE FIGHTER   Hats, raincoats, boots, short length of garden hose.

FARMER   Shovel, rake, hoe, seeds.

PLUMBER   Wrench, plastic pipes, tool kit.

GAS STATION ATTENDANT   Shirt, hat, tire pump.

HOUSE PAINTER   Paint brushes, buckets filled with water.

WINDOW WASHER   Bucket, soap, sponges, squeegee, water.

POLICE OFFICER Hat, badge.

MILK DELIVERER Plastic bottles and cartons, wagon, white hat and coat.

Bibliography of Resources

BOOKS ABOUT CREATIVE EXPRESSION FOR THE TEACHER

Gowan, John Curtis, et al. (eds.). *Creativity: Its Educational Implications.* 2nd ed. New York: Wiley, 1981. A collection of readings that gives the teacher some insights into the creative potential of children and provides ideas for practical application of research in the curriculum.

Torrance, E. Paul. *Guiding Creative Talent.* Englewood Cliffs, N.J.: Prentice-Hall, 1962. A discussion of creative talent at all ages and educational levels. The author presents information based on research and gives examples of specific tasks used to assess creativity. He examines some of the difficulties that educators face in understanding and maintaining creativity.

Creative Movement

Some types of dancing involve following a pattern of movements the dancer has already been taught. These movements are "right" and "wrong" according to the teacher's judgment, the goal being a performance for others of a practiced and perfected skill. However, creative movement is not such a performing art. It is, rather, a nonintellectual activity in which the dancer forgets about himself or herself and allows the music to carry the body away from careful, conscious thinking. Under this philosophy, dancing becomes a successful experience filled with music, freedom, and joy for the child. The feeling of success is engendered by the teacher's positive and approving attitude. Therefore, the role of the teacher in guiding creative movement is of primary importance. Keep these basic concepts in mind as you work with young children in this area:

1. You should make it clear that anything the child does that is safe for himself or herself and others is all right.
2. The child should realize that he or she needn't do anything that anyone else does; the child can do anything the music "tells" him or her to do.
3. The dance is an integrating experience, strengthening and uniting the whole person.
4. Creative dance should provide a rewarding interaction among muscular, emotional, and intellectual growth.
5. You can explain that it is all right if the child wants to "copy" someone for a start, as they could never look exactly alike.
6. Make it very clear that each child is different and that we all move in a different way.
7. You can explain that dancing is a healthy form of exercise for everyone and that it takes no special talent or skill.
8. Children should be helped to experience the feeling of freedom in movement, the relationship of movement to space, and moving in relationship to others.
9. Some children find it difficult to be creative and follow their own movement ideas if they are inexperienced in this area. The teacher should begin by introducing some "watch and follow" games, such as "Did You Ever See a Lassie," and some "listen and follow" games, such as "Looby-Loo" and the "Hokey Pokey." Then branch out from these by asking for new ideas on ways to move. Say:
   Can someone show me a new way to jump?
   Who can move their arms a different way?
   These suggestions give the child a point of reference from which to begin thinking creatively.
10. As the dancing activity progresses, you may need to give further verbal cues. Say:
    Can you turn yourself around?
    Can you swing your arms while you walk?
    Commenting on any new movement ideas members of the group may be using will also help children expand their own movement ideas if they so choose.

The following is an example of the procedure to use for the activities in this section:

1. Have available a variety of types of musical recordings and a simple long-playing phonograph. Premarking records can help you find appropriate music easily.
2. Suggest that all the children stand in a circle, facing in.
3. Play a bouncy kind of record — for example, songs by the Tijuana Brass — and tell the children to feel the bouncing from their tummies and to begin by lightly jumping up and down.
4. Explain that the stomach area is the center of the whole body and after bouncing it the children can start bouncing other parts of the body — hands, head, legs, ears, nose — so that everything is looser than it was.

HELPFUL HINTS

1. Movement activities should be presented in a noncompetitive way. Every child should have the feeling of success; the child should not be compared with someone else.
2. There should be no standard of performance for the class.
3. Children should be challenged to progress individually with questions that are specific, yet allow for different interpretations. For example:
   Can you show me another way to move from here to there?
4. Do not expect success the first few times you try movement activities. Practice timing your questions, reinforcing different children, and redirecting challenges.
5. Pacing is an important part of any movement lesson, even if only one activity is involved. With young children, the most successful group experience usually involves short explorations repeated at various times. Introduce and practice movement skills in spurts of a few minutes. Pacing influences movement activities in these ways:
   a. Pacing allows a transition between vigorous and less active movements so that no one becomes overtired. (Equally important, children should be given frequent breaks from sedentary activities.)
   b. Pacing provides a shift from moving through space to coming back together and sitting in a group.
   c. Pacing allows a transition between loud and quiet sounds and activities.
   d. Pacing lets children progress from moving, singing, and playing an instrument as part of a group to taking turns demonstrating individual efforts. (Small groups are best for turn-taking with young children.)

5. Tell the children they can go anywhere in the room and do anything the music tells them to do.
6. Play a quiet bit of music to allow rest and to give the children a sense of contrast.
7. Play music with a strong beat or staccato rhythm and ask the children to clap as they hear it.

BODY PARTS

▶ **PURPOSE**   **To learn to relax**

MATERIALS   — One small, limp rag doll
               — Recording of slow, quiet music[11]

PROCEDURE   1. Have the children sit on the floor around you.
               2. Hold the rag doll with both hands and show the children how limp it is. Shake it gently and call their attention to the way its head, legs, and arms hang loosely.
               3. Have the children shake their hands and arms and let them hang limp. Then have the children do the same with their heads and bodies.
               4. Play the record and let the children move around the room as if they were rag dolls.
               5. Ask the children to lie down. Go to each one and lift arms and legs and let them drop gently, saying:
                   Feel like a rag doll. Make your arms and legs heavy and floppy.
               6. Other forms of imagery that stimulate relaxation are melting ice or jello. Let the children experience ice cubes or jello melting — watching, touching, and verbalizing the process.

Note: In addition to enriching children's lives creatively, imagery of all kinds — in literature, music, dance, and singing — can also help develop visual memory skills.

▶ **PURPOSE**   **To learn to stretch**

MATERIALS   — Chinese jump ropes (stretchy ropes)
               — Records appropriate for stretching movements[12]

PROCEDURE   1. Demonstrate how the Chinese jump rope stretches.
               2. Give each child a jump rope.
               3. Say:
                   Show me how you can stretch this rope with your hands and arms.
                   Show me another way you can do it (holding rope with foot and stretching with the arm; holding rope with both feet; holding rope around various parts of the body).
               4. Play the record and ask children to stretch to the music.

---

[11]"Songs in Spanish for Children" (Columbia 91A02029); "Duets with Spanish Guitar" (Capitol 8406). Try the different bands to find the most suitable mood.
[12]"Natay, Navajo Singer" (Arizona 6160); "Balalaika" (Elektra EKS7194).

CREATIVE MOVEMENT · *Body Parts*   **79**

HELPFUL HINTS

1. Use a whistle (only outdoors) to signal *stop.* Practice with the children so they respond to the whistle before you introduce difficult tasks. (Indoors, use a drum beat, a hand clap, or tone blocks as a signal to stop. Young children often are quite sensitive to loud sounds.)
2. Keep activities simple for very young children; do not expect the children to respond to a large number of variations.
3. If a child's response is "incorrect," rephrase the question, rather than telling the child that he or she is wrong. For example, if a child starts throwing a ball and bouncing it wildly when you ask the child to show you how to bounce the ball, say:
   Can you bounce the ball and keep it in this circle?

---

5. Suggest long, slow movements.
6. Collect the ropes and continue to play the music.
7. Say:
   Now stretch to the music. Stretch all parts of yourself. Stretch your arms, stretch your legs, stretch your body as you move to the music.
   You should stretch along with the children. Say:
   Remember how it felt when you were pulling the rope?
   Stretch as if you were still pulling on the rope.
   Stretch your hands up; feel the top of your head reaching up toward the ceiling. Lie on the floor and stretch your fingers and arms and legs. Stretch your fingers as far as you can from your toes. (For this activity, see Illustration 2.3.)

HELPFUL HINTS

1. Provide ample space for children to observe.
2. Not everyone has to participate.
3. Invite children with comments like: "We have a place here, Mary"; "We need another dancer"; "You can hold my hand, Jimmy"; "There's room if you decide you'd like to join us later."

▶ **PURPOSE**   **To learn to move every part of the body**

MATERIALS   — Records of both fast and slow music[13]
               — Small finger puppets

PROCEDURE   1. Have children sit in a circle.
               2. Say:

[13]"Music of Golden Africa" (Universal DC 6485).

Illustration 2.3   **Learning to stretch**

We can dance with many parts of our body. We don't have to use just our feet. Our fingers can dance too.
3. Demonstrate with the finger puppets.
4. Let each child play with a finger puppet.
5. Play the recording and suggest that the children let their fingers dance to the music. Say:
Pretend your fingers are candles with flames moving.
Pretend your fingers are sparklers with sparks flying from them.
6. Suggest that children sit still and dance with other parts of their body. Say:
Dance with your whole arm.
Move your head to the music.

Dance with one arm and your shoulder.
Move just your arms and head.

▶ PURPOSE **To learn to isolate body parts in movement**

MATERIALS — Any record with a bouncy, spirited beat

PROCEDURE
1. Have the children stand in a circle.
2. Say:
   Let's pretend there is popcorn popping inside of us. Here it goes inside of our hands — pop, pop, pop. See our hands go popping.
3. Show the children how to bounce and shake just their hands. If a child is using total body movement, you can hold the child gently by the wrists to isolate that body part.
4. Then let the popcorn move inside different body parts — head, shoulders, elbows, knees, hips, fingers, toes.
5. Name each body part so the children learn to identify them. Encourage their suggestions. This type of practice will help young children develop total body coordination and increase body awareness.
6. Have children bounce the whole body up and down as if popping. This will lead into jumping, hopping, galloping, and other movements that children enjoy.

HELPFUL HINT

Precede the activity with an actual corn-popping session. Place a large sheet on the floor with a corn popper in the middle. Have the children sit around the outside edges of the sheet. Play the bouncy tune and when the corn pops, remove the cover and let the corn pop out onto the sheet. Have children listen for the popping sounds and watch how the corn pops up and out.

MOVEMENT IN SPACE

▶ PURPOSE **To learn to relate movement to space**

MATERIALS
— Large and small cardboard containers
— Records of medium to slow music[14]

PROCEDURE
1. Play a record and suggest that children dance in and around the cartons.
2. Say:
   We all need space to move. Move into a small space.

[14]"Hadjidakis, Lilacs out of the Dead Land" (Odeon).

Now use big spaces.

3. Suggest climbing, crawling, hiding in and under various spaces in the room. Tell them to fit into different spaces.
4. Say:
When you are in a small space, you make small movements. Show me how you moved when you were inside the box.
When you are in a large open space, you can make big movements. Show me how you moved when you had lots of space.

HELPFUL HINTS

1. Use books by Helen Borten (such as *Do You Move as I Move? Do You See What I See?*) to start a discussion of different kinds of movement. Have children create their own movements based on themes from the books.
2. Take color slides of children painting to music; project these slides to the same music and have each child create dance movements in front of the projector so his or her shadow is superimposed on the painting.

▶ **PURPOSE**   **To learn to make heavy and light movements**

MATERIALS   — Balloons, scarves, heavy blocks
— Records of slow "heavy" music and "light" music[15]

PROCEDURE   1. Ask children to watch how the balloon moves when you toss it in the air. Reach up with stretching movements to grasp the balloon as it comes down.
2. Say:
A balloon is very light. Move like the balloon.
3. Give each child a balloon and comment on the way each one moves and stretches and lifts up on his or her toes, and so on.
4. Praise the movements that convey the feeling of lightness:
I like the way you bounce so lightly on your feet, Mei-ling.
Max, that's a lovely way to move your arms. Your whole body is moving in such a light way.
5. If balloons are too distracting, use scarves.
6. Demonstrate with heavy blocks by having each child move with a block in his or her hands.
7. Play heavy-sounding music and say:
Move as though you are as heavy as a block. Move your feet and arms and body in a heavy way.
8. Contrast heavy and light music and comment as children move to each kind of music:

---

[15]"Shalom" from "Orcha Bamidbar" for heavy mood (Elektra ELK146); Geula Gill: "Newest Hits in Israel" (Epic LF18045); "Iron Butterfly" — drum part in middle of record (Altco SD33-250); "Bantu Folk Songs" (Folkways FW6912).

I see you're putting your whole foot down at once.
You're dragging your shoulders, and your arms and hands are
so heavy. Listen to what the music tells you to do.

MOVEMENT WITH OTHERS

▶ **PURPOSE** **To learn to move with a partner (for ages 5 and up)**

MATERIALS — Scarves
— Chinese jump ropes
— Records appropriate for dancing and skipping[16]

PROCEDURE 1. Ask children to hold hands with partners and skip.
2. If some children can't skip, let those who know how hold hands with those who don't. Skipping-like movements are all right. Practice the activity in pairs.
3. Let pairs of children hold hands and skip around the room, trying not to bump.
4. Give a Chinese jump rope or a scarf to each pair of children to share.
5. Play music and say:
   It feels different to move with someone else. Show me how you move with your partner using the rope or scarf.
6. Keep each pair together and comment on movements that indicate that a child is aware of the other child's presence:
   I like the way you both move so close to each other without touching.
   That's nice the way your back and arms touch while you move and turn to the music.

Note: Remember that preschoolers are more concerned about themselves than others and need to be encouraged to work with partners.

▶ **PURPOSE** **To learn to relate movements to others**

MATERIALS — Scarves or ribbon streamers for each child
— Recorded music of a soft, swaying melody and a bouncy, spirited tune

PROCEDURE 1. While the children are seated, hand each of them a scarf or streamer. Ask the children to feel the prop and touch it to their bodies.
2. Then have the children stand and begin to move their scarves to the soft music.
3. Say:
   Listen to the gentle music. Let's see how we can move our scarves with that sound.

---

[16]"Original Score of Butch Cassidy and the Sundance Kid" (A&M Records SP4227).

4. Encourage new ideas and incorporate movements that you see the children using.
5. You may wish to let the children move about the room swaying their scarves as they go.
6. After a period of free movement, have the children sit together in pairs. Say:
   We are going to move our scarves again with the music. When it stops, you and your partner will put your scarves together on the floor.
7. Look for interesting designs the two scarves make on the floor and comment on the patterns you see.
8. Keep the music segments short. Change from gentle to more spirited music. Encourage the children to listen and move appropriately to the different sounds.
9. Once the children are interrelating well with their partners, let them hold hands as they move their scarves and walk around the room.
10. You may wish to continue using the pauses in the music as a *stop* signal while the children move around on their feet.

Bibliography of Resources

BOOKS ABOUT CREATIVE MOVEMENT ACTIVITIES

Barlin, Anne Lief. *Teaching Your Wings to Fly.* Santa Monica, Calif.: Goodyear Publishing Co., Inc., 1979. An excellent collection of movement activities including relaxation, emotional expression, and body techniques. Generously illustrated with photographs. Two 33⅓ records included with the book.

Birkenshaw, Lois. *Music for Fun/Music for Learning.* Toronto: Holt, Rinehart and Winston of Canada Ltd., 1974. Songs for relaxation, spatial relations, and singing.

Carr, Rachel. *Be a Frog, a Bird, or a Tree: Creative Yoga Exercises for Children.* New York: Harper & Row, 1977. Encourages children to use their imaginations and pantomime in conjunction with exercises. The book has a section of helpful guidelines for teaching yoga, accompanied by illustrations and photographs of young children demonstrating the yoga postures. Exercises can be selected to suit children's abilities.

Cherry, Clare. *Creative Movement for the Developing Child.* Belmont, Calif.: Pitman, 1971. A nursery-school teacher's collection of ideas on involving the young child in such activities as creeping, crawling, walking, and balancing games.

Gray, Vera, and Rachel Percival. *Music, Movement & Mime for Children.* London: Oxford University Press, 1962. A useful book based on British Broadcasting Company Programs for Music and

Movement. Includes suggested lessons based on time, weight, and space, plus an appendix of music suitable for movement.

Jones, Elizabeth. *What Is Music for Young Children?* Washington, D.C.: National Association for the Education of Young Children, 1969. A discussion of how to plan music experiences for the young child. Some observations of music experiences in the classroom are included.

Sheehy, Emma D. *Children Discover Music and Dance.* New York: Teachers' College Press, 1968. A useful text for the teacher of children of all ages. Includes discussions of the use of singing, instruments, dance, movement, records, and so forth in the classroom.

Sullivan, Molly. *Movement Exploration for Young Children.* Washington, D.C.: National Association for the Education of Young Children, 1982. Movement exploration as a teaching method for the total development of the child. Encourages children to apply problem-solving techniques to activities and to explore fantasies and relationships with others.

Wax, Edith, and Sydell Roth. *Mostly Movement.* New York: Mostly Movement, Ltd., 1979, 1982. Book I *(First Steps)* and Book II *(Accent on Autumn)* contain many original movement activities for preschoolers.

Werner, Peter H., and Elsie C. Burton. *Learning Through Movement.* St. Louis: C. V. Mosby, 1979. Activities designed to teach movement concepts to children and to assess learning outcomes.

RECORDS TO STIMULATE MOVEMENT ACTIVITIES

Instrumental Only

Lee, Karol. *"Music for Movement Exploration — Let Them Discover."* Freeport, N.Y.: Educational Activities, Inc. A delightful mixture of melodies with different moods and tempos. Excellent as background music for motor equipment or motor skills activities.

Palmer, Hap. *"Movin'."* Freeport, N.Y.: Educational Activities, Inc. A collection of original melodies with mostly moderate tempos. Good for use with motor activities. Includes a booklet of suggestions for motor activities useful with preschoolers and up.

———. *"Sea Gulls — Music for Rest and Relaxation."* Freeport, N.Y.: Educational Activities, Inc. Original tunes that are slow and restful in nature. Includes a guide for the teacher in leading relaxation techniques. Good for toddlers and up.

Wonderful World of Music Series. *"Joy — Classical Music for Children, Popular Songs Taken from the Classics."* Newark, N.J.: Peter Pan Records. An excellent array of the well-known classical melodies, some serene, some spirited. Can be used for background music during movement activities, for creative movement, and with motor equipment.

Instrumental and Narration with Music

Johnson, Laura. "Simplified Lummi Stick Activities." Long Branch, N.J.: Kimbo Educational. Prepared for prekindergarten through second grade, these familiar tunes and simple, repetitive routines are fun to use with rhythm sticks. A booklet of useful suggestions is included.

Mullane, Jack, with music by Stevie Wonder. "Keep on Steppin'." Freeport, N.Y.: Educational Activities, Inc. A variety of fitness and movement activities set to music with a unique and catchy style. Although designed for elementary grades, these activities can be adapted for use with much younger children. Further suggestions are included within the record jacket.

Stewart, Georgiana L. "Bean Bag Activities and Coordination Skills." Long Branch, N.J.: Kimbo Educational. A series of games, dances, and activities using bean bags. Useful for preschoolers and children with special needs. The music is delightful and the activities are highly successful. An illustrated booklet is included.

———. **"Toes Up Toes Down — Sensory Motor Skills for Body Identification, Spatial Awareness and Listening."** Long Branch, N.J.: Kimbo Educational. An assortment of original music and activities to develop sensorimotor skills. Useful for preschoolers and for older children with special needs. An easy-to-follow illustrated manual is included.

BODY AWARENESS

▶ **PURPOSE**   **To learn parts of the body**

MATERIALS   None[17]

PROCEDURE   1. Say:
   Do you know what your body is? It's you from head to toe. It's all of you.
   2. Tell the children that you and they are going to play a game. They will touch the part of the body that you name.
   3. Work from top to bottom — head, eyes, nose, ears, mouth, chin, neck, shoulders, chest, back, arms, and so on.
   4. Repeat. Then name parts of the body in random order.
   5. Ask if anyone would like to be the leader. As the children learn the names for their body parts, they can name the part as they touch it.

HELPFUL HINTS

1. As the children develop their body awareness have them concentrate on two or more body parts. Say:
   Can you touch your elbow to your knee?
   Show me how quickly you can balance with only one hand and one foot touching the floor.
2. Elementary-level children may enjoy playing this game with partners. Give directions such as:
   Stand with your shoulders touching your partner's shoulders.
   Show me how you can walk with one leg stuck to one of your partner's legs. This version calls for increased team work, balance, and problem solving.
3. For more variation at the preschool level, give each child a prop such as a cotton ball, a feather, or a soft foam ball. As you call out the body part they are to tap it with their prop. Body awareness is increased by this additional stimulation of the child's sense of touch.

▶ **PURPOSE**   **To learn how body parts move**

MATERIALS   None

PROCEDURE   1. Tell children they are going to play a game about moving parts of their bodies. Have everyone stand up.

[17]See Bibliography of Resources at the end of this section for records and books useful in enhancing motor explorations.

2. Ask how they can move their heads. Note the different kinds of responses and repeat them with the children. Ask how children can move their eyes, mouth, necks, shoulders, elbows, chests (move when they breathe), arms, fingers, waists, hips, legs, knees, ankles, toes.

3. Play a game in which you say:
Move your _____.
Allow children to use their own type of movement.

CROSS-REFERENCE   To learn parts of the body, left and right side, p. 87.

SPACE AWARENESS

▶ **PURPOSE**   **To experience space in relation to the body**

MATERIALS   None

PROCEDURE   1. Ask children to sit on the floor and curl up and try to make themselves round as a ball. You might show them a party noisemaker (one that unrolls when you blow it). Ask them to roll up as it does. Go around looking for spaces. Show them where the empty spaces are by patting — for example, behind calves.

2. Ask children to use more space by stretching their arms, then their legs.

3. Ask them how they can use more space behind themselves, to the side.

4. Have them repeat the entire sequence with their eyes closed.

VARIATIONS   1. Have the children start the exercise by lying on their backs or on their sides.

2. Have the children place one part of the body in relation to another part. Say:
Put your arms between your knees.

▶ **PURPOSE**   **To experience limitations of space**

MATERIALS   — Several large cardboard boxes

PROCEDURE   1. Set the boxes on their sides in a circular pattern like a corral. Leave enough room so that when the children are standing in the middle, they will have to take at least three steps to reach the boxes.

2. Ask children to walk slowly and stop when they touch the boxes. Ask them to walk back to the middle of the circle.

3. Move the boxes farther out. Have the children walk out again and back. Then ask them if they had more space to move in or less.

4. Ask them to repeat steps 2 and 3 with their eyes closed.

5. Remove the boxes and ask the children to walk out as far as they can until something stops them. Return.

6. Have the children sit down. Talk about how sometimes we can change the size of the space around us, sometimes we can't. For example, ask if there is any way to change the space when we are

riding in a car (rolling windows down, putting seat of station wagon down). Ask whether they have more space in their bathroom or their living room, their living room or their front yard or the street. Talk about how sometimes it feels good to have a small space — when tucked into bed, for example.

HELPFUL HINT

Over, Under & Through by Tana Hoban (New York: Macmillan, 1973) provides picture presentations of twelve spatial concepts that you can use to reinforce movement exploration activities. Photographs show children crawling through a pipe, leapfrogging over a hydrant, and so on.

▶ **PURPOSE** To experience spatial relationships

MATERIALS
— One chair per child
— Table
— Group of objects to place on or under chair: dolls, books, cars, blocks

PROCEDURE
1. Direct each child to take a chair and put it someplace so that he or she can walk around it without touching someone else.
2. Tell children to walk around their chairs. Ask if they can move around their chairs in another direction.
3. Ask whether they can move around their chairs without walking.
4. Ask if they can get on top of their chairs:
   Who can get in front of his or her chair, behind it, to the side of it?
5. Ask whether they can get under their chairs. (If not, why not?)
6. Ask if they see anything they can get under (the table). Let them get under in suitable groups.
7. Ask:
   Do you see anything on top of the table?
   Pick one of those objects and put it on top of a chair.
   Put your objects under the chair.
   Who can think of another place to put his or her object?

CROSS-REFERENCE To learn relational concepts, p. 157

FORM AWARENESS

▶ **PURPOSE** To experience form through touch

MATERIALS
— Enough boxes to form the outline of a square with a 3' x 3' base and 3' sides
— Enough boxes to outline a triangle with 4' base and 3' walls
— Corrugated cardboard 3' x 12' to make a circle
— One or two aides

PROCEDURE

1. Allow one child at a time to get inside the circle and walk around it, running his or her hand on the side to feel the curve.
2. Let the same child get inside the boxes that form the square and walk or skip around running his or her hand on the side to feel the straight plane and sharp angles. While the first child is doing this, another child can start in the circle.
3. Introduce the triangle in the same manner.
4. After everyone has had a chance to experience the shapes until they are satisfied, sit down and talk about how each space felt different. Ask what was different about each one — curves, straight lines, number of angles (corners).
5. Arrange the boxes so each child can be directed to go in the circle and come out of the square, and so on.

LOCOMOTOR SKILLS[18]

Locomotor movement is defined as that which carries one through space on a moving base. This base can be either "footed" or "non-footed." Typically children first move on a non-footed base, propelling themselves by rocking, rolling, scooting on their bottoms, crawling (with tummy in contact with the floor), and later creeping on hands and knees. When children are able to stand, they learn the eight locomotor skills that are basic to all movement activities. The first five locomotor movements are done to a single, steady rhythmic beat: walking, running, jumping (with two feet leaving the floor together), hopping (on one foot only), and leaping (moving off from one foot and landing on the other). The next three movements are done to an uneven, short-long rhythmic beat: galloping (a step sequence with the same foot consistently leading the other); sliding (a step sequence with one foot consistently sliding behind the other on the floor, often done moving sideways); and skipping (a step-hop sequence with a leg swing). One rarely sees preschoolers use leaping movements because of the strength required to perform more than one leap. Skipping is a complex locomotor skill that requires the child to use both sides of the body in a cross pattern. The left arm swings forward as the right leg swings up. Because the awareness of left and right body sides does not occur until sometime between four-and-a-half and seven years of age, skipping is generally the last locomotor skill a child acquires. Most children use the galloping pattern until they are ready to internalize the skipping process.

▶ PURPOSE   **To experience the changing forms of shadows**

MATERIALS   None

PROCEDURE

1. Have children stand in the sun to cast a shadow.
2. Say:
   What is a shadow?

[18]A particularly helpful film is "Movement Exploration" (Robert G. Jenson and Layne C. Hackett, Documentary Films, 3217 Trout Gulch Rd., Aptos, Calif. 95003).

Is your shadow bigger or smaller than you?
Can you make your shadow move?
How can you make your shadow bigger? Smaller?
Make your shadow bounce up and down.
Make the arms of your shadow move like the wings of a bird.
How can you make your shadow say "yes"?

3. Encourage the children to show one another how they create different shadow patterns.

VARIATION   Have the children work in pairs. Encourage the pair to move together with their bodies touching in some way. They might hold hands and stretch, bend, jump, or walk to make a shadow design together.

This version helps develop a child's ability to interrelate in movement with others and improves balance skills.

▶ **PURPOSE**   **To learn the feeling of direction (up, down, forward, and so on), and to develop strength and coordination**

MATERIALS   — Drum or whistle

PROCEDURE   1. Have children stand far enough apart so they can put their arms out without touching anyone else. Explain that when you hit the drum (or blow the whistle), you want them to stop and listen.
2. Ask:
Who can jump?
3. As children jump around, watch and comment on each child.
Can you jump another way? I see you are jumping forward (backwards, sideways, crouched, and so on). Can you take a big jump towards me? A little jump?
Can you move a part of your body while you are up in the air?
Find someone to jump with.
How would you jump if you were mad? How would you jump if you were sad? How would you jump into a swimming pool?
4. Use the drum to call children's attention to the objectives you have in mind — different ways of moving in different directions, for example.

Note: There is no right or wrong way to move; the goal is to have each child explore a variety of ways.

VARIATIONS   Do the same with hopping, walking, tip-toeing, and so on:
Who can hop? Can you hop and change feet? How tall can you make yourself while you hop? Who can walk without touching anyone?

▶ **PURPOSE**   **To learn the feeling of direction (across and over)**

MATERIALS   — Large mattress (king-size, if possible) with sturdy box springs covered with canvas

PROCEDURE   **Note:** Allow only one child at a time on the mattress when doing these directed exercises.

1. Have the child jump from one corner of the mattress to the other corner.
2. Suggest that the child land on all fours and jump up again.
3. Have the child turn while jumping so that she or he changes direction.
4. Have the child land on his or her seat and bounce up again.
5. Ask the child to close his or her eyes and jump from one end of the mattress to the other.
6. Have the child roll over and over again from one end of the mattress to the other.
7. Then ask the child to "log roll" over and over again across the mattress. The log roll is done with arms extended over the head and legs out straight. This movement helps the child integrate use of both sides of the body together.

VARIATIONS
1. Use a waterbed mattress to provide a more flexible surface and to increase tactile input as the child rolls or jumps across the mattress. This activity stimulates the inner-ear balance center as well.
2. This activity can be varied even further by changing the surface material. Cover the mattress with a rough canvas tarp, a nylon parachute, or a carpet remnant. New tactile experiences are provided as the child rolls, creeps, or jumps across the surface.

Note: These are all appropriate activities for toddlers, preschoolers, and primary-level students.

HELPFUL HINTS

1. Teachers sometimes assume that a child who is highly verbal and intellectually above average is also physically well coordinated. This is not necessarily true.
2. Children who need more practice in physical coordination may be resistant, requiring firm but gentle guidance.
3. Be supportive of children who need help. Hold the child's hand while he or she jumps on the balance board, praise the child, let the child have more turns, and protect the child from those who are faster and more likely to push him or her aside. Provide many positive experiences and lots of praise.
4. Observe individual children and keep a record of the activities each favors and those each avoids.

▶ **PURPOSE**   **To learn the feeling of direction while walking**

MATERIALS   — Drum or whistle

PROCEDURE   1. Tell children:
             When I hit the drum (or blow the whistle), it means I want you

to stop. I'm going to watch how you walk. Show me how you walk.

2. Give directions:
Show me how slowly you can walk.
Now show me how fast you can walk.
See how close to someone else you can walk without touching.
Walk taking giant steps. Walk taking small steps.
Walk using a lot of space. Walk using a little bit of space.

3. Ask the following questions:
How can you walk and make noise with your feet? (shuffle, stamp)
Can you walk and then turn and walk in a different direction when I beat the drum twice?
How would you feel if you were walking to the store to buy ice cream?
How would you walk if you were going someplace you didn't want to go?

HELPFUL HINTS

1. Children often need help moving to a specific tempo such as fast or slow. Be prepared to clap or drum the speed you want them to follow.
2. For further variation, select instrumental music with a moderate tempo. Have the children walk with the beat, which you accent further by clapping. When the music stops, the children are to stop also.
3. This activity helps build listening skills as well as co-ordination and sense of direction.

▶ **PURPOSE**   **To learn the feeling of direction while running**

MATERIALS   — Four barrels, large storage cylinders, or boxes
— Drum or whistle

PROCEDURE   1. Find an area (preferably grassy) at least 20′ long for the running distance and wide enough for the children to stand side by side in a row, about an arm's length apart.
2. Before setting up the barrels, ask the children to line up on one side of the grass. Stand at the other side.
3. Ask them to show you how they can run to your side of the grass as you play the drum and stop quickly when the drum stops.
4. Ask:
Can you run quickly and reach to the sky, be as tall as you can?
5. Set up the barrels in a line with about three feet of space between them. If the children need more space, use only three barrels spaced farther apart.
6. Have them run in and out around the barrels quickly, then slowly, then moving another part of the body along with their feet.

7. Ask:

How would an airplane fly around those barrels?
Can you show me how a train would move around the barrels?
What else could you be?

▶ **PURPOSE**   **To learn the feeling of direction while bouncing**

MATERIALS   — Large ball

PROCEDURE   **1.** Ask the children to watch the ball while you bounce it.
2. Ask if they can bounce exactly the same way.
3. Tell them to stop when you stop.
4. When the children's bouncing is coordinated with the bouncing ball, vary the action by bouncing the ball to the right or left; in a circular pattern; fast, slow, and so on.

HELPFUL HINTS

1. Be sure to verbalize the directions in which you are moving the ball.
2. Say:
Now the ball is going quickly.
Now it is moving backwards.
This time I'll move the ball to the right side.
3. This activity helps children build their vocabulary of direction words. It also helps them coordinate their physical movements with the visual cues from the ball and the auditory cues from the teacher.

▶ **PURPOSE**   **To learn to skip**

MATERIALS   — Drum or sand blocks
— Barrels (optional)

PROCEDURE   **1.** Ask children to show if they know how to skip. If some children can and some cannot, ask them all to join hands and skip toward you. Those who are learning to skip will receive movement and rhythm cues from those who can already skip. Children also can do a slow step-hop pattern together.
2. Play an uneven rhythm pattern with the sand blocks to accompany the skipping movement (two beats in an uneven, short-long combination).
3. If the children have mastered the skipping pattern, they can go on to explore other movement possibilities, such as jumping, hopping, walking, and running.

Note: Skipping is a difficult motor skill for children to master, requiring an internal integration of both sides of the body. Children master this skill between the ages of four-and-a-half to seven.

▶ **PURPOSE**   **To learn directional placement of the feet**

MATERIALS   — Vinyl tiles
              — Water-base paint

PROCEDURE   **1.** Paint the bottoms of a child's bare feet and make a dozen or more prints of each foot on separate tiles.
              2. Arrange the printed tiles in a path the children can walk. Vary the footprints so children must criss-cross, go sideways, and move their feet in different directions.
              3. Ask each child to place his or her foot to match the pattern.
              4. When all are familiar with the pattern, ask them to move more quickly along the path.
              5. Move the tiles to form different patterns.

BALANCE

▶ **PURPOSE**   **To experience directional changes in space**

MATERIALS   — A walking board (1′ wide x 8′ long x 2″ thick) supported by small saw horses 8″ off the ground

PROCEDURE   **Note:** Use a grassy area. Work with one child at a time.

              1. Say:
              Show me how you can walk across the board.
              Can you walk across touching your heel to your toes?
              Try walking backwards.
              Can you walk sideways on the board? Can you go the other way?
              Show me how you can walk to the middle, turn around, and walk back towards me.
              How else can you get to the middle and change?
              2. Ask what other ways the child can get across the board. (Possibilities include jumping and hopping sideways and backwards or using different body positions, such as squatting and stooping.)

VARIATIONS   **1.** Place the walking board at a slight slant by putting a 6″ block under one end.
              2. Place the walking board on a mat or mattress to further emphasize the uneven surface.
              3. Place a bean bag on the walking board. First have the children step over it as they walk across the board. Next have them stop, pick up the bean bag, and carry it to the end.

              Note: These variations require children to shift their center of gravity even further and stimulate the inner-ear balance system as well. All these activities are equally important for preschoolers and for primary-level children.

HELPFUL HINTS

1. Provide an object at eye level for the children to focus on (such as another adult or a streamer tied to a branch). The children should be encouraged to watch the target rather than their feet.
2. For preschoolers, start with the walking board placed on the ground. Raise it later.

▶ **PURPOSE**   **To learn to coordinate weight shift and to experience right and left sides of the body**

MATERIALS   — A wooden balance board (16″ x 16″ x 1″)
              — A wooden base (5½″ x 5½″ x 2″) placed under the center of the board

PROCEDURE   **Note:** Use a grassy area. Work with one child at a time.

1. Show the child the equipment. Say:
   See what happens when you push with your foot on this side of the board?
   What happens when you push the other side with your foot?
2. Ask the child to get up on the balance board. He or she may need to hold your hands at first in order to maintain balance. Try to keep most of the child's weight on the board rather than your hands.
3. Ask the child to push down on one foot, then the other. The goal is a smooth shifting of weight and the child will probably need a good deal of practice before the goal is reached. Singing "See-Saw, Margery Daw" might help the child to develop a smooth, rhythmic pattern of movement.
4. Ask:
   What happens if you lean on your toes? What else could you lean on? (heels)
   Ask the child to combine the movements.
5. As the child becomes skilled, you can talk about pushing forward, backward, and side to side.

▶ **PURPOSE**   **To practice balance and to experience directional changes**

MATERIALS   — One hula hoop for each child
              — One red cardboard circle and one red cardboard square (8″ x 8″) for each child

PROCEDURE   1. Give each child a hula hoop. Ask children to put them on the ground in a place where they have room to move around the hoops.

Ask children to stand behind their hoops, facing you. Call that their "home" position.

2. Say:

   Can you jump into your hoop with both feet? Can you jump out the other side? Turn around and jump back through.

3. Ask who can hop on one foot into the hoop and hop out the other side. Ask if they can hop back through. Then ask them to hop through using their other foot.

4. Ask them to hop into the hoop using both feet and stop. Ask if they can see a place to jump where they haven't been yet (to the side). Have them practice jumping to the side on both feet, then on one foot.

5. Tell them they are going to play a game. Put the red circle on the side of the hoop which is to their right; put the red square to their left.

6. Play the game by asking who can jump into the hoop and out onto the circle. Ask them to jump into the hoop and out onto the square, then back again. After the children are aware of the possible bases, encourage them to explore different combinations (for example, jump in and out toward you and go back and land on the circle). Ask what different way they could go back besides straight to "home."

HELPFUL HINTS

1. Jumping on an uneven surface is an excellent activity for developing the child's inner-ear balance system.

2. This activity is appropriate for two-year-olds and up, as long as the trampoline will bear the child's weight.

3. As the child nears kindergarten age, he or she should be able to answer questions, recite simple rhymes, count, or say his or her phone number while continuing to jump. This demonstrates the ability to perform a cognitive or learned skill while performing a basic motor skill and maintaining balance.

▶ **PURPOSE** **To practice balance on an uneven surface**

MATERIALS — Small circular trampoline or rebounder. (These are sold in most sporting-goods stores. Be sure the edges are padded, the legs are secure, and that the trampoline is no more than a foot high off the floor.)

— Recorded music and record player

PROCEDURE **Note:** Let children use the trampoline only when an adult is in attendance or when it is surrounded by tumbling mats. Children may go on the trampoline in stocking feet indoors or may keep their shoes on if outdoors.

1. Have children jump on the trampoline one at a time. (With very young children, two may go at a time.)
2. Stand next to the trampoline as a "spotter" while each child is jumping.
3. Play some recorded music with a steady, moderate beat to set the pace.
4. To help inexperienced children maintain balance while jumping, hold one side of a hula hoop as you stand on the floor while the child faces you and grasps the other side of the hoop with both hands.

COMBINING MOVEMENTS

▶ **PURPOSE**   **To combine movements using tires**

MATERIALS — One automobile tire for each child (get used ones free from a service station), placed flat on the ground with space between them

PROCEDURE
1. Assign each child a tire.
2. Ask how the child can get from one side of the tire to the other side without touching the tire (walk around it, hop into the middle and out).
3. Ask how the child can get from one side of the tire to the other by touching the tire (walk around the edge, hop on one edge, jump into the center, jump over the edge and out, jump around the edge). Encourage the children to explore all the possibilities by offering indirect clues (to use one foot, to touch twice, and so on).

HELPFUL HINTS

1. Begin with simple activities and do not end on a failure.
2. Demonstrate what you want before distributing materials.
3. If the group is large, use a whistle to signal the beginning and ending of an activity.
4. Don't expect children to stand still and pay attention after you hand them a ball, a tire, or a hula hoop. Let the children experiment with free movements.
5. Play recorded music as a background. Use a moderate tempo appropriate for jumping and hopping. Tell the children that when the music stops they are to "freeze." This helps maintain control of the group and also reinforces the tempo at which you wish to maintain the activity. The "freeze" will allow the children to rest as well.
6. Remember that hopping is difficult for young children. By age four-and-a-half, a child may be hopping on one leg, usually the dominant one. By age five, the child will be able to hop on one leg and then the other.

▶ **PURPOSE** **To use various body postures**

MATERIALS — Walking board
— Saw horses
— Mattress

PROCEDURE 1. Use a grassy area. Set up the walking board so that it is at the edge of the mattress.
2. Let the children take turns moving across the board in any manner they choose and end by jumping on the mattress. Encourage them to try new movement combinations by saying you like what they are doing. Help them think of new things to do by asking if they can move their hands or whether they can use one foot, and so on. Other possible questions include:
Can you look somewhere different when you land?
Can you go higher as you move across?
3. Once they land on the mattress, the children can explore the space available, the movement combinations, and the various body postures.

▶ **PURPOSE** **To move through a maze**

MATERIALS Any or all of the following to make a maze:

— big wooden blocks (for walking around, jumping over, hopping onto and off of)
— four chairs
— two or more yardsticks (use with chairs or blocks for going over or under)
— walking board
— mattress
— big boxes or barrels
— auto or bicycle tires (for hopping into, running through, walking on)
— chalk for drawing guidelines through the maze
— rope at least 9′ in length
— footprint patterns (see following activity)

PROCEDURE 1. Set up maze.
2. Allow the children to go through the maze any way they want the first time as long as they follow the guidelines. Keep the children spaced 15 feet apart.
3. The second time they go through, ask them to do something specific at one point (hop off the blocks, for example).
4. Each time change the point at which they are to do something specific.

▶ **PURPOSE** **To make footprints on butcher paper**

MATERIALS — One sheet of butcher paper (10′ long) per child
— A plastic dishpan holding ½″ of easel paint (see "Easel Paint Recipes," p. 11)

— Two child-sized chairs
— A basin of soapy water
— A towel

PROCEDURE   **Note:** Use an aide to help the children wash their feet.

1. Seat the barefooted child on the chair, which has been placed at one end of the butcher paper.
2. Have the child put his or her feet in the dishpan of paint. Help the child to step onto the paper.
3. Say:
   Show me how you can move on your feet across the paper to the other end. (He or she may simply walk straight across the paper.)
4. Have the aide stand at the other end of the paper with the other chair placed beside the pan of soapy water and a towel. The aide can help the child be seated, place his or her feet in the soapy water, and clean and dry the feet.
5. Note on the paper who walked across it and when.
6. As a follow-up within the next day or so, show the child his or her footprints from that first experience and have the child walk on the prints. Set up a blank sheet of paper and ask the child to go across the paper differently than he or she did before. Should the child balk while on the paper, the teacher can guide him or her by asking:
   Can you hop?
   Other movement possibilities are jumping on both feet, stepping sideways with one foot or the other, crossing one foot in front of the other.

▶ **PURPOSE**   **To walk and crawl through inner tubes**

MATERIALS   — Ten or more inner tubes

PROCEDURE   1. Arrange inner tubes in a variety of patterns.
2. Ask the children to put one foot in each inner tube and walk through the pattern.
3. Ask them to put two feet in each tube as they move through the pattern.
4. Ask them to show you how quickly they can go through the pattern.
5. Ask them to show you other ways they can go along the tubes (using hands and feet, on their knees, touching only the tops of the tubes).

▶ **PURPOSE**   **To combine clapping with body movements**

MATERIALS   — Record player and square-dance record

PROCEDURE   1. Listen to the regular beat of the square dance.
2. Have children follow you in clapping in unison.

3. When children are familiar with clapping to the beat, ask them to slap their thighs.
4. Call out other parts of the body:
   Touch your toes; squeeze your waist; nod your head; touch your elbows; rub your tummies.
5. Combine clapping with hopping, jumping, walking, skipping, and so on.

▶ **PURPOSE**   **To combine movements using a parachute**

MATERIALS — One small cargo parachute (available from surplus stores)[19]
          — Two or three lightweight balls about 8–10″ in diameter

PROCEDURE 1. Have children grip the edge of the chute and pull back tightly.
          2. Ask if they can shake the chute.
          3. Ask them to shake it up and down in unison to fill the chute with air.
          4. Have them hold the parachute up as high as they can.
          5. Ask for a volunteer to run under the chute from one side to the other without letting it touch them. (You may want to demonstrate and to tell each child when it is time to start running.)
          6. Have everyone let go and run under the chute at the same time.
          7. Place one or more balls on top of the parachute and ask the children to bounce the balls up and down.
          8. Ask if they can shake the chute to make the balls bounce off it.
          9. For variation and to provide further sensory stimulation, have a few children lie in the center of the parachute while it is on the ground. Have the others shake the chute up and down so that it ripples around those in the center. They can pretend to be noodles cooking in a pan of bubbling water.

Note: It may be helpful to use a whistle to signal when to start and stop.

▶ **PURPOSE**   **To exercise to music**

MATERIALS — Record player and records suitable for exercise movements. (The theme from *Rocky* works well.)

PROCEDURE 1. Have children sit on the floor or a mat facing you. Allow three to four feet on either side of each child for movement.
          2. Have the children start with slow movements to the music — nodding the head and moving the head from side to side.
          3. Ask them to reach high with the arms, stretching at the waist and sitting very tall.
          4. Have the children bring their arms down and extend them be-

[19]Varying sizes of parachutes are available from Mosier Materials, Inc., 61328 Yakwahtin Court, Bend, Oregon 97702.

hind the body, leaning forward and letting the head touch the knees.

5. Tell the children to stand up with their hands at the waist, then bounce on the balls of the feet.
6. Have children hop to the left and then to the right.
7. Let them climb an imaginary ladder with arms and legs.
8. Show them how to do jumping jacks.
9. Have children lie on their stomachs, face down. Tell them to reach back with their hands and hold their feet and then rock back and forth.
10. Have children lie on their backs with legs extended over head; have them pedal an imaginary bicycle.

Bibliography of Resources

BOOKS ABOUT SENSORIMOTOR EXPLORATIONS

Academic Therapy Publications. *Sensorimotor Activities for the Remediation of Learning Disabilities.* San Rafael, Calif.: 1977. Based on the theories of A. Jean Ayres, this book is highly useful for teaching young children who are still in the process of integrating their sensory and motor systems, as well as children with special needs. Practical, simple explanations and a great many activities for use in the classroom.

Allen, Marsha. *Sensory-Motor Integration.* Bend, Oreg.: Mosier Materials, 1983. A practical book with a simple explanation of sensory integration, diagnostic tests, and 30 lesson plans for grades K–8. Includes a wide range of activities and equipment. Many suggestions can be applied to the preschool child as well.

Ayres, A. Jean. *Sensory Integration and the Child.* Los Angeles, Calif.: Western Pyschological Services, 1982. A basic text for any teacher interested in the theory of sensory integration.

Bentley, William G. *Learning to Move and Moving to Learn.* New York: Citation Press, 1970. Concisely prepared booklet with simple outlines for movement activities covering such skills as directionality, laterality, and axial movements. Designed primarily for elementary-age children, but also useful with preschoolers. Includes selected bibliography and list of related audiovisual materials.

Braley, William T., et al. *Daily Sensorimotor Training Activities: A Handbook for Teachers and Parents of Pre-school Children.* Freeport, N.Y.: Educational Activities, Inc., 1968. A manual with activities that can be integrated into the preschool curriculum. The daily lesson plan of activities progresses through a thirty-four week training period designed to develop body image, space and direction, balance, hearing discrimination, and form perception.

Capon, Jack. *Perceptual-Motor Lesson Plans.* Byron, Calif.: Front Row Experiences, 1975. A book and cards presenting activities for preschool through first grade. Included are plans for 25 weeks of activities with evaluation scales, objectives, introductory information, and illustrations. Many of the lessons can be simplified further as needed. Detailed technical presentation of the tactile and inner-ear balance systems.

Cratty, Bryant J. *Movement, Perception and Thought: The Use of Total Body Movement as a Learning Modality.* Mt. View, Calif.: Peek Publications, 1969. The author explores activities that involve total body movement and action that reflect understanding of certain kinds of concepts and are especially useful for children with learning difficulties. For example, one exercise in pattern recognition suggests that the child be given a triangle to hold while he or she walks that same pattern into the sand. Another in number recognition requires that the child look at a number on the chalkboard and then jump onto that same number in a grid of numbers placed on the ground.

Curtis, Sandra R. *The Joy of Movement in Early Childhood.* New York: Teachers College Press, 1982. Photographs are used to illustrate various stages of fundamental motor patterns—walking, running, jumping, kicking, throwing, and catching. The author offers games and activities for preschoolers based on these patterns and suggestions for setting up creative play spaces.

Furth, Hans, and Harry Wachs. *Thinking Goes to School: Piaget's Theory in Practice.* New York: Oxford University Press, 1981. Designed for use in the classroom from kindergarten on up, many of the activities are appropriate for preschoolers as well. Offers games that develop movement thinking (eye-movement thinking games, auditory thinking, logical thinking, social thinking, etc.). The emphasis is on the development of visual skills.

Graselli, Rose N., and Priscilla A. Hegner. *Playful Parenting.* New York: Perigee Books, 1981. Games and exercises for infants to three years of age designed to encourage physical and mental skills according to developmental stages.

Hackett, Layne C. *Movement Exploration and Games for the Mentally Retarded.* Mt. View, Calif.: Peek Publications, 1970. Noncompetitive, child-centered activities that provide successful experiences. For example, children are asked to show "how far you can reach with your hands" or "how you can put your heels together." Most of the activities are designed for older children, but the teacher can adapt the ideas to suit younger children.

Hackett, Layne C., and Robert G. Jenson. *A Guide to Movement Exploration.* Mt. View, Calif.: Peek Publications, 1973. The movement exploration activities are designed for the elementary-school child but can be adapted for the preschooler. These tasks allow the child to develop and progress at his or her own rate. Helpful teaching techniques are given.

Kamii, Constance, and Rheta DeVries. *Group Games in Early Education: Implications of Piaget's Theory.* Washington, D.C.:

National Association for the Education of Young Children, 1980. This book is based on the premise that play is a powerful factor in fostering the social life and constructive activity of the child. It outlines the criteria for meaningful group games and then presents examples of the following: aiming, chasing, hiding, and guessing games; races; and games involving verbal commands. Appropriate for preschool and the elementary grades.

Levy, Janine. *The Baby Exercise Book.* New York: Pantheon, 1975. Simple exercises by a kinesiotherapist based on natural movements. For newborns through fifteen months.

Lovinger, Sophie L. *Learning Disabilities and Games.* Chicago, Ill.: Nelson-Hall, 1979. Describes the procedure and intrinsic developmental tasks of the standard and beloved games of childhood. Emphasizes the usefulness of these games in contributing to the self-esteem and skill development of the learning-disabled child. Appropriate for elementary level, but some games easily adapted for preschool.

The Parent-Child Early Education Program. *Shaping a Curriculum for Fours and Fives.* Ferguson, Mo: Ferguson-Florissant School District, 1980. Contains screening tests for language, math, and gross and fine motor coordination. There are daily lesson plans complete with goals, activities, and materials as well as suggestions for simplifying or making the activities more complex. Available from Mosier Materials, 61328 Yakwahtin Court, Bend, Oregon, 97702.

FILMS

Films on creative and sensorimotor movement are available from the following sources:

Bradley Wright Films, 1 Oak Hill Dr., San Anselmo, CA 94960. Provides films on basic motor and perceptual activities.

Documentary Films, 3217 Trout Gulch Rd., Aptos, CA 95003. Provides films on fun with parachutes and movement exploration activities.

Film Fair Communications, 10900 Ventura Blvd., Studio City, CA 91604. Provides films on such topics as balance skills, ball skills, and basic movement skills.

WHERE TO WRITE FOR ADDITIONAL RESOURCE MATERIALS

Bowmar Music and Records, Belwin Mills Publishing Corp., Melville, NY 11747. (516) 293-3400.

Children's Book and Music Center, 2500 Santa Monica Blvd., Santa Monica, CA 90404. (213) 829-0215.

Educational Activities, Inc., P.O. Box 392, Freeport, NY 11520. 800-645-3739.

Folkways Records, 632 Broadway, New York, NY 10012. (212) 777-6606.

Kimbo Educational, P.O. Box 477, Long Branch, NJ 07740. (201) 229-4949.

Linden International, 1955 Camino De Los Robles, Menlo Park, CA 94025. (415) 321-5445.

Melody House Publishing, 819 NW 92nd Street, Oklahoma City, OK 73114. (405) 840-3383.

Pacific Cascades, 47534 McKenzie Hwy., Vida, OR 97488-9707. (503) 896-3290.

PART THREE

Math Experiences

Introduction

Young children learn mathematical concepts in many of their daily activities. An awareness of one-to-one relationships is evidenced by comments like "one cracker for you, one for Mary, and one for me." An understanding of ordinal numbers is apparent when children say things like "I get to go first," "You're next," and "She's last." Young children are also capable of comparing numbers and quantities: "I have more than you do."

Numbers are all around young children. It is *10* o'clock, time for juice; *five* children can go for a walk today; *2* cups of flour are needed for the play dough recipe. Numbers are also part of songs and stories.

In cooking activities, children learn sequence and how different measures correspond: "You put the flour in first, the sugar second, and the baking powder last"; "Three of these (teaspoons) equal one of those (tablespoon)."

Geometric shapes are all about the room. Children learn to recognize the circle of a clock face and the edge and angle of the corner of a table, and to differentiate the square and rectangular blocks.

Mathematical concepts can be woven into every area of the preschool curriculum. Numbers, shapes, sizes, sequences, correspondence, and other relationships are so much a part of a child's daily experience that teaching opportunities arise naturally. Concepts and skills acquired during the early years lay the foundation for an understanding of mathematics later in life.

The acquisition and understanding of mathematical concepts during the early years are related to the child's level of cognitive development. In the view of Jean Piaget, a famous Swiss psychologist, cognitive development progresses through several identifiable stages, characterized by particular cognitive activities or *mental operations*. A summary description of each stage is given on the next page.

Piaget's Stages of Cognitive Development

Stage	Approximate age range[1]	Mental operations
Sensorimotor	Birth to 2 years	Makes contact with external world through senses; lacks object permanence (that is, believes an object ceases to exist when it is hidden from sight). Between the ages of one and two, discovers that something or someone out of sight can still exist.
Preoperational	2 to 7 years	Ages two to four: Begins to discriminate patterns and shows awareness of consistent patterns in the environment (a ball is round, a block is hard, a pillow is soft), but is still easily misled by perceptions. Ages four to seven: Makes accurate perceptual comparisons and deals with immediate and observable events, but cannot hold abstract ideas in mind to compare with unseen events.
Concrete operations	7 to 11 years	Able to conserve and hold information in mind; can articulate consequences; shows a rudimentary grasp of logic (for example, can handle two dimensions of object simultaneously).
Formal operations	11 years through adult	Able to use symbols to reason and solve problems on an abstract level; can consider alternatives by using symbols; is less dependent on visual or tactile information; can see logical possibilities.

[1] The ages provided are approximate averages and will vary with individual children.

Preschool teachers are most concerned with the first and second stages of cognitive development. In the *sensorimotor* stage, infants begin to organize into patterns the mass of sensations that come from the environment. One jumble of sensations becomes a face, another becomes a bottle, and a moving cluster of stimuli becomes a hand. The stimuli are received through the various sensory modalities — vision, touch, taste, hearing, and smell. During this period, children accumulate ideas about the world, and around eighteen months to two years of age, they begin to represent these ideas with simple words. At about this time they also begin to plan and to think in advance of what they are about to do. When faced with a problem, a two-year-old will try a new strategy if the first one does not work. Although thought is beginning to be independent of action, these planned acts take place only with objects with which the child is in direct contact. That is, thinking is still tied to things that are immediately before the child in space and time, not in the other room, or in the past or future.

During the later part of the sensorimotor stage, a fascinating process takes place: the development of *object permanence*. At this time, the child realizes that objects, including people, continue to exist even when they are not visible. Memory plays a crucial role in object permanence: if mommy continues to exist as an image in memory, the child can accept the notion that she hasn't disappeared for good, but still exists in some place out of sight and will return.

The second, or *preoperational*, stage is the basis for many preschool activities. At this stage, symbols, ideas, imagery, and other internal representations become a familiar part of the child's mental system. Between the ages of two and four, children begin to develop certain logical concepts about their environment. They are beginning to learn that certain characteristics of an object are enduring, that such things as quantity and number do not change just because the appearance of the object is transformed. But children in the preoperational stage are still easily misled by their perceptions. Pour all the juice from a tall glass into a shallow bowl and the child is apt to say there was more juice in the tall glass. Several pieces of candy spread out over a larger space will look like more than the same number of pieces in a smaller space. Children in the preoperational stage are misled by one characteristic of an object or set of objects because they have difficulty holding perceptual information in mind and applying it to new situations. They are only beginning to realize that some properties remain constant despite a change in some features of an object. This awareness of the constancy of properties is known as *conservation*. Problems of conservation apply to numbers and to length, width, and volume. Youngsters in the preoperational stage should be given many opportunities to pour liquids, stack blocks, bounce balls from different heights, measure cooking ingredients, and so on. Through such activities, children begin to develop notions of cause and effect and an understanding of concepts like conservation.

Many teachers and parents want to know if a child's progress from one stage to another can be accelerated. Efforts to do so have been only partially successful. It appears that children can learn a concept such as conservation more quickly if given plenty of firsthand experiences in that area and only *when they are old enough to learn* (age five is usually the earliest a child can master conservation).

The activities in this section are presented in a general order of simple to more complex. However, the teacher needs to assess the developmental level of *each* child before presenting specific tasks. For example, conservation of various attributes do not occur at the same time in the same order for all children. One child may be a conserver of length but not of number. By presenting one or more of the activities, the teacher can determine where there is conflict between logical understanding and the child's perception.

These activities need not, however, be carried out as though they were formal tests. They can be adapted for use in spontaneous situations at the play dough table or the sandbox, during snacks, or whenever a natural teaching moment arises. Knowing the child's level of cognitive development helps the teacher plan activities that lay the foundation for learning more complex concepts and relationships.

The terms listed below represent important mathematical concepts. Familiarity with them will help you recognize more quickly an opportunity to incorporate them in the daily activities and learning experiences of the children.

Terms	Definitions
Cardinal	The names of the numbers or the counting numbers; the numbers that tell us *how many*. Examples: *one, five, fifty;* he has *two* hands and *ten* fingers
Ordinal	Numbers that tell us *which one* and express succession in a series. Examples: *first, last, second, tenth;* the *fifth* child in the *first* row.
Comparison of numbers	When numbers are in sequence, such as 1, 2, 3, 4, 5, then 5 > (is greater than) 3 3 < (is less than) 5
Pairing or matching	One-to-one correspondence; when one set is equal to another; when one set has the same number of members as another set. Examples: 2 beads and 2 blocks or ☐ ☐ and △ △
Set	A collection of things. Things belonging to a set are its *members* or *elements*. A set

Terms (cont.)	Definitions (cont.)
	may have many or few members, or *no* members (empty set). Example: members of the class = a set.
Subset	A set within a given set. Examples: set = members of the class. subset = members of the class with brown shoes.
Comparison of sets	*More than* and *fewer than* are the words used in comparing sets. *Are there more members in this set than in that set? Which set has fewer members?*

□ □ □ □   △ △
(more than)   (fewer than)

This concept is taught more easily after *pairing,* and *more than* is more easily grasped than the concept *fewer than.*

Conservation of quantity	The quantity of matter remains constant no matter what shape it assumes.

Math Activities

NUMBERS

▶ **PURPOSE**   **To practice using names of the cardinal numbers**

MATERIALS   — Flannelboard with five identical pieces. For example:

△△△△△

PROCEDURE   **1.** Have objects arranged horizontally:

△△△△△

Count 1, 2, 3, 4, 5, left to right, with the children.

2. Rearrange vertically:

Count again: 1, 2, 3, 4, 5.

3. Rearrange objects:

Count again (left to right): 1, 2, 3, 4, 5.

VARIATIONS
1. Teach the song "Ten Little Indians."
2. Count the number of toys in the doll corner, painting corner, sandbox, and so on.
3. Count the number of people present — boys, girls, adults.
4. Bounce a ball and call on a child to clap his or her hands the same number of times. The child who does this correctly becomes the leader. If bouncing a ball is too difficult, let the child beat on a drum.
5. Do finger plays using numbers.

HELPFUL HINTS

1. Help children become conscious of numbers: count the number of children at each table; count napkins, cups, eating utensils.
2. Send number tasks home with each child and suggest that family members help to reinforce the concepts.
3. Write out numerals in each child's life: his or her age, address, phone number, number of people in the family or school.

▶ **PURPOSE** **To practice using cardinal numbers**

MATERIALS — Chairs, crackers, people

PROCEDURE
1. Have children sit at the table during snacktime.
2. Count the number of chairs, crackers, and people with the children.
3. Hold up four fingers and ask the children to count how many there are.
4. Hold up your fingers in a different combination (for example, two fingers of each hand) and ask if that is the same number.
5. Change combinations in presenting a number concept to be certain children have a logical understanding of numbers.

▶ **PURPOSE** **To practice using cardinal numbers by counting**

MATERIALS — Egg carton
— Twelve plastic eggs (the hollow kind that twist open), all the same color
— One larger hollow plastic egg
— Objects suitable for counting such as buttons, Styrofoam packing materials, Cheerios, and so on

PROCEDURE 1. With felt-tip pen, number each egg from 1 to 12. On each egg, make the corresponding number of dots.
2. Place any number of eggs in the carton, depending on the child's ability.
3. Place uniform counting materials in the larger egg.
4. Have the child place correct number of buttons (or other counting material) in each egg to correspond to the number indicated.
5. Be sure to check for correct counting after each series.
6. Say:
How many buttons are in the larger egg? (None.) **Then we say that there are** *zero* **buttons in the larger egg because zero is the same as none.**
7. Have the child place a card with the number zero printed on it next to the larger egg.
8. As children become more capable, add different numbers and mix up the eggs.

VARIATION Carry out addition and subtraction problems in the same way.

▶ **PURPOSE** **To practice using cardinal numbers with dice**

MATERIALS — Dice
— Pebbles, play coins, or other uniform small objects

PROCEDURE 1. Have children take turns throwing the dice.
2. Let the child count the number showing on the dice and take an equal number of pebbles or objects from the kitty.
3. With very young children, use only one die or make a wooden cube with a low number of dots painted on it.
4. Have children count out loud.

VARIATION 1. Cut out or mark spaces on tagboard.
2. Have the children throw the dice and move their marker the equivalent number of spaces, making certain that they are counting correctly and moving one space for each number.

▶ **PURPOSE** **To practice using cardinal numbers with dots and numerals**

MATERIALS — Cardboard (11″ × 14″)
— Sandpaper or fabric
— Dot stickers of the same size, shape, and color

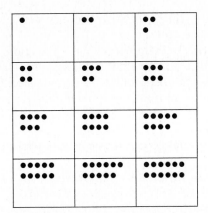

Illustration 3.1 **Box to practice cardinal numbers**

PROCEDURE   **1.** Cut the numerals 1 to 12 out of fabric and mount each one on a separate piece of cardboard.

2. Have the child name each numeral as he or she traces over them with his or her finger.

3. Using a felt-tip pen, make twelve boxes on the piece of cardboard.

4. Moving consecutively from left to right, place the appropriate number of dots in each box. (See Illustration 3.1.)

5. Have the child count the number of dots in a box out loud and place the corresponding numeral in the box.

▶ **PURPOSE**   **To practice using ordinal numbers with bean bags**

MATERIALS   — Four bean bags

PROCEDURE   **1.** Have four children gather in a group.

2. Give a bean bag to each child.

3. Say:
How many bean bags are there?
Let's count them: 1, 2, 3, 4.
If you all throw them, could I catch them all at once? (No.)
We could take turns. (Give each child a number.)
You are first; you are second; you are third; and you are fourth.
We will throw them in that order. Let's say your numbers together: first, second, third, fourth.

4. Have children throw the bean bags in order.

5. On another day, also ask:
***Who* was first, second, third, and so on?**

▶ **PURPOSE**   **To practice using ordinal numbers**

MATERIALS   — Four paper cups labeled 1st, 2nd, 3rd, and 4th
— Button

PROCEDURE   **1.** Place the four cups on a table.

2. Have the children close their eyes while you hide a button under one of the cups.

3. Have the children open their eyes and guess which cup the button is under. (The child must say "The button is under the [first/second/third/fourth] cup," not simply point or say "that one.")

4. Label and add more cups as children learn the ordinal numbers.

▶ **PURPOSE**   **To practice using ordinal numbers with blocks**

MATERIALS   — Blocks or other common objects

PROCEDURE   1. Begin with a group of four children and four blocks.

2. Say:
   Let's count the blocks: 1, 2, 3, 4. There are four blocks. I will give each of you a block in a certain order. You will be first (give block to a child), **you are second** (give block to another child), **you are third, and you are fourth.**

3. Have the children repeat *first, second, third, fourth* together. Point to or touch each child as he or she is labeled.

4. Say:
   Now I would like you to return the blocks to me in order: first, second, third, fourth.

5. Increase the size of the group as children indicate their understanding of the concept.

6. Group children according to their ability.

▶ **PURPOSE**   **To practice using ordinal numbers with matching and nonmatching items**

MATERIALS   — Box filled with matching pairs of items: bottle caps, buttons, spools, marbles, small toys, and the like

PROCEDURE   1. Place seven nonmatching items in a row. This row will serve as a model.

2. Ask the child to select matching items and copy the model, making certain that his or her row is at least ten inches away from the model.

3. Help the child order his or her items in the same way the model is ordered.

4. Have the child verbalize the label (for example, "The first item is a marble, the second item is a button, the third item is a bottle cap," and so on).

▶ **PURPOSE**   **To practice using ordinal numbers with music**

MATERIALS   — Record player and records, or piano, or some other form of musical accompaniment

PROCEDURE   1. Have a small group of children line up.

2. Say:

We're going to play a game called "Jumble Up."
I will give each of you a number in order. (Assign ordinal number to each child—first, second, third, and so on.)
When the music starts, you can move around and get "jumbled up." When the music stops, I want you back in the right order.

3. Play the music and let the children move around.
4. Stop the music and ask the children to get back in order. When children are back in line, have them repeat the original order as you point to them ("I am first," "I am second," and so on).
5. The number of children in the group and the length of time the music is played should depend on children's abilities.

VARIATION   Children can remain "jumbled up" when the music stops and can wait until you call out "first," "second," "third," and so on before taking their places.

▶ **PURPOSE**   **To practice using ordinal numbers and to learn sequence**

MATERIALS   — Pictures showing sequence of events, cut from magazine
— Photographs showing sequence of experiences familiar to children
— Drawings of experiences in sequence
— File box

PROCEDURE   1. Have each sequence of pictures in a separate folder or envelope in the file.
2. Let children work in small groups or separately.
3. Have them sort the pictures into proper sequence.
4. Have them tell what happened first, second, third, and so on.

▶ **PURPOSE**   **To compare numbers**

MATERIALS   — Flannelboard with different shapes cut from construction paper:
♡ ♡ ♡ ♡ and ◇ ◇

PROCEDURE   1. Have children stand or sit near the flannelboard.
2. Say:
Are there as many diamonds as hearts?
Which set has more? How many hearts are there? How many diamonds?
The set of 4 is greater than the set of 2.
We say that 4 *is greater than* 2.
3. Let each child take a turn manipulating the shapes and demonstrating *greater than* and *less than*.

▶ **PURPOSE**   **To compare numbers using bean bags**

MATERIALS   — Five bean bags (or other common objects)

PROCEDURE   1. Have children gather in groups of a convenient size.
2. Say:

Let's count the bean bags together (as you count, push the bean bags aside): **1, 2, 3, 4, 5 bean bags.**
Which is greater — 5 bean bags or 3 bean bags? 5 is greater than 3.

3. Use other objects such as buttons or beads; use amounts that are greater than or less than.

HELPFUL HINTS

1. Count children as they sit down at the juice table.
2. Count the steps involved in getting dressed.
3. Count the steps involved in doing an art project: first, cut; second, paste; third, color.
4. In a cooking activity, point out the order in which ingredients are added.
5. Use appropriate stories, such as "The Three Bears" or "Caps For Sale," for practice in repeating ordinal numbers.
6. Ask a child to assign the correct number of children to a particular number of chairs.
7. Sing "Ten Little Indians." Have the children say which is greater: three Indians, two Indians, four Indians, and so on.
8. Compare ages of grandmother, mother, and child. Ask which is greater and so on.

FORMS

▶ **PURPOSE**   **To identify and match geometric forms**

MATERIALS   — Geometric forms cut from construction paper:

     ○ □ △ ▭

— Paper clip attached to each form
— Pole (more than one, if possible)
— Magnet attached to pole with string

PROCEDURE
1. Spread forms on the floor.
2. Hold up a shape (△) and ask a child to "fish" for a shape that matches.
3. Let the child fish for the shape; when he or she finds it, ask the name of the shape.
4. Hold up another shape, and ask another child to fish for that shape. Repeat until each child has had a chance to fish.

▶ **PURPOSE**   **To sort geometric forms**

MATERIALS   — Large assortment of each of four shapes: triangle, circle, square, and rectangle

— Box divided into four equal compartments, with one of the shapes pasted on each of the compartments.

PROCEDURE
1. Mix all shapes together on a table.
2. Have child sort shapes into appropriately labeled compartments, naming the shapes as he or she works.

VARIATIONS
1. Use large and small shapes.
2. Use shapes of different colors.
3. Have the child sort shapes in any way he or she chooses. Have the child tell why he or she categorized them in that way. Most young children will sort according to color, then shape, and finally size.

HELPFUL HINTS

1. Have the children help make a large poster of different shapes and label them. Post the names of the children who can identify each shape.
2. Cut sandwiches, cookies, and snacks into geometric shapes and talk about shapes as children eat.
3. Cut sponges into different shapes and use them for making paint designs on construction paper.

▶ **PURPOSE**   **To match geometric forms**

MATERIALS
— Flannelboard with at least two cutouts of each of four shapes: triangle, circle, square, and rectangle

PROCEDURE
1. Place a triangle on the flannelboard.
2. Say:
   Who can find a shape to match this one? (Let a child find it.)
3. Repeat the same procedure with each shape.
4. Let each child pick a shape and then choose someone who has a matching shape.

▶ **PURPOSE**   **To name and match geometric forms**

MATERIALS
— Cards of heavy tagboard, each marked like a grid with different shapes in each square
— Cutout cardboard shapes to match

PROCEDURE   1. Have children place matching shapes on the card.
             2. Have children name the shapes as they select them.

VARIATIONS   1. Have children take turns drawing shapes from a box. After each child pulls a shape out, he or she should place it in the appropriate square. If the child has no square left to cover, he or she may choose to give the shape to another child who needs that particular shape.
             2. Each child can be given a handful of shapes and the teacher or another child can draw shapes from a box one at a time calling them out as in Bingo.

▶ **PURPOSE**   **To make geometric forms**

MATERIALS   — 12″ square of wood, ¾″ thick
             — Twenty-five nails, 1 to 1¼″ long
             — Box of rubber bands

PROCEDURE   1. Hammer the nails into (but not through) the board in a 5 x 5 array.
             2. Use a rubber band to make a square shape and ask the children to make a shape just like the one you made. (See Illustration 3.2.)
             3. Do the same with triangular and rectangular shapes.
             4. Name each shape as you make it.
             5. Let children experiment with the shapes they can make and help them make them.

VARIATION   The form board can also be made with golf tees glued into a pegboard.

Illustration 3.2 **Using nailboard to learn geometric shapes**

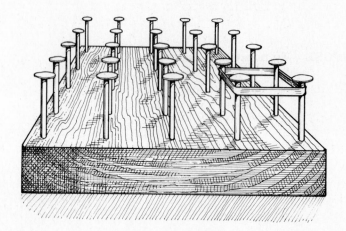

HELPFUL HINTS

1. Construct shapes with yarn or tape.
2. Mark geometric shapes on the floor with chalk or tape and have children singly or in a group reproduce those shapes with their bodies by lying on top of them.
3. Have children look around the room for shapes in the windows, doors, chairs, bookcases, blocks, balls, musical instruments, and so forth.
4. Distribute geometric shapes to children at dismissal time or transition time:
   The children with triangles may go to the juice table.
   The children holding circles may get ready to go home.
5. Cut sandwiches into geometric shapes at lunch time. Identify the shapes. Have children bite their cookies or sandwiches into other shapes and name them.

PAIRING AND MATCHING

▶ **PURPOSE**   **To pair and match assorted stickers**

MATERIALS — Blank index cards (3″ x 5″)
— Assorted pairs of stickers

PROCEDURE 1. Attach one sticker to each card.
2. Place all the cards face down on a table.
3. Have each child take turns picking out two cards.
4. Say:
   Are your pictures the same? (Yes.) **Then we say they are a pair because both pictures match and they are the same.**
5. Have the child place the pair of cards next to him or her and take another turn.
6. If the child selects two cards that are not the same, state that they are not a pair because they do not match. Replace those cards face down on the table.
7. Let another child take a turn.
8. When the game is over, let each child count the number of pairs he or she has collected.

Note: This activity is especially popular with five-year-olds. It is a good memory and recall game.

▶ **PURPOSE**   **To pair and match sets**

MATERIALS — Assorted pairs (sets) of objects: 2 forks and 2 crayons, 2 scissors and 2 pencils, 2 paper clips and 2 safety pins

PROCEDURE 1. Arrange children in three small groups at a table.
2. Say to the first group:

Here is a set of forks and a set of crayons. Let's count the members in each set (2). **Are they the same in each set?** (Yes.) **Then we say that they are pairs. The sets match. Each one has the same number of members.**

3. Say to second group:

    Here is a set of scissors and a set of pencils. Let's count the members in each set (2). **Are they the same?** (Yes.) **Then we can call them pairs. Each set has the same number of members.**

4. Do the same for the third group.

▶ **PURPOSE**   **To pair and match groups of objects**

MATERIALS   — Flannelboard
            — Cutouts of three different-colored pigs, three kinds of houses (straw, twig, and brick with a chimney), and three arrows

PROCEDURE   1. Tell the story of "The Three Little Pigs," emphasizing which pig goes with which house and using the arrows to show the correct pairing.
            2. When the children are familiar with the pairing, mix the houses and pigs and let children use the arrows to indicate which pig goes with which house.

VARIATION   Use cutouts of the three bears and different-size chairs, bowls, beds, and so on.

▶ **PURPOSE**   **To pair and match two sets**

MATERIALS   — Flannelboard with cutouts of at least three each of the following shapes:

✚   ◯   ♡   △

PROCEDURE   1. Have children stand in a group around the flannelboard. Take two ✚ 's and two ♡ 's.
            2. Say:
               Are there more crosses or more hearts?
            3. Rearrange in two similar groups of three. For example:

△△△   ♡ ♡ ♡

            4. Ask if the sets match. Do they have the same number of members?
            5. Arrange in unlike (dissimilar) sets:

△ ♡ ◯   ✚ ◯ △

Do these match? They are pairs because they have the same number of members.

▶ **PURPOSE**   **To pair and match more than two sets**

MATERIALS   — Flannelboard and cutouts used in previous activities
— A cutout circle to use as a marker

PROCEDURE   **1.** Place groups of different shapes on the flannelboard:

$$\bigcirc \ \bigcirc \ \bigcirc \qquad\qquad \heartsuit \ \heartsuit$$
$$\triangle \ \triangle \ \triangle \ \triangle \ \triangle \qquad\qquad \square \ \square \ \square$$

2. Say:
Who can show me the sets that match? Come and make a ring around them. Why do they match? (Because these groups have the same number of objects.)

3. Make other combinations:

$$\bigcirc\bigcirc \qquad\qquad\qquad \heartsuit \ \heartsuit \ \heartsuit \ \heartsuit$$

Have children come to the flannelboard and circle the matching sets using the marker or their hands.

▶ **PURPOSE**   **To pair and match sets with unequal members**

MATERIALS   — Flannelboard with cutouts used in previous activities

PROCEDURE   **1.** Have children gather in group around you.
2. Say:
Here are two sets:

$$\triangle \ \triangle \qquad\qquad \heartsuit \ \heartsuit$$

Let's count the members in each of these sets. Are they the same? (Yes.)

3. Arrange two more sets:

$$\square\square \qquad\qquad \bigcirc\bigcirc$$

4. Say:
Let's count the members. Are they the same? (Yes.)

5. Rearrange so that the sets are unequal.

$$\square\square\square \qquad\qquad \bigcirc\bigcirc$$

6. Say:
Let's count the members again. Are they pairs? (No.) **Why not?** (Because they have different numbers of members.)

7. Do as often as necessary to teach matching concept.

EQUIVALENCE

▶ **PURPOSE**   **To practice one-to-one correspondence by matching**

MATERIALS   — Collection of buttons or other easily manipulated objects, all uniform in size and shape, but in two colors (for example, black buttons and white buttons)

PROCEDURE
1. Give a child a handful of buttons (about twelve).
2. You take a handful of the opposite color.
3. Make a row of six buttons equally spaced.
4. Ask the child to make a row just like yours with his or her buttons.
5. If the child does not understand the concept of one-to-one correspondence, he or she is likely to use all of the buttons or to make a row that is not equivalent, even though the two end buttons may match.
6. After each trial, change the number of buttons.
7. Give the child many opportunities to learn about one-to-one correspondence through manipulation. (See Illustration 3.3.)

HELPFUL HINTS

1. Have children set the table matching the correct number of napkins, cups, and so on to the number of chairs.
2. During stories or music time, have children close their eyes and listen while you clap your hands three times. Have children open their eyes and clap their hands the same number of times. Increase in number and variety of patterns.
3. Match ordinary items (for example, paintbrushes to containers of paint or coats to children).

Illustration 3.3 **Using buttons to practice one-to-one correspondence**

▶ **PURPOSE** To practice one-to-one correspondence by pairing

MATERIALS — Flannelboard
— Ten or more circles to represent heads
— Ten or more cone shapes to represent hats

PROCEDURE 1. Place a circle on the flannelboard and say:
This is a head and I want to put a hat on it. (Place a cone on top of the circle.)
2. Place another circle on the board and say:
Here is another head.
3. Continue to place circles on board and ask:
How many hats do we need?
If children begin to guess, ask:
How can we find out?
4. Let each child show how he or she understands pairing.
5. Let each child pick up (or count out) the number of hats he or she thinks you will need each time you put up a series of circles.
6. Do not correct and teach the child; rather, watch how the child tries to figure out the problem. Children who do not understand equivalence need to be given many opportunities to do pairing and matching activities.

COMPARISONS

▶ **PURPOSE** To practice making comparisons *(more than, fewer than)* using a balance scale

MATERIALS — Balance scale
— Small blocks

PROCEDURE 1. Have the child place the same number of blocks in each tray.
2. Have the child take some blocks out of one tray.
3. Have the child count the number of blocks in both trays.
4. Ask:
Which one has more blocks? Which one has fewer blocks? What do you need to do to make them weigh the same?
5. Let the child tell you the number of blocks that need to be added or subtracted in order to achieve a balance.

▶ **PURPOSE** To practice making comparisons *(more than, fewer than)* using blocks

MATERIALS — Set of blocks

PROCEDURE 1. Have children count the blocks with you.
2. Then distribute varying numbers of blocks to each child, counting each block as you hand it to the child. Example:
I am giving Emilio one block, two blocks, three blocks. Now I am giving Françoise one block, two blocks. I wonder who has

more? Let's count them together. Emilio has more blocks than Françoise. There are *more* blocks in Emilio's set. Françoise has *fewer than* Emilio.

3. Vary the activity in difficulty according to the children's abilities.
4. Similar comparisons can be made with equipment and toys in other areas of the school and home.

▶ **PURPOSE**   **To practice making comparisons** *(more than, fewer than)* **using buttons**

MATERIALS   — Collection of buttons or similar objects, all uniform in color, shape, and size

PROCEDURE
1. Place four buttons on a table in a random design.
2. Have children look at the buttons and count them.
3. Have children close their eyes while you take away one button.
4. Have children open their eyes and tell if there are *more* or *fewer* buttons than before.
5. Begin at a level at which the children can succeed. Place buttons in a straight line for those who become confused with random design.
6. Increase and vary in difficulty by using more buttons and removing varying numbers, or sometimes leaving the *same* number.

▶ **PURPOSE**   **To practice making comparisons** *(more than, fewer than)* **using beads**

MATERIALS
— Container with separate compartments, such as egg carton or muffin tin
— Beads for stringing in assorted colors (be sure the beads have large enough holes so children can string them easily)
— Strings of equal length, knotted at one end and dipped in melted wax at the other end for easier stringing

PROCEDURE
1. Have beads sorted in the compartments according to color.
2. Have children copy your pattern of stringing.
3. Increase difficulty of pattern by adding more colors and more beads, varying the numbers each time. Do not move on to more difficult steps until the children have had many opportunities to indicate that they understand the concept.
4. Let children string beads any way they like, but check with each one and have the child tell you as he or she is stringing beads which are *fewer than* and *more than* and *the same number as.* (See Illustration 3.4.)

VARIATIONS
1. Compare the number of pieces in two puzzles.
2. Compare the number of boys to the number of girls.
3. Compare color of hair — blonde to brown, and so on.
4. Compare room fixtures — windows to doors, lights to doors, and so on.

Illustration 3.4 **Using beads to make comparisons**

5. Compare foods — crackers and cookies, celery and carrots, and so on.
6. Compare stacks of paper juice cups (count the number in each stack).

▶ **PURPOSE**   **To practice making comparisons *(more than, less than)* using containers**

MATERIALS   — Cans of varying sizes and shapes: tall, thin, small, wide
— Pan full of rice

PROCEDURE   1. Select two cans. Say:
Which do you think holds the greater amount? (Let children guess.)
How can we find out?
2. Have a child fill one can with rice.
3. Let the child pour the rice into the other can.
4. Help the child to indicate with words the appropriate concept:
The green can holds a greater amount of rice than the red can.
The blue can holds less than the green can.

VARIATION   The same activity can be carried on by measuring sand in the sandbox or water in the housekeeping area.

SETS

▶ **PURPOSE**   **To learn about sets having like members**

MATERIALS   — Sets of objects having *like* members: blocks, paintbrushes, crayons, scissors, and so on

PROCEDURE   1. Have a small group of children sit at a table or on the floor.
2. Show them one set of like objects (blocks).
3. Say:
   What are these? These are all blocks. They belong to a group. This is a group of blocks.
4. Show the children another set of objects. Say:
   What are these? These are all brushes. This is a group of brushes. We can call this a *set*.
5. Continue with other sets of objects and repeat that each group can be called a *set*.
6. When all objects have been shown, repeat the identification:
   This is a set of blocks. This is a set of brushes.
7. Ask:
   Can you name some other sets in this room? (Help children identify other like objects by the word *set*.)

HELPFUL HINTS

1. Use the children's natural experiences to introduce the concept of set. For example, at the juice table, let children help distribute a set of cups. Talk about groups of things that are alike and refer to them as sets. Talk about groups of things that are used for the same purpose and refer to them as sets.
2. Other properties of sets that children can easily recognize are color, size, texture, shape, weight, and length.

▶ **PURPOSE**   **To learn about sets having unlike members**

MATERIALS   — Sets of objects having *unlike* members: sandbox toys, playhouse dress-ups, cooking utensils, equipment used in the art corner

PROCEDURE   1. Have a small group of children sit on the floor in a group.
2. Say:
   Here are a strainer, eggbeater, spoon, and measuring cup. What are these things used for? (Cooking.)
   Are they all alike? (No.) **But they are all used for cooking. They are all members of the same set that we will call the "cooking set."**
3. Do the same for each group that you have. Finish by saying:
   We will call these members of the same set the _____ set.

▶ **PURPOSE**   **To learn about subsets**

MATERIALS   — Large assortment of buttons

PROCEDURE   1. Have a group of children sit at a table.
2. Distribute a handful of buttons to each child, saying:
Here is a *set* of buttons for Mary, here is another *set* of buttons for John, and a *set* of buttons for Jim.
3. Take a handful of buttons for display purposes.
4. Sort buttons and indicate what you are doing:
I am sorting the red buttons and putting them here. This is my *subset*. These red buttons are a *subset* of my buttons.
5. Have the children sort their buttons. As they work, reinforce the concept of *subset:*
I see John is sorting his blue buttons into a separate pile. I wonder if someone knows what we call that pile of buttons?

HELPFUL HINTS

1. Story time: Discuss the fact that everyone is a *member of the class.* Have all the children wearing brown shoes stand up. They are the *brown shoes subset.* Have all the girls stand up. They are the *girls subset.* Select other qualities familiar to the children, such as color of hair or style of clothing.
2. Juice time: Refer to a basket of crackers as a *set;* each child is given a *subset* of crackers. Do the same with napkins, cups, and other objects to reinforce the concept.
3. Music time: If children remove their shoes for dancing, have them place all their shoes together and discuss the fact that these constitute a set of shoes. The brown shoes are a *subset.* Let the children determine other ways to establish subsets, such as tennis shoes, sandals, and oxfords.

CONSERVATION

▶ **PURPOSE**   **To learn conservation of quantity (volume) using play dough**

MATERIALS   — Two pieces of play dough of equal size and quantity

PROCEDURE   1. Give one piece of play dough to a child and ask:
Do you have as much as I do?
2. Roll one piece of play dough into a rope shape and ask:
Now, do you have as much as I do?
3. Re-form your piece of dough into the original shape and ask the same question again.
4. Give the child opportunities to shape and reshape the play dough in order to experience conservation of quantity.

> **HELPFUL HINTS**
> 1. Provide large containers, such as dishpans, buckets, or sandtables, filled with fine-grain sand, rice, flour, or water; and measuring utensils, such as measuring spoons, sifters, scales, and plastic measuring cups with ounce as well as milliliter markings on them.
> 2. Talk about pouring, measuring, sifting, comparing, and use words provided in the activities.
> 3. Have children pour different kinds of materials, such as beans, gravel, and liquids, from a small to a large measuring cup, then from the large to the smaller cup. Discuss weight and conservation of quantity *(more, less, same)*.

▶ **PURPOSE**   **To learn conservation of quantity (volume) using liquid**

MATERIALS   — Clear plastic measuring cups
                — Glasses of sizes and shapes different from the measuring cups

PROCEDURE   1. Set up several measuring cups with equal amounts of water in each (a few drops of blue food coloring added to the water helps children see the level of measure more easily).
                2. Give each child a cup of liquid and a glass.
                3. Have children pour their liquid from the measuring cups into the glasses.
                4. Place your measuring cup of water next to each child's glass and ask:
                   Is there as much water in here as in there?
                5. Let children pour liquids back and forth and compare amounts. (See Illustration 3.5.)

▶ **PURPOSE**   **To learn conservation of quantity (number)**

MATERIALS   — Flannelboard
                — Cutouts of same size and shape, but two different colors (for example, black and white)

PROCEDURE   1. Place six black circles in a row.
                2. Have a child place an equal number of white circles in a row beneath the black ones.
                3. Pick up the black circles and place them farther apart in a row:

                4. Ask:
                   Is this the same number (pointing to the black) **as this** (pointing to the white)?

Illustration 3.5 **Using liquid to learn conservation**

5. Use other arrangements to be certain the child is not using space as the basis for judgment:

▶ **PURPOSE**   **To learn conservation of quantity (number) using beads**

MATERIALS — Egg carton
— Black beads and white beads

PROCEDURE **1.** Place one black bead in each of the six compartments on one side of the egg carton.

2. Ask a child to count the number of beads.
3. Pick up one bead from a compartment and place it in an adjoining compartment.
4. Ask the child:
   Now are there the same number of beads?
5. If the child answers correctly, place six white beads on the other side of the egg carton, one bead in each compartment (your side). Ask:
   Do I have the same number of beads as you have?
6. Pick up two white beads and place them in adjoining compartments. Ask:
   Now do I have the same number as you have?
7. Vary the location of beads to be certain the child understands the concept of conservation.
8. Add an extra bead and ask:
   Now do I have the same number as you have?

HELPFUL HINTS

1. With groups of children, regroup according to the suggestions of the class: hair color, color of shoes, boys, girls, and so on.
2. Arrange four or five blocks in a row; then stack them. Explain that it is the same quantity each time.
3. Assemble two groups of children (five in each group). Have one group form a circle and one group sit in a straight line. Point out that each group contains the same number.
4. Make different shapes from pieces of heavy string or yarn of equal lengths.

Bibliography of Resources

The following books may be useful to the teacher who wants to adapt additional curricular ideas to the classroom or wants to do some additional reading about instruction in number readiness.[2]

Baratta-Lorton, Mary. *Mathematics Their Way.* Menlo Park, Calif.: Addison-Wesley, 1976. Photographs and descriptions of activity-centered games and tasks for teaching math concepts to young children.

————. **Workjobs.** Menlo Park, Calif.: Addison-Wesley, 1972. Photographs illustrate well-designed activities for an open classroom. Provides the teacher with ideas for development of language, math, and other concepts.

[2] See also page 193 for books about shapes and numbers.

————. **Workjobs II.** Menlo Park, Calif.: Addison-Wesley, 1979. Photographs illustrate twenty new inexpensive, teacher-made activities that provide young children with concrete experiences in math.

Beberman, Max (ed.). *Young Math Books.* New York: Crowell. A series of books designed for the young child, covering such concepts as long, short, high, low, thin, wide, circles and other shapes, and weighing and balancing. Some of these books are too difficult for the very young, but others can be adapted or used as resource material for the teacher.

Branley, Franklyn M. *Think Metric!* New York: Crowell, 1972. Conversion to the metric system may cause some problems for adults who are unaccustomed to the International System of Units. Young children should be introduced to the system early, and teachers of young children will find this book a valuable aid. Written and designed for elementary ages, but very helpful for the adult.

Brown, Sam (ed.). *One, Two, Buckle My Shoe.* Mt. Ranier, Md.: Gryphon House, Inc., 1982. Activities of varying degrees of difficulty designed for parents and preschool teachers to use with young children. Describes the materials needed, the concept being taught, and the vocabulary to be stressed.

Carmichael, Viola S. *Curriculum Ideas for Young Children.* Los Angeles: Southern California Association for the Education of Young Children, 1971. See pages 63–73 for exercises that illustrate weight, size, and shape concepts. Includes a bibliography of children's books and records dealing with these concepts.

Charlesworth, Rosalind, and Deanna J. Radeloff. *Experiences in Math for Young Children.* Albany, N.Y.: Delmar, 1978. Provides teachers with an organized, sequential approach to developing math activities for young children.

Dawes, Cynthia. *Early Maths.* New York: Longman, 1977. Covers the development of math experience in children ages three to five. The author discusses stages of development and how math concepts can be introduced in any nursery school using common materials and objects. The book includes diagrams and illustrations to provide prenumber, measurement, and shape experiences.

Debelak, Marianne, Judith Herr, and Martha Jacobson. *Creating Innovative Classroom Materials for Teaching Young Children.* New York: Harcourt Brace Jovanovich, 1981. Provides teachers with ideas for developing games that teach young children basic math concepts.

DeFranco, Ellen B. *Learning Activities for Preschool Children.* Salt Lake City, Utah: Olympus, 1975. Provides activities that help young children grasp basic math concepts. Includes a list of the concepts, skills, and vocabulary words to be learned.

Ekberg, Marion Hopping. *Games for All Seasons.* Marion Hopping Ekberg, 1982. A game book designed to teach prereading and prewriting skills to children between the ages of three and six.

Hans, Elizabeth, and Dolores M. Hibbard. *The Learning Box.* Elizabeth A. Hans and Dolores M. Hibbard, 1981. Contains visual and auditory discrimination, art, prenumber, and reading-readiness activities for three-, four-, and five-year-olds.

Hibner, Dixie, and Liz Cromwell (eds.). *Explore and Create.* Livonia, Mich.: Partner Press, 1979. An activity book that provides many concrete experiences in premathematical skills for young children.

Kamii, Constance. *Number in Preschool and Kindergarten.* Washington, D.C.: National Association for the Education of Young Children, 1982. A Piagetian-based resource encouraging teachers to build on number relationships derived from children's personal experiences rather than using workbooks.

Kay, Evelyn. *Games That Teach for Children Three Through Six.* Minneapolis, Minn.: T. S. Denison, 1981. Photographs and descriptions of handmade activities that help develop a child's prereading and premathematical skills.

Lavatelli, Celia. *Early Childhood Curriculum: A Piaget Program.* Boston: American Science and Engineering, 20 Overland St. This set of materials includes a book; classification kits; number, measurement, and space kits; and seriation kits for use in teaching basic math concepts.

Nuffield Mathematics Project. *I Do, and I Understand.* New York: Wiley, 1967. Deals with the rationale for teaching math to young children and discusses many of the problems involved in setting up a classroom in which math instruction can take place. Useful for the teacher who wants more general information about math instruction.

————. *Mathematics Begins.* New York: Wiley, 1967. An excellent booklet designed to help young children perceive the patterns and relationships of mathematics. The section devoted to the preschool experience is especially useful in planning projects and activities that give children experiences of space, shape, size, matching, measuring, and so on.

————. *Pictorial Representation.* New York: Wiley, 1967. This booklet provides ideas about the use of pictures and graphs to communicate and simplify information. Much of the material is suitable for older children, but some can be easily adapted for use with younger children.

San Felipe Kindergarten. *A Kindergarten Guide for Indian Children.* Available through the Commissioner of Indian Affairs, 1951 Constitution Ave. N.W., Washington, D.C. 20242. This program was created and adapted to serve Indian children. It includes number concepts, counting, sets, geometric shapes, positional relationships, measurement, and basic operations of addition and subtraction.

Sharp, Evelyn. *Thinking Is Child's Play.* New York: Dutton, 1969. Forty games based on Piaget's work stressing learning concepts through manipulation of objects. Each activity is presented in a simple format with purpose, materials, and comments accompanied by illustrations. This book should make it possible for teachers and parents to put into practice and appreciate Piaget's impressive research work.

Tarrow, Norma Bernstein, and Sara Wynn Lundsteen. *Activities and Resources for Guiding Young Children's Learning.* New York: McGraw-Hill, 1981. An activity book designed to help children learn math concepts at various developmental stages.

Warren, Jean. *Learning Games.* Palo Alto, Calif.: Monday Morning Books, 1983. Provides illustrations and directions for making mathematical games for young children.

Weikart, David P., et al. *The Cognitively Oriented Curriculum: A Framework for Preschool Teachers.* Washington, D.C.: ERIC-NAEYC, 1971. A description of a curriculum based on Piagetian theory. The second half of the book provides helpful guides to activities in teaching classification, seriation, spatial relations, and temporal relations.

PART FOUR

Language Arts

Introduction

One of the most exciting and complex achievements of a preschooler is learning to talk. As teachers, we are privileged to be part of the period of language development that is probably the most dramatic of the child's life. Teachers share in the daily discovery of words and phrases as a child's language skills mature and new avenues of communication are explored. Observing the change from the compressed style of a toddler's message ("all gone" or "more milk") to the complex forms of a three-year-old's "I don't want to do that," the teacher encounters one of the most impressive feats of a young child's development.

By the age of six, a child has learned most of the adult patterns of speech. But children seem not to be taught a language so much as they acquire it on their own. Preschoolers are not passive learners. They absorb words as they play, they imitate the teacher's conversational phrases, and they repeat stories read to them. Often, to the surprise of adults, youngsters will mimic patterns of speech they hear with astonishing accuracy.

Although imitation and modeling are important factors in speech development, researchers are not clear about the exact ways in which children learn to speak. One principle of significance to early education, however, is that *children learn to speak by speaking.* Opportunities for children to practice speaking are very important.

Several basic principles that describe things adults can do to facilitate children's language development can be summarized from research findings:

1. Get children to talk.
2. Children talk more if there is something of importance to them to talk about.
3. Children will talk more to an adult they like. Continuity in the adult-child relationship makes for richer content in conversation.
4. Provide activities that lend themselves to verbal interaction.
5. Whenever possible, connect words and phrases to actions rather than to linguistic exercises.
6. Use language that is more precise and complex than that which the child is presently using.

7. Informative comments evoke responses from children more often than commands or directives.

8. For children who do not talk easily, structured speaking situations may make them feel more comfortable.

Monitor teacher-child conversations for a period of time and certain patterns will become clear. With some adults, the tendency is to rely on the interview technique: "What is your name?"; "How old are you?"; "Where do you live?"; "How many brothers or sisters do you have?"; and so forth. These questions usually prompt simple one- or two-word replies. The teacher who consciously refers to topics and activities that are of interest to the children will get many more elaborate verbal responses: "I see you're carrying a red lunch box with your name on it, David. I wonder what you like to eat." When the topic is of importance to the youngster, he or she is more likely to become engaged in conversation.

The stress of a busy teacher's workday can often induce a monologue of directives: "Put the brush in the paint can"; "Be careful not to spill"; "Use your inside voices"; and "Time to sit down for juice." Such utterances do not encourage extended conversations; conversational give-and-take between adult and child does not happen accidentally. Teachers have to monitor themselves in conversation and plan an environment that allows equal interaction to take place naturally.

When snacks and other meals are served to small groups, or when stories and sharing activities allow plenty of time and space for individual children to express themselves verbally, conversation is natural and enjoyable. When adults ask open-ended questions ("What do you think we should do when the rabbit has her babies?") and make comments that encourage thinking responses ("I wonder why the little girl in the story was sad"), children are more likely to respond and carry on extended conversations.

The teacher who is most likely to succeed in motivating children to talk is the one who listens very carefully to the child and watches for clues that tell more about the child's interests and concerns. Attending totally to children means not finishing their sentences for them or assuming that one already knows what they want to say. Ask children to elaborate and explain what it is they mean when they make comments. For example, a child might complain that another "won't share." Ask the youngster to tell you what he or she means and to verbalize in greater detail how such a conclusion was reached. When children are encouraged to expand their ideas, they gain practice in verbalizing, they clarify their thought processes for themselves, and they learn from the teacher the value of listening attentively.

We all appreciate a good listener — a person who genuinely wants to understand what it is we are trying to communicate. Likewise, children respond favorably to the adult who attends to and appreciates what they are saying. Children like to be praised and rewarded for expressing themselves verbally and using language correctly. The best reward and reinforcement is an appreciative and attentive listener.

Sometimes teachers rely on comfortable, pat phrases ("That's very nice, honey"; "I like that"; "You're doing a good job"; and "How are we doing here?") without really expecting any response from the child. Such phrases do not encourage a child to think. They become hollow and the child soon learns to tune them out. When questions and comments are geared to children's level of understanding, however, and are intended to engage them in thought and conversation, the adult-child interaction is greatly enriched.

Teaching language does not require a formal teacher-directed setting in which the child sits and listens passively and then responds to the teacher's questions. Young children learn language best when they are actively engaged in doing something of real interest to them and are relating their physical activities to appropriate speech. Children are easily motivated to practice speaking in natural settings like cooking, building, dramatic play, and similar group projects.

Teachers can help stretch a child's verbal abilities by using an extended vocabulary and a wide variety of expressions. Instead of saying, "Marty, think of another way to do that," the teacher might say, "Marty, have you considered other possibilities?" Although the child may not be able to understand all the teacher's words, he or she will be challenged in a nonthreatening way to think about the meanings of those words within a given context. Of course, the teacher must be careful to see that the child does not have to stretch too much. Since children have difficulty following abstract language, they are more likely to learn, use, and understand the words they hear when verbal interactions are directly related to their activities.

Adults tend to talk to children who respond. Unless the teacher is sensitive to this tendency, the shy or quiet child is likely to be overlooked. Sometimes there may be a language deficiency or other handicap of which the teacher should be aware. It is important that the teacher initiate conversations and plan activities to engage reluctant youngsters in conversation. Sometimes quiet children respond most favorably to the friendly, warm, and chatty teacher who makes no demands for verbal response. At other times, they may appreciate the safety of a more structured, pattern-response activity. Young children whose primary language is something other than English may have difficulty making the transition to a second language, even when they understand what they hear. A sensitive and loving teacher — one who does not give up on these children or treat them as though they were less intelligent than the rest of the group — can do much to help these children risk speaking in a less familiar tongue.

The teacher should not assume that the highly verbal child always understands what others are saying. For example, when the teacher points to an object and says, "There it is under the table," the child may appear to understand the word *under* when the teacher's pointing actually provided a cue. Children may also repeat phrases they have heard without understanding their meaning. They are often impressed by language they hear within a dramatic context, such as phrases from television commercials and curse words.

Although the exact nature of how a child learns a language may not be clear to researchers, it is safe to assume that children are likely to learn best in a setting that is warm, friendly, safe, and designed to engage them actively in verbal exchange. Children learn language by practice, and teachers develop competence in motivating language by practice. A setting rich in language-motivating experiences makes talking enjoyable. And when teachers and children are enjoying themselves and each other, language competence will grow and flourish.

The activities in this section are designed to encourage children's participation in a variety of language experiences. Some of the activities may appear drill-like in form and content, but they are merely simplified so that teachers can adapt and revise them as needed. Corrective feedback and verbal rewards are supplied by the teacher's responses to the individual child's participation. Suggested dialogue is also included in many of the activities to offer examples of the kinds of comments and questions that lead a child to respond.

The language skills covered in this part are those included in most preschool curriculums — speaking, listening, reading,[1] and writing. The activities are divided into five sections:

1. Speaking — developing fluency
2. Speaking — acquiring new words and concepts
3. Learning to listen and to discriminate sounds
4. Reading — learning to identify letters and numbers and to discriminate visual patterns
5. Writing — developing motor skills and familiarity with writing

A number of different techniques may be used to develop competence in these skill areas. Although these techniques overlap, applying to more than one area, some are relatively focused on one skill or another:

— *Storytelling* falls in the listening skill area, but also contributes to vocabulary development and concept formation.
— *Games* may be used for evoking verbal responses, as in "I have a secret," or for guided expression of emotion. Both techniques help develop fluency in speaking.
— *Dramatic play*, which is included in the section on creative activity, encourages fluency in speaking, practice in taking roles, and the use of a variety of speech styles.
— *Visual cues*, including flashcards, objects displayed to be named, and flannelboards, help develop skills needed in reading, such as visual perception and discrimination of shapes, numbers, and letters.
— *Sensorimotor activity* helps children learn to coordinate visual perception with motor skills, obviously relevant to the development of writing ability.
— *Auditory cues* facilitate listening skills and help develop the ability to discriminate among sounds.
— *Conversation* is so obvious that it is easily neglected. Activities

---

[1] In most preschools, reading is included in the sense that prereading skills — letter recognition, vocabulary, familiarity with printed materials, encouraging the children to follow a story through pictures or other visual materials, developing perceptual skills — are taught or encouraged.

that encourage children to talk with one another and with adults are important for both speaking and listening skills.

Variations of some of the activities may be used to challenge all levels of ability in the group and to provide additional practice of a particular skill. The activities can also be modified for bilingual children when necessary. Use the space provided alongside each task and at the end of the section to note your own modifications.

Materials required for many of the activities are easily made or obtained by a teacher. The use of familiar objects is most effective in introducing a skill or concept for the first time. Pictures and object-props are a teacher's best friends!

The love of books and an appreciation of the beauty and power of words are an outgrowth of a well-developed language arts program. Teachers can do much to engage young children in exciting language experiences by using stories. Activities involving telling and reading stories are especially effective with very young children and children who have not had many positive experiences with language activities in the past. Probably the most important ingredient in the success of a language arts program is your own appreciation for literature and the enthusiasm you bring to the experience of sharing a story with your children. This section also offers some suggestions in the form of helpful hints for effective storytelling and for teachers who want to enhance their language arts programs.

Finally, this section concludes with an extended annotated bibliography, listing books suitable for young children as well as resource texts for teachers. The descriptions should be helpful in selecting appropriate stories for the curriculum. Some of the books are out of print, but they can be found in libraries. Others have been reprinted in paperback editions.

Language Activities

SPEAKING — DEVELOPING FLUENCY

The activities in this section are designed to give children the opportunity to practice speech. The emphasis is not on learning new words, but on active participation in verbal exchanges with adults and other children. Some activities involve labeling and identifying objects, but others give the children an opportunity to develop their own speech patterns by describing situations, objects, or their own experiences.

▶ **PURPOSE**   **To use complete sentences to describe an activity**

MATERIALS   — Group of photographs, mounted on tagboard, showing candid shots of the children engaging in activities at the school (leave space under each picture to write a descriptive sentence)
— Felt-tip pen

PROCEDURE   1. Hold up a picture and ask the children to tell what is happening in the picture.
2. Invite each child to help dictate what you should write under the picture.
3. Encourage each youngster to use a complete sentence in the description.
4. Have the child repeat the sentence after it is written.
5. Help children associate speaking with writing.
6. Let them add more descriptive sentences each time you show the pictures.
7. Add new pictures from time to time.

HELPFUL HINTS

1. Use large pictures so all children can see.
2. Hold pictures so children do not have to strain their necks.
3. Design activities to suit the size of the group.
4. Keep up interest level in large groups by using faster-paced activities.

▶ **PURPOSE**   **To understand and talk about action words**

MATERIALS   — Pictures, mounted on tagboard, showing actions such as running, hopping, skating, and talking

PROCEDURE   1. Hold up a picture and say:
Something is happening. Or **Look what is happening in this picture.**
2. Say:
Tell me about the picture.
What is happening?

HELPFUL HINTS

1. Plan activities for individual children or small groups of children who are reluctant to speak up in a large group.
2. Give instructions before showing the items.
3. Keep in mind the sequence of activities so you can make a quick transition from one to another. (Hesitate and you're lost!)
4. Sometimes it helps to start an activity with a finger play or short song, then introduce the learning activity when you have everyone's attention.
5. If you're yelling a lot, it's time to stop and reassess your presentation method.
6. Make mental note of children who don't participate.

What do you think happened before this?
What do you think will happen next?
3. Record the children's answers and read them back.
4. Display the pictures with each child's answers.
5. Encourage each child to tell you what he or she said about each picture. Children will want to have you change their responses; let them know it is all right to make up new stories.

▶ **PURPOSE**   **To use complete sentences to describe an object**

MATERIALS   One each of objects such as the following:

— red ball
— blue block
— yellow chalk
— green play dough

PROCEDURE   1. Hold up one of the objects and make a statement about it, using a complete sentence. For example:
This is a red ball.
2. Have the children respond in a complete sentence when you ask what the object is. For example:
TEACHER   **What is this?**
CHILDREN   **This is a red ball.**
3. Do the same with the other objects.
4. When children become familiar with the technique of responding with a complete sentence, introduce two qualities as descriptors:
TEACHER   **This is a round, red ball.**
        What is this?
CHILDREN   **This is a round, red ball.**

Note: Learning to use complete sentences is accomplished most effectively when children have many opportunities to hear adults using complete sentences in natural and spontaneous conversation. Drill-like activities are not designed to be forced on children, but to serve as reminders for teachers to incorporate patterning and modeling in practicing language skills.

HELPFUL HINTS

1. When working with very young or inattentive children, try involving them first by drawing or painting large pictures of the characters in a story such as "The Gingerbread Man" or "The Three Bears."
2. Encourage the children to help color or paint the characters. (They need not paint within the lines.)
3. Cut and mount the pictures on tagboard or flannel backing.
4. Talk about the story while the children are helping with the art work.
5. Finally, tell the story using the characters.
6. On another day read the story and show the book.

► **PURPOSE** **To recognize and describe objects**

MATERIALS — Pictures of objects, mounted on cardboard, such as animals, furniture, vehicles, food, and play equipment

PROCEDURE
1. Play the game called "I've Got a Secret."
2. Do not show the pictures to the children.
3. Discuss each picture in turn, giving clues about the object in the picture, such as physical description; group it belongs to (animal, vehicle, etc.); how it is used; where it is found.
4. Let children guess after each clue.
   This animal has a long neck. What is it? (giraffe)
5. When a child guesses correctly, give him or her the picture.
6. When all pictures have been handed out, let each child hold up his or her picture and ask, "What is this?"
7. Encourage the children to answer in complete sentences.

VARIATIONS
1. Have children describe objects and let others guess.
2. Make animal sounds and have children guess the animal.
3. For children with limited vocabularies, use pictures of one class of objects (food, cars, or animals), and line pictures up to provide a visual clue.

HELPFUL HINTS

1. Use language to help children focus on their activities: "Joshua uses both hands to hold on"; "Carmelita is hopping on her right foot"; "Peter knows how to go down the slide slowly. Now he's going very, very slowly."
2. Make comments that encourage responses: "I wonder how you make this design"; "That's an interesting way to do it"; "I'd like to have you tell me more."
3. Phrase comments and questions that require more than a yes or no answer. Instead of "Do you want to read a story?" you might say, "I wonder if you remember the funny story we read yesterday about the silly bear."

► **PURPOSE** **To recognize and name colors**

MATERIALS — Red, blue, and yellow construction-paper strips ¾″ wide and 6″ long; ten strips of paper in different colors for each child
— Paste and paste brushes
— Containers for paste (plastic coffee lids, foil tins)

PROCEDURE
1. Give each child strips of construction paper and pasting material.
2. Show children how to make a loop chain:
   Put paste on one end of a strip of construction paper.
   Bring the two ends together to form a ring.
   Thread the next strip through the first ring and paste the two ends together.

Continue this process until you have made a chain of at least eight loops.

3. Conduct an exercise in naming colors:

   Show a strip of red paper.

   Have each child find the same color strip.

   Name the color and have the children repeat it.

   Select another strip of the same color and let one child name the color.

   Use the same method in teaching the other colors.

4. Conduct an exercise in pattern recognition and reproduction:

   Make a model chain of three colors, repeating the color pattern three times.

   Have children duplicate the model chain.

   Have one child explain how the pattern was put together.

▶ **PURPOSE**   **To recall members of a group of objects by color**

MATERIALS — Plastic spoons of different colors

PROCEDURE 1. Show the children four spoons of four different colors.
2. Review the colors.
3. Say:

   I am going to hide one spoon and you can take turns telling me which one is missing.

4. Encourage children to answer in complete sentences. For example: "You are hiding the red spoon."
5. When a child guesses correctly, he or she may hold the spoon.
6. Children can play this game together, once they have learned it.

HELPFUL HINTS

1. Squat or kneel down to the child's eye level when you talk with him or her.
2. Get into the habit of putting your arm around a child or making some kind of physical contact when you communicate verbally.
3. Be conscious of the way you stand and sit. Your posture invites or rejects physical contact from others.

▶ **PURPOSE**   **To name and describe single and plural objects**

MATERIALS — Collection of cardboard or construction-paper fish
— Picture of a single object pasted on each fish
— A paper clip attached to each fish
— Small pole with string and magnet on the end

PROCEDURE 1. Give each child a chance to fish.
2. If the child can identify the object by saying "This is a ____," he or she keeps the fish.

3. The child with the most fish wins.

4. After all the objects have been identified, children can fish again.

5. This time they must say one other thing about the object to keep the fish. For example: "This is a car. This car is red."

6. When the children can easily make two simple statements, encourage them to make compound statements, such as "This car is red and has wheels."

VARIATIONS **1.** Put objects behind a screen or partition, and use a larger pole with a clothespin on the end.

2. If flannel objects are used, children can catch two of the same thing. Make it clear that the statement "This is a ___" refers to one thing and the statement "These are ___" means more than one.

▶ **PURPOSE** **To sort and describe objects by size and/or color**

MATERIALS — Red and white buttons (include large and small buttons of each color as well as buttons with different numbers of holes)
— Cigar box or shoe box
— Two small boxes for sorting or two paper mats

PROCEDURE **1.** Work with one child at a time and ask the child to determine what is in one of the boxes.

2. Say:
Can you tell me about this object? (Give the child a large red button.)

3. Encourage the child to name the button and describe the shape, color, and number of holes it has.

4. Give the child time to think about what he or she wants to say.

5. If necessary, direct the child by asking:
If a button were missing from your coat and you needed a new one just like this one, how could you tell what it looked like?

6. Compare a red button with a white one to encourage the child to see the color difference.

7. Compare the number of holes in the buttons.

VARIATION **1.** Ask a child to sort buttons in any manner he or she wishes, putting the buttons in as many piles as he or she thinks necessary.

2. Then ask the child to put the buttons into two piles, using the mats or small boxes. If he or she sorts the red ones from the white ones, ask the child if the buttons can be put together in another way (small and large, two holes and four holes, and so on).

SPEAKING—ACQUIRING NEW WORDS AND CONCEPTS

As children gain proficiency in using the words they know, new words and new concepts are added to their vocabulary at a rapid rate. The activities in this section are designed to help expand their knowledge of words and how to use them.

▶ **PURPOSE**   **To learn parts of the body, left and right side**

MATERIALS   — Large roll of butcher paper
            — Large black crayon
            — Tempera paints and paintbrushes
            — Scissors

PROCEDURE   **1.** Conduct a discussion about parts of the body. Say:
            Can anyone tell me what the word "body" means?
            Does Hans have a body? Does Lisa? Do I?
            What are some of the parts of our bodies?
            Do we all have arms? (Hold arms in air and shake them.)
            We all have arms; what else do we all have?
            2. After some discussion, show children the paper, crayon, and paint.
            3. Explain that they will lie on the paper and you will trace around them. Then they can cut out the shapes and paint them; after that they can put in a face and draw the clothes. Encourage naming and discussion of body parts.
            4. When tracing around the child, start at the head, saying:
            I am starting at the top of your head. (See Illustration 4.1.)
            5. Mention the body parts as you trace, stressing right and left sides.
            6. The figures can be hung on the walls with name cards under them.

HELPFUL HINTS

1. Children like teachers to share in a learning experience.
2. Join in activities and laugh with the children.
3. Let children draw your outline while you lie on a large piece of butcher paper.
4. Play "Simon Says." Use directions such as "pat your head, shake your left leg, and wriggle your right-hand fingers."
5. Make a puzzle. Draw figures of a boy and a girl. Mount them on cardboard. Cut the cardboard into parts of the body.
6. Act out and sing "Put Your Finger in the Air."
7. Occasionally, use more difficult or different words in familiar finger plays and chants, like "My neck, my elbow, my thigh, my heel" instead of "My head, my shoulders, my knees, my toes."

▶ **PURPOSE**   **To learn directional words (in, out, up, down, across, through, into)**

MATERIALS   Playground equipment or substitutes:

            — big cement pipe (3′ in diameter) or wooden barrel, steel drum, or large cardboard box (use for crawling *through*, going *into*)
            — slide or a kitchen chair-stool (climbing *up* and sliding *down*)

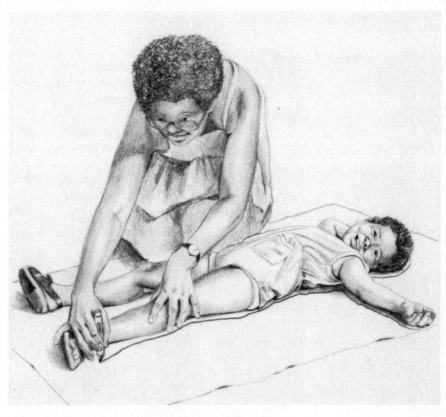

Illustration 4.1 **Learning about parts of the body**

— board (4'–5' long) supported on either end by wooden boxes or bricks (walking *across*)
— a wagon or large box (sitting *in* and getting *out* of)
— camera to take pictures of children performing the actions

PROCEDURE
1. Play "Follow the Leader."
2. Explain that the leader has to tell what he or she is doing and the others are to copy his or her actions and words.
3. First time through, help the children know what words to use by asking the leader to do something. Say:
   Show us how you go up.
4. As children do various activities, have someone take pictures to be used for a discussion at a later date.

VARIATION
1. Show the pictures to the children.
2. Write down their conversation when they discuss the pictures.
3. Make a book using the pictures and the dictation, underlining the action words.

▶ **PURPOSE** **To learn to say names, addresses, and telephone numbers**

GAME NO. 1
MATERIALS
— List of name, address, and telephone number of each child
— Police officer's hat, if available

PROCEDURE
1. Have children form a circle.
2. Tell the children they are going to play a game about being lost.
3. Talk about how it feels to be lost.
4. Ask who might help them find their way home; ask how they could tell someone where they live; ask how they could let their parents know they were all right.
5. They may need to be guided by your saying,
   Do you think a police officer could help you? How would you tell the police officer where you live?
6. Let one child wear the police officer's hat and assume the role of the officer; have other children pretend to be lost.
7. It may be necessary to help the first few children by feeding them their lines.

GAME NO. 2

MATERIALS
— List used in Game No. 1
— Small chair

PROCEDURE
1. Have the children play a "pretend" game in which they live in a magic town that has a fairy.
2. Once a year all the children can ask the fairy for anything they want; they then leave their names and addresses so the fairy can send what they asked for.
3. You play the fairy and each child comes to you and tells what he or she wants and leaves his or her name and address.

HELPFUL HINTS

1. Children relate more easily to a book if they are familiar with the story through some other personal experience, such as having it told to them or having acted it out.
2. "The Great Big Enormous Turnip" by Alexei Tolstoy (Weston Woods, Conn.) lends itself well to acting out. Show a filmstrip of the story.
3. Weston Woods Studios, Weston Woods, Conn. also sells filmstrips of other popular titles.

▶ **PURPOSE**   **To identify and classify foods**

MATERIALS   Samples of one of the following classes of foods:

— fruits (apples, oranges, grapefruit, apricots, plums, prunes, figs, tangerines, bananas, avocados, tomatoes, cherries)
— vegetables (peas, green beans, carrots, turnips, celery, collard greens, pea pods, radishes, lettuce, green peppers, squash)
— meats (pictures of different cuts of meat or ways of serving; examples of precooked meat such as hot dogs, weiners, beef jerky, and luncheon meat)
— fish and fowl (shrimp, chicken, turkey)

— grains (cereals, breads, rice, noodles, macaroni, crackers)
— dairy products (cheeses, milk, ice cream, butter, eggs)

PROCEDURE

1. Consider explaining this project to the parents and asking them about some of the foods served frequently at home.
2. Parents might be willing to prepare one food for the child to bring to school.
3. Discuss with the children the kinds of things they eat at home to provide a basis for classification.
4. If you start with fruit, for example, bring in five common varieties.
5. Talk about color, shape, and skin texture.
6. Hold up an apple and ask if anyone can tell what it is.
7. Hold up an orange and have it identified.
8. Introduce three more fruits.
9. Cut open the fruit and show the children what it looks like inside.
10. Call attention to the seeds and to the fact that all fruit contains seeds.
11. Cut fruit into sections and give to each child to taste.
12. Talk about taste (sour, sweet) and whether pulp is crisp or hard or soft or juicy.
13. Talk about ways we can use fruit (pies, dried, juices, salads, and so on).
14. Follow up with tasting experiences of processed fruit.
15. Consider taking a field trip to a grocery store.

VARIATION

After the children have learned some of the different kinds of food, set up a store using wooden boxes, benches, or bookcases. Ask children to bring in empty food boxes, cartons, meat trays, and cans from home. Children can make papier-mâché fruit, meat, and other foods and paint them with tempera, or put pictures mounted on cardboard over the empty containers. Let the children sort the items into groups of fruit, vegetables, and so on. Help them make signs and then let them play store.

▶ **PURPOSE** **To match, sort, and classify objects**

GAME NO. 1 — MATCHING

MATERIALS

— Pictures pasted in two rows on cardboard covered with construction paper (protect pictures with clear contact paper), with knotted shoestrings inserted next to each picture on the left side and punched holes on the right side
— Examples of objects that might be included in pictures: face, tree, apple, wheel, wagon, plate with food, leaf, eye

PROCEDURE

Have children connect pairs of objects that can be matched conceptually by inserting shoestring in the proper hole. For example: face—eye.

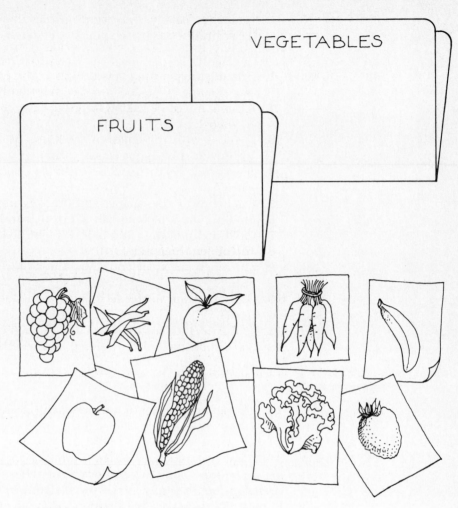

Illustration 4.2   **Materials for sorting game**

GAME NO. 2 — SORTING

MATERIALS
— Two large manila folders, each labeled with a different category
— Pictures of objects representing the two categories (See Illustration 4.2.)
— Examples of categories:

fruits	flying things
animals	vegetables
wheeled things	plants
objects of same color	objects of same shape

PROCEDURE
1. Have children divide pictures into two categories.
2. Then have them place each picture in the appropriate folder.

GAME NO. 3 — CLASSIFYING

MATERIALS
— Flannelboard and shapes of animals commonly owned by children (each category of animal — such as dogs, cats, or guinea pigs — should be the same shape and color)

PROCEDURE   **1.** Ask children:
           Who owns a dog?
    2. Count the number of children who own a dog and place the appropriate number of dog shapes on the flannelboard.
    3. Repeat the same procedure with each animal.
    4. After figures are placed on the board, ask:
           How many animals do you children have? Let's count them.
           How many are dogs? (Count)
    5. Do the same with all the other animals. Be sure also to stress those that *do not* belong to a category.
    6. As children become more sophisticated, add other categories (clothing, food, color of hair and skin, types of transportation, and so on).

HELPFUL HINTS

1. Teach concepts over and over again in different areas of the school; incorporate them into other parts of the curriculum.
2. Remind children of the concepts they learned earlier.
3. Have them demonstrate what they learned.
4. Review and repeat learned concepts frequently.

▶ **PURPOSE**   **To learn names of different shapes, colors, and patterns**

MATERIALS   — Three blue squares (10″ × 10″) for each child (Make the squares from construction paper; mark the center of each square with an X, designating area for paste.)
    — Paste and brushes
    — Containers for paste (plastic coffee-can lids or tin-foil pans)
    — Three-sectioned TV-dinner foil trays filled with the following three groups of items cut from construction paper: yellow circles, 3″ diameter; red squares, 3″ square; green triangles, 3″ to a side

For teacher's demonstration purposes:

    — Two large blue squares decorated with two yellow circles
    — One large blue square decorated with one small red square

PROCEDURE   **1.** Use groups of four children.
    2. Show children the squares, circles, and triangles.
    3. Have children repeat the names of the shapes.
    4. Note the color of each shape.
    5. Have children repeat both the color and the shape.
    6. Give each child three blue squares, with the centers marked, and pasting materials.
    7. Have each child choose one square or one circle or one triangle from the TV-dinner tray.
    8. Have the child glue this shape to the blue square.
    9. Stop the activity and demonstrate matching and nonmatching patterns:

Have children hold squares.

Show them similar patterns — two blue squares decorated with two yellow squares. Ask if they are alike.

Introduce another blue square, decorated with a smaller red square.

Ask children if the patterns are now all alike.

Ask which squares have the same shapes glued on them.

Ask which squares are different.

10. Have children choose two more shapes from the foil tray, one like the first one they chose, and one that is different.

11. Proceed with the activity by decorating the blue squares with different shapes. (The object of the activity is to have two matching shapes pasted on two different blue squares and one nonmatching shape pasted on a blue square.)

12. Gather the squares as the children finish. Squares can be backed with sandpaper and used on the flannelboard for discussion purposes. You can discuss why certain members of a group are alike and why some members are not alike.

HELPFUL HINTS

1. Have all materials organized before starting the activity.
2. Limit group size.
3. Plan more than one activity to reinforce each type of learning.
4. Keep instructions simple and clear.
5. Repeat instructions from time to time.

▶ **PURPOSE**   **To learn concepts of shape (round and square)**

MATERIALS
— Round objects such as ball, bottle cap, marble, can, plastic drinking glass, and pencil
— Square objects such as blocks, tiles, containers, and cardboard squares

PROCEDURE
1. Put round objects on a table.
2. Ask children to name the objects.
3. Ask if anyone knows what the word *round* means.
4. Hold up the ball and say:
   The ball is round.
   Trace around it with your fingers.
5. Have the children trace a circle in the air.
6. Pass the other objects around and let children establish the roundness of the objects and trace around them.
7. Place a block or other square object on the table and ask:
   Is this round?
   How do you know this isn't round?

8. Help children talk about the differences by asking:
   Do round things have corners? Do round things have sides?
   What shape is this? This is square.
   What do you think will happen if we try to roll this block?
   What will happen if we roll the ball?
9. Pass the square things around and let the children trace them.

HELPFUL HINTS

1. Listen carefully and attentively to each child.
2. Look at each child while he or she is speaking.
3. Correct immediately when a child gives a wrong response.

▶ **PURPOSE**   **To learn concepts of large and small**

MATERIALS   — Large cardboard box or block
              — Very small cardboard box or block

PROCEDURE   1. Let children see the large box.
              2. Let them crawl inside it and explore it.
              3. Talk about the concept of large and have them name things they think are large.
              4. Show them the small box and let them hold it.
              5. Talk about the things they think are small.

▶ **PURPOSE**   **To learn concepts of loud and soft**

MATERIALS   — At least one of the following: drum, wood blocks, or party horn

PROCEDURE   1. Say something to the children in a soft voice and ask if you spoke in a loud or a soft voice.
              2. Say something loudly and ask how you were talking.
              3. Ask them to say something softly.
              4. Ask them to say something loudly.
              5. Discuss when we need to use loud voices and when we need to use soft voices.
              6. Talk about how important it is to speak in a loud voice when we have to warn someone of danger, yell for help, or call a dog.
              7. Talk about times when we speak in a soft voice, such as when people are sleeping and we do not wish to disturb them, when we are at the hospital or library, sometimes when we are in school, or when we have a secret.
              8. Use wood blocks, drum, or party horn to demonstrate loud and soft. Let children practice making loud and soft sounds with instruments. (See Illustration 4.3.)

Illustration 4.3   **Using instruments to learn meaning of "loud" and "soft"**

▶ **PURPOSE**   **To learn concepts of hot and cold**

MATERIALS   — Hot-water bottle filled with hot water
              — Bowl of ice cubes

PROCEDURE   **1.** Pass the hot-water bottle around.
              2. Ask how it feels.
              3. Ask:
                 Who can think of something we eat or drink that is hot?
              4. Pass the bowl of ice cubes around.
              5. Ask how it feels.
              6. Ask:
                 Who can think of something we eat or drink that is cold?
                 How do you feel when the weather is hot? When it is cold?

▶ **PURPOSE**   **To learn concepts of fast and slow**

MATERIALS   — Pictures of things that are fast: airplane, speedboat, racing car,
                bus, train
              — Pictures of things that are slow: baby crawling, turtle, snail, worm,
                old person with a cane

PROCEDURE   **1.** Introduce pictures of things that go fast.
              2. Talk about why people use them.
              3. Introduce contrasting pictures.
              4. Talk about why some things are slow.
              5. Find things in the classroom that go slow or fast.

▶ **PURPOSE**   **To learn concepts of light and dark**

MATERIALS — Light-colored objects: piece of pastel cloth, picture of a sunny scene, toy or stuffed animal that is light colored
— Dark-colored objects: piece of dark-colored cloth, picture of dark cloudy scene, toy or stuffed animal that is dark colored

PROCEDURE
1. Let children handle and look at the light-colored objects.
2. Discuss light-colored things.
3. Ask questions about their clothing, their hair, their skin.
4. Ask what happens if the shades are pulled or if the lights are shut off. Demonstrate.
5. Provide contrasting objects so children can see and talk about the opposite concept.

▶ **PURPOSE**   **To learn concepts of hard and soft**

MATERIALS — Hard objects: block, thick plastic, wood, rock, spoon
— Soft objects: cotton ball, sponge, pillow, marshmallow

PROCEDURE
1. Let children handle the hard objects.
2. Discuss things that are hard.
3. Ask if their heads are hard or soft; if their stomachs are hard or soft.
4. Provide a soft object for contrast.
5. Let children handle soft objects.
6. Discuss soft things they know about.
7. Have children look around the room for hard and soft objects.

▶ **PURPOSE**   **To learn relational concepts (behind, on top, inside, outside, in front, beside)**

MATERIALS — Three boxes covered with colorful paper: small box with a top; medium-sized box; large box
— Three stuffed animals or dolls

PROCEDURE
1. Place boxes in a row.
2. Ask children to identify what you have and how many there are.
3. Talk about the parts of a box (sides, bottom, top).
4. Ask how they could use boxes (for keeping things, toys, presents, small parts of games, etc.).
5. Put each doll with one box and tell the children you are going to talk about where each doll is.
6. Put one doll on top, one behind, and one inside.
7. Ask:
   Where is this doll? (Point to doll on top of small box.)
8. Continue with the other dolls.
9. Review the questions and answers.
10. Put a doll beside the box and ask where it is.

11. Place the next doll in front of the box and proceed with the questioning.
12. Review the last two positions.
13. Put a doll underneath a table or chair and talk about that.
14. Let children put the doll in a place and tell where they put it. Then ask them to put the doll on top of, behind, under, and so on.
15. Play "Simon Says," using a box for each child.

▶ **PURPOSE**   **To learn names of objects and concepts of same and different**

MATERIALS — A deep cigar box or shoe box
           — Two construction-paper mats on which to place sorted objects
           — Round objects: beads, buttons, thumb tacks, spools, bottle caps, pebbles, marbles, fake money, corks, small paper plates or toy dishes
           — Square objects: bolts, empty matchbooks, sugar cubes, dice, individual ice-cube molds, erasers
           — Alternatives: round buttons and square buttons, red buttons and white buttons (or any two colors), two-holed buttons and four-holed buttons

PROCEDURE 1. Sit down with one child at a time and take an object out of the box.
           2. Ask the child to name the object. (Encourage the child to reply in a complete sentence.)
           3. Have the child take out each object, one at a time.
           4. Have the child tell what each object is.
           5. When he or she is finished, put two round objects and one square object on the table.
           6. Ask:
              Is there anything the same about these objects?
              Is one different? How?
           7. Encourage the child to feel the roundness or squareness of the objects.
           8. Put all the objects back in the box.
           9. Put down the two paper mats.
           10. Have the child put all the same shapes on one mat and the other shapes on the other mat.

VARIATION Provide a box full of objects that can be sorted according to size, shape, and color. Specify criterion, such as round or red, and have the children take turns selecting an object that fits the criterion.

▶ **PURPOSE**   **To learn concepts of right and left**

MATERIALS None

PROCEDURE 1. Play the game "Follow the Leader."
           2. Explain the game:

Children are to follow what you do.

You will be making turns to the right and to the left.

Children will be told when you change direction.

Children will slap the right side of their thigh when you tell them you are turning right. They will slap the left side of their thigh when you tell them you are turning left.

3. Demonstrate the game:

Have children stand in a semicircle so they can see and hear better.

Turn your back to the children.

Turn to your right two or three times and tell children you are turning right.

Slap your right thigh when you tell children you are turning right.

Turn to the left two or three times, telling children that you are turning left.

Slap your left thigh when you tell the children you are turning left.

4. Practice the game with the children:

Have someone observe the children to make sure they understand the game.

Select a leader.

You can then observe children.

VARIATIONS   Different motions for the game:

— hopping to the left and right
— taking giant steps to the right or left
— skipping
— jumping
— taking a little step

HELPFUL HINTS

The following articles offer many helpful suggestions for storytelling:

— Baker, A., and E. Greene. "Storytelling: Preparation and Presentation." *School Library Journal*, 24, No. 7 (March 1978), 93–96.
— Sherman, J. L. "Storytelling with Young Children." *Young Children*, 34, No. 2 (January 1979), 20–27.
— Williamson, Paul M. "Literature Goals and Activities for Young Children." *Young Children*, 36, No. 4 (May 1981), 24–30.

LEARNING TO LISTEN AND TO DISCRIMINATE SOUNDS

These activities are designed to help children attend to words and to the speech of others and to become aware of differences among a variety of sounds that are common in their environment.

▶ **PURPOSE** **To recognize sounds**

MATERIALS — Bag or box with lid
     — Noise-making objects: bell, rattle, whistle, paper (to tear), pieces of sandpaper (to rub together), cricket, horn

PROCEDURE **1.** Say:
      We are going to play a listening game.
      When we are listening what do we hear? Noises. Every day we hear lots of noises.
      What do we hear the noises with? Ears.
      Take your hand and wiggle your earlobes, like this.
      I have a box with some things in it that make noises. I am going to make a noise and then ask who can tell me what is used to make that sound.
      Cover your eyes with your hands.
     2. Make a sound with one of the objects and ask who knows what object made the sound.
     3. Go through the entire selection of objects, trying to call on each child.
     4. When the children become more adept at identifying the sounds, have them cover their eyes while you make two sounds. Ask if the sounds were the same.
     5. After this first introduction, the children can play the game in a group by taking turns at choosing the noisemakers.

▶ **PURPOSE** **To hear and repeat sound sequences**

MATERIALS — Noise-making objects: bell, rattle, sandpaper, paper (to tear), wooden blocks (to hit together)

PROCEDURE **1.** Start with three objects on the table.
     2. Hold up one object and ask if anyone knows what it is called and what it does.
     3. Pass it around and let each child use it. Do the same with the other two objects.
     4. Say:
      I am going to make three noises. First I will shake this rattle, then I will ring the bell, and last I will tear the paper.
      What noise did you hear first?
      What noise did you hear next?
      What noise did you hear last?
     5. Give another example.
     6. Ask the children to cover their eyes with their hands.
     7. Have them listen carefully to more noises and then have them make the same noise.
     8. Add new objects and increase the number of noises in the sequence.
     9. Introduce sounds the children can make (clapping, stamping, tongue-clicking).

HELPFUL HINTS

1. When working with children for whom English is a second language, take slides of their experiences at school — even their unhappy moments.
2. Include pictures of the child's parents to show what they are doing while the child is in school.
3. Write a story about the child's adjustment to school over a period of time.
4. Have the story translated into the child's native language.
5. Tape-record the story, synchronizing the tape with the slides.
6. The audio portion accompanying each slide should present the child's native language first, followed by the English translation.
7. There are fairly inexpensive tape recorders and slide projectors that a child can operate.

▶ **PURPOSE**   **To hear rhyming sounds and match rhyming objects**

MATERIALS   — Box (whose base measures approximately 6″ × 9″) with lid
— Collection of small toy objects with rhyming names: tire, wire; hook, book; shell, bell; fork, cork; cane, plane; mouse, house
— Construction-paper mat (6″ × 9″) marked off into six 3″ × 3″ squares (See Illustration 4.4.)

PROCEDURE   1. Give a child the box (filled with the small toy objects) and ask him or her to take everything out of it.

Illustration 4.4   Materials for rhyming activity

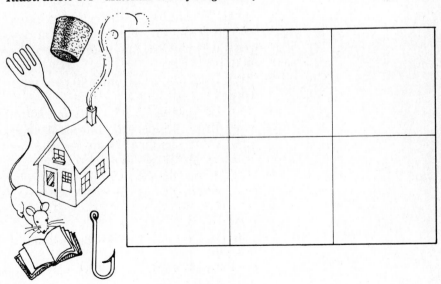

2. Ask if the child can tell you the name of each object.
3. If the child cannot name each object, help by asking:
   Is it a ___?
4. If the child still does not know, name the object and have the child repeat after you:
   This is a ___.
5. Follow the same procedure with all the objects, naming each.
6. Ask the child if the names of any two of these things sound the same.
7. If the child seems confused, line up three objects, two that rhyme and one that doesn't. Have the child name these three objects, and ask the child which names rhyme.
8. When the child hears the rhyming sounds and can find matching items, he or she can put each pair in a square on the construction-paper mat.

▶ **PURPOSE**　**To identify familiar sounds**

MATERIALS　— Tape recorder and microphone

PROCEDURE
1. In preparation for the class experience, tape-record sounds of common activities. For example:
   In the kitchen — getting things out of the cupboard and placing them on the counter, using the egg beater, frying bacon or anything else that sizzles, washing dishes
   In the bathroom — brushing teeth, washing hands, flushing the toilet, taking a bath or shower
   In the yard — running the sprinkler (hearing the rhythm of it hitting the sidewalk), pruning a hedge, edging the grass, running the lawnmower, raking leaves
   At the market — sound of the door opening, the cart being pulled apart from the others, cans being piled on one another, opening the cooler door to get milk, hearing the paper bag being popped open, hearing the cash register ringing
2. Ask the children to listen closely and see if they can tell where the person was when the sounds were recorded and what was happening.
3. Encourage them to remember as many different sounds as they can.
4. Play the tape again and ask what sound they heard first.
5. Play three sounds, then stop the tape and ask what sound was first, what was next, and what was last. Increase the number of sounds as children demonstrate success.
6. After doing this activity once, the children might have some ideas as to what sounds they would like recorded.

▶ **PURPOSE**　**To learn to listen and follow directions**

MATERIALS　— Noise-making objects: bell, rattle, two wooden blocks, egg beater
　　　　　　— Other objects: book, chair, ball, baseball cap

PROCEDURE   1. Say:
This game we are going to play is about careful listening.
See this bell? What can you do with it?
See that chair? What can you do with it?
I am going to ask you all to listen carefully while I tell you what to do.
Then I will ask who wants to do it.
First shake the rattle, then put on the baseball cap. Who wants to do that?
2. Continue, giving only two directions until the group seems to find that easy.
3. Then give three tasks in a row.

VARIATIONS   1. You can select one child and ask him or her to do two tasks. Then let the child choose someone else, and so on.
2. Ask which child would like to do four tasks. If the school has a play store, then the game could be about shopping for certain items.
3. You can move around the room, touching three or four children or objects. You can then ask who remembers who or what was touched. If a child has difficulty, give hints as to hair color, clothes worn, or shape and color and so on of an object.
4. When children are outside, give directions such as:
Take two big steps, hop, and turn around.

HELPFUL HINTS

1. Browse in bookstores; go to book sales.
2. Ask the local librarian about library book sales.
3. Start your own collection of favorite books.
4. Write your own "custom-designed" story just for your class.

▶ PURPOSE   **To follow the sequence of action in a story[2]**

MATERIALS   A book that includes a conflict, real or unreal, and expresses negative as well as positive feelings and actions. For example:

— Margaret W. Brown, *The Runaway Bunny*, New York: Harper & Row, 1972
— Margaret W. Brown, *The Dead Bird*, New York: Scott, 1958
— Charlotte Zolotow, *The Quarreling Book*, New York: Harper & Row, 1963
— H. A. Rey, *Curious George*, Boston: Houghton Mifflin, 1941

[2]Reprinted by permission from *Young Children*, Vol. 22, No. 1 (Oct. 1966), pp. 31–43. Copyright © 1966, National Association for the Education of Young Children, 1834 Connecticut Avenue, N.W., Washington, D.C. 20009.

PROCEDURE   **1.** Read intimate passages softly, exciting passages more forcefully; read slowly for suspense and faster for action.

2. Check to discover if the children understand the following:

Words If you think a word might not be familiar to the children (for example, *lost, curious, sad, friendly*), then ask if they know what the word means. If the action in the story explains the word, ask how the story explains it and discuss it.

Abstract concepts If a book is about an abstract concept (such as fast, soft, round, secret, or mystery), ask if anyone knows what the key word means. Encourage the children to give examples or descriptions and to look for what the story tells them about that word.

Character motivations Ask, for example, why the boy is sad, how they know he is sad, and what they think would make him happy. Pictures and words in the book can be used as clues.

Processes Ask why something happened, what will happen next, and what the subject of the story could do to solve the problem in another way.

3. Encourage children to participate by accepting their answers and expanding them. If necessary, clarify meanings. Show them that their thoughts are important and interesting to you.

HELPFUL HINTS

1. Make flannelboard cutouts and slides from the illustrations in *Pig Pig Grows Up* by David McPhail (New York: Dutton, 1980).

2. Let the children help act out the story.

3. Tell the story using the flannelboard and let the children help put up the pictures as you hand them the proper ones.

4. Show the slides while they help tell the story.

5. Show the children the book after they have become familiar with the story. Leave the book in the reading area where they can look at it themselves.

Reading-Readiness Activities

LEARNING TO IDENTIFY LETTERS AND NUMBERS AND TO DISCRIMINATE VISUAL PATTERNS

The following activities facilitate the skills that lead naturally to reading. Recognition of letters and numbers, learning the sounds of letters, and familiarity with printed materials are tasks included in this section. Additional tasks can be added for children who are ready to move beyond these preliminary stages.

▶ **PURPOSE**   **To recognize addresses**

MATERIALS — Flash card for each child
— Address of each child printed on the flash card

PROCEDURE
1. Talk about numbers on houses.
2. Talk about names of streets.
3. Mention why addresses are important.
4. Play a game:
Read one child's address and ask the group if anyone knows who lives there.
Give clues, such as boy or girl, hair color, or clothing color.
When the children guess correctly, read the address and hand the flash card to the child who lives there.
Follow this procedure for each child.

VARIATIONS
1. The same procedure can be used for telephone numbers.
2. Make a simple map of the city, showing streets where the children live, and let each child pin a colored square on his or her own street.

HELPFUL HINTS

1. Do not say the *child* is wrong, but that the *response* is wrong. Say "No, that letter is B," rather than "You're wrong, Charles. That letter is B."
2. Tell children when their response is wrong. Give the correct response, have the child repeat it, and follow this with praise.
3. Stop a teaching activity while children are still motivated and interested.

▶ **PURPOSE**   **To practice the beginning sounds of words**

MATERIALS — Shoe boxes
— Variety of toys that children can easily identify

PROCEDURE
1. Print one letter of the alphabet (in upper- and lower-case) on the end of each shoe box. Next to the letters, draw or paste a picture of a common object whose name begins with that letter. Place five or six objects whose names begin with that letter in each box.
2. Place one shoe box on a table.
3. Let children examine and name objects in the box.
4. Pass the box around to a small group of children and let each child take one object.
5. Ask each child to name what he or she has.
6. When a child responds, reinforce by repeating the name of the object:

Roberto has a bat.

7. Have the group repeat the name of each object and collect each object as it is named.
8. If a child cannot name the object, say:
   Marcelle, show everyone your object. Can anyone name it?
9. After all objects are collected, hold each one up and ask:
   What is this?
   Did you hear anything special about the names of these things?
   Who can tell me the name of the letter on the shoe box?
10. Bring out a second shoe box with a different letter on it. Repeat above procedure.
11. Mix all the objects from both boxes.
12. Let each child pick one object, name it, and place it in the appropriate shoe box. Continue, varying degrees of difficulty according to children's abilities.

HELPFUL HINTS

1. Invite parents to share stories and food to celebrate special holidays.
2. Send notes home to let parents know what books their children enjoy in school.
3. Suggest good books to buy for gifts.
4. Make annotated lists of favorite stories available in the local library and suggest parents take their children there.

▶ **PURPOSE**   To identify and group objects whose names begin with the same sound

MATERIALS
— Sources for pictures: coloring books, catalogues, magazines
— Scissors
— Crayons
— Paste and paste brushes
— Cards
— Box for storage (on outside of box, print upper- and lower-case letters and paste picture of object)

PROCEDURE
1. Show the children the box with the identifying letters and picture.
2. Ask:
   Who can tell me the name of this letter?
   What is this? (picture)
   This box is for pictures of things whose names begin with the "b" sound such as a bicycle. Can you say *bicycle*?
3. Pass out the picture books and ask the children to show you when they have found a picture beginning with the same sound as bicycle; have them identify the object and say the word *bicycle* for comparison.
4. If correct, the child can color the picture or cut it out and paste it on a card.

5. Repeat this activity with all the consonants.
6. After two or three cards have been collected, they can be used by individual children for sorting into beginning-sound groups or used to play "Which One Doesn't Belong" (display three cards with the same letter, one with a different letter).
7. It is helpful to place a strip of paper over the letters at the top of the card so that the only clues are similarities or differences of the sounds.

HELPFUL HINTS

1. Make puppets of storybook characters.
2. Have the children help tell the story with the puppets. (See Illustration 4.5.)
3. Finally, read the story from the book.

Illustration 4.5 **Using finger puppets to tell stories**

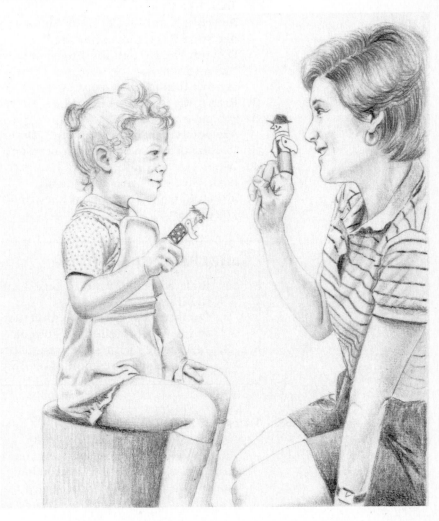

▶ **PURPOSE**   **To recognize right and left hands**

MATERIALS   Simple, homemade picture book showing:

— top of left hand with fingers and thumb spread, the word *left* printed beneath it
— top of right hand with fingers and thumb spread, the word *right* printed beneath it
— left hand, palm up
— right hand, palm up
— left and right hand on same page, palms down
— left hand and right hand, one palm up, one down
— same as picture above, reversing positions

Trace your own hands to make the pictures or trace a child's hands.

PROCEDURE   **1.** Say:
This is a book about hands. That word on the cover says *hands*. There are pictures in the book of hands. See if you can make your hands look like the hands in the pictures.
Here is a picture of a left hand. Can you make one of your hands look like this?
Put your hand on the table below the picture in the book.
Are your fingernails showing?
Do your thumb and the finger next to it make a shape that looks like an *L*?
Is your thumb in by your stomach or out by your shoulder?
2. Repeat for top of right hand.
3. For palm up, ask:
Are your fingernails showing? Do you see lines on the hands? Is your thumb nearest your stomach or your shoulder?
4. When using a picture of two hands, help the child to get one hand positioned first, then the other.
5. If a child copies hand positions right away, talk about how he or she did it.

HELPFUL HINTS

1. Start a special fund to buy duplicate books for a lending library.
2. Contact local libraries, storytellers guild, and book clubs to invite storytellers to school.
3. Tell stories with slide transparencies.
4. Encourage expression of feelings with words.

▶ **PURPOSE**   **To match identical symbols**

MATERIALS   — Handmade Christmas tree ornaments (can be made from construction paper) such as the following: a pair of candy canes; a pair of angels; a pair of Christmas trees; pairs of different-shaped ornaments (round, square, triangular, and the like); pictures of

Christmas themes cut from catalogues and reinforced by construction-paper backing
— Paste and brushes
— Containers for paste (foil pans or milk-bottle lids)
— Felt tree pinned to wall
— Straight pins on tips of branches or wherever possible on the felt tree
— Paper punch and strings
— Alternatives: live tree and real ornaments

PROCEDURE

1. Have children paste matching pictures or ornaments onto matching-shaped paper ornaments.
2. Punch hole at the top of each ornament and string the ornament.
3. Give each child one ornament from a set.
4. Hang the matching ornament on the felt tree where straight pins have been placed.
5. Have each child find the matching ornament on the felt tree and hang his or her ornament beside it.
6. Have children work in pairs.

VARIATION

Have children make Chanukah decorations. These can include:

— a pair of six-pointed stars
— a pair of menorahs
— a pair of candles
— pairs of differently clothed warriors

Have the children paste matching decorations on a large sheet of butcher paper to make a mural.

▶ **PURPOSE** **To recognize patterns**

MATERIALS

— White glue or paste and brushes
— Triangles, cut from 2″-square pieces of construction paper
— Cardboard strips, 2″ x 8″
— Sample cards with different triangular designs, four triangles to a card (See Illustration 4.6.)

PROCEDURE

1. Hand each child pasting material, four triangles, and a cardboard strip.
2. Show children the sample cards with different triangular designs.
3. Ask children what they see on the cardboard strips.
4. Ask if they know what shape is used in the design.
5. Ask:
   Where would I put my first triangle if I wanted to make a design just like the sample card? (Put it in the wrong corner and let children tell where it should be placed.)
   Where would I put my second triangle?
6. Give each child a sample cardboard strip.
7. Have them make a design duplicating the one on their sample.
8. Help when necessary, but do not actually place the triangle for

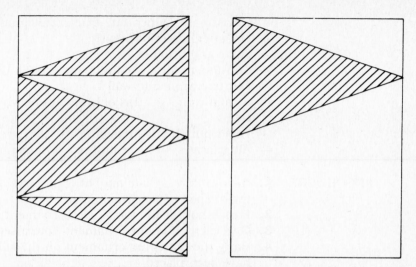

Illustration 4.6   **Sample cards for recognizing patterns**

them. Instead, help them decide which corner the triangle goes in, or whether the shapes are touching, and so on.

9. Say:
    When you have finished, I will come and see what you have done. Then you may glue your pieces on the cardboard and take the design home with you.

▶ **PURPOSE**   **To match identical letters**

MATERIALS   —   One cardboard square per child, divided into nine small squares with a different letter of the alphabet printed in each square
            —   Plastic or cardboard letters of the alphabet
            —   Box or tin can with deep sides (three-pound coffee can) to hold letters

PROCEDURE   1. Give each child a card.
            2. Explain that there are letters of the alphabet on each card.
            3. Say:
                In the can are letters of the alphabet. Some of these letters will match the ones on your card.
            4. Have the children take turns drawing the letters from the can.
            5. As each one draws, ask if the child knows the name of the letter.
            6. Ask the child to repeat the name as he or she looks at the letter.
            7. Ask if the child can find it on his or her card.
            8. Give help when needed.
            9. If there is no match, the child puts the letter back in the can.
           10. The next child takes a turn.
           11. The first child to fill in a row across or down wins the game.

HELPFUL HINTS

1. Cut heavy construction paper or good quality scrap paper into flash cards approximately 3″ x 6″.
2. Let each child think up a word he or she would like to have written on the card.
3. Print each word with a felt-tip pen in large, neat letters.
4. Give the cards to the children and encourage them to keep a collection to share with the class and with their families.

▶ **PURPOSE** **To learn names of letters**

MATERIALS — A magnetized board with two sets of lower-case letters and upper-case letters (or a flannelboard with two sets of lower- and upper-case letters)

PROCEDURE
1. Place four lower-case letters in the column on the left-hand side of the board.
2. Place identical letters on the right-hand side of the board, making certain that no two identical letters are opposite each other.
3. Point to the first letter in the left-hand column and ask if anyone knows what the letter is called.
4. When it has been identified, ask if anyone can show you a letter in the second column that looks the same.
5. When a matching letter has been identified, pick it up and place it beside its mate in the left-hand column for close comparison.
6. Match remaining letters in the same way.
7. Repeat several times, encouraging different children to respond.
8. Do this with all the lower-case letters. Then work through the alphabet using the upper- and lower-case together.
9. Then work with only the upper-case letters to be sure the children associate each symbol with its name.

▶ **PURPOSE** **To learn to arrange in logical sequence**

MATERIALS — Manila folder or envelope for each child, with four to six squares drawn and numbered on the outside
— A set of four to six pictures for each child, showing the sequence of an activity, mounted on cardboard cut to fit the squares and placed inside each envelope (pictures of a child in bed, getting up, dressing, eating, and going to school, for example) (See Illustration 4.7.)
— First picture in sequence glued in place on the folder

PROCEDURE
1. Using one folder as an example, show children the squares and ask what is happening in the first picture.

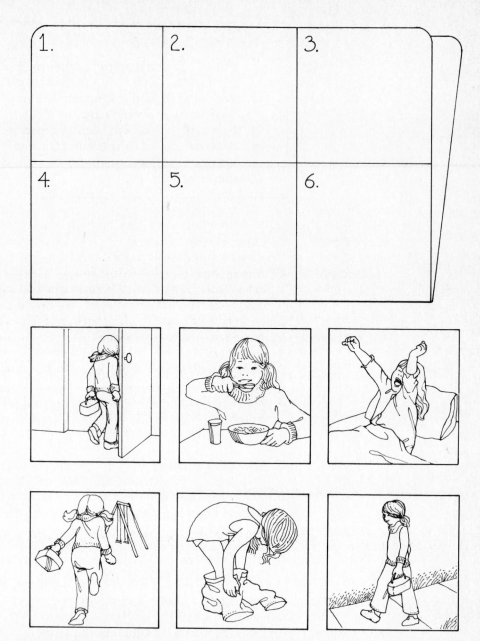

Illustration 4.7   **Materials to use for sequence activity**

2. Show two other pictures and ask that they be described.
3. Put these pictures in an illogical sequence.
4. Say:
   Is that the way you do this in the morning?
   What might be a better way to put these pictures?
   Why?
5. Give each child a folder and ask the child to put the pictures in order.
6. Give help to the children who need it.
7. Talk about the pictures with each child when he or she finishes.

▶ **PURPOSE**   **To recognize differences in objects**

MATERIALS   Strips of cardboard 4″ x 20″ on which have been drawn four objects that are identical and one that is different. Examples:

— four squares and one circle
— four balls and one bat
— four triangles and a fifth upside down
— four *F*'s and one facing backward
— four cups with spoons, one cup without a spoon
— four *B*'s and one *D*
— four hats with feathers, one hat without a feather

PROCEDURE   **1.** Start with objects that have obvious differences; proceed to the less obvious. Place the different object in different places, so the children don't use position as a clue.
2. Say:
I have some cards with pictures on them.
On each card all the shapes will be the same except one.
I would like you to see if you can find the one that is different and tell why it is different.
3. Help children notice the differences in shape. Note, for example, that squares have four sides and pointed corners and that the circle has no corners.
4. Allow children to trace shapes with their fingers to help them understand the different shapes.

Prewriting Activities

DEVELOPING MOTOR SKILLS AND FAMILIARITY WITH WRITING

Children scribble and try to draw long before they are taught to write. They recognize their names in written form and are aware of the importance of writing from their own experience. They try to write with crayons and large pencils. Most children of preschool age can learn to make simple letters and can recognize the difference between printed letters and script. The activities selected for this section include practice in motor skills that are essential for writing and in tracing and making lines that follow a pattern.

▶ **PURPOSE**   **To learn to draw a line that follows a pattern and changes direction**

MATERIALS   — Self-sticking colored dots or circles
— Felt-tip pen, crayons, or colored pencils
— Large sheet of paper

PROCEDURE   **1.** Play the game "Dot to Dot":
Place a dot on the paper and ask the child to put the pen on the dot.
Place another dot a short distance away.
Have the child draw a line from the first dot to the second. Be sure the child keeps his or her pen on the last dot until the next dot is in place.
2. Continue to place dots so the child must make lines going in different directions.
3. Avoid crossing lines until the child does the task easily.
4. Increase the length of the lines and the difficulty of pattern as the child becomes more adept.

▶ **PURPOSE**   **To develop eye-hand coordination in preparation for writing**

MATERIALS   — Mimeographed sheets with rows of dots. (Directions: Make six heavy dots about ⅛″ thick. For first row, space dots ½″ apart across one quarter of the page. Gradually increase the distance between the dots within each row. Gradually lengthen the rows until they stretch across the page.) (See Illustration 4.8.)
— One large crayon for each child
— One mimeographed sheet clipped to clipboard for demonstration purposes
— Simple story book

PROCEDURE   **1.** Pass out mimeographed sheets.
2. Ask children to tell what they see on the paper.
3. Explain that dots were made one right after another; dots were made in a straight line; dots were made in row formation.
4. Review with children the above explanation. Say:
What are the marks on the sheet called?
Put your finger on each dot (left to right).
5. Pass out crayons and instruct children to place crayon on the first dot in the upper left-hand corner. (Point at the dot on your own sheet.)
6. Have them draw lines from one dot to another, from left to right across the row. (Demonstrate.)

Illustration 4.8   **Materials for developing eye-hand coordination**

7. Check each child's work and make sure that all the children have followed directions.
8. Start other rows and remind children to draw lines from one dot to another, always moving from left to right.
9. While they are drawing, explain to the children that they are drawing lines from left to right.
10. Point to words in a book and read each sentence aloud.

▶ **PURPOSE**   **To develop eye-hand coordination and to learn the concept "circle"[3]**

MATERIALS   — Portable or wall chalkboard
— Oversized chalk (easier to handle)
— Two or three pieces of colored chalk per child
— Templates made out of ⅛"-thick cardboard (use sides of boxes), cut in shapes of circle, square, triangle, and diamond

PROCEDURE   1. Have the child stand at the chalkboard. (Give the child enough room to make a large circular arm movement.)
2. Begin by letting the child draw anything he or she wishes.
3. Have the child draw a large circle. If the child does not know how to do this, take his or her hand and guide the movement; encourage the child to relax.
4. Have the child trace the circle at least six times.
5. Let the child use colored chalk to decorate the circle.

VARIATIONS   1. Use circle template.
2. Help the child hold the template against the board with the hand not used for drawing.
3. Have the child trace inside the template, pushing against the edge of the template. Contact with the edge of the template gives the child a feeling of roundness.
4. Have the child trace around six times, rest, then trace around another six times.
5. Tell the child that the templates can be used to make a design or a picture. If a child wishes to make a design or a picture, give the child colored chalk to do so.
6. Introduce templates of square, triangle, and diamond, in that order.

▶ **PURPOSE**   **To develop eye-hand coordination and to learn the concept "square"[4]**

MATERIALS   — Two or three pieces of thick white and colored chalk for each child
— Chalkboard

---

[3]Adapted from Newell C. Kephart, *Slow Learner in the Classroom.* Columbus, Ohio: Charles E. Merrill. 1960, pp. 185–187. Used by permission.
[4]Adapted from Newell C. Kephart, *Slow Learner in the Classroom.* Columbus, Ohio: Charles E. Merrill. 1960, p. 202. Used by permission.

— Eraser
— A square template (Directions for making template: Using a matte knife or single-edge razor blade, cut out a piece of cardboard from the side of a box. Draw a square 10″ x 10″ on the piece of cardboard and cut it out. Draw an inner square 7″ x 7″ on the 10″ square and cut it out.)
— Substitute for the template: Make an outline of a square on the chalkboard. Use the side of a piece of chalk to illustrate the outline.

PROCEDURE
1. Practice tracing squares with template on the chalkboard, telling children they will be tracing a square.
2. Show them the template with a square; have them repeat the word *square* several times.
3. Tell children you will be helping them hold the template while they trace the square to the chalkboard.
4. Have children help to hold the template with their free hand.
5. Tell them to push gently against the edge of the cardboard while tracing the square. You can help by guiding their hand movements.
6. Trace the square six times. Help children count the number of times they have traced the square.
7. After a short rest, the children may like to resume tracing.
8. Make sure each child is making pointed corners instead of rounded ones.
9. Use colored chalk to decorate squares.

▶ **PURPOSE**   **To print first and last names in upper- and lower-case letters**

MATERIALS
— Clear plastic folder for each child
— Name of child printed on a piece of paper inserted into each folder
— Felt-tip pen or crayon for each child
— Paper towel or sponge for wiping ink or crayon off folder
— Alternative materials: piece of cardboard with child's name printed on it

PROCEDURE
1. Give each child a folder with his or her name on it.
2. Read the child's name aloud.
3. Tell children they will be printing their own names.
4. Explain to children how to use their materials:
Tell children their name is printed on a piece of paper and inserted inside the plastic cover.
They are to use the felt-tip pen to trace over letters on the plastic cover.
Wipe printing off with paper towel or sponge.
5. Instructions for printing letters:
Start by printing the big letters.
Do one letter at a time.
Begin with the big letters on the left, working toward the right.

Observe children to make sure they are printing each letter from left to right.

6. Give children a chance to ask questions.

VARIATIONS
1. This same procedure can be used to copy shapes. Start with the circle and progress to the square, rectangle, triangle, and diamond.

2. The procedure can be used to teach children to print letters of the alphabet. Start with lower-case letters, one at a time.

HELPFUL HINTS

1. Print parts of a favorite story on a large chart. Let children run their hands along the lines of the story and "read" along with the teacher.

2. Tell children the title, author, and illustrator of each story. Show them several books by one illustrator. Help them become familiar with and identify the style of an illustrator.

3. Print portions of stories on 3″ x 5″ cards. Read familiar passages and have children guess what story the passages are from.

4. Make some large, colorfully illustrated book envelopes that children can use to check out favorite books to take home. As a child learns to write, let the child copy the title and author of a book.

▶ **PURPOSE** **To recognize printed names**

MATERIALS
— Manila envelope for each child
— Rectangular piece of tagboard for each child
— Letters needed to make the child's name cut out of cardboard
— Flannelboard or bulletin board for demonstrating

PROCEDURE
1. Have children draw their own faces on the envelopes.
2. Have them write their names on the pieces of tagboard in upper- and lower-case letters.
3. Place name card and letters inside each envelope.
4. Print the child's name in upper left-hand corner of the envelope.
5. Pin a name card on the flannelboard.
6. Pin the required letters at random on the board.
7. Say:
Remember when you drew your face on an envelope?
I am going to show you some things you can keep in your envelope.
On the board is a card with the name "Mike" on it.
Here are some letters that can be used to make the name "Mike."
We will start here, on the left-hand side, and work to the right.

Who can find the big "M" and place it under the one just like it on the card? (Point to "M" on card.)

8. Complete the name.
9. Mix up the letters and let several children make the name.
10. Give each child his or her envelope.
11. Tell the children they may each make their own name and that you will help if they need it.
12. Later each child can learn his or her last name in the same manner.
13. When children can copy their names easily, show them the card and ask them to make their names from memory.

► **PURPOSE** **To form associations among talking, writing, and reading**

MATERIALS — Source for story information, such as photograph of a child engaged in a school activity; picture cut from magazine, catalogue, and the like; storybook character with whom the child can identify; a picture that a child has painted; a tempting question, such as "If you had three wishes, what would they be?"
— Paper for story dictation
— Construction paper for cover
— Stapler

PROCEDURE 1. Initiate storytelling, using one of the sources listed, or take advantage of a child's spontaneous interest.
2. Print the story as the child tells it.
3. Staple together the pictures and dictation pages.
4. Suggest that the child make a cover and put his or her name and a title on it.
5. Place a "library card" in each book and let the children check them out.

HELPFUL HINTS

1. Choose a story you like that is easy to memorize (for example, "Caps for Sale").
2. There is no need to memorize word for word, but do stick to the plot.
3. Repeat the story to yourself while driving, doing the dishes, and the like.
4. Visualize the incidents in your story.
5. Watch the children and speak directly to them.
6. Use pauses for effect.
7. Show enthusiasm.
8. Create a parent-child diary (for example, "Karen and Daddy's Diary"). Each evening, the child dictates events of the day for the parent to enter in the diary. After the entry is made, both help to illustrate something to highlight what was written. Part of story time can be spent rereading earlier pages in the diary.

Bibliography of Resources

ALL-TIME FAVORITES

Allard, Harry. *The Stupids Step Out.* Boston: Houghton Mifflin, 1974. The Stupids are a family different from most. A funny story filled with slapstick that young children will enjoy.

Anglund, Joan Walsh. *A Friend Is Someone Who Likes You.* New York: Harcourt, Brace & World, 1958. See next entry for description.

————. *Love Is a Special Way of Feeling.* New York: Harcourt, Brace & World, 1960. Both of these books by Anglund are excellent to look at, read, and talk about with one child. They are small, easy to hold, and delightfully illustrated. Topics are geared to the young child's experiences.

Austin, Margot. *Barney's Adventure.* New York: Dutton, 1941. A favorite story for telling without a book and showing the pictures afterwards or adapting to the flannelboard. Barney is a little boy who wants to see the circus, but has no money for a ticket. On his way home he sees large tracks and follows them into the woods, hoping to capture and return one of the circus animals in exchange for a ticket. Instead he finds a clown who gets him into the circus after all.

Bannon, Laura. *The Scary Thing.* Boston: Houghton Mifflin, 1956. A boy and his farm-animal friends are frightened by some scary eyes and noises. They see a shape that is dark, lumpy-like, and hides in the bushes. The scary thing turns out to be a newborn calf.

Barrett, Judi. *Animals Should Definitely Not Wear Clothing.* New York: Atheneum, 1971. Illustrates how uncomfortable it would be for certain animals to wear clothing. Clear bright graphics by Ron Barrett showing how silly each animal would look wearing hats, sweaters, and other clothes. Funny to children. Good for discussion.

Borten, Helen. *Do You Move As I Do?* London: Abelard-Schuman, 1963. The text calls attention to the various kinds of movement all around us. The child can see movement as "lazy as a yawn" or flowing movements "that ooze as smoothly as honey," and as other common experiences that challenge the child to think about and try movements. This book is one of a series including *Do You See What I See?* and *Do You Know What I Know?*

Brown, Margaret Wise. *Goodnight Moon.* New York: Harper & Row, 1947. An old standby about a bunny in bed who says goodnight to the moon, stars, and noises until he falls asleep.

————. *The Indoor Noisy Book.* New York: Harper & Row, 1942. A book about the noises a little dog named Muffin hears. Encourages children to participate and guess about noises indoors. The teacher can use this story for telling without a book. Other books in this series include *The Quiet Noisy Book, The Summer Noisy Book,* and *The Winter Noisy Book.*

————. *The Noisy Book.* New York: Harper & Row, 1939. A good story for young children about the noises Muffin hears as he walks around the city. The children enjoy guessing about and making the noises.

————. *The Runaway Bunny.* New York: Harper & Row, 1972. A bunny tells his mother he is going to run away, but his mother tells him she will find him because he is her little bunny. A pretend story told and illustrated in a gentle, tender way.

Burton, Virginia Lee. *The Little House.* Boston: Houghton Mifflin, 1942. A Caldecott Medal winner about a little house in the country that eventually becomes surrounded by urban development and the happy ending when it is jacked up and moved back to the country again.

Chapman, Carol. *Fortunately.* New York: Four Winds Press, 1964. A humorously illustrated story of Ned who has a series of unfortunate experiences, but something fortunate saves him each time.

————. *The Tale of Meshka the Kvetch.* New York: Dutton, 1980. A woman who spends all her time complaining soon finds her complaints coming true.

Charlip, Remy. *Mother, Mother, I Feel Sick. Send for the Doctor, Quick, Quick, Quick.* New York: Parents' Magazine Press, 1966. A child has a stomach ache and the doctor finds all kinds of hilarious things in his stomach from a plateful of spaghetti to a two-wheeled bike. This funny story can be adapted for the flannelboard or presented as a shadow play.

Daugherty, James. *Andy and the Lion.* New York: Viking, 1938. Andy removes a thorn from a lion's paw and the grateful lion helps to make Andy a hero.

De Regniers, Beatrice Schenk. *May I Bring a Friend?* New York: Atheneum, 1964. When the king and queen invite the hero of the story to tea, he asks to bring a friend. His friend turns out to be an animal. He is invited to lunch, dinner, breakfast, Halloween, and more, and each time he brings different kinds of animals until the king and queen finally go with him to the zoo. The teacher can adapt this to the flannelboard by using sandpaper backing with cutouts of crowns to represent the king and queen and with simple silhouettes or magazine pictures of zoo animals.

————. *Something Special.* New York: Harcourt, Brace & World, 1958. A book of poems with titles such as "A Sugar Lump Is Good to Have in Case of," and "What's the Funniest Thing?" This is an all-time favorite for children and their parents and teachers.

DiNoto, Andrea. *The Star Thief.* New York: Macmillan, 1967. A storyteller's delight about a thief who steals all the stars from the sky and nails them into barrels for safekeeping. The story theme is easy to learn without memorizing every word. Show the pictures after telling the story.

Emberley, Barbara. *Drummer Hoff.* Englewood Cliffs, N.J.: Prentice-Hall, 1967. A brightly illustrated adaptation of a folk tale in rhyme about all the soldiers who help to build a cannon, but Drummer Hoff "fires it off" in a colorful blast at the end. Trace the figures to adapt to the flannelboard. Repetitive rhyme is fun to recite.

Ets, Marie Hall. *Play with Me.* New York: Viking, 1955. A little girl goes out to the meadow to play but the animals are frightened of her. When she sits quietly they gradually come out to "play." Record and cassette also available.

————. *Talking Without Words. (I Can, Can You?)* New York: Viking, 1968. Animals can make their wishes known without words. The book calls attention to the many ways we can communicate without words. Look for other titles by this well-known author. Sound filmstrip, record, and cassette also available.

Flack, Marjorie. *Ask Mr. Bear.* New York: Macmillan, 1958. An old favorite about a little boy who doesn't know what to give his mother for her birthday, so he asks a series of animals who make suggestions, which he rejects. Finally he asks Mr. Bear, who gives him a wonderful solution. Good for adaptation to flannelboard. Also easy to tell without the book.

Forrester, Victoria. *The Magnificent Moo.* New York: Atheneum, 1983. When a cow trades her moo for a cat's meow because she thinks it too loud, the moo gets traded in turn to several other animals until it finally returns to a more satisfied cow.

Freeman, Don. *Corduroy.* New York: Viking, 1968. A little girl falls in love with a teddy bear no one else wants. Look for other books by this popular author. Sound filmstrip, record, cassette.

Gag, Wanda. *Millions of Cats.* New York: Coward-McCann, 1928. An old classic, which is familiar to many who tell and enjoy Wanda Gag's stories. The story of an old man and an old woman who collect so many cats that they end up with "hundreds of cats, thousands of cats, millions and billions and trillions of cats." Fun to read and an easy story to tell without the book. Show the pictures after telling the story.

Green, Mary McBurney. *Is It Hard? Is It Easy?* Menlo Park, Calif.; Addison-Wesley Children's Books, 1960. Silhouette-type photographs of children doing such things as skipping, tying shoes, catching a ball and doing a somersault. Encourages sharing and discussion of individual skills.

Harper, Wilhelmina. *The Gunniwolf.* New York: Dutton, 1967. A suspenseful and humorous tale about a little girl who wanders too far into the woods to gather flowers and is accosted by the gunniwolf. Excellent story for telling without the book. Show pictures afterward.

Hitte, Kathryn. *Boy, Was I Mad!* New York: Parents' Magazine Press, 1969. A little boy is so angry he decides to run away from home, but he sees so many interesting things when he goes out that he forgets he is running away.

Hobart, Lois. *What Is a Whispery Secret?* New York: Parents' Magazine Press, 1968. A delicately illustrated book about quiet things like leaves whispering in the breeze, kittens and frogs making soft sounds, and holding someone close and whispering "I love you." A good lap book.

Holdsworth, William Curtis (illus.). *The Gingerbread Boy.* New York: Farrar, Straus & Giroux, 1968. The classic story about the gingerbread boy who runs away from the little old woman and the little old man and the cow and the horse, etc., until he meets up with the sly old fox. Good for telling without the book or can be easily adapted for the flannelboard.

Hutchins, Pat. *Happy Birthday, Sam.* New York: Greenwillow Books, 1978. Sam turns a whole year older, but he still can't reach the light switch or the front door knob. His parents give him a beautiful boat for his birthday, but he can't reach the sink to sail it. But then his grandfather's present arrives.

Keats, Ezra Jack. *Over in the Meadow.* New York: Four Winds Press, 1972. A familiar counting rhyme about the activities of meadow animals and their young. Beautifully illustrated by this well-known artist. Useful for flannelboard counting.

Krasilovsky, Phyllis. *The Man Who Didn't Wash His Dishes.* New York: Doubleday, 1950. An amusing story about a man who was always too tired to do his dishes after dinner, so he let them pile up until he finally had to eat out of his ash trays, soap dish, and flower pots. He finally piles all his dirty dishes into his truck, sprinkles soap on them, and drives around on a rainy day.

———. *The Very Little Girl.* New York: Doubleday, 1953. The story about a very little girl and how small she was in comparison with the big chair, a kitchen stool, a rose bush, and other things, until she realizes one day that she is bigger than all these objects. Can be adapted for the flannelboard to show relative size.

Krauss, Ruth. *The Bundle Book.* New York: Harper & Row, 1951. Children identify easily with the strange bundle under the blankets, which moves and puzzles mother, who tries to guess what it is.

———. *The Growing Story.* New York: Harper & Row, 1947. A little boy watches the animals and plants around him grow, but his arms and legs look the same to him until he tries on some of his old clothes and discovers he has grown too.

Leydenfrost, Robert. *The Snake That Sneezed!* New York: Putnam 1970. Harold is a snake who leaves his forest home to make his way in the world. Good for adapting to flannelboard.

Lifton, Betty Jean. *One Legged Ghost.* New York: Atheneum, 1968. Japanese folk tale about a boy who finds an umbrella and doesn't know what it is. Show the lovely pictures after you tell the story so as not to give away the surprise.

Lionni, Leo. *Inch by Inch.* New York: Astor-Honor, 1962. An inchworm uses his ingenuity to stay alive by measuring different birds, but a nightingale decides to eat him.

McCloskey, Robert. *Blueberries for Sal.* New York: Viking, 1948. A standard book for most preschool children about a little girl who goes out with her mother to pick blueberries, and a little bear who goes with his mother to eat blueberries. The babies get mixed up to the surprise of both mothers. McCloskey's story and illustrations are excellent. Other titles by this author are highly recommended *(One Morning in Maine; Make Way for Ducklings).*

McPhail, David. *Pig Pig Grows Up.* New York: Dutton, 1980. A charmingly illustrated book about a pig who doesn't want to grow up until his mother collapses pushing him up a hill in his stroller. Then the adventure begins and pig pig grows up in a hurry. Excellent for telling with a flannelboard or slides.

————. *The Bear's Toothache.* Boston: Little, Brown, 1972. What do you do when a huge bear with a big toothache sits under your window at night and cries so loudly you can't sleep? Do you tell him to go away, send him to a dentist, or try to help? An imaginative, humorous story, simple to read. A good attention-getter when the reader starts the story by howling like the bear.

Nash, Ogden. *Custard the Dragon and the Wicked Knight.* Boston: Little, Brown, 1961. An imaginary tale in rhyme about a cowardly dragon named Custard. Every child should be familiar with Ogden Nash's humorous story.

Potter, Beatrix. *The Tale of Peter Rabbit.* Grand Rapids, Mich.: The Fideler Company, 1970. Children love this classic tale of Peter Rabbit and his adventures in Mr. McGregor's garden. Good for telling without the book. Show pictures later.

Rogers, Joe (illus.). *The House that Jack Built.* New York: Lothrop, 1968. Simple Mother Goose tale. Repetitive and excellent for use on the flannelboard. These illustrations can be traced onto Pellon or flannel.

Roy, Ron. *Three Ducks Went Wandering.* New York: Houghton Mifflin/Clarion Books, 1979. One fine day three little ducks wander away from their mother's nest and are confronted by many dangerous animals, but they luckily escape harm to return home to Mother. Another of Paul Galdone's well-illustrated books. Adaptable for flannelboard storytelling.

Sendak, Maurice. *In the Night Kitchen.* New York: Harper & Row, 1970. A highly imaginative story about a child's dream of falling into cake batter and bread dough. A good story to tell with dramatic gestures. Be sure to show the imaginative illustrations.

————. *Where the Wild Things Are.* New York: Harper & Row, 1963. A fantasy about a little boy named Max, who is sent to his room for misbehaving. He imagines that he sails away to a place where the wild things are. Illustrations are highly imaginative. Some teachers like this book very much; others think the pictures are frightening. Winner of the Caldecott Medal.

Shaw, Charles G. *It Looked Like Spilt Milk.* New York: Harper & Row, 1947. Some large white shapes look like all kinds of things but turn out to be clouds in the sky. This is excellent for flannelboard use. Trace the shapes onto Pellon and let the children answer "no" as each shape is named and placed on the flannelboard.

Shulevitz, Uri. *One Monday Morning.* New York: Scribner, 1967. A boy in a city tenement dreams of royalty coming to visit him. A good story to adapt to the flannelboard to teach days of the week.

———. *Rain, Rain Rivers.* New York: Farrar, Straus & Giroux, 1969. A girl listens to the rain outside her window and imagines it falling on places near and far away. She thinks about her friends and how they will play in the puddles. Lovely "rainy-day" type illustrations.

Skorpen, Liesel Moak (Emily McCully, illus.). *That Mean Man.* New York: Harper & Row, 1968. A delightful story about a mean man and his family who did "mean" things like crayoning on the walls, spilling their cocoa, slopping their soup, and other things that young children can easily identify with.

Slobodkin, Louis. *Moon Blossom and the Golden Penny.* New York: Vanguard, 1963. A poor child in Hong Kong receives a lucky penny when she helps an old woman. Tell the story and let children look at the little illustrations in small groups.

Slobodkina, Esphyr. *Caps for Sale, A Tale of a Peddler, Some Monkeys & Their Monkey Business.* Menlo Park, Calif.: Addison-Wesley Children's Books, 1947. One of the all-time favorites of teachers and children. Easy to tell without the book. Children always love to hear this story about a peddler trying to sell the colored caps that he carries around on top of his head.

Steadman, Ralph. *Jelly Book.* New York: Stroll Press, 1970. Charming illustrations and a humorous story about the very "complicated" process of making gelatin.

Steig, William. *Sylvester and the Magic Pebble.* New York: Simon & Schuster, 1969. Sylvester is a donkey who loves pebbles. He finds a magic pebble and turns it into a big rock. Ends with a happy family reunion. Caldecott Medal winner. This story is good for telling even though there is a lot of text.

Stobbs, William. *Henny-Penny.* Chicago: Follett, 1969. Here is another classic for telling with the flannelboard. Repetitive tale about Henny-Penny who says the "sky's-a-going to fall!"

Ungerer, Tomi. *Crictor.* New York: Harper & Row, 1958. A story about the imaginative antics of a snake named Crictor, who is the friend of a French lady, Madame Bodot.

———. *Zeralda's Ogre.* New York: Harper & Row, 1967. A suspenseful tale about an ogre who loves to eat children, especially for breakfast, until Zeralda teaches him to like her exotic cooking. Large colorful illustrations. Fun to tell.

Viorst, Judith. *I'll Fix Anthony.* New York: Harper & Row, 1969. Younger children can relate to this humorously written story about little brother who is planning all kinds of revenge on big brother Anthony.

Waber, Bernard. *"You Look Ridiculous," Said the Rhinoceros to the Hippopotamus.* Boston: Houghton Mifflin, 1966. An amusing story in which a hippopotamus learns to appreciate what he looks like. Fun to tell without the book.

Weil, Lisl. *Fat Ernest.* New York: Parents' Magazine Press, 1973. The tale of what happens when a preschooler and his two pet gerbils move into a big housing project building with an unfriendly neighbor across the hall.

Welber, Robert. *The Winter Picnic.* New York: Pantheon, 1970. Adam wants to go on a picnic, but it is snowing outside and his mother feels that it might be better to postpone the picnic until summer. Mother is too busy to play with him, but Adam finally convinces her to go out, and she discovers that he has fashioned plates, cups, and bowls from snow. Warm feelings of sharing. Encourages a child's imagination and ingenuity.

Withers, Carl. *The Tale of a Black Cat.* New York: Holt, 1966. Well-known drawing story, which the author (narrator) illustrates as the story unfolds. Line drawings accompany each episode. Encourages storytellers to invent and illustrate their own creations.

Zion, Gene. *Harry the Dirty Dog.* New York: Harper & Row, 1956. A dog named Harry hides his bath brush and proceeds to get very dirty. His family no longer recognizes him when he tries to convince them he is Harry. He finally retrieves his brush and is happy to be bathed.

Zolotow, Charlotte. *Sleepy Book.* New York: Lothrop, 1958. Interesting descriptions of how birds and beasts settle down for the night. Ends with children tucked in their beds.

BOOKS OF POETRY AND NURSERY RHYMES

Abercrombie, Barbara. *The Other Side of a Poem.* New York: Harper & Row, 1977. Very inviting introduction to poetry. The poems, cleverly organized under headings such as "Discoveries" and "Secret Messages," are written by familiar authors as well as new, contemporary writers. The poems can be enjoyed by children of all ages.

Bean, Cheryl A., and Sandra D. Albertson. *Just in Time with Nursery Rhymes.* Longview, Wash.: Just In Time, 1980. A curriculum guide using rhymes and activities for two- and three-year-olds.

Ciardi, John. *You Know Who.* Philadelphia: Lippincott, 1964. A book of poems about children who pout, hide, misbehave, and are mischievous. Titles include "Someone Showed Me the Right Way to Run Away," "Get up or You'll Be Late for School, Silly!"

deAngeli, Marguerite. *Book of Nursery and Mother Goose Rhymes.* Garden City, N.Y.: Doubleday, 1954. Large, colorfully illustrated book with index of first lines and familiar titles.

Field, Eugene. *Wynken, Blynken and Nod.* New York: Hastings House, 1970. Barbara Cooney's dream-like illustrations capture the mood of this classic children's poem.

Fisher, Aileen, and Eric Carle. *Do Bears Have Mothers, Too?* New York: Crowell, 1973. Colorful, close-up illustrations of animal babies and their mothers. Accompanying verses describe animal mothers who, like all mothers, are careful of their children, proud of them, anxious to teach them how to behave, and want to just have fun together.

Frank, Josette. *Poems to Read to the Very Young.* New York: Random House, 1982. A selection of poems about common events and topics of interest to preschoolers.

Kuskin, Karla. *In the Middle of the Trees.* New York: Harper & Row, 1958. Poetry good for use with one child or small group.

Livingston, Myra Cohn. *Listen, Children, Listen: An Anthology of Poems for the Very Young.* New York: Harcourt, Brace Jovanovich, 1972. An excellent collection for any program of early education. Illustrations by Trina Schart Hyman.

Lord, John Vernon. *The Giant Jam Sandwich.* Boston: Houghton Mifflin, 1973. "One hot summer in Itching Down/Four million wasps flew into town." Imaginatively detailed illustrations by John Lord and verses by Janet Burroway tell a delightful story of how a town cooperates to rid itself of wasps with a giant jam sandwich. Encourage children to look at and talk about all the details.

Mullins, Edward S. *The Big Book of Limericks (to Laugh At).* New York: Platt, 1969. Large, humorous torn-paper illustrations with one limerick per page.

Petersham, Maud. *The Rooster Crows.* New York: Macmillan, 1955. Caldecott Medal winner. Rhymes, skipping games, and finger plays.

Pomerantz, Charlotte. *The Tamarindo Puppy.* New York: Greenwillow Books, 1980. A unique collection of poems in two languages, English and Spanish. Spanish words are interspersed in the poems quite naturally. Simple themes of interest to young children.

Prelutsky, Jack. *Lazy Blackbird and Other Verses.* New York: Macmillan, 1969. Catchy verses designed to accompany childlike illustrations by Janosch.

Prelutsky, Jack (ed.). *The Random House Book of Poetry for Children.* New York: Random House, 1983. A wonderful anthology of poetry to delight children of all ages. Most are twentieth-century poems accompanied by Arnold Lobel's humorous illustrations. Poems grouped by subject matter include "City, Oh City," "I'm Hungry," "Some People I Know," and a wealth of the best in child-oriented verse.

Raskin, Ellen. *Who, Said Sue, Said Whoo?* New York: Atheneum, 1973. "The cross-eyed owl said whoo/The polka dot cow said moo/Then who, said Sue, said chitter-chitter-chatter, and titter-tatter, too?" That's the question woven into a nonsense rhyme in which more and more silly animals climb aboard Sue's car until they find the answer to her question.

Stevenson, Robert Louis. *A Child's Garden of Verses.* New York: Franklin Watts, 1966. A classic combining poetry with storytelling. Illustrated by Brian Wildsmith.

Tripp, Wallace (illus.). *A Great Big Ugly Man Came Up and Tied His Horse to Me.* Boston: Little, Brown, 1973. A compilation of silly verses accompanied by illustrations that tickle the reader's sense of humor.

Updike, John. *A Child's Calendar.* New York: Knopf, 1965. Book of poetry.

Wells, Rosemary. *Noisy Nora.* New York: Dial, 1973. "Jack had dinner early, Father played with Kate, Jack needed burping/So Nora had to wait. . . ." Being the middle child in a family means having to wait and wait, so Nora gets into all kinds of mischief and finally decides to run away. The story of a family of mice portraying familiar experiences in simple verse.

Wildsmith, Brian (illus.). *Mother Goose.* New York: Franklin Watts, 1965. Well-illustrated and colorful.

MULTI-ETHNIC BOOKS

Adoff, Arnold. *Big Sister Tells Me that I'm Black.* New York: Holt, Rinehart and Winston, 1976. Black and white drawings illustrate this story in poetry about children growing up proud to be black. ". . . a story, a series of poems, and a song of love."

Baker, Betty (Arnold Lobel, illus.). *Little Runner of the Longhouse.* New York: Harper & Row, 1962. Little Runner is envious of his older brothers, who are allowed to participate in the Iroquois New Year's ceremonies. Young children will be able to identify with his persistence in trying to convince his mother that he is not too young. He finally persuades her to give him a bowl of maple sugar.

Battles, Edith. *What Does the Rooster Say, Yoshio?* Chicago: Albert Whitman, 1978. A Japanese boy who knows no English plays with an American girl by comparing animal sounds in the two languages. A little book, excellent for small groups and discussing language differences.

Berger, Terry. *Big Sister, Little Brother.* Chicago: Children's Press, 1974. A small boy tells his mixed feelings about having a protective older sister. Beautiful photographs of a black brother and sister help convey feelings all children with siblings can relate to.

Cannon, Calvin. *Kirt's New House.* New York: Coward, McCann & Geohegan, 1972. The excitement of helping to build a new house through the Self-Help Housing Program is shared by a black child and his family in Macon County, Alabama. See also *What I Like to Do,* by the same author, about the life of a seven-year-old and the warmth of his family in Alabama.

Cheng, Hou-tien. *The Chinese New Year.* New York: Holt, 1976. A factual, colorful account of the Chinese New Year celebration, illustrated with paper cuts.

Clark, Ann Nolan. *In My Mother's House.* New York: Viking, 1941. A book of simple verses describing the Pueblo Indian — their land, the people, their homes and animals. Velino Herrera's stylized illustrations depict the Pueblo lifestyle.

Ets, Marie Hall. *Gilberto and the Wind.* New York: Viking, 1963. A little Mexican boy finds in the wind a temperamental playmate — one who can fly kites, capture balloons, scatter leaves, and run races. The wind can be a stormy and quiet companion. Charming pencil sketches.

Ets, Marie Hall, and Aurora Labastida. *Nine Days to Christmas.* New York: Viking, 1959. A story about Ceci, a five-year-old Mexican girl who selects her piñata for Christmas. Illustrations and text give the child a picture of how Christmas is spent by children in modern-day Mexico. The story may be a bit long for reading to a large group of very young children, but it lends itself to sharing with a small group who can look at and talk about the pictures.

Flack, Marjorie, and Kurt Wiese. *The Story About Ping.* New York: Viking, 1933. An old favorite about a little duck who lives on a boat on the Yangtze River and his adventures when he hides from his master in order to avoid getting a spank on the back. Children identify easily with not wanting to be spanked.

Greenberg, Polly. *Oh Lord, I Wish I Was a Buzzard.* New York: Macmillan, 1968. A black girl goes to work in the cottonfield "with the sun shining pretty on the land." Before the day's end, she has imagined changing places with a buzzard, a butterfly, a dog, and other creatures. Written in a simple, rhythmic style, with bright, warm illustrations.

Keats, Ezra Jack. *Goggles!* Toronto: Collier-Macmillan, Canada, Ltd., 1969. Two black children find a pair of motorcycle goggles but have to outsmart a gang of "big guys" in order to keep them. The author is well known for his excellent stories and illustrations and in this book he "tells it like it is" for a little boy in the big city.

Keats, Ezra Jack, and Pat Cherr. *My Dog Is Lost!* New York: Crowell, 1960. Juanito, who speaks only Spanish, has just arrived in New York from Puerto Rico and is sad because he lost his dog. His search takes him to Park Avenue, Chinatown, and Harlem where he meets friends who help him find his dog. Some simple Spanish phrases are introduced.

Mao-chiu, Chang. *The Little Doctor.* Peking: Foreign Languages Press, 1965. Ping Ping, the little girl doctor, helps make her sister's doll well, gives her brother's teddy bear a check up, and even repairs a broken rocking horse with hammer and nails. Typical story used with young children in China.[5]

---

[5] Chinese story books are written in English and are available from Guozi Shudian (China Publications Centre), P.O. Box 399, Peking, China. U.S. distributor: China

Martin, Patricia Miles. *The Rice Bowl Pet.* New York: Crowell, 1962. Ah Jim lives in a crowded apartment in San Francisco's Chinatown. He roams the streets looking for a pet small enough to fit in his rice bowl. Authentically illustrated by Ezra Jack Keats.

Moon, Grace. *One Little Indian.* Chicago: A. Whitman, 1967. Ad-di wakes up feeling all shiny inside. It is his fifth birthday. Mother tells him that a surprise awaits him in the desert if he can find it. Children will enjoy the unexpected surprise that he finds.

————. *Moy Moy.* New York: Scribner, 1960. Authentic story of a little Chinese-American girl who celebrates Chinese New Year in Los Angeles. Includes some Chinese phrases.

Scott, Ann Herbert. *On Mother's Lap.* New York: McGraw-Hill, 1972. The author of *Sam* has created another favorite. Michael, a young Eskimo boy, loves to rock on his mother's lap. But when the baby cries, he is sure there will not be enough room for both of them. Charming illustrations by Glo Coalson.

————. *Sam.* New York: McGraw-Hill, 1967. Everyone in the family is too busy to pay any attention to Sam until he finally begins to cry. Then they find a job that is just right for him.

Showers, Paul. *Your Skin and Mine.* New York: Crowell, 1965. This book shows three boys (an Oriental, a black, and a Caucasian) examining and finding out about skin — how it protects you, its different colors, and so forth. Good for use with a small group of children to allow each one to share in the discussion. Illustrated by Paul Galdone. Filmstrip with record or cassette available.

Sonneborn, Ruth A. *Friday Night Is Papa Night.* New York: Viking, 1970. The tender story of a black family looking forward to having Papa come home on Friday night.

Steptoe, John. *Stevie.* New York: Harper & Row, 1969. Robert, a black child, is jealous when his mother takes care of a younger child, Stevie, in their home. The text is witten as if Robert were telling the story. He learns about his sensitive feelings for Stevie when his mother no longer has to babysit.

Yashima, Mitsu, and Taro Yashima. *Momo's Kitten.* New York: Viking, 1961. Momo finds a kitten who becomes her "nyan-nyan." She nurses her pet back to health and takes on new responsibilities when her cat becomes a mother.

Yashima, Taro. *Umbrella.* New York: Viking, 1958. Beautiful illustrations and text about Momo, a little Japanese girl who lives in New York, and how eager she is to use her new umbrella.

Yi, Yang, and Ko Liang. *I Am on Duty Today.* Peking: Foreign Languages Press, 1966. This simple story colorfully illustrated by Ku Yin shows a typical day in a Chinese nursery school where a little girl helps the teacher set up the classroom, do daily exercises, pass out pencils and paper, get the children ready for nap, and distribute the snacks. Very similar to activities in American

---

Books & Periodicals, 125 Fifth Ave., New York, NY 10003; 2929 Twenty-fourth St., San Francisco, CA 94110.

schools, but this is a good example of how emphasis is placed on teaching cooperation and concern for others before oneself.

BIBLIOGRAPHIES OF MULTI-ETHNIC BOOKS

Griffin, Louise. *Multi-Ethnic Books for Young Children: Annotated Bibliography for Parents and Teachers.* Washington, D.C.: National Association for the Education of Young Children for the ERIC Clearinghouse on Early Childhood Education, 1970. Books are annotated and categorized according to age groups. Ethnic books focus on American Indians and Eskimos, Appalachia and the Southern Mountains, Afro-Americans, Hawaii and the Philippines, Latin-American, Asian, Jewish and European. Included also are books for parents and teachers.

National Association for the Advancement of Colored People. *Integrated School Books: A Descriptive Bibliography of 399 Preschool and Elementary School Texts and Story Books.* New York: NAACP, 1967.

White, Doris. *Multi-ethnic Books for Head Start Children, Part I: Black and Integrated Literature.* Also *Multi-ethnic Books for Head Start Children, Part II: Other Minority Group Literature.* Urbana, Ill.: ERIC Clearinghouse on Early Childhood Education, 1969. Both booklets contain annotated lists of children's books and materials covering such subjects as poetry, fiction, folklore, music, math, science, social studies, health, adult readings, records, and films.

CHRISTMAS STORIES

Ets, Marie Hall, and Aurora Lambastida. *Nine Days to Christmas.* New York: Viking, 1959. The story tells about Mexican customs at Christmas time. This is a Caldecott Medal winner. (See Multi-Ethnic Books for further description.)

Geisel, Theodor (Dr. Seuss, pseud.). *How the Grinch Stole Christmas.* New York: Random House, 1957. Dr. Seuss' imaginative treatment of a grinch who tried to put a stop to Christmas. The rhythmic format is familiar to children and teachers who like to read Dr. Seuss books.

Moore, Clement C. (Leonard Weisgard, illus.). *The Night Before Christmas.* New York: Grosset & Dunlap, 1954. One of the most popular treatments of this classic tale. Also in several paperback editions.

Wenning, Elizabeth. *The Christmas Mouse.* New York: Holt, 1959. A true story of "Silent Night, Holy Night," written in an appealing way for young children. Good for telling without the book and then showing the pictures afterward.

EASTER STORIES

Brown, Margaret Wise. *The Golden Egg Book.* New York: Simon & Schuster, 1947. A beautiful, simply written story. Large, colorful illustrations.

Holl, Adelaide (Roger Duvoisin, illus.). *The Remarkable Egg.* New York: Lothrop, 1968. A coot finds a round red egg in her nest and demands to know who laid it there.

Kraus, Robert. *Daddy Long Ears.* New York: Simon & Schuster, 1970. "Once there was a rabbit who was called Daddy Long Ears because he had many children and long ears. After the birth of their thirty-first child, Mrs. Long Ears ran away with a muskrat and Daddy Long Ears was left with thirty-one bunnies to be both father and mother to. It wasn't easy." An amusing and touching story of how a Daddy rabbit earned the title of Easter Rabbit.

Milhous, Katherine. *The Egg Tree.* New York: Scribner, 1950. Children will want to help make their own egg tree after hearing this story. The teacher can use hollow decorated eggs to demonstrate. A Caldecott Medal winner. A good book for the teacher to use in making an egg tree is *Easter Eggs for Everyone,* by Evelyn Coskey (New York: Abingdon, 1973).

Tresselt, Alvin (Roger Duvoisin, illus.). *The World in the Candy Egg.* New York: Lothrop, 1967. The miniature landscape inside a candy egg is seen by a tiny bird, a chicken, a lamb, and a rabbit, but the make-believe world of the egg goes to a little girl.

Zolotow, Charlotte (Betty Peterson, illus.). *The Bunny Who Found Easter.* Berkeley, Calif.: Parnassus, 1959. A bunny goes searching through summer, autumn, and winter for Easter until he finds its true meaning in the spring. A good lap book.

HALLOWEEN STORIES

Adams, Adrienne. *A Woggle of Witches.* New York: Scribner, 1971. On a certain night when the moon is high, all the witches fly on their brooms 'way up into the dark sky. They have fun on their night out until they run into a parade of little monsters who frighten them. Beautifully imaginative illustrations.

Balian, Lorna. *Humbug Witch.* New York: Abingdon, 1965. A little girl dresses up like a witch and tries to make magic potions with such things as paprika, hair tonic, pickle juice, and peanut butter. Can be adapted to the flannelboard.

Bright, Robert. *Georgie's Halloween.* New York: Doubleday, 1971. One of a delightful series about Georgie, a friendly ghost.

Calhoun, Mary. *Wobble, the Witch Cat.* New York: Morrow, 1958. It wasn't easy for Wobble the witch cat to ride on his mistress's broom with the slippery handle. The thought of falling off again made him cranky enough to do some mean things, including pushing the broom into the trash barrel. Wobble has the last laugh when, riding comfortably on his vacuum cleaner, he flies by all the other witch cats.

Low, Alice. *Witch's Holiday.* New York: Pantheon, 1971. A little boy's imaginary witches escape from his closet on Halloween and create all kinds of mischief.

Varga, Judy. *Once-a-Year Witch.* New York: Morrow, 1973. Booboolina the witch snatched every little girl she could find until the townspeople raided her cottage. What they discover is the surprise. The clever plot suggests a way the custom of trick-or-treating may have started.

von Hippel, Ursula. *The Craziest Halloween.* New York: Coward-McCann, 1957. A little witch wants to prove that she is a real witch. Amusing.

CHANUKAH STORIES

Bial, Morrison David. *The Hanukkah Story.* New York: Behrman House, 1952. This book gives instructions on how to play the dreidel game, which children like.

Cedarbaum, Sophia N. *Chanuko.* New York: Union of Hebrew Congregations, 1960. Two children plan for the Chanuko festival. May not be appropriate for those who are unfamiliar with the holiday, but the teacher can use the book for background material to adapt to her needs.

Morrow, Betty, and Louis Hartmon. *A Holiday Book of Jewish Holidays.* Champaign, Ill.: Garrard, 1967. Easy explanations and readable history of Jewish holidays including Chanukah, Purim, Passover, Yom Kippur, and Rosh Hashanah. Good for teachers' background material.

HOLIDAY STORYBOOKS FOR THE TEACHER

The following books include some good selections of stories that the teacher can learn for telling on special occasions.

Burnett, Bernice. *The First Book of Holidays.* New York: Franklin Watts, 1974. Short, factual information with photos describing holidays, including ethnic holidays celebrated in the United States. Another section describes festivals of other nations. Useful resource for the teacher.

The Child Study Association of America (comp.). *Holiday Storybook.* New York: Crowell, 1952. One of the few books containing stories about some of the less popular holidays, including Purim, Chanukah, United Nations Day, Lincoln's Birthday, and Labor Day. Among some of the best for telling to preschoolers are "A Valentine Story," by Evelyn Davis; "Mr. Plum and the Little Green Tree," by Helen Earle Gilbert (Arbor Day); and "Horace the Happy Ghost," by Elizabeth Ireland (Halloween). Very few illustrations.

Purcell, John Wallace. *The True Book of Holidays and Special Days.* Chicago: Children's Press, 1955. This book gives a brief description of each holiday and why we celebrate it.

BOOKS ABOUT SHAPES

Atwood, Ann. *The Little Circle.* New York: Scribner, 1967. A story about a little circle who starts out being a zero and goes through a series of adventures, becoming the circle of a daisy, a nest in a tree, a ripple in a fountain of water, and many other circles found in nature. Lovely color photographs.

Budney, Blossom. *A Kiss Is Round.* New York: Lothrop, 1954. Colorful illustrations of common objects that are round — a ring, balloon, pie, doughnut, money, clock, and others.

Charosh, Mannis. *The Ellipse.* New York: Crowell, 1971. An ellipse is a flattened circle. If you point a flashlight beam directly at a darkened wall you will see a circle, but if you tip the flashlight up just a little you will see an ellipse. This book has many similar simple experiments that young children can do. This is one in the series of Young Math Books edited by Dr. Max Beberman to acquaint the child with the concepts indicated by the titles: *Bigger and Smaller, Odds and Evens,* and *Circles.*

Children's Television Workshop. *The Sesame Street Book of Shapes.* New York: Preschool Press, Time-Life Books, 1971. Photographs and illustrations developed from material provided by the Sesame Street series so well known on television.

Hoban, Tana. *Shapes and Things.* New York: Macmillan, 1970. Common articles such as comb, brush, hammer, letters in white on black background without words.

Lerner, Sharon. *Square Is a Shape.* Minneapolis, Minn.: Lerner, 1970. Different shapes done in torn colored paper.

Matthiesen, Thomas. *Things to See: A Child's World of Familiar Objects.* New York: Platt, 1966. Lovely color photography of familiar objects.

BOOKS ABOUT NUMBERS

Anno, Mitsumasa. *Anno's Counting Book.* New York: Crowell, 1977. Children who read this counting book will get not only a mathematical learning experience, but also an aesthetic one. The scene is a rural village. Readers must search to find what has been added to the village to make one more. Contrasting groups emerge also, such as fruit trees versus evergreens. Children will surely be stimulated by this beautiful and imaginative counting book.

Hutchins, Pat. *One Hunter.* New York: Greenwillow Books, 1982. One hunter walks through the forest observed by two elephants, then three giraffes, and so on.

McLeod, Emile. *One Snail and Me.* Boston: Little, Brown, 1961. A good book to use with one child or a small group so children can look for the snail on each page.

Oxenbury, Helen. *Numbers of Things.* New York: Franklin Watts, 1968. The child can count the number of colorful illustrations on each page, such as two cars, four mice. Good for one child with adult. The illustrations encourage putting a finger on each object while the child counts.

Steiner, Charlotte. *Ten in a Family.* New York: Knopf, 1960. Teaches adding and subtracting as well as counting from one to ten. Can be adapted for use with a flannelboard.

Ungerer, Tomi. *One, Two, Where's My Shoe?* New York: Harper & Row, 1964. The artist disguises drawings of all kinds of shoes in his illustrations, and the child must go on a pictorial search through the pages. Good for use with one or two children.

———. *Snail, Where Are You?* New York: Harper & Row, 1962. Same format as above except the snail is hidden in illustrations.

Wildsmith, Brian. *Brian Wildsmith's 1, 2, 3's.* New York: Franklin Watts, 1965. Numbers are illustrated with bright shapes, such as one colorful circle, five different-size triangles, and so on. The combinations of numbers, shapes, and forms may be confusing for the beginner.

BOOKS ABOUT COLORS

Freeman, Don. *A Rainbow of My Own.* New York: Viking, 1966. A child sees a rainbow and runs out to catch it for his own. This is a book to encourage the imagination and interest in colors. Sound filmstrip, cassette.

Hoffmann, Beth Greiner. *Red Is for Apples.* New York: Random House, 1966. A book in rhyme calling attention to familiar objects and their colors.

Lionni, Leo. *Little Blue and Little Yellow.* New York: Astor-Honor, 1959. Torn paper illustrations showing how two colors can make a third. Good for adapting for use on the flannelboard with cellophane or tissue paper mounted on flannel or sandpaper frames.

BOOKS ABOUT THE ABC's

Alexander, Anne. *ABC of Cars and Trucks.* New York: Doubleday, 1971. A favorite, especially with children who enjoy looking at the cars and trucks.

Brown, Marcia. *All Butterflies.* New York: Scribner, 1974. These brightly colored butterflies, which fly through the ABC's, will trigger the imagination of any child.

Gag, Wanda. *The ABC Bunny.* New York: Coward-McCann, 1933. An old-time favorite with original lithographs and hand lettering.

Hoban, Tana. *A, B, See!* New York: Morrow, 1982. A collection of objects that begin with a particular letter of the alphabet. Hoban's books are generally well-designed selections for the preschool.

Munari, Bruno. *Bruno Munari's ABC.* New York: World, 1960. Clear, bright, simple, and large illustrations.

Newberry, Clare. *The Kittens' ABC.* New York: Harper & Row, 1964. Reissue of a favorite large book with illustrations of kittens on each page.

Wildsmith, Brian. *Brian Wildsmith's ABC.* New York: Franklin Watts, 1963. Large, modern, colorful illustrations, each accompanied by a word in upper-case and lower-case letters.

BOOKS ABOUT COMMUNITY WORKERS

Rubinger, Michael. *I Know an Astronaut.* New York: Putnam, 1972. A little boy accompanies his Uncle Bill, an astronaut, to the space center, where he takes a tour and learns about the kind of work astronauts do. This book is one of the Community Helper Books published by Putnam to acquaint the young child with various community workers. Written and illustrated by different authors, titles include *I Know a Policeman, I Know a Librarian, I Know a Bank Teller,* and *I Know a Teacher.*

Note: A good series of "Let's Visit" books illustrated with photos of children visiting such places as the hospital, doctor's office, supermarket, and the police and fire stations, is published by Taylor Publishing Company *(Your World Series),* Dallas, Texas.

BOOKS FOR CHILDREN ABOUT DEATH

Aliki. *The Two of Them.* New York: Greenwillow Books, 1979. A sensitive description of the relationship of a grandfather and his granddaughter from her birth to his death. Growth and change are realistically portrayed. "She knew that one day he would die. But when he did, she was not ready, and she hurt inside and out."

Bernstein, Joanne E., and Steven V. Gullo. *When People Die.* New York: Dutton, 1977. In this reassuring book about death, many of the questions young children ask are answered in a sensitive way. Throughout the book, emphasis is placed on the chain of life, touching on a variety of beliefs, but not identifying with any one of them. This book is not only full of sadness, it is also full of love.

Brown, Margaret Wise. *The Dead Bird.* New York: Young Scott Books, 1958. A simple story touchingly illustrated by Remy Charlip about some children who find a dead bird and bury it in the woods. The description of death is factual and handles the subject in a way that a child can understand and accept.

Bunting, Eve. *The Happy Funeral.* New York: Harper & Row, 1982. A Chinese-American girl deals with her feelings after her grandfather dies and assists in the preparations for his funeral. Excellent, simple descriptions of entire funeral. Probably best for five-year-olds, though could be adapted for younger children.

Coutant, Helen. *First Snow.* New York: Knopf, 1974. A snowflake changing to water helps a Vietnamese-American girl understand the meaning of dying.

de Paola, Tomie. *Nana Upstairs & Nana Downstairs.* New York: Putnam, 1973. "Nana Downstairs kept busy in the kitchen by the big black stove. Nana Upstairs rested in her bedroom. She was ninety-four years old. Tommy loved visiting them on Sunday afternoons. But one day, when Tommy ran up the steps to see Nana Upstairs, her bedroom was empty." This is the heartwarming and very real story of that special relationship between the very young and the very old and the moment when the two must part.

Fassler, Joan. *My Grandpa Died Today.* New York: Behavioral Publications, 1971. Realistic treatment of a young boy's close relationship with his grandfather and his adjustment to the grandfather's death. Written by a child psychologist. Look for other books from this publisher's series dealing with sensitive topics.

Freschet, Burneice. *The Old Bullfrog.* New York: Scribner, 1972. A beautifully written book about the understanding of survival.

Harris, Audrey. *Why Did He Die?* Minneapolis, Minn.: Lerner, 1965. A mother's poem explaining to her child about the death of his friend's grandfather. Good for use with young children.

Kantrowitz, Mildred. *When Violet Died.* New York: Parents' Magazine Press, 1973. They knew Violet was going to die, so when the little bird lay down in her cage, the children give her a wake and burial with songs, poems, and strawberry punch.

Miles, Miska. *Annie and the Old One.* Boston: Little, Brown, 1971. When the new rug is taken from the loom, Annie's grandmother, The Old One, will return to Mother Earth. Her family all understood the cycle of nature, but Annie couldn't. A poignant story of a little Navajo girl and her very special relationship with her grandmother. Lovely illustrations by Peter Parnall of life in a hogan. Read with a small group or with one child.

Tobias, Tobi. *Petey.* New York: Putnam, 1978. A girl's family helps her face her pet gerbil's dying and death.

Viorst, Judith. *The Tenth Good Thing About Barney.* New York: Atheneum, 1975. A young boy tenderly narrates the story of his pet's death. He must remember ten good things about his cat, Barney, to tell at the funeral. Realistic treatment of the death of a pet and how the boy comes to deal with his loss.

Zolotow, Charlotte. *My Grandson Lew.* New York: Harper, 1974. A boy lovingly recalls his grandfather, who died when the boy was quite young.

BOOKS FOR CHILDREN ABOUT DIVORCE, THE SINGLE PARENT, AND WORKING PARENTS

Adams, Florence. *Mushy Eggs.* Children of divorced parents are saddened by the departure of their very special baby sitter.

Blaine, Marge. *The Terrible Thing that Happened at Our House.* New York: Parents' Magazine Press, 1975. Things were fine until Mother went back to being a science teacher. That's when everything began to be different. The confusion, frustration, and lack of attention perceived by the young child is finally solved with cooperation from family and friends.

Caines, Jeannette. *Daddy.* New York: Harper & Row, 1977. This book about the children of separated parents deals with one aspect of the situation that has often been overlooked: What do Daddy and his daughter do on their Saturday visiting days? Here we read not only about the places they go, but also the things they do with Daddy's new wife. The people in this black family have warm, loving relationships, beautifully expressed by the artist.

Goff, Beth. *Where Is Daddy?* Boston: Beacon, 1969. Very few stories are written for the preschooler about divorce. This one was written by a psychiatric social worker to help a child adjust to her parents' divorce. This story is good for reading aloud on a one-to-one basis, giving the child plenty of opportunity to discuss and identify with the child in the story. An honest, realistic treatment of a subject that is difficult for the young child to understand.

Hazen, Barbara Shook. *Two Homes to Live In.* New York: Human Sciences Press, 1978. Gives a child's-eye view of a painful divorce. It shows the child that he or she did not cause the divorce and that life will stabilize again. It helps the child face his or her feelings honestly and will hasten adjustment.

Lexau, Joan M. *Me Day.* New York: Dial, 1971. Rafer wakes up on his birthday with good feelings inside, but he quickly grows disappointed. His parents are divorced and he has not heard from his father. Then his mother sends him on a mysterious errand. . . . Children can identify with Rafer's reaction to his parents' divorce and how important the celebration of a special day can be. Written in black dialect style, the text may be too wordy at times for a preschooler. Good for discussion of feelings.

Lindsay, Jeanne Warren. *Do I Have a Daddy?* Buena Park, Calif.: Morning Glory Press, 1982. A story about a little boy who wonders why he never sees his father. Designed to help children increase their understanding of different lifestyles and acceptance of single-parent friends. The book includes a special section for single mothers and fathers, giving suggestions for dealing with a young child's feelings and discussing the roles of never-married parents as well as divorced parents.

Merriam, Eve, and Beni Montresor. *Mommies at Work.* New York: Knopf, 1961. Gives a view of mothers at work in airport towers, on assembly lines, as train conductors, as dancers, with blueprints, and even as bridge-builders.

Perry, Patricia, and Marietta Lynch. *Mommy and Daddy Are Divorced.* New York: Dial, 1978. A sensitive, realistic look at the feelings of two children when their parents are divorced. The photos and text are honest and direct about family relationships, making this book a wise choice.

Saul, Wendy. *Butcher, Baker, Cabinetmaker.* New York: Thomas Y. Crowell, 1978. Black and white photographs by Abigail Heyman of women at work. Includes doctors, firefighters, letter carriers, zookeepers, airplane pilots, astronauts, butchers, and cabinetmakers. Good for discussion.

Thomas, Ianthe. *Eliza's Daddy.* New York, Harcourt, Brace, Jovanovich, 1976. Eliza's father remarries and even though she and her daddy have good times together, Eliza wonders about his other family. Finally, she asks to meet her new stepsister.

SEX EDUCATION BOOKS FOR CHILDREN

Andry, Andrew C., and Steven Schepp. *How Babies Are Made.* New York: Time-Life Books, 1968. Honest answers to children's questions about sex. Photographs of colored cut-out paper.

De Schweinitz, Karl. *Growing Up.* New York: Macmillan, 1968. One of the best books for preschoolers dealing with the topic of growing up. Good for use with one child or for discussion in a small group.

Gruenberg, Sidonie Matsner. *The Wonderful Story of How You Were Born.* New York: Doubleday, 1970. Good book to look at with a child but too many words for the preschooler. Use this for the excellent illustrations showing sperm, ovum, fetus.

Manushkin, Fran. *Baby.* New York: Harper & Row, 1972. Mrs. Tracy was growing a baby and baby didn't want to be born. Humorously illustrated tale showing the various positions and facial expressions of a baby inside the mommy and its responses to other members of the family waiting for it to be born. Pictures by Ronald Himler.

Selsam, Millicent E. *How Puppies Grow.* New York: Four Winds Press, 1977. Actual photographs by Esther Bubley showing six newborn pups and how they grow until they are old enough to be adopted.

Sheffield, Margaret. *Where Do Babies Come From?* New York: Knopf, 1973. A very explicit book designed for use by parents with their children. Simple, direct explanations of conception, reproduction, and the life cycle. Sheila Bewley's softly colorful illustrations convey feelings of tenderness and warmth. Adapted from the award-winning BBC program of the same title in England, this is by far the most honest book available on sex education for children.

Showers, Paul, and Kay Sperry Showers. *Before You Were a Baby.* New York: Crowell, 1968. Simply written and well-illustrated book appropriate for use with preschoolers. Allow plenty of time for discussion.

STORIES ABOUT A NEW BABY IN THE HOUSE

Arnstein, Helene S. *Billy and Our New Baby.* New York: Behavioral Publications, 1973. A good book for preschoolers who must deal with feelings of jealousy over the new baby. Billy acts out his conflicts by being aggressive, by crying, by regressing to bottle feeding. He learns that it's all right to have angry feelings, but that he may not hurt others. Gradually, Billy's parents help him to understand his importance in the family. There is a helpful guide at the end with suggestions and information about sibling rivalry.

Borack, Barbara. *Someone Small.* New York: Harper & Row, 1969. A child's daily experiences with a new baby in the house and with her bird that dies.

Hamilton-Merritt, Jane. *Our New Baby.* New York: Julian Messner, 1982. A boy adjusts to the birth of a new baby brother and looks forward to being friends with him. Beautiful photographs illustrate this sensitive book for young children.

Hoban, Russell. *A Baby Sister for Frances.* New York: Harper & Row, 1964. One of several books about a badger named Frances. When a new baby comes to the house, Frances is unhappy because she does not get enough attention.

Holland, Vicki. *We Are Having a Baby.* New York: Scribner, 1972. Four-year-old Dana is just as excited as her mother and father about the birth of their baby. But when the baby arrives at home, Dana is not sure if she likes the idea. Dana narrates the story, and the expressive photographs capture her reactions to this new event.

Iwasaki, Chihiro. *A New Baby Is Coming to My House.* New York: McGraw-Hill, 1970. A young girl muses on the arrival of a new baby brother. What will he look like? What can she give him for a present? Lovely watercolor illustrations complement simple text.

Keats, Ezra Jack. *Peter's Chair.* New York: Harper & Row, 1967. Peter's old cradle, high chair, and crib are all painted pink for his new baby sister. He is so unhappy that he decides to take his little blue chair and run away from home.

Weiss, Nicki. *Chuckie.* New York: Greenwillow Books, 1982. When Chuckie arrived, Lucy was as disagreeable to him as she knew how to be. Whatever Lucy did was fine with Chuckie, but whatever he did was wrong with Lucy. Finally, Chuckie speaks his first word! A humorous book that touches on jealousy of a new baby.

STORIES ABOUT MOVING TO A NEW HOME

Viklund, Alice R. *Moving Away.* New York: McGraw-Hill, 1967. One of the best books available on the subject of moving. A small book, easy to hold, sensitively written, and delicately illustrated. "Moving away is leaving behind people and places you know so well. It is a time when everything is different . . . It is a time to put things in boxes, decide which toys to take with you, and who to give your goldfish to. . . ." The child discovers that a new home can be nice too and that things are not so different.

Wise, William. *The House with the Red Roof.* New York: Putnam, 1961. Jimmy likes his house with the red roof and all the familiar things about his life. He thinks he is going to live there forever, but one day his father tells him they will move far away. Jimmy is reluctant and uncertain, but after the routine of moving he discovers he doesn't mind his new house with the brown roof.

BOOKS ABOUT OTHER CHILDHOOD EXPERIENCES

Alexander, Martha. *We're in Big Trouble, Blackboard Bear.* New York: The Dial Press, 1980. Anthony teaches his "blackboard bear" about leaving other people's things alone. A charming little book. Good for small groups.

Babbitt, Natalie. *The Something.* New York: Farrar, Straus & Giroux, 1970. Mylo the monster is afraid of the dark — or rather, of The Something he believes will come in through his window at night. His mother gives him some clay to make a statue of The Something. Mylo begins to wish The Something would appear so that he could make a better likeness. One night he has a dream and meets The Something. Mylo finds he is no longer afraid and decides to keep the statue next to his bed. Children may be amused at the prospect of a monster being afraid. Creative resolution to a child's fears.

Barrett, John M. *Oscar the Selfish Octopus.* New York: Human Sciences Press, 1978. A beautifully illustrated book about a young, self-centered octopus who is alienated from his friends and wonders why.

Berger, Knute, Robert A. Tidwell, and Margaret Haseltine. *A Visit to the Doctor.* New York: Grosset & Dunlap, 1960. A detailed discussion about a child going to the doctor for a physical examination, with illustrations of the little boy who has his height, weight, temperature, and pulse recorded; the doctor listens to his chest with a stethoscope and he gets a booster injection. The text is factual and written for the young child, but there may be too many explanations for the three-year-old. Good to use as a basis for discussion.

Bradbury, Ray. *Switch on the Night.* New York: Pantheon, 1955. A little boy overcomes his fears of the dark by learning to "switch on" the night — seeing and hearing the crickets, frogs, stars, and moon come alive.

Bulla, Clyde Robert. *Keep Running, Allen!* New York: Thomas Y. Crowell Co., 1978. The youngest in the family has to keep up with his sister and brothers who always run too fast, until he shows them the pleasure of being quiet and observing things around him. An excellent book for any young child who has ever tried to keep up with older siblings or friends.

Castle, Sue. *Face Talk, Hand Talk, Body Talk.* New York: Doubleday, 1977. Photographs of children with simple text showing how many ways people say things to each other without using words. Communications of anger, fear, doubt, love, need, yes, no, maybe, and please are some of the expressions. An excellent resource for discussion about feelings.

Chase, Francine. *A Visit to the Hospital.* New York: Grosset & Dunlap, 1957. A well-written and accurately illustrated book about a boy who goes to the hospital to have his tonsils removed. A shorter version is published under the same title by Wonder Books (1958).

Chorao, Kay. *Lester's Overnight.* New York: Dutton, 1977. This book about a child's first night away from home expresses well those feelings of misery experienced in a house so very different from one's own. The tender illustrations show Lester's imaginings and the intriguing details of Auntie Belle's house.

Cohen, Miriam. *Will I Have a Friend?* New York: Macmillan, 1967. Jim wonders if he will have a friend at nursery school. The children easel paint, play with clay, have juice and stories. When Jim goes home he realizes he has a friend at school.

de Paola, Tomie. *Now One Foot, Now the Other.* New York: G. P. Putnam's Sons, 1981. When his grandfather suffers a stroke, Bobby teaches him to walk, just as his grandfather had once taught him. An exceptional book dealing with a child's relationship with his grandfather and his feelings when the grandfather suffers a stroke.

Fassler, Joan. *All Alone with Daddy.* New York: Human Sciences Press, 1975. A tender story about a little girl who, while her mother is away on a trip, tries to take her mother's place. Ellen's daddy helps her to understand that she can't take mommy's place, but that she has a very special place in his heart.

———. *Don't Worry Dear.* New York: Human Sciences Press, 1974. This story is about Jenny, a little girl who sucks her thumb, stutters, and wets the bed. Jenny has a loving family who support her and reassure her that they accept her and will help her overcome her problems.

———. *Howie Helps Himself.* Chicago: A. Whitman, 1975. The story of a wheelchair-bound boy and his efforts to push his wheelchair across the classroom by himself. We see pictures of Howie doing his exercises and lessons, preparing himself for this stupendous task. Children and adults will be touched by Howie's life.

Fleisher, Robbin. *Quilts in the Attic.* New York: Macmillan, 1978. Two small sisters, playing imaginative games with quilts on a rainy day, quarrel and make up.

Garn, Bernard J. *A Visit to the Dentist.* New York: Grosset & Dunlap, 1959. Illustrations and text about a little boy who goes to the dentist for a regular checkup. Many details and factual information. If this book is too wordy, the same publisher has a shorter version in its Wonder Book series (1959) listed under the same title and author.

Gauch, Patricia Lee. *Grandpa and Me.* New York: Coward, McCann & Geoghegan, 1972. Story describes the special relationship between a grandparent and a child. Beautiful pencil/wash drawings by Shimlin.

Hickman, Martha Whitemore. *When Can Daddy Come Home?* Nashville, Tenn.: Abingdon, 1983. A good portrayal of the confusion and embarrassment a child feels when his father is imprisoned.

Hurd, Edith Thacher. *Come with Me to Nursery School.* New York: Coward-McCann, 1970. "What will I do at my school?" The text and a collection of photographs by Edward Bigelow show everyday activities in a nursery school setting. Useful to help introduce children to nursery school.

Hutchins, Pat. *Titch.* New York: Macmillan, 1971. Titch's older brother and sister always have bigger and better things than he does. They have bicycles and he has only a tricycle; they have kites while he has a pinwheel. But when the threesome decide to plant a tree, Titch becomes the hero because he has the seed. Bright, simple illustrations accompany the sparse text.

Jeffers, Susan. *All the Pretty Horses.* New York: Macmillan, 1974. Dreams and their beauty and mystery are depicted in this delicate book.

Keats, Ezra Jack. *Dreams.* New York: Macmillan, 1974. The story of how children who live in apartment houses amuse themselves. This book stimulates the imagination of the readers.

————. *Whistle for Willie.* New York: Viking, 1964. How Peter wished he could whistle! He saw others whistle, but try as he might, Peter couldn't. Young children identify easily with Peter, who finally experiences the joy of being able to whistle.

Lapsley, Susan. *I Am Adopted.* New York: Bradbury, 1975. The story of Charles and Sophie, who explain that their mommy and daddy adopted them when they were very little. The book tenderly depicts family experiences.

Mayer, Mercer. *There's a Nightmare in My Closet.* New York: Dial, 1976. A child frightened by nightmares finally invites the scary thing to join him in bed.

Memling, Carl. *What's in the Dark?* New York: Parents' Magazine Press, 1971. "What's in the dark? After they've clicked the light off. . . ." Shadows on the wall, moon in the sky, animals asleep, trucks on the street. The dark of night becomes more familiar and less frightening to the child. Big, bright illustrations accompany simple text.

Paullin, Ellen. *No More Tonsils!* Boston: Beacon, 1958. Good photography of a little girl going to the hospital to have her tonsils taken out.

Peterson, Jeanne Whitehouse. *My Sister Is Deaf.* New York: Harper & Row, 1977. A small deaf girl can understand by reading people's lips and eyes. She can say with her face and shoulders what many people cannot say with words. Soft charcoal sketches enhance this first-person text.

Preston, Edna Mitchell. *Squawk to the Moon, Little Goose.* New York: Viking Press, 1974. The delightful story of Little Goose, who almost loses his life by being disobedient, but learns a lesson in self-reliance. The book contains delightful water colors, which contribute much to the book. Filmstrip, cassette.

Rappaport, Doreen. *But She's Still My Grandma!* New York: Human Sciences Press, 1982. A young child learns to accept the senility of a beloved grandparent.

Rockwell, Harlow. *My Doctor.* New York: Macmillan, 1973. Story of a child's first visit to a doctor's office. The doctor reassuringly tells the child how she will use each of her instruments for the check-up. Also, *My Dentist*, 1975.

Schwartz, Amy. *Bea and Mr. Jones.* Scarsdale, N.Y.: Bradbury Press, 1982. Bea is tired of all her kindergarten activities, and her father (Mr. Jones) has had all he can take of the business world. So naturally they decide to trade places.

Serfozo, Mary. *Welcome Roberto.* Chicago: Follett, 1969. A Mexican-American child's first experience in school.

Shay, Arthur. *What Happens When You Go to the Hospital.* Chicago: Reilly & Lee, 1969. Photographs of a black girl named Karen, who goes to the hospital for two days to have her tonsils removed. Details show routine procedures of taking temperature, blood test, x-rays, and so on, and finally the operating room and recovery.

Showers, Paul. *How Many Teeth?* New York: Crowell, 1962. Well-written book on learning about the teeth and their care. Filmstrip, record, cassette.

Silverstein, Shel. *The Giving Tree.* New York: Harper & Row, 1964. A touching parable that tells of the child who took more and more from his tree — the apples, its branches, its wood, until only a stump was left. A sad and effective interpretation of "the gift of giving and a serene acceptance of another's capacity to love in return."

Simon, Norma. *I Know What I Like.* Chicago: A. Whitman, 1971. This well-written book helps the young child to be more sensitive to the feelings and ideas of others — ideas that may be quite different from one's own. It also encourages an acceptance of one's own feelings. A good book to use for discussion and further exploration and expression of feelings.

Skorpen, Liesel Moak. *All the Lassies.* New York: Dial, 1970. Peter wants a dog for a pet, but his parents try to persuade him to have another animal. He ends up with a fish, a turtle, a bird, and a cat, all of which he names Lassie. Finally, Peter gets his wish for a dog. He chooses the largest dog in the pet shop and names it Walter! Charming pencil sketches by Bruce Martin Scott.

Stanton, Elizabeth, and Henry Stanton. *Sometimes I Like to Cry.* Chicago: A. Whitman, 1978. Depicts real-life situations in a family. This story will help children to realize that not only do people cry when they are sad, but sometimes they cry when they are happy.

Tamburine, Jean. *I Think I Will Go to the Hospital.* New York: Abingdon, 1965. Susy doesn't want to go to the hospital to have her tonsils out. She plays hospital with her pets, visits friends who have been hospitalized, and soon realizes that the hospital is a good place to be when you are sick.

Viorst, Judith. *Alexander and the Terrible, Horrible, No Good, Very Bad Day.* New York: Atheneum, 1972. Poor Alexander has a terrible day with all sorts of things happening to him. Young children can identify with the humor.

Watson, Jane Werner, Robert E. Switzert, and J. Cotter Hirschberg. *Read-Together Books for Parents and Children.* New York: Western, 1971. These authors have written a series of books in cooperation with the Menninger Foundation for Solving Problems of Childhood. Titles include *Sometimes I Get Angry, Sometimes I'm Afraid, Sometimes I Get Jealous.* A worthwhile series to use in discussing feelings.

Williams, Barbara. *Kevin's Grandma.* New York: Dutton, 1975. A book about a grandma who is not only calm, giving, and warm, but has very ungrandmotherly experiences that delight her grandson. This is a funny and loving story about a very important person in a child's life.

Zolotow, Charlotte. *A Father Like That.* New York: Harper & Row, 1971. "I wish I had a father. But my father went away. . . ." A boy imagines what his father would be like. A touching story of a child's imaginary ideal family.

————. *William's Doll.* New York: Harper & Row, 1972. William wanted a doll more than anything else. His family tried to discourage him. Only William's grandmother understood how he felt. Sympathetic treatment, although text may be a bit wordy for preschoolers. Color illustrations by William Pene Du Bois.

PICTURE BOOKS WITHOUT WORDS

The following are excellent lap books that encourage language development and use of the imagination. They are used most effectively with one child at a time.

Alexander, Martha. *Bobo's Dream.* New York: Dial, 1970. Bobo is a dachshund whose master saves his bone from a large mongrel.

Bobo dreams of returning the favor. Martha Alexander's first book without words, *Out! Out! Out!*, is another excellent selection.

Amoss, Berthe. *By the Sea.* New York: Parents' Magazine Press, 1969. A fantasy of line drawings showing children at the beach. The hero wears red trunks, holds a red kite, and has a dog with a red collar. The kite pulls the little boy up into the sky, and the little dog goes after him with a red balloon. This is a small book, fun for little hands to hold.

Goodall, John S. *The Adventures of Paddy Pork.* New York: Harcourt, Brace & World, 1968. A charmingly illustrated book with detailed black and white line drawings of a pig who runs away to join the circus. A second book by the same author, also without words, is *The Ballooning Adventures of Paddy Pork* (1969), which has our hero saving a piglet from a band of gorillas. Good for use with children who have been exposed to many stories and will not be frightened by ferocious-looking animals.

———. *The Midnight Adventures of Kelly, Dott, and Esmeralda.* New York: Atheneum, 1973. Soft, detailed watercolors without words tell the story of three toys, a koala bear, a doll, and a mouse, who wake up at midnight and begin their adventures by climbing into a landscape picture on the wall. The effective use of half-pages heightens the child's interest and imagination.

———. *The Surprise Picnic.* New York: Atheneum, 1977. This book without words will allow even very young readers to follow the action entirely through its lovely, detailed pictures. It shows the suspenseful adventures of a mother cat and her two kittens and a clever coping with catastrophe!

Hoban, Tana. *Look Again!* New York: Macmillan, 1971. Look once, look twice. Look again! Collection of black and white photographs in an amusing format. They show that there is more than one way of seeing a picture. Children enjoy guessing the surprise answers. Good for language involvement. Look for other books by Hoban on teaching concepts *(Push, Pull, Empty, Full; Count and See; Shapes and Things)*.

———. *Round and Round and Round.* New York: Greenwillow Books, 1982. Color photos featuring objects that are round.

Mayer, Mercer. *A Boy, a Dog and a Frog.* New York: Dial, 1967. A small book with delightful drawings of a boy and his dog and their attempt to catch a frog for a pet. The sequel to this book, *Frog, Where Are You?* (1969), shows the frog escaping from a jar at night and the little boy and his dog finding their friend in the pond.

———. *Bubble, Bubble.* New York: Parents' Magazine Press, 1973. A little boy buys a magic bubble-maker and blows bubbles in all kinds of shapes, including some scary animals. But he can always pop his bubbles — or can he?

Wezel, Peter. *The Good Bird.* New York: Harper & Row, 1966. A large, colorfully illustrated book about a bird who makes friends with a fish in a gold-fish bowl by sharing a worm. See also *The Naughty Bird* (New York: Follett, 1967).

LANGUAGE ACTIVITY BOOKS FOR THE TEACHER

Included in this list are books that provide teachers with guidelines for telling a story without using a book. Also included is a variety of language activity books that suggest a number of projects, games, and storytelling activities designed primarily to develop language skills.

Bauer, Caroline. *Handbook for Storytellers.* Chicago: American Library Association, 1977. Covers detailed aspects of all phases of storytelling, including techniques for different age groups, exhibits, and the use of slides, films, and multimedia presentations. There are also sections on the use of flannelboards, chalkboards, puppetry, and magic.

———. *This Way to Books.* New York: H. W. Wilson Co., 1983. Collection of ideas, programs, techniques, and activities designed to involve children in books. Includes use of toys, puppets, crafts, music, costumes, and banners as devices to bring children and books together. Material suitable for preschool and up. Bibliographies throughout.

Caballero, Jane A. *The Handbook of Learning Activities for Young Children.* Atlanta, Ga.: Humanics Limited, 1984. Presents more than 125 activities in such areas as: math, health and safety, play, movement, science, social studies, art, language, and puppetry.

———. *Art Projects for Young Children.* Atlanta, Ga.: Humanics Limited, 1984. An excellent book with more than 100 activities in drawing, painting, cut and paste, flannel and bulletin boards, puppets, clay, printing, textiles, and photography.

Carlson, Bernice Wells. *Listen! And Help Tell the Story.* New York: Abingdon, 1965. Emphasis on encouraging the child to listen and participate in telling a story. The contents include sections on finger plays, action verses, action stories, poems and stories with sound effects, poems with a refrain and with a chorus. Some can be easily memorized by the teacher; others can be used with the book.

Cohen, Monroe D. (ed.). *Literature with Children.* Washington, D.C.: Association for Childhood Education International, 1972. Contains short, helpful articles by outstanding authors covering such subjects as the classics, poetry, storytelling, dramatizing literature, creative experiences, using multimedia with literature, and teacher resources.

Commins, Elaine. *Early Childhood Activities.* Atlanta, Ga.: Humanics Limited, 1984. Consists of more than 500 projects, games, and activities for three- to seven-year-olds in the areas of art, language arts, mathematics, music, physical education, science, and social studies.

Coyne, John, and Jerry Miller. *How to Make Upside-Down Dolls.* Washington, D.C.: Bobbs-Merrill, 1977. Dozens of "how-to" diagrams, patterns, and photographs showing how to make the famed upside-down dolls of the mountain craftspeople of North Carolina. A Goldilocks doll turns upside-down to reveal the three bears.

Engler, Larry. *Making Puppets Come Alive: A Method of Learning and Teaching Hand Puppetry.* New York: Taplinger, 1973. A useful resource for teachers who want to use puppets for storytelling. Also has suggestions for teaching children how to make and use puppets in the classroom.

Flemming, Bonnie Mack, and Darlene Softley Hamilton. *Resources for Creative Teaching in Early Childhood Education.* New York: Harcourt Brace Jovanovich, 1977. An excellent reference book that integrates ideas and activities in all areas of the curriculum. The subject areas include self-concept, families, family celebrations, seasons, animals, transportation, day and night, food, water, color, tools, machines, and math.

Hunt, Tamara, and Nancy Renfro. *Puppetry in Early Childhood Education.* Austin, Tex.: Nancy Renfro Studios, 1982. Describes how to make and use puppets in all areas of the curriculum.

Hutchings, Margaret. *Making and Using Finger Puppets.* New York: Taplinger, 1973. A useful book for designing and making finger puppets.

Karnes, Merle B. *Helping Young Children Develop Language Skills.* Arlington, Va.: The Council for Exceptional Children, 1976. A very good book covering such areas of language as listening skills, motor expression, and auditory and visual memory. Each chapter includes suggestions for activities and games to use with the child.

Kay, Evelyn. *Games that Teach for Children Three Through Six.* Minneapolis, Minn.: T. S. Denison & Co., 1981. Photographs and descriptions illustrate language games that can be made inexpensively.

Kimmel, Margaret Mary, and Elizabeth Segel. *For Reading Out Loud!* New York, Delacorte Press, 1983. A good book describing why it is important to read aloud during early years and how to do it effectively at home and in the classroom. The authors provide a recommended reading list of more than 140 books for children, mostly appropriate for the early elementary grades, but some appropriate for grades K–3.

Sawyer, Ruth. *The Way of the Storyteller.* New York: Viking, 1977. This is not a book on "how to tell stories and what to tell" according to the author, but every teacher should be familiar with Ruth Sawyer's philosophy on the creative art of storytelling.

Schimmel, Nancy. *Just Enough to Make a Story: A Sourcebook for Storytelling.* Berkeley, Calif.: Sister's Choice Press, 1978. Tips on choosing, learning, and telling a story. Includes songs, finger plays, paper folding, and selected bibliography.

Schubert, Delwyn G. (ed.). *Reading Games that Teach.* Monterey Park, Calif.: Creative Teaching Press, 1965. A series of teaching games designed to reinforce reading skills. Some are for older children who can read, but many can be adapted for use in the preschool. Games in the readiness section include suggestions for activities that require the child to tell "what happened next," select the "best path for bunny," and "cover the odd one."

Scott, Louise Binder. *Learning Time with Language Experiences for Young Children.* New York: McGraw-Hill, 1968. Describes what language is and its stages of development. Offers a variety of activities, including exposure to poetry. It suggests ways of helping children with speech problems and those for whom English is a second language.

Scott, Louise Binder, and J. J. Thompson. *Rhymes for Fingers and Flannelboards.* St. Louis, Mo.: Webster Division, McGraw-Hill, 1960. Includes an interesting introduction regarding finger plays of long ago, value of finger plays, and suggestions for purpose and devices the teacher can use. Descriptions of suggested materials to use in acting out a rhyme and illustrations of figures to prepare for the flannelboard are included, as well as a section on fingerplays in foreign languages. Other sections focus on holidays, numbers, active and quiet times, and more.

Sims, Judy. *Puppets for Dreaming and Scheming.* San Francisco: Early Stages Press, 1978. Illustrations and directions that show how to make puppets and a stage as well as prepare for a performance.

Steiner, Violette G., and Roberta Evatt Pond. *Finger Play Fun.* Columbus, Ohio: Merrill, 1970. A collection of old and new finger plays, with photographs or illustrations accompanying each one. Sections include those on quiet time, counting, animals, and holidays.

Trencher, Barbara R. *Child's Play.* Atlanta, Ga.: Humanics Limited, 1984. Presents ideas and materials needed to make such things as puppets and mobiles. Also contains songs and poetry.

Warren, Jean. *Language Games.* Palo Alto, Calif.: Monday Morning Books, 1983. A collection of more than 100 language activities that can be made from inexpensive materials.

WHERE TO WRITE FOR ADDITIONAL RESOURCE MATERIALS

The following organizations will provide bibliographies of books, records, tapes, and other helpful resource aids. Some of the pamphlets are free and others carry a small fee. Inquire about specifics.

American Library Association, Children's Service Division, 50 East Huron St., Chicago, IL 60611.

Association for Childhood Education International, 3615 Wisconsin Ave., N.W., Washington, D.C. 20016.

Association of Children's Librarians of Northern California, San Francisco Public Library, San Francisco, CA 94102.

The Child Study Association of America, Inc., 9 East 89th St., New York, NY 10028.

The Consumer Information Center, Dept. 60, Pueblo, CO 81009. (Annual editions of children's books published by the Library of Congress.)

Encyclopedia Brittanica Educational Corporation, Reference Division, 425 N. Michigan Ave., Chicago, IL 60611.

National Association for the Education of Young Children, 1834 Connecticut Ave., N.W., Washington, D.C. 20009.

Two excellent aids for the teacher published by NAEYC in conjunction with ERIC are *Books in Pre-school,* a guide to selecting, purchasing, and using children's books, and *Multi-ethnic Books for Young Children,* an annotated bibliography for parents and teachers. Both were compiled by Louise Griffin.

PART FIVE

The Physical World

Introduction

Young children are constantly exploring the world around them. Their urge to touch, see, hear, and taste brings them information about the physical world. The natural curiosity of young children can be guided to make learning more specific. Planned activities can help in several ways:

1. Children gain knowledge about the physical world.
2. They become aware of basic "laws" (such as gravity) and processes (for example, seeds need water to grow).
3. They learn about the methods of science — observation, testing ideas, and measurement.
4. They develop attitudes about ecology and conservation.

Knowledge about the physical world grows out of observing events, questioning or investigating hunches about why things work the way they do, manipulating objects to see what will happen, and measuring the results. Young children start learning about their world by observing and recording their ideas about things that happen. They may not observe systematically or come up with hypotheses on their own, but they are able to check their ideas ("Let's see what will happen if we put this saucer of water in the sun."). Children can learn to ask questions, and they can help find answers for themselves. They can see what happens as a result of what they do. Organized activities based on these principles will help young children learn the most they can about the physical world.

You can help children begin to acquire the *knowledge, skills and methods,* and *attitudes* of science and conservation in a number of ways.

1. Help children get firsthand experience with materials, living animals, and plants. Let them see how substances act or react to certain conditions or situations (evaporation, plant growth, gravity, the movement of a pendulum, the process of heat producing steam, and so on).
2. Give children repeated experience with a particular principle. They may observe *causal relationships,* where one thing happens as the result of something else. For example, when you push chil-

dren on the swings, a certain back and forth motion follows. If they "pump," the motion is maintained. If they stop, the motion stops. Children may also learn *predictability* of events or results. If a block is dropped from a child's hand, it will fall to the floor; if a seed is planted and watered, it will usually sprout; if a plant is not watered, it will die.

3. Use modeling to develop a questioning attitude and to encourage experimentation. You can ask a question or express doubt and proceed to measure or weigh or check something out. Comments appropriate for this kind of teaching include:

Let's see what happens if. . . .
Let's try it again and see if the same thing happens.
Let's be sure. Let's measure again.
We won't really know what will happen unless we try it out.

4. Keep emphasizing the processes and methods that you or the children are using. Help children be clear about what it is they want to discover. Encourage them to ask specific questions. Use labels for methods that are understandable and phrases that can become familiar:

Look carefully.
Say what you want to find out.
Try it out.
Watch to see what happens.

Children should be given experiences and experiments they may not completely understand but that will give them the basis for future knowledge. The principle of conservation — that matter may change in form and composition but continues to exist — is not an easy concept to teach, but there are many examples of such transformations that you can use to demonstrate the principle. Changing water into ice is one example: the water is still there but in a different form. Another example is the difference in reactions that take place when sugar is put into one glass of water and sand into another glass of water. The sugar seems to disappear but is still in the water, as the children can observe by tasting it. It is important that children have experiences that begin to lead them to new levels of understanding, even though full understanding may not be reached until after they leave the nursery school or child-care center.

Children's curiosity about the physical world is also a natural opportunity for teaching ecological conservation. The damaging effects of litter, waste, and pollution can be demonstrated through curriculum activities. In areas where drought is sometimes a problem, young children can be made aware of the need to save water and can recognize some of the obvious ways to avoid waste. They learn that it is not a good idea to leave the faucet running or to throw paper and soft-drink cans out of the car, even though they may not be able to explain the logic of recycling.

Young children can be taught to save, to avoid pollution, and to value clean air and water. The central concept of ecology — the interdependence of life forms on one another and on their physical surroundings — isn't something children are prepared to explain, but the foundation of attitudes toward specific behavior, such as littering, wasting, and polluting, can be learned *and* taught. We believe that preschool is the time to teach such attitudes that, for this generation of children, may be a matter of survival. In addition, the sense of cooperation and of consideration for others that conservation and ecological principles represent are themselves well worth the effort required to include them in the preschool curriculum.

Most of the tasks suggested in this part draw on resources that exist in the natural environment of the school or home. They allow for maximum participation by the children, and they encourage independent investigation. You need to remember that children are active investigators, not passive observers. By asking pertinent questions yourself, you can teach them to phrase questions that will help them make discoveries on their own.

Different kinds of questions call for quite different types of responses from children. Questions that begin with words such as *can*, *is*, *will*, or *did* can often be answered by a *yes* or *no*. Questions that include words such as *why* or *how* are usually very difficult for young children because they call for much more complex answers. Questions using the words *who*, *what*, and *when* often require specific information by way of response, and may or may not be easy to answer. Your task, obviously, is to ask questions to which the child can respond. You may ask, "Does the ball always fall to the floor?" and expect a reasonable reply from a young child. But if you ask, "Why does the ball fall to the floor?" you will only mystify and confuse. If you ask, "When [how soon] does the ball fall?" the children will probably be able to respond in a way that makes sense both to them and to you. You may ask, "What does a tadpole turn into?" and expect the children to know or to learn the answer; if you ask, "How does a tadpole become a frog?" you won't get very far. The point is to select questions carefully and to phrase them so that they are answerable by the children or so that they will lead the children to find the answer.

A science table or discovery corner provides opportunities for exploration. You can display rocks, plants, a terrarium or aquarium, and many other interesting things for children to feel, smell, listen to, look at, and experiment with. The display can be changed to offer varied learning experiences. Children can also be encouraged to bring their own contributions to share with others.

Centering activities on a particular theme, such as "changes," "how things feel," or "growing things," is another useful technique. For "changes," you might make cinnamon toast for snack time and talk about how the bread changes to toast, discuss ways boys and girls can and can't change as they grow, and talk about how leaves change color in different seasons. The science table can reflect the same theme with displays of how a dry sponge changes in water or how a starfish can grow back an arm. Pictures on this same theme can also be displayed.

Every teacher has the opportunity to do some spontaneous teaching during the daily routine. A snail from the garden, a bird's nest a child may have found, some seashells from a recent trip — all provide the teacher and child with an opportunity to gain more information about the physical world. When a school has many kinds of animals, the children learn that they need food and water just as humans do and that animals are born and grow.

The outside environment presents many areas for discovery: leaves change colors, die, and drift to the ground; a bud blossoms into a flower; and sand comes from rocks. The weather offers many opportunities for discussion: rain falls from clouds; puddles dry up on a sunny day; the wind causes certain sensations and things happen when it blows.

The area inside the school or child-care center also offers many places for discovery. The idea of balance comes naturally when children are building with blocks or walking on high heels in the playhouse; the awareness of resonance and tone changes develops as children listen to the piano, autoharp, or guitar; some understanding of why an open scrape or cut should be washed with soap and water can be fostered while you administer first aid. As in all areas of the curriculum, some of the best times for teaching will occur spontaneously.

The activities you select must involve concepts and mental operations that the young child is able to handle. But it is the teaching strategies underlying the activities, not the activities themselves, that determine the quality of an effective program in science and ecology. Keep these suggestions in mind as you plan activities in this area:

1. Give children plenty of opportunity to explore and experiment on their own.
2. Provide enticing materials that will encourage experimentation.
3. Do not give answers too readily. Instead, ask questions that will stimulate thinking. Try to discover *what* the child is thinking.
4. Ask questions that will encourage children to
   a. *hypothesize:* "What do you think will happen if we drop the balsa wood into the water? What do you think will happen if we drop the clay into the water?"
   b. *identify the result:* "What happened?"

HELPFUL HINTS

1. Refer to the bibliographies in this part for books to display in the science and ecology area.
2. Write to publishers for additional materials (Thomas Y. Crowell, New York, is especially good for children's books on science).
3. Display large posters of subjects relating to science and ecology projects.
4. Take photographs of the children engaged in conservation activities and display them.
5. Tape-record interesting facts about the project and provide a playback machine for the children to operate. (The "play" and "reverse" buttons can be color-coded.)
6. Cover the holes in a Halloween eye mask to use in tasks that call for children to close their eyes.

  c. *predict:* "What will happen if we do this again?"

  d. *explore other possibilities:* "What other things will sink? "What other things will float?" (The child should not be expected to understand the concept of specific gravity. Some children will continue to predict that large objects will sink and small ones float, despite demonstrations that there are exceptions.)

5. Young children learn best when information is given in response to their own questions.

Science Activities

SENSORY PERCEPTION

▶ **PURPOSE** **To experience how different things smell**

MATERIALS — Baby food jars
— Cloves, mint, flower petals, sawdust, leather, onions, apples, and other items with a distinctive scent

PROCEDURE **1.** Place one ingredient in each jar.
2. Punch holes in the lids.
3. Ask children to close their eyes and take turns smelling each jar.
4. Have them guess what they smell.

CONCLUSION Different things smell different.

▶ **PURPOSE** **To differentiate common sounds**

MATERIALS — Common objects in the room

PROCEDURE **1.** Have children close their eyes.
2. Produce various sounds by rubbing a piece of chalk on the chalkboard, dropping a pencil on the floor, opening and shutting a door, closing a window, and turning on a faucet.
3. Ask the children to guess the source of each sound.
4. Ask children to describe how each sound was made.
5. Stress accuracy in description as well as perception.

CONCLUSION Different things make different sounds.

▶ **PURPOSE** **To experience how different things feel**

MATERIALS — Objects differing in texture and hardness, such as foam rubber, cork, pennies, velvet, satin, burlap, eraser, and marshmallow

PROCEDURE **1.** Let children see all the objects.
2. Have them close their eyes.
3. Hand them one object at a time to feel or let one of the children hand out the objects.
4. Have children guess what object they are holding.

CONCLUSION Different things feel different.

VARIATION Place several objects in a bag or box. Have one child put his or her hand in and select, describe, and guess what the object is before he or she pulls it out.

217

▶ **PURPOSE**   **To experience how different things taste**

MATERIALS   — Variety of common foods, such as apples, popcorn, bread, dry cereal, and peanut butter

PROCEDURE   1. Have children close their eyes.
2. Put a small amount of food in each child's mouth.
3. Have the child guess what he or she is tasting.
4. Have the child hold his or her nose and close his or her eyes.
5. Place food in the child's mouth and have the child guess what it is.

CONCLUSION   1. Different things taste different.
2. Smelling something helps to tell how it tastes.

▶ **PURPOSE**   **To learn about objects that feel the same but look different**

MATERIALS   — Objects that feel the same but look different, such as different colored apples, crayons, or cups; paper with and without pictures or printing; and so on

PROCEDURE   1. Have children close their eyes.
2. Let each child hold an object and tell what he or she thinks it is.
3. Have the child describe all the properties of the object without looking.
4. Ask questions about each object, such as:
Is it rough or smooth?
Is it hard or soft?
Is it round or flat?
What color is it?
Is there a design on it?

CONCLUSION   1. Your eyes can tell you about the color of things.
2. Your eyes can tell you if things have designs or printing or pictures on them.

HELPFUL HINTS

1. Supervise and plan experiments carefully.
2. Repeat experiments and help children to ask questions and arrive at answers for themselves.
3. Keep small sorting objects in designated places and set limits for their use.
4. Do not put out materials without adequate supervision.

DEMONSTRATING PHYSICAL PROPERTIES

▶ **PURPOSE**   **To classify objects that are alike and different**

MATERIALS
— Three cigar boxes
— Self-sticking paper
— Assortment of buttons
— Large variety of different shapes and materials, such as marbles, dice, erasers, bolts, bottle caps, coins, spools, plastic objects, pieces of cloth, and paper clips

PROCEDURE
1. Cover cigar boxes with the self-sticking paper.
2. Draw buttons on the lid of one box and fill with buttons.
3. Draw pictures of objects with round, triangular, square, and rectangular shapes on another box.
4. Draw pictures of objects made of different kinds of materials on the last box.
5. Fill each box with appropriate objects for sorting.
6. Have children sort the objects according to size, shape, color, texture, or materials from which each is made (metal, plastic, wood, cloth).

CONCLUSION
Things are alike and different because of their color, shape, size, the way they feel, and the things they are made from.

▶ **PURPOSE**   **To learn about air**

MATERIALS
— Bowl of water
— Empty glass
— Tissue or napkin

PROCEDURE
1. Turn the glass upside down and force it straight down into the bowl of water.

OBSERVATION
The glass did not fill up with water.

2. Tilt the glass to one side.

OBSERVATION
Bubbles rise and break at the water's surface. These bubbles show that the glass was full of air.

3. Take the napkin and crumple it. Place it in the bottom of a clean, dry glass.
4. Force the glass straight down into the bowl of water and then lift it straight out again.

OBSERVATION
The napkin is dry.

5. Now force the glass straight down into the water and then tilt the glass to one side.

OBSERVATION   Water enters the glass and wets the napkin.

CONCLUSION   Air takes up space even though we can't see it or taste it.

VARIATIONS   Other similar experiments show us that air is present all around us:

1. Blowing bubbles.
2. Blowing up a balloon.
3. Feeling the wind blowing against you.
4. Watching all the things the wind blows (smoke, clouds, trees, clothes, kites, flags or banners, pinwheels, curtains).
5. Using an air pump for bicycle or car tires.

HELPFUL HINTS

1. Type out instructions about how to present tasks and experiments so that volunteers can supervise an activity.
2. Post interesting facts about animals and science displays so that adults can read them to the children.

▶ **PURPOSE**   **To learn what air can do**

MATERIALS   — Book
                — Balloon
                — Air pump

PROCEDURE   1. Place the balloon under the book.
                2. Inflate the balloon with the pump. (See Illustration 5.1.)

OBSERVATION   The book is rising.

CONCLUSION   1. Air can lift things up.
                2. Air can push things.

▶ **PURPOSE**   **To learn how water gets into the air**

MATERIAL   — Dish of water

PROCEDURE   1. Place dish of water in the sun.
                2. After a few hours, check to see what has happened to the water.

OBSERVATION   The water is gone.

CONCLUSION   1. The sun heats the water.
                2. The water evaporates and goes into the air.
                3. Water from oceans, rivers, and lakes rises into the air when the sun heats it.

Illustration 5.1 **Demonstrating that air can lift things**

HELPFUL HINTS

1. Save plastic six-pack bottle holders, funnels, and the like to use for blowing bubbles.
2. A teaspoon of glycerin added to water and detergent will make bigger, better bubbles. Blowing bubbles is a good activity for restless children and provides opportunities to talk about rainbows and air.

▶ **PURPOSE** **To learn about rain**

MATERIALS — Saucepan partially filled with boiling water
— Lid of the pan or a plate

PROCEDURE Keep the water boiling in the saucepan and take the lid or the plate and hold it over the pan, but not on it.

OBSERVATION First, a thin film of steam covers the plate or lid, and when more steam rises, tiny drops of water form on the lid and fall back into the pan.

CONCLUSION When water is heated it evaporates and becomes steam. When it is cooled, it condenses and becomes water again. The water droplets are like rain that falls. There are lots of tiny drops of water that make a cloud. When these drops are cooled and get too heavy, they have to fall to the ground, and we get rain.

▶ **PURPOSE**   **To learn about snowflakes**

MATERIALS
— Piece of heavy acrylic or glass
— A can of clear spray lacquer
— Snow

PROCEDURE
1. Place both the can of lacquer and piece of glass in the freezer for two minutes.
2. Take them outdoors before they warm up.
3. Spray a thin coat of lacquer on the glass.
4. Hold the glass so snow falls on it.
5. Place the glass in the freezer for fifteen minutes.

OBSERVATION
The snowflakes will be "captured" on the glass. Children can study them closely through a magnifying glass.

CONCLUSION
A snowflake is formed high above the earth when water vapor freezes around a tiny dust particle. The snowflake turns and spins as it falls, forming many different shapes. No two snowflakes are alike. Snow and ice are important to our environment. Snow is a warm blanket for the earth that keeps the soil from freezing. Many animals and plants would die in the winter without a snow blanket.

▶ **PURPOSE**   **To learn about lightning**

MATERIALS
— Two inflated balloons
— A darkened room or closet

PROCEDURE
1. Rub the two balloons on your clothes, a rug, or draperies.
2. Hold the balloons end to end, almost touching.

OBSERVATION
If the room is dark enough, you can see a spark jump between the two balloons. That spark is electricity.

CONCLUSION
Sparks result from friction. If the balloons had been clouds, the sparks would have been lightning. Lightning is electricity that we see in the sky.

▶ **PURPOSE**   **To learn about thunder**

MATERIAL
— Empty paper bag

PROCEDURE
1. Blow up the paper bag and hold the neck tightly so air cannot escape.
2. Hit the bag with the other hand.

OBSERVATION   The bag will break with a loud bang.

CONCLUSION   When air rushes together it makes a loud noise. Lightning forces air apart, and when the air rushes together again it makes a loud noise. Whenever there is lightning forcing the air apart, you will then hear thunder as the air rushes back together.

▶ **PURPOSE**   **To learn about rainbows**

MATERIALS   — Garden hose
— Small mirror
— Glass of water

PROCEDURE   **1.** Turn the hose on to a fine spray. Stand with your back to the sun.

OBSERVATION   You will see a rainbow in the fine spray of water.

2. Place a small mirror in a glass of water. Place the glass so that the sun can shine on the mirror. Turn the glass until the rainbow is reflected against the wall or ceiling.

OBSERVATION   Look around on the walls or ceiling to find colors of the rainbow.

CONCLUSION   The sun is made up of all the colors in the rainbow mixed together. When sunlight hits raindrops or water, the colors are separated.

Note: This conclusion is often too complex for very young children to understand. If they are at the preoperational stage, their response might be: "Oh, that's magic. Do that again!" or "Let us do it." You should encourage this interest and excitement by letting each child make his or her own rainbow. You can help develop an attitude of "things happen for reasons" and "we can look for answers." Arriving at the "correct" conclusion should not always be the only objective in an experiment.

▶ **PURPOSE**   **To learn about gravity**

MATERIALS   — Any objects that can be dropped

PROCEDURE   **1.** Give each child an object and have the child drop it. Where does it go?

OBSERVATION   It falls to the floor.

2. Have each child repeat this several times. Each time the child drops the object ask a question such as:
Will it fall to the ground this time?
Will it fall up?
Will it fall to the side?
What will happen the next time you drop it?
What do you think will happen every time you drop it?

OBSERVATION   The object falls to the floor every time. You can predict that the next time you drop the object, it will fall to the floor.

CONCLUSION   There is a force that pulls everything downward to the center of the earth. This force is called *gravity*.

Note: Young children will have difficulty understanding or explaining gravity. They will be able to predict that something will fall to the ground based on their experiences, but if you ask them why, they are likely to answer: "Just because I know it will." It is sufficient to focus on consciously recognizing that objects will fall to the ground every time and that this is predictable.

LEARNING ABOUT LIVING THINGS

▶ **PURPOSE**   **To learn about the birth and care of animals**

MATERIALS   — Guinea pigs,[1] rabbits, hamsters, rats, or kittens

PROCEDURE   Let children care for the animals.

OBSERVATION   Watch as the female becomes pregnant and bears her litter.

CONCLUSION   Explain that animals like these (as well as people) grow inside the mother. The father plants a seed inside the mother and the baby grows from this seed. Every animal has both a mother and father.

DISCUSSION   Point out that many animals need to be cared for when they are first born. Explain to the children that when they were babies, they could not walk or talk or feed themselves. Their mothers and fathers had to take care of them. Other animals, such as guinea pigs, kittens, rats, and dogs, also need someone to take care of them. Some babies have more than just their parents to take care of them. Bees have many worker bees to care for the babies. The queen bee lays the eggs, but she does not take care of the babies.

HELPFUL HINTS

1. See Bibliography of Resources for good books to use to reinforce science concepts.
2. Introduce children to simple concepts about the balance of nature, ecology, and conservation. (Refer to books described at the end of this part.)

---

[1] See L. Meshover and S. Feistel (with photographs by E. Hoffmann), *The Guinea Pigs that Went to School* (Chicago: Follett, 1968). This book depicts a classroom of children learning about and caring for some guinea pigs and their babies.

▶ **PURPOSE**   **To learn about the different ways living things are born**

MATERIALS   — Chickens, snakes, spiders, ducks, or turtles

PROCEDURE   Let children care for animals and insects.[2]

OBSERVATION   Watch when eggs are laid and hatched.

CONCLUSION   Some living things are hatched from eggs laid by the mother.

DISCUSSION   Explain that different types of living things are born in different ways. All chicks are born the same way; all snakes are born the same way; all humans are born the same way. Some babies, such as turtles, frogs, fish, and most insects, have to take care of themselves as soon as they hatch. The seahorse is a good example of one of the different ways living things are born. The female gives her eggs to the male, and he carries them until the babies are born.

You might use this opportunity to explore social and physical concepts, with questions such as:
Could an elephant have a baby dog?
Can boys have babies?
Were your parents once babies?
Do your mom and dad have a mommy and daddy?
Is an animal a living thing? Is a plant? A rock?

▶ **PURPOSE**   **To learn how tadpoles turn into frogs**

MATERIALS   — Terrarium
— Frog eggs from stream, pond, or lake
— Plenty of pond water and some of the plants
— Extra food: boiled spinach, hard-cooked eggs, bugs, spiders, worms, and insects
— Rocks

PROCEDURE   1. Put frog eggs, pond water, and plants in the terrarium and watch daily for tadpoles to hatch.

OBSERVATION   Soon tadpoles or pollywogs will hatch.

2. Boiled spinach or other leafy vegetables and the yolk of a hard-cooked egg can be added as an extra food supply for the growing tadpoles.

OBSERVATION   The hind legs will begin to grow first, then the front legs. The tail gets smaller and lungs replace the gills.

---

[2] See Sylvia Greenberg and Edith Raskin, *Home-Made Zoo* (New York: David McKay, 1952), listed in annotated bibliography under "Books About Science for the Teacher."

3. Large rocks and dry areas are needed in the terrarium as the frogs develop, or the frogs can be returned to their natural environment. If you keep the frogs, they will need food.

OBSERVATION   Grown frogs like to eat bugs, spiders, worms, and insects.

CONCLUSION   Some animals don't look like their parents when they are born. Tadpoles do not look like frogs when they are born, but they grow into frogs.[3]

HELPFUL HINTS

1. Let children collect snails in baby food jars containing a small amount of water and some pebbles and grass.
2. Read *The Snail's Spell* by Joanne Ryder (New York: Frederick Warne, 1982).
3. Make slides from the book and let children share in the imaginary experience suggested.

▶ **PURPOSE**   **To learn about earthworms**

MATERIALS   — Large container of dirt
— Earthworms
— Worm food: ½ cup raw oatmeal, ½ cup coffee grounds, and 1 tablespoon milk mixed together

PROCEDURE   **1.** Scratch worm food into the dirt each week. Add enough water to keep dirt damp, but not soaked.
2. Loosen dirt and distribute earthworms throughout.
3. Have the children look at the earthworms through a magnifying glass.
4. Place an earthworm on a table and shine a flashlight at it. Watch to see if the worm prefers light or dark.
5. Place some dry soil on one side of the box and damp soil on the other. What does the earthworm do?

DISCUSSION   Earthworms have no eyes or ears, but they have very sensitive cells beneath the skin to detect vibrations, light, and dark.

Earthworms like the dark. They come to the surface at night to search for food. They do not push the dirt aside but swallow it. Their digestive tracts can break down the earth's chemicals into useful food. The earthworm eats its own weight in leaves, grass, and worm food every twenty-four hours.

An earthworm breathes through the skin, taking oxygen from the air. In order to do this, the skin must be moist at all times. Too much water, such as a heavy rain, fills up all the air spaces in the

---

[3] See Leo Lionni, *Fish Is Fish* (New York: Pantheon, 1970).

soil, causing the worm to suffocate. That is why worms wiggle to the surface of the earth to get air after it rains.

Earthworms reproduce by laying eggs.

If you accidentally cut off an earthworm's head or tail, it will grow another.

Earthworms are very valuable because they help plow, cultivate, and fertilize our soil. They are also a food source for birds, frogs, toads, and moles. Insecticides spread on the ground can kill earthworms, disturbing the balance of nature.

▶ **PURPOSE**   **To explore how caterpillars turn into butterflies**

MATERIALS   — Caterpillars
— Jars
— Leaves
— Gauze
— Rubber bands

PROCEDURE   **1.** Find some caterpillars.
2. Place one or two in each jar with some leaves from the plant from which the caterpillars were taken.
3. Cover the jar with some gauze. Secure with a rubber band.
4. Give the caterpillars a fresh leaf every day.
5. Clean the jar of wastes and dead leaves every day.
6. Soon each caterpillar will spin a ladder and climb to the top of the jar. Then it will spin a pad and hang from it by its feet. By the next day the caterpillar will change into a chrysalis.
7. Do not open the jar again until the butterfly comes out of the chrysalis.
8. In a week or two, the chrysalis will split open and the butterfly will come out.
9. *Do not touch* the butterfly for twelve hours. Then let it go.

▶ **PURPOSE**   **To learn about how different plants grow**

MATERIALS   — Assorted seeds: radish, carrot, corn, bell pepper, tomato, flowers
— Glass jars
— Blotter paper, cotton, or paper towels

PROCEDURE   **1.** Sandwich the seeds between the blotter paper or towels and the inside of the glass jar.
2. Pour enough water in the jar to soak up into the blotter. Keep the jar in a sunny place.

OBSERVATION   Soon the seeds will grow. Watch the roots grow downward toward the water and the stems upward toward the sunlight.

3. Seedlings may be transferred to soil cups or planted in the ground.

OBSERVATION   Plants take food from the soil and need space to grow.

CONCLUSION   Some plants grow from seeds. Wind, water, insects, and animals carry seeds to new and different places for them to grow into more plants.

HELPFUL HINTS

1. Plant wheat in flower pots. (See Illustration 5.2 for a depiction of Steps, 1, 3, and 4.)
2. Use stories and illustrations to show children how farmers plant and harvest wheat.
3. Let children separate wheat from the chaff.
4. Purchase kernels of whole wheat and let children grind the wheat into flour for pancakes and bread. (Use a blender or food processor if a grinder is unavailable.)
5. A free poster on grains of wheat can be obtained by writing to the Kansas Wheat Commission, 1021 N. Main St., Hutchinson, KS 67501.

▶ **PURPOSE**   **To learn how plants get their food**

MATERIALS   — Growing plants
— Celery stalks
— Red food coloring
— Water

PROCEDURE   **1.** Put a celery stalk into a glass of colored water.

OBSERVATION   In a few hours the leaves turn red.

2. Cut across the stem of the celery stalk.

OBSERVATION   The red spots are the veins that carried the water up to the leaves.

3. Observe the root system of other growing plants.

OBSERVATION   Plants carry food up from the ground through their roots and veins.

CONCLUSION   Plants can make their own food with the help of the sun and water and minerals from the soil.

SUGGESTION   Collect and identify leaves common to the immediate environment. Discuss the fact that leaves are necessary to plants because plants take water and minerals from the soil and gases from the air, and, with the help of sunlight, the leaves manufacture food for the plant. When the food is stored, such as in nuts and seeds, the leaves drop off because they are no longer needed. Food is stored in various parts of plants: leaves (lettuce, spinach, cabbage); stems (asparagus, celery, green onions); bulbs and tubers (onions, potatoes); roots (beets, carrots, radishes, sweet potatoes); flowers (artichokes, broccoli, cauliflower); fruits (apples, pears, tomatoes, peaches, plums, apricots); and seeds (nuts, peas, beans).

Illustration 5.2 **Learning about planting, separating, and grinding wheat**

HELPFUL HINTS

1. Collect shells, fossils, and rocks on a nature walk.
2. Ask parents to bring their collections of science materials to share.
3. Encourage girls as well as boys to participate in science activities.
4. Save old clocks, radios, motors, and so on to take apart.

► **PURPOSE**   **To learn how plants grow**

MATERIALS   — Carrot tops
— Sweet potatoes
— Onions
— Cuttings from plants such as ivy

PROCEDURE   1. Place the sweet potato in a jar of water.
2. Place the carrot top with leaves removed in a dish of water.
3. Place onion in a jar of water.
4. Put ivy cuttings in a glass of water. (See Illustration 5.3.)

OBSERVATION   Roots and new leaves, or new plants will begin to grow.

CONCLUSION   Some plants do not need seeds to grow.

► **PURPOSE**   **To learn how plants grow from spores**

MATERIALS   — A large jar
— Piece of bread

PROCEDURE   1. Expose a piece of bread to the air overnight.
2. Put the bread in a closed jar.
3. Make sure the bread is kept moist.

OBSERVATION   Soon a bread mold will start to grow that is blue, gray, and green in color.

4. Turn the bread upside down and gently tap it.

OBSERVATION   The spores will fall off.

CONCLUSION   Plants such as yeast, mushrooms, ferns, lichens, and molds grow from spores. Most spores do not form new plants.

► **PURPOSE**   **To explore chemical growth**

MATERIALS   — Glass bowl or plate (not metal)
— Broken pieces of brick or charcoal briquets
— Porous rocks

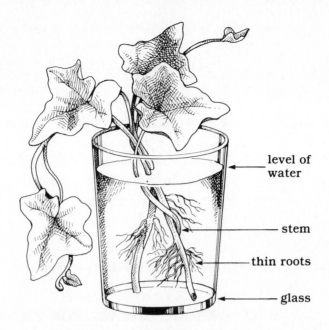

level of
water

stem

thin roots

glass

Illustration 5.3   **Learning that some plants do not need seeds to grow**

— Pieces of sponge or synthetic foam rubber
— Jar
— 6 tablespoons water
— 6 tablespoons salt (3 for solution, 3 for sprinkling)
— 6 tablespoons laundry bluing
— 3 tablespoons household ammonia
— Food coloring
— Plastic flowers or succulents

PROCEDURE
1. Dampen rocks, briquets, and sponge.
2. Arrange these materials in a glass plate or shallow bowl.
3. Mix chemicals in jar, using 3 tablespoons salt.
4. Pour mixture to saturate all the rocks, briquets, and sponge. Dampen thoroughly. A few drops of food coloring can be dropped on the tops of the high points of the arrangement. Sprinkle remaining salt evenly over the display. Add small plastic flowers or succulents to give more of a garden effect.

OBSERVATION
In a few hours, a coral-like growth of crystals will begin to form on the solid materials and the rim of the bowl.

5. Add more chemicals if some places seem bare. Allow growth to continue for several days.

OBSERVATION
Within a day the growth will spread and will continue spreading for several days.

CONCLUSION
Chemical growth is made up of complex salts that form as the liquid evaporates. The porous materials soak up the liquid and carry it to the surface where it evaporates, leaving the salts behind. The deposit

continues to grow because each of the crystals that has formed is likewise able to carry the liquid through itself and to the surface, leaving even more crystals behind. Growth can be started again by adding a teaspoon or so of ammonia.

HELPFUL HINT

The Educational Development Center, 55 Chapel St., Newton, MA 02160, is a good source for science, math, and social studies materials for teachers.

Bibliography of Resources

BOOKS ABOUT SCIENCE FOR THE TEACHER

Blackwelder, Sheila Kyser. *Science for All Seasons.* Englewood Cliffs, N.J.: Prentice-Hall, 1980. Packed with scores of safe, easy-to-do experiments that require only inexpensive objects found in the home or classroom, this science activity book can help parents and teachers satisfy a young child's natural curiosity about the world around us.

Brandwein, Paul F., and Elizabeth K. Cooper. *Concepts in Science.* New York: Harcourt, Brace & World, 1967. An illustrated book without text, showing scenes such as children playing with magnets and levers and chicks hatching. Sections cover investigating matter, investigating force, and investigating plants and animals. Another section shows pictures of children from different ethnic groups, and there is also a page of living and nonliving things. A list of science words is supplied at the end of the book.

Brown, Sam (ed.). *Bubbles, Rainbows and Worms.* Mt. Ranier, Md.: Gryphon House, 1981. Science experiments for preschool children. Parents and teachers can help give very young children practical, hands-on experiences in science. Experiments provide ways for children to learn by doing, rather than by being told or shown.

Carmichael, Viola. *Science Experiences for Young Children.* Los Angeles: Southern California Association for the Education of Young Children, 1982. Sections of this book are devoted to plants, animals, weather, the human body, cooking, machines, and developing concepts. Each section provides the teacher with background information, suggested class projects, arts and crafts ideas, and book lists.

Forte, Imogene, and Marjorie Frank. *Puddles and Wings and Grapevine Swings.* Nashville, Tenn.: Incentive Publications, 1982. Exciting ways to use nature's materials! Clear directions for outdoor or indoor projects and adventures. Includes crafts for all seasons, games, weather and ecology experiments, and loads of recipes for fun and food.

Gale, Frank C., and Clarice W. Gale. *Experiences with Plants for Young Children.* Palo Alto, Calif.: Pacific Books Publishers, 1975. The pages are filled with ideas to help teachers and parents provide sensory experiences; guide children's attention to help them explore, compare, and see relationships; and enlarge children's understanding of the world in which they live.

Greenberg, Sylvia S., and Edith L. Raskin. *Home-Made Zoo.* New York: David McKay, 1952. Teachers and parents will find this book a useful guide for the care of small animals such as hamsters, rabbits, mice, guinea pigs, birds, turtles, and fish. The authors provide helpful information on the buying of pets, how to build cages, sanitation, feeding, and some common ailments.

Haupt, Dorothy. *Science Experiences for Nursery School Children.* Washington, D.C.: National Association for the Education of Young Children. This booklet offers a discussion of the teacher's role in providing science experiences in the nursery school, with some examples and a list of resource materials.

Hibner, Dixie, and Liz Cromwell. *Explore and Create.* Livonia, Mich.: Partner Press, 1979. Discovery and exploration is the basis for a child's learning and playing. Adults extend the curiosity of the child by providing an environment that lends itself to observation and exploration. A variety of experiences will produce discovery and learning. The hands-on activities will help increase awareness by means of observation, discussion, and experimentation.

Holt, Bess-Gene. *Science with Young Children.* Washington, D.C.: National Association for the Education of Young Children, 1977. Helps the teacher understand why science is important in the curriculum and provides suggestions for setting up activities, including a section on ecology.

Kranzer, Herman C. *Nature and Science Activities for Young Children.* Jenkintown, Pa.: Baker, 1969. A booklet of activities grouped according to subjects such as plants, animals, weather, light, time, tools, and machines. Each page provides ideas for a display, an activity, or an experiment, with suggestions to the teacher on how to extend these learnings in the classroom.

McGavack, John, Jr., and Donald P. La Salle. *Guppies, Bubbles, and Vibrating Objects: A Creative Approach to the Teaching of Science to Very Young Children.* New York: John Day, 1969. This book lives up to its title very successfully. Emphasizes children's involvement with simple, carefully designed activities to help them develop healthy attitudes and to increase their curiosity through active exploration. An excellent resource book.

Morris, Loverne. *Frogs as Wild Pets.* Chicago: Children's Press, 1973. A useful resource of scientific information about different kinds of frogs and how to find, capture, feed, and tame them. Includes a glossary of scientific terms. Illustrations by Arnold Mesches.

Piltz, Albert, et al. *Discovering Science: A Readiness Book.* Columbus, Ohio: Merrill, 1968. Large pictures and illustrations are presented with only a word or short sentence accompanying each picture. Includes a section titled "Finding Out," showing pictures of children using their five senses to explore materials (children blindfolded touching, tasting, and smelling objects, and so on). Other sections include pictures about sound, magnets, gravity, weather, seasons, animals, and plants. Pictures are good for discussion. Some of the simple questions can help the children clarify what they need to know in order to have a better understanding of a concept.

Ranger Rick's Nature Magazine published by the National Wildlife Federation, 1412 16th St., N.W., Washington, D.C. 20036. This magazine presents simply written and informative articles about wildlife. The lovely photographs in every issue make it a particularly valuable resource.

Rieger, Edythe. *Science Adventures in Children's Play.* New York: The Play Schools Association, 1968. This book was written for teachers of elementary school science, but the preschool teacher will find it useful as a resource for ideas to incorporate into the curriculum. Helpful suggestions and background information on such topics as exploring the neighborhood, insects, collections, and ideas for program enrichment. Bibliography of resource books included.

Russell, Helen Ross. *Ten-Minute Field Trips.* Chicago, Ill.: J. G. Ferguson Publishing Co., 1973. Dr. Russell's method of inspiring both children and teachers to investigate city deserts is wonderful. The book shows how each individual can explore the natural history of his or her own area. The elementary school teacher, trained in pedagogy but not in science, now has a guide for fascinating, easy-to-do explorations.

Science Books: *A Quarterly Review* published by the American Association for the Advancement of Science, 1515 Massachusetts Ave., N.W., Washington, D.C. 20005. Short reviews and recommendations for science publications. Annotations include listings for various age groups including kindergarten and preschool. Useful, timesaving resource.

Selsam, Millicent E. *Animals as Parents.* New York: Morrow, 1965. A good resource for background information. Topics include birds and mammals as parents and the book provides much interesting information, such as the fact that different species of birds lay different numbers of eggs. There is also a simply written and interesting section about mother love among monkeys and apes and the role of early experience. The author has written other books about plants and animals, all worth having in the teacher's library. Nicely illustrated by John Kaufmann.

Stetten, Mary. *Let's Play Science.* New York: Harper & Row, 1979. Science projects designed especially for preschool children. These activities will enrich any early childhood curriculum.

BOOKS ABOUT SCIENCE FOR CHILDREN

Arneson, D. J. *Secret Places.* New York: Holt, 1971. Beautiful, vivid photographs of a young boy's secret places in the countryside around his home. He takes the reader on a tour and expresses the hope that "progress" — machines and construction — will never find his secret places. Good feeling for the preservation of natural open spaces. Photos by Peter Arnold.

Baer, Edith. *The Wonder of Hands.* New York: Parents' Magazine Press, 1970. The text, accompanied by Tana Hoban's sensitive photography, portrays the many ways hands communicate: hands can heal, plant a seed, finger-paint, and wave goodby.

Bartlett, Margaret Farrington. *The Clean Brook.* New York: Crowell, 1960. The story of the changing life of a brook, how the natural water filters the sediment, and the various animals that frequent the brook. Clear, realistic illustrations by Alden A. Watson. Good book for introducing children to the natural environment. Look for other books from the "Let's Read and Find Out" science series.

Branley, Franklyn. *What Makes Day and Night.* New York: Crowell, 1961. A simple, detailed explanation describing the mechanics of the earth's rotation.

Brenner, Barbara. *Faces.* New York: Dutton, 1970. Photos and script about the sense organs on the face — eyes, ears, nose, and mouth. Simple, concise text. Photos by George Ancona show how one uses each of the organs and illustrates how every face is different but has some things in common. Good to use in conjunction with body parts and exploration of the senses.

Bulla, Clyde Robert. *A Tree Is a Plant.* New York: Crowell, 1960. This simple text with colorful illustrations takes the young child through the life cycle of the apple tree, from seed to flower to fruit. Very helpful and easy to understand.

Carle, Eric. *The Very Hungry Caterpillar.* New York: World, 1971. A simple and colorful book showing stages of growth in a caterpillar. There are holes in the bright illustrations of leaves and fruit showing what the caterpillar consumes as it grows.

Collier, Ethel. *Who Goes There in My Garden?* New York: Young Scott Books, 1963. With his birthday money, a boy buys seeds to plant a spring garden. The book discusses planting and garden insects. A good book to read to children before planting a garden.

Gans, Roma. *It's Nesting Time.* New York: Crowell, 1964. An informative and highly educational book designed to teach young children to observe and respect the nests of various birds. Illustrations by Mizumura show how different birds build their nests with different kinds of materials and designs.

Gans, Roma, and Franklyn M. Branley (eds.). *Let's Read and Find Out Science Books.* New York: Crowell. A very well-planned series of books designed for children on topics indicated by the titles: *Air Is All Around You; How a Seed Grows; What Makes a Shadow?; Your Skin and Mine;* and many more.

One book in the series, *My Hands* (by Aliki, 1962), describes the fingers and thumb, shows how hands are necessary for work and expression, and gets the child to think about his or her own hands. The concepts are written for the young child, and the easy-to-read text is colorfully illustrated. *My Five Senses* is written by the same author.

Find Out by Touching (by Paul Showers, 1961) suggests that the child feel common objects such as the book, a window, or a carpet, and learn how the sense of touch can tell him or her many things about the world. Through touch, the child learns about the concepts of hard, soft, smooth, rough, cold, warm, and so on.

Garelick, May. *Where Does the Butterfly Go When It Rains?* New York: Young Scott Books, 1961. Story concerns the "mystery" of where the butterfly goes when it rains. The author shows what happens to other creatures — the bee flies back to its hive, water slides off a duck's back. Encourages children to look and discover the answers for themselves. Blue-hued illustrations give the impression of rain.

Goldreich, Gloria, and Esther Goldreich. *What Can She Be? A Veterinarian.* New York: Lothrop, 1972. Children who have had to take a pet to the veterinarian will appreciate the photographs by Robert Ipcar showing a typical day in the life of a female vet caring for injured and sick puppies, cats, and bunnies.

Hawes, Judy. *What I Like About Toads.* New York: Crowell, 1969. "I didn't used to like toads. I thought toads gave me warts." The author helps children see the usefulness of toads and their habits.

Krauss, Ruth. *The Carrot Seed.* New York: Harper & Brothers, 1945. There are some things little children just know, that's all. And even when everyone said it wouldn't come up, the little boy knew his very own carrot seed would grow.

Leaf, Munro. *Who Cares? I Do.* New York: Lippincott, 1971. Cartoon-like figures alongside photographs supplied by the U.S. Forest Service, The National Park Service, and Keep America Beautiful, Inc., help the child see that "our country is getting to be a mess. And we seem to be the best ones to do something about it."

Leen, Nina. *And Then There Were None.* New York: Holt, 1973. Over one hundred species of wildlife in the United States are endangered, and prize-winning photographer Nina Leen has presented more than fifty of these rare animals in a book well worth showing to children. Commentaries by zoologist Joseph A. Davis explain the causes of endangerment.

Lionni, Leo. *Fish Is Fish.* New York: Pantheon, 1970. "The minnow and the tadpole were inseparable friends. . . ." But the tadpole grows up and becomes a frog and goes off to explore the world. He returns to tell his friend about the extraordinary things he has seen and convinces Fish that he too should venture out of the pond. Humorous sketches of Fish's dreams. A good book to use with tadpoles and fish in a science project.

Lowery, Lawrence F., and Evelyn Moore. *I Wonder Why Readers.* New York: Holt, 1969. A series of twenty-four books designed for early grades but also useful for the preschool. They cover general topics of language arts and science activities. *Quiet as a Butterfly* stresses listening as an observational skill. It suggests that the teacher ask the class to think of things that make a sound and to finish stories that start with lines like "If I were a yellow butterfly, I would. . . ." The series contains titles such as *Soft as a Bunny; Look and See; Up, Up in a Balloon; What Does an Animal Eat;* and *Larry's Racing Machine.* The accompanying teacher's guide contains valuable ideas and suggestions for using these books in language and science. Can be easily adapted for use in the preschool. Well-illustrated in color with sturdy covers.

Mallinson, George G., et. al. *Science 1.* Morristown, N.J.: Silver Burdett, 1965. Excellent color photos that encourage discussion. Some portions are rather sophisticated, but most cover topics that the preschooler can discuss, such as "Plant Life on the Earth," "You and Your Body," "The Sounds You Hear," and "How Work is Done" ("Some things are too big to push and pull. Your muscles are not strong enough. Big machines help do the work.").

Mari, Iela, and Enzo Mari. *The Apple and the Moth.* New York: Dial, 1970. Lovely picture book without words that shows the metamorphosis of a moth and its stages — egg on leaf, caterpillar, cocoon, moth. All occur in one apple tree. Teacher and children can make up their own descriptions to accompany the drawings. Use with display of caterpillars and cocoons.

————. *The Chicken and the Egg.* New York: Pantheon, 1969. A hen lays an egg and the following sequence of pictures shows the development of the chick until it finally hatches. Can be used in studying growth cycles.

Podendorf, Illa. *The True Book of Science Experiments.* Chicago: Children's Press, 1972. Experiments for the young child about gravity, magnets, air, water, sound, heat, and cold.

Selsam, Millicent E. *Is This a Baby Dinosaur?* New York: Harper & Row, 1972. Photographs stress the importance of careful observation. With a photograph of lentil seeds, for example, the caption asks "Are these pebbles?" This author produces consistently excellent books on science for the young child.

Shuttlesworth, Dorothy E. *Clean Air — Sparkling Water: The Fight Against Pollution.* New York: Doubleday, 1968. "We can live without many things. But not without air. Not without water. And the air must be clean. The water must be pure." A series of photographs with a text designed for the older reader helps tell the story of pollution and how people can fight back. The teacher can read the captions of the pictures to young children and underline the simpler concepts in the text.

Stone, A. Harris. *The Last Free Bird.* Englewood Cliffs, N.J.: Prentice-Hall, 1967. Lovely watercolor illustrations by Sheila Heins enhance a very simple text, which tells of human destruction of the nesting and feeding places of birds.

Tresselt, Alvin. *The Dead Tree.* New York: Parents' Magazine Press, 1972. The reader is helped to appreciate the natural cycle of life in the forest where even a dead tree serves to enhance new growth. A good book for ecology.

Udry, Janice May. *A Tree Is Nice.* New York: Harper & Row, 1956. An old favorite showing why trees are nice to have around. You can climb on them, eat their fruit, hang a swing, picnic in their shade, and plant your very own. Encourages observation of nature.

Ecology Activities

CONSERVATION AND ENERGY

▶ **PURPOSE** **To illustrate a food chain**

MATERIALS
— Large sheet of mural-size paper
— Blue, green, and brown paint
— Various colors of construction paper
— Glue
— Paintbrushes

PROCEDURE
1. Make a mural for the classroom. Let the children help paint a blue backdrop for the sky and use green and brown for the earth. Add the sun, clouds, rain, lakes, trees, and plant life. Show a food chain by depicting plants and food getting energy from the sun; insects eating leaves; a chicken, toad, or snake eating insects (snakes also eat toads); and people eating a chicken. Show how everything in nature is linked and interdependent.
2. Discuss how the destruction or interruption of such a chain eventually affects everyone. Talk about what it would be like to live without the sun, rain, and food.
3. Discuss water cycle, and show water evaporating from the ocean, forming clouds that travel across the sky to rain in mountains, and water rolling down a hill to the ocean.
4. Another topic that can be depicted and discussed is erosion. Show wind, water, and ice wearing away mountains, boulders, and rocks.

▶ **PURPOSE** **To show that water is needed for life**

MATERIALS
— Plants, such as geranium cuttings, in flower pots
— Cut flowers in plastic or glass vases

PROCEDURE
1. Look at and talk about the flowers and let the children feel the leaves and petals.
2. Talk about the colors and how they look when the flowers are alive.
3. Ask the children what they think the plants need to live.
4. Ask them what they think will happen to the plants and cut flowers if they do not get any water.
5. Put one potted plant and one vase of cut flowers under a sketch or sign that indicates those plants have water.
6. Put one potted plant and one vase of cut flowers under a sign that indicates the plants have no water.
7. Have the children observe daily the changes that occur in the leaves, petals, and colors.
8. Ask them about other living things that need water.

▶ **PURPOSE**   **To understand the importance of conserving water**

MATERIALS   — Bucket or pitcher
— Garden hose or faucet
— Display of plants and animals that need water

PROCEDURE   1. Discuss the importance of water to living things.
2. Leave a pitcher or bucket under a dripping faucet or at the end of a dripping garden hose.
3. After a time, observe how much water has collected in the container.
4. Have the children use that water to replenish the animals' water dishes, water the plants, or mix juice for snack time.
5. Ask how they can help prevent waste of water: shut off faucets; flush toilets only when necessary; use a stopper in the sink; take short showers.
6. Talk about the ways they can save water: collect rain water for plants; save water used for washing vegetables and fruit for the garden.
7. Post illustrations over wash basins and faucets showing a child turning the faucet off.
8. Ask the children questions about their daily routines, such as: **Do you leave the water running when you brush your teeth?** Ask them to explain why they shouldn't. Praise them for correct answers.

DISCUSSION   Water is needed for drinking; washing; growing food; working (power, cooling, transportation); and playing (swimming, boating).

HELPFUL HINTS

Talk about reducing waste by suggesting that children:

1. Reuse plastic bags.
2. Reuse large envelopes.
3. Color and draw on scrap paper.
4. Use newspapers to wrap inedible things.
5. Buy milk in bottles rather than cartons.
6. Pick up litter.
7. Use a shopping bag rather than the store's paper bags.

▶ **PURPOSE**   **To learn responsibility for conserving paper and paper products**

MATERIALS   — Disposable paper goods: cups, plates, napkins, towels, wax paper, newspaper, paper bags
— Reusable counterparts to the above: ceramic dishes, cloth napkins, plastic containers

PROCEDURE   1. Ask what each of the paper items is used for. Ask what happens to each item after it has been used.

2. Do the same with reusable items.

3. Refer to the activity on erosion, page 249, and talk about the importance of saving our trees.

4. Ask children to help identify other ways we can save paper: not wasting toilet paper and cleansing tissues; recycling newspapers; using both sides of art papers; reusing paper bags for groceries.

▶ **PURPOSE** **To understand the importance of conserving energy resources**

MATERIALS
— Pictures of electrical appliances: radio, TV, light bulb, iron, refrigerator, fan
— Pictures of items that require gasoline, natural gas, or oil: heaters, cars, airplanes, and so on

PROCEDURE
1. Ask the children to identify each item.

2. Ask what would happen if the electrical cords on the TV, a lamp, or the radio were unplugged from the wall outlet.

3. Explain that electricity goes through the wires to make the appliances work.

4. Explain that electricity, like water, has to be conserved.

5. Explain that when people use too much electricity and there isn't enough to go around, we sometimes have a black-out and all our lights and electrical appliances go out.

6. Discuss the same idea about heating our homes with gas or oil, operating machines, and so on.

7. Talk about how we can help conserve our energy resources by turning off lights, keeping the refrigerator door shut, turning off the TV, and keeping the heat in our homes turned down.

HELPFUL HINT

A good resource book about energy for young children is *Energy* by Carolyn Diener, et al., Atlanta, Ga: Humanics Limited, 1984. This activity book introduces preschoolers to several basic concepts of energy.

▶ **PURPOSE** **To understand how the sun can be a source of energy**

MATERIALS
— A terrarium or other large glass container
— Insulation, such as sheets of thick plastic, roofing insulation, or corrugated cardboard
— Sheets of aluminum foil
— Juice cans
— Black paint
— Piece of glass large enough to cover top of terrarium

PROCEDURE
1. Make a solar unit by lining the inside of the terrarium with insulation material.

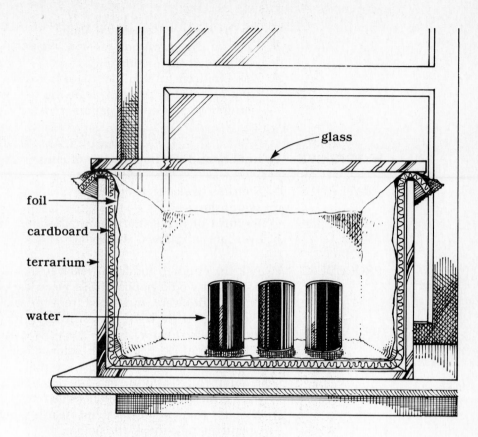

Illustration 5.4   **Setting up a solar unit**

2. Cover the insulation material with foil so that the foil faces the inside of the terrarium.
3. Paint the outside of juice cans with black paint.
4. Fill the juice cans with water and place them inside the terrarium.
5. Cover the terrarium with the sheet of glass.
6. Place the solar unit where it will collect the maximum amount of sunlight. (See Illustration 5.4.)
7. If the sun is at an angle, remove insulation and foil from one of the sides so that sunlight can enter the box.
8. After a few hours of collecting solar heat, let the children feel the water inside the terrarium.
9. Talk about the sun as a source of heat.
10. Point out that if we use the sun to heat our water, we can save gas and electricity.

▶ **PURPOSE**   **To appreciate the balance and harmony of nature**

MATERIALS   — Terrarium, aquarium, earthworm farm, or ant farm

PROCEDURE   1. Let children help plan and set up an ecosystem for living things.
2. Talk about and list the things that are necessary to keep plants, ants, worms, or fish alive.
3. Let the children be responsible for creating the ecosystem. Ask

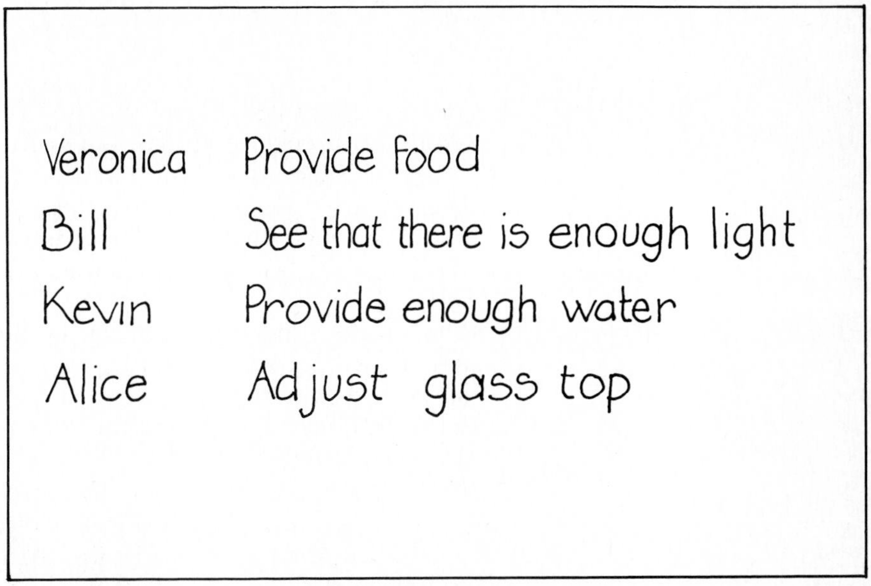

Veronica   Provide food

Bill   See that there is enough light

Kevin   Provide enough water

Alice   Adjust glass top

Illustration 5.5   **Chart to show children's responsibilities for maintaining an ecosystem**

them what they think would happen if they did not provide water, air, food, and so on.

4. List the names of the children who helped develop the ecosystem. Print a description of the ecosystem and what it needs.

5. List the names of the children who will be responsible for maintaining the proper balance of the ecosystem by watering, feeding, and the like. (See Illustration 5.5.)

DISCUSSION   Explain that a terrarium with animals in it is a small ecosystem. Earth is made up of millions of ecosystems. An ecosystem may be as small as a snail, a plant, and some dirt in a jar, or it may be as large as a forest, but it always contains all the requirements for the life of everything in it.

HELPFUL HINT

Plants in a tightly sealed terrarium can grow successfully for a long time because they are efficient recyclers. The plants will last longer if the terrarium also houses some small animals such as earthworms, a cricket, a slug, or a snail. The animals must be the kind that live on dead or living plant material.

▶ **PURPOSE**   **To see how organic materials can be returned to the earth to be used again**

MATERIALS   — Grass clippings
            — Food scraps, eggshells, vegetable peelings

— Animal manure
— Weeds

PROCEDURE   1. Identify an isolated area of the yard for your compost pile. A shaded area near a deciduous tree is good. A small fenced area, a large container like a barrel, or a shipping crate is also appropriate.

2. Let children help layer grass clippings and other organic compost materials with dirt. The ideal time to start a compost pile is in the fall or spring. Mix leaves and grass with wood shavings; each layer should be no more than six inches thick. Droppings of rabbits, ducks, and chickens can be added. Sprinkle the compost pile with enough water to equal the moisture of a wrung-out sponge. Cover the pile with plastic. The material takes several weeks to "cure." Turn and mix the compost as you add more organic materials and dirt.

3. Examine how materials break down. The smaller the pieces of material, the more quickly they will break down. Compare compost with nonorganic materials, such as plastic, that do not decompose.

4. Discuss the value of and need for nutrients in the earth to make plants and food grow.

5. Use compost for planting. Compare with plants that have been grown in soil without compost.

6. Plant quick-sprouting seeds, like beans, in pots of different kinds of soil (clay, sand, rocky soil, and composted soil). Label each pot and compare growth.

HELPFUL HINT

Use the following "insecticide" as needed in gardening projects with the class.

Safe Repellent

6 garlic cloves
3 hot chili peppers (dried or fresh)
6 cups water

Place garlic, peppers, and 1 cup water in a blender. Blend until finely ground. Let mixture stand 10 minutes; strain through cheesecloth. Add remaining 5 cups water. Mix well and pour into spray bottles. Shake well, then spray plants and vegetables as needed to repel insects. Makes 1½ quarts.

▶ **PURPOSE**   **To learn to create and care for a miniature ecosystem**

MATERIALS   — Baby food jars
            — Gravel
            — Aged water (tap water that has been sitting 24 hours or longer)

— Aquarium plants
— Snails

PROCEDURE
1. Give each child a baby food jar. Label each jar with the child's name. (Make the label small so child can see into the jar easily, or place the name on the jar top.)
2. Fill the jar about a quarter of the way with gravel. Pour enough aged water to barely cover the gravel. Place some small aquarium plants into the gravel. Put a snail in the jar. Cover the jar.
3. Let each child be responsible for his or her snail.
4. Discuss the need for gravel and moisture so algae can form for the snail to eat. The gravel is also a place for the snail to walk and rest. Aged water has no chemicals to hurt the snail. The plants are also food for the snail.
5. Have children watch and care for their snail each day. Note the gradual change in water level and watch what happens to the plants.
6. Introduce another snail to provide opportunity for reproduction.

Note: Ecosystems can also be created for ants, praying mantis, ladybugs, sowbugs, and spiders.

HELPFUL HINTS

Build a simple breeding box:

1. Get a large cardboard box with top.
2. Cut out a large window on one or two sides of the box.
3. Cover the window with clear plastic attached with tape.
4. Line the bottom of the box with aluminum foil to prevent moisture from weakening it.
5. Introduce larvae of insects such as moths, butterflies, beetles, caterpillars.
6. Be sure to include some of the plant food and leaves they thrive on.
7. Snails, slugs, and pill bugs will feed on lettuce leaves, raw apple, or raw potato.
8. Add a small container of water to provide moisture.

FORMS OF POLLUTION

▶ PURPOSE
To become aware of surroundings and maintain a clean environment

MATERIALS
— Paper bags, cleansing tissue boxes, small cartons, or other such containers
— Paint materials and/or crayons

PROCEDURE
1. Have children decorate their litter containers with paintings or collages of a lion or other animal of their choice. (See Illustration 5.6.)

Illustration 5.6   **Decorated litter containers**

2. Ask the children:
 What is litter? (Anything out of its proper place.)
 Other questions to help children think about litter might be:
 Should candy wrappers be in the street? Where do they belong?
 Should soft-drink cans be out in the yard?
 Should your sweater be on the floor?
 Should your toothbrush be in the basin?
 Children enjoy "ridiculous" questions such as:
 Should your hat be in the guinea pig cage?
 Should your toothpaste be in the car?

3. Take a short walk around the school grounds and help the children identify and pick up litter.

4. Help each child show and tell what each "litter lion" found.

5. When children become competent at identifying litter, let small groups take ten minutes each to collect as much litter as they can find.

6. As each child brings back his or her litter, let the group help decide where each object should go: back on the toy shelf, on the table, in the garbage.

7. Ask each child to tell how he or she helped to clean up after litterbugs at home.

8. Reminders that are useful for children:

Use trash cans. Remind others to use trash cans.
Pick up clothes and toys at home.
Keep a litter bag in the car.

HELPFUL HINTS

1. Refer to the annotated list of books at the end of this part for more ideas on teaching children about conservation and ecology.
2. Take children on a nature tour where guides are available to explain ecology and conservation measures.
3. Take children on a field trip to a lake or pond. Give them plastic bags and cups to collect tadpoles, pond water, and plant life. Use these for making an ecosystem in the school.

▶ **PURPOSE**   **To see some of the things polluting the air**

MATERIALS   — Pieces of heavy plastic, glossy cardboard, or white 3 x 5 cards
— Shortening or vaseline
— Masking tape and string

PROCEDURE   1. Spread shortening or vaseline on plastic or cards.
2. Tape or hang cards or plastic in different places indoors and outdoors.
3. Look at them each day for three or four days.
4. Notice the things collected on the cards or plastic.
5. Ask children where the air is dirtiest.
6. Talk about different things that pollute the air, such as exhaust, smoke, and sprays.

▶ **PURPOSE**   **To understand the meaning and causes of air pollution**

MATERIALS   — Flannel cutouts of the following for use on the flannelboard: mountains, sun, blue sky, horses, bicycle, cars, factories, trees, houses, strips of grey and brown to represent smog

PROCEDURE   1. Use the flannelboard to tell the children a story that illustrates how people lived many years ago. Show people working on farms, using horses, and riding bicycles for transportation. Show lots of trees and clear landscape. Then tell how more babies were born, grew up, and began to build cities, factories, and cars. (Take down trees; put up more houses.) Tell about new modes of transportation. (Take down horses and bicycles; put up cars and airplanes.) Show how the cities grew; show more factories, buildings, and houses. Show how the smoke from cars, planes, and factories got heavier and heavier and became so thick that it began to cover the sun. On days when there was no wind or rain, the smog stayed in the air and bothered people's eyes and throats. (Cover blue with gray and brown.) Soon the smog was so thick that the people couldn't see the mountains anymore.

2. Ask the children how to help clean the air: we can walk and ride bikes whenever possible; instead of each child coming to school in a separate car, the people who drive them can form car pools; we can put smog control devices on cars.

3. Explain that if each person does a little bit, it can help.

HELPFUL HINT

The Little House by Virginia Lee Burton (Boston: Houghton Mifflin, 1942) is an excellent story to introduce children to the importance of caring about the environment. (See annotated listing under "All-Time Favorites" in Part Four, "Language Arts.")

▶ **PURPOSE**   **To show how smoke pollutes the air and damages living things**

MATERIALS
— Two small plants that are the same size
— Two glass jars, large enough to cover each of the plants
— Small scraps of paper

PROCEDURE
1. Let children examine the two same-size plants, talking about the color of leaves and petals.
2. Ask them if they know what pollution means. Explain that the clean air plants and animals need to be healthy is polluted by smoke.
3. Ask what they think will happen if one of the plants is placed in air that has been polluted by smoke.
4. Cover one of the plants with a glass jar.
5. Surround the other plant with small wads of paper. Burn the paper and cover the plant with the second glass jar so that the plant is contained within the smoke-filled environment.
6. Repeat the smoking process several times over the next few days.
7. Compare the plants. Examine leaves and petals to see how air polluted by smoke can damage living things.

Note: A tropical plant, such as a prayer plant, reacts to smoke more quickly than hardier plants do.

▶ **PURPOSE**   **To become aware of noise pollution**

MATERIALS
— Flannelboard with cutouts of two mice and of things that make noise: airplane, trucks, jackhammers, and the like
— Other props as desired
— Record or tape of loud noises and of soothing sounds

PROCEDURE **1.** Tell a story about a country mouse who goes to the city to visit his friend. Introduce flannelboard pictures of jackhammers, trucks, cars with loud horns, airplanes, garbage cans, loud radios, people yelling, and motorcycles. A tape recording of the noises these things make can be used in the background as the story is being told.

2. Tell how the noises frighten and upset the country mouse and how he becomes tired of having to yell. Tell how his body gets tense and how he feels nervous and irritable. He finally has to wear a pair of earplugs in order to get to sleep.

3. Show how happy he is to get back to the country where he can hear the wind in the trees, the babbling brook, the crickets chirping, and all the quiet sounds around him.

4. Play some quiet sounds and have the children listen carefully.

5. Turn the lights down low and talk quietly about the importance of having quiet times.

▶ **PURPOSE** **To understand the meaning of pollution and how water becomes polluted**

MATERIALS — Two fish tanks or large containers of fresh water
— Flannelboard cutouts of fish, litter, and polluting materials, such as beer cans, paper, oil, plastic containers, and other common objects
— Bits of garbage, such as plastic bags, pieces of metal, napkins, and leftover food

PROCEDURE **1.** Tell the children a story about a little fish that swims happily in her fresh clean pond. Then day by day, thoughtless people throw things into the water. Show how the fish has to confine herself to smaller and smaller spaces until she has no place to swim. Ask the children how they can help to make more space for the fish. Let them each remove some bit of garbage.

2. Talk with the children about the water they drink. Ask if they would like to drink water with pieces of plastic, dirty oil, or garbage in it.

3. Let the children be polluters by dropping garbage into one tank. After a few days ask them to smell the water in each tank. Compare how the water in each tank looks, feels, smells. Ask them what the water in each tank would be good for now.

▶ **PURPOSE** **To understand the meaning of erosion and how it occurs**

MATERIALS — Sweet potato, avocado pit, or other quick-rooting plant
— Glass jars
— Large deep trays
— Dirt

PROCEDURE **1.** Place the sweet potato or avocado pit in water in the glass jar and wait for roots to grow.

2. Let the children look at roots and talk about other plants. Ask them if they think a flower has roots or if trees have roots.
3. Let the children help transplant the rooted plant from the glass to dirt, either in the deep tray or in the yard. Build the dirt up to a mound before planting the potato or avocado.
4. Place another similar mound of dirt next to the plant.
5. Let children pour water over the rooted plant; have them water the dirt also.
6. Observe how the dirt washes away where there is no plant to hold the dirt with its strong web of roots.
7. Talk about the way dirt washes away when trees are cut down. Discuss the importance of planting trees on hillsides.
8. Talk about mudslides during heavy rains.
9. When children are thoroughly familiar with the concept of erosion as presented in this task, move on to related discussions. (Be careful not to introduce too many problems or new ideas at one time).
10. Other questions might include:
   What happens when we cut down trees?
   How do we get new ones?
   How long does it take for a tree to grow big enough to give us wood for a house?

VARIATION   A related project might include pictorial materials and discussions of how trees are cut down to make paper, furniture, houses, pencils, paper bags, napkins, paper towels, toothpicks, and cardboard boxes. Tie this in with conservation projects.

Bibliography of Resources

BOOKS FOR THE TEACHER ABOUT ECOLOGY, THE ENVIRONMENT, AND CONSERVATION

Dasmann, Raymond F. *Planet in Peril: Man and the Biosphere Today.* New York: World, 1972. Technological progress is now dictating our life conditions. The delicate balance of nature is threatened. We can either ignore the problem or cooperate internationally to plan our environment. This book helps the teacher understand the growth and change in ecosystems and points toward new goals.

Farb, Peter. *Ecology.* New York: Time-Life Books, 1970. A beautifully illustrated book to share with a child. Not a child's book, but the lovely color illustrations in the large format lend themselves to discussion of topics such as why living things are where they are, food chains, and the different realms of the earth.

Harrah, David F., and Barbara K. Harrah. *Conservation — Ecology: Resources for Environmental Education.* Metuchen, N.J.: Scarecrow Press, 1975. Includes numerous activities and crafts and discusses available support and teaching aids in the field of ecology.

Hillcourt, William. *Outdoor Things to Do.* New York: Western, 1975. Clearly illustrated book designed for older girls and boys. Helpful for the adult who wants to adapt nature activities for the younger child. Illustrations show how to make terrariums, collect leaves and rocks, study insects, and the like.

Knight, Michael E., and Terry Lynne Graham. *Leaves Are Falling in Rainbows.* Atlanta, Ga., Humanics Limited, 1984. Science activities that teach children the concepts and properties of water, air, plants, light, shadows, magnets, sound, and electricity.

Lauwerys, J. A. *Man's Impact on Nature.* New York: Natural History Press, 1970. A well-designed book to help the teacher understand the complexity of life on this planet — a network of interrelated forms that can be easily deflected. Food and overpopulation are discussed.

Lipschitz, Ceil. *An Ecology Craftsbook for the Open Classroom.* New York: The Center for Applied Research in Education, 1975. Crafts and activities, most requiring scrap items and materials, for the classroom. Includes hints on how to teach the subject on a budget.

National Geographic Society. *As We Live and Breathe: The Challenge of Our Environment.* Washington, D.C.: 1971. A beautifully illustrated volume designed to point out the environmental problems of our age. More than three hundred illustrations gathered throughout the United States show the impact of people living on the earth and the efforts to restore and preserve the balance of nature.

Pringle, Laurence. *Ecology: Science of Survival.* New York: Macmillan, 1971. Ecology is the study of living organisms in their surroundings. It is the science of survival because if people fail to learn its lessons, they risk the destruction of the world on which they depend. Many photographs illustrate this easy-to-understand book exploring the intricate web connecting humans to the environment. This book deals with a complex subject in one of the clearest formats available.

Russell, Helen Ross. *Earth, The Great Recycler.* Nashville, Tenn.: Nelson, 1973. An interesting, well-written book explaining the building blocks of our planet. Explains how plants function and how all the components of the earth's many cycles of life-giving activity contribute to the ecosphere. Describes how we can observe interrelationships in nature by building a terrarium, aquarium, and other observable ecosystems.

Saltonstall, Richard, Jr. *Your Environment and What You Can Do About It.* New York: Walker, 1970. A practical guide for the person who wants to do something about air pollution, noise, chemical pollution, waste, and litter. The suggestions offered can be adapted to activities for young children and included in parent newsletters.

Schwartz, George I., and Bernice S. Schwartz. *Food Chains and Ecosystems: Ecology for Young Experimenters.* New York: Doubleday, 1974. An excellent book for older boys and girls containing thirty-nine projects that can be adapted for the younger child. Topics include investigation of life on land, in and around the water, and indoors. The experiments presented in the book include exploring a microcommunity in a tide pool, study of desert plants, setting up a terrarium with a forest-floor community, and using breeding cages to observe the development of insects.

BOOKS FOR CHILDREN ABOUT ECOLOGY, THE ENVIRONMENT, AND CONSERVATION

Blocksom, Claudia. *It's Your World.* San Francisco: Troubador Press, 1979. A short, well-illustrated discussion of the environment.

Collins, Patricia. *Chain of Life: A Story of a Forest Food Cycle.* New York: Doubleday, 1972. The story of a forest and the living things one can find there. It is also the story of how the native plants and animals get their food — how plants live on other plants and animals; how animals live on plants and other animals. Delicately illustrated in line sketches and soft pastels.

Crawford, Mel. *The Turtle Book.* New York: Western Publications, 1965. An illustrated discussion of the various water and land reptiles having toothless jaws and soft bodies enclosed in a bony shell. Appropriate for preschool to the fourth grade.

Freschet, Berniece. *Year on Muskrat Marsh.* New York: Scribner, 1974. "In the half-wet, half-dry world of the marshland, creatures come on swift wings, swooping down to the water. They come on webbed feet, splashing near the reeds. They come thirsty, trudging along well-worn paths. They come to the marsh, and all depend on it for life." Elegant black-and-white illustrations of wildlife around a marsh.

Grossman, Shelly, and Mary Louise Grossman. *The How and Why Wonder Book of Ecology.* New York: Grosset & Dunlap, 1971. A big picture book with photographs of wildlife, such as hawks, snakes, owls, and crabs. The text is too advanced for preschoolers, but the teacher can adapt the information to suit the child's level of curiosity and understanding.

Hamberger, John. *Birth of a Pond.* New York: Coward, McCann & Geoghegan, 1975. Clear illustrations and simple text show the reader the process of creating a people-made pond. This book shows how we can contribute to nature and the interdependence of wildlife.

Miles, Betty. *Save the Earth! An Ecology Handbook for Kids.* New York: Knopf, 1974. An enjoyable book of information and guidance for children in the areas of conservation and ecology.

Paulsen, Gary. *The Small Ones: Real Animals.* Milwaukee: Raintree Editions, 1976. Sketches and photographs show the natural habitats of animals such as the rabbit, mouse, and fox. The text is too detailed for young children, but the teacher can adapt the useful information.

Peterson, Ottis. *Junior Science Book of Water.* Champaign, Ill.: Garrard, 1966. People are 86 percent water. They need large quantities of water to drink, wash, and irrigate. Our cities and industrial plants have poisoned the streams, lakes, and seashore. Many fisheries have been destroyed. Photos and text illustrate pollution and what we can do to prevent further destruction of our water supplies. Text is easily adaptable to the interests of the young child.

Pringle, Laurence. *City and Suburb: Exploring an Ecosystem.* New York: Macmillan, 1975. Sometimes a city seems to be entirely constructed by humans, but it is one of the most complicated ecosystems in the world. Photos and text help reader to explore a city's insects, wildflowers, birds, and mammals. Text is for older children, but photos are good for discussion with preschoolers.

Ravielli, Anthony. *The World Is Round.* New York: Viking, 1963. A picture book illustrating the size and shape of the earth by having the child imagine a ball the size of a house and a fly standing on the ball. Illustrations are large and good for discussion. Some concepts, such as sphere and circumference, are beyond the understanding of young children.

Shapp, Martha, and Charles Shapp. *Let's Find Out About the Sun.* New York: Franklin Watts, 1975. Colorfully illustrated picture book for preschoolers, which calls attention to the heat of the sun, its size, and why it rises and sets.

Stone, Lynn M. *Marshes and Swamps.* Chicago: Children's Press, 1983. An examination of the ecosystems in wet, marshy environments. Illustrated.

Wosmek, Frances. *The ABC of Ecology.* Los Altos, Calif.: Davenport Press, 1982. Guide to the subject of plant and animal relationships. Written for preschool and the early elementary grades. Available in both English and Spanish.

PART SIX

Health and Safety

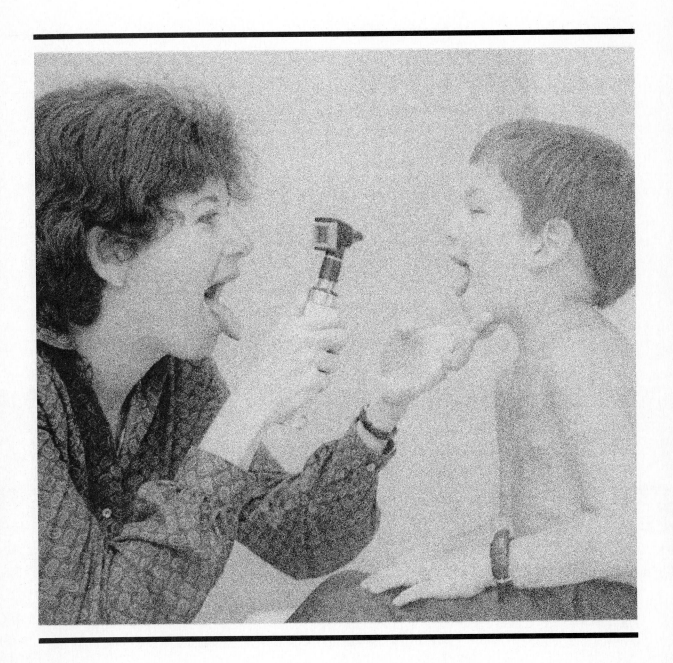

Introduction

At one time, health and safety issues such as brushing teeth, toilet training, and learning to avoid strangers were the exclusive purview of the child's parents. Today, when many youngsters spend most of their waking hours in day-care situations, teachers and child-care workers are beginning to take on some of these responsibilities.

The areas of health and safety are especially important at the pre-school level. Young children are susceptible to colds and other infections and are more vulnerable than older children to many kinds of accidents. As teachers we are in a unique position to observe the varying degrees of health in young children and to insure their physical safety. We are with them long hours and are often more attuned to subtle changes in a child's physical and emotional state than parents can be. Frequently the teacher is the first to suspect the onset of an illness simply by observing a change in the child's behavior.

Teachers also realize that health is not an objective or static condition. A child's state of health is constantly changing and affects the way he or she behaves at a particular moment, especially the way the child learns and socializes. Health is not simply the absence of illness. Rather, health is a state of being that can be viewed as a continuum with varying degrees of fitness and vitality at one end and of illness and abnormal functioning at the other. As any teacher can verify, the degree of health and well-being of a child can dramatically affect his or her attention span, attitude toward others, and in fact, the mood of the entire classroom or day-care center.

Teachers of young children need to be concerned about three aspects of health and safety:

1. prevention of illness and injury;
2. detection of illness and knowledge of first aid;
3. promotion of good health and safety habits.

Because children spend long hours in child-care facilities, teachers need to emphasize the importance of good hygiene in order to prevent the spread of infection. Highly contagious infections like *giardiasis*[1] spread so quickly that health departments must fre-

---

[1] See "To practice washing hands" on page 258 for further information about this disease.

quently intervene and close facilities. Practicing the basic principles of good hygiene can prevent such occurrences. The activities offered in this section are designed not to frighten youngsters, but to help them develop good health habits through specific strategies.

To prevent injury, children should be taught the proper ways to use toys and gym equipment; how to use the swings without hurting others; when it is safe for them to run; and other safety measures.

A good detection program in the school will include screening for dental, hearing, and vision problems. If professionally trained technicians are not available through the local health department, teachers and parents can be trained to do screening by the Red Cross, community day-care associations, or the local college or university. Early detection can prevent many serious problems, such as *ambliopia* (lazy eye), which can be corrected if caught between the ages of three and six.

Teachers have many opportunities to provide the child with information about first aid and basic treatment of simple injuries. For example, when a child suffers minor bruises, the teacher can talk about how to report an accident — how and where it happened, the extent of the injury, and so on — and can discuss hygienic measures as well as methods for preventing future accidents.

Promoting good health and safety habits can be reinforced throughout the curriculum by offering dramatic play materials in the dress-up area, preparing nutritious foods, reading appropriate stories, and using music.[2] The school is the natural setting in which to teach safety precautions, such as appropriate ways to use toys and play equipment. Other safety and health habits are more appropriately taught by parents, with support from the school staff (such as use of car seats and safety belts, how to use the telephone to call for help in an emergency, and avoiding strangers). Concern about child abuse and abduction can be addressed in parent-education meetings, and further resources and support can be provided by the school.

However the teaching is approached, attitudes about health and safety are best taught by the important adults in a child's life. Teachers and parents need to encourage children to communicate with them about how they feel and to ask questions about health and safety matters. Activities and teaching strategies should help children to see health-care professionals as helpful, not frightening, individuals and safety rules as beneficial precautions rather than restrictive measures.

Please see the bibliography at the end of this part to help build and expand the ideas presented here to fit the individual needs of your school or child-care center.

[2] Try Hap Palmer's recording on health and safety: "Learning Basic Skills Through Music" (AR 526) available from Educational Activities, Inc., Freeport, N.Y.

Health Activities

▶ **PURPOSE**   **To see what bacteria (germs) look like**

MATERIALS
— One envelope unflavored gelatin
— Two cups hot water
— Two small, clean containers (such as cottage cheese cartons)
— Masking tape
— Marking pen
— Soap and water

PROCEDURE
1. Dissolve gelatin in hot water.
2. Pour one cup of the dissolved gelatin in each of the clean containers.
3. When the gelatin is cool, have one child with dirty hands touch the surface of the gelatin in one of the containers with his or her finger. Label this container "dirty finger."
4. Wash the same child's hands well with soap and water. (See next activity, "To practice washing hands.")
5. Have the child touch the surface of the gelatin in the second container with a clean finger. Label this container "clean finger."
6. Cover the containers and place them in a warm, dark place (near a heater or in an oven with a pilot light).
7. Check the containers in five days. In the "dirty finger" container, colonies of bacteria can be seen. In the "clean finger" container, few or no bacteria colonies will be visible.

DISCUSSION
Explain that the growth in the "dirty finger" container is called *bacteria*. Bacteria are very tiny plants that are found everywhere. Most of the time we cannot see them. But with food (the gelatin) and warmth, they divide and grow and make more bacteria that can cause disease and sickness. Bacteria is likely to grow on food that is not properly refrigerated, damp towels, handkerchiefs, and clothing. Thorough washing removes most bacteria.

▶ **PURPOSE**   **To practice washing hands**

MATERIALS
— Dispenser soap or bar soap such as Lifebuoy, Safeguard, or Dial
— Paper towels
— Nail brush (optional)
— Timer (optional)

PROCEDURE
1. Wet hands thoroughly with warm water.
2. Use enough soap from dispenser or bar soap to work up a good lather.
3. Use vigorous rubbing motions for at least thirty seconds (use a timer so that children can experience how long thirty seconds is).
4. Be sure the child washes the palms and backs of hands, wrists, between the fingers, and under the nails (using a brush if one is available).

5. Rinse hands thoroughly.
6. Dry hands thoroughly with clean paper towel.
7. Turn off the faucet using the paper towel.

DISCUSSION   Talk about the things we do with our hands and how they collect bacteria. Discuss times when it is important to have clean hands. Ask children if they think they should wash hands before and after toileting, eating, holding hands, blowing the nose, and going to bed. When should the teacher or parent wash hands? Why? **Note to child-care workers:** Germs hide in jewelry and chipped nail polish.

VARIATION   Use a puppet during story time to reinforce the importance of frequent and thorough handwashing. Have the puppet help clean the animal cage, help cook, go to the toilet, play in the sand, sit down to eat, and so on, forgetting to wash its hands each time. Let the children "remind" the puppet to wash hands. Inspect the children's hands periodically and give children plenty of praise for remembering to wash their hands.

COMMENTS   In recent years a highly contagious infection, *giardiasis*, has forced the closing of many child-care centers. It is caused by an intestinal protozoan, *giardia lamblia*, which can be spread by people who do not have the symptoms themselves. The onset of this illness may be gradual or sudden, and is characterized by diarrhea, abdominal cramps, loss of appetite, nausea, and sometimes vomiting and fever. Transmission of the disease is by the fecal-oral route (usually by putting contaminated food, hands, or other objects into the mouth). Therefore, thorough handwashing with soap after bowel movements, after changing diapers, and before handling food is extremely important.

▶ **PURPOSE**   **To learn the correct way to sneeze and wipe the nose**

MATERIALS   — Photo or sketch of a person sneezing, showing explosive spread of droplets
            — Box of cleansing tissues
            — Puppet

PROCEDURE   **1.** Have the puppet sneeze at the children while it is talking to them.
            2. Tell the puppet to cover its nose and mouth and turn away from others when sneezing.
            3. Have the puppet ask why.
            4. Show the puppet and the children the photo of a person sneezing and ask what is happening in the picture.
            5. Let the children help the puppet answer.
            6. Discuss things the puppet and children can do to prevent the spread of droplets and germs when they sneeze.
            7. Ask what can happen if they cover their noses and mouth with their hands but do not wash their hands.
            8. Ask what can happen if they use a cleansing tissue and then put it in their pocket.

9. Talk about other ways germs are spread (coughing, touching, kissing, sharing the same eating and drinking utensils).

10. Have the puppet and children practice using cleansing tissues to wipe their noses. Discard the tissues and be sure that children wash their hands.

▶ **PURPOSE**   **To practice the correct way to brush teeth**

MATERIALS — One toothbrush and paper cup for each child (use small toothbrushes with soft bristles that are straight across the top)
— Disclosing tablets
— Unbreakable hand mirrors
— Oversized model of teeth and toothbrush (optional; often available on loan from the local American Dental Association)
— Toothpaste and dental floss (optional)
— Styrofoam egg carton
— The story "D is for Dentist" and the film "Tooth Brushing with Charlie Brown," both available from the American Dental Association[3]

PROCEDURE 1. Read the story and show the film to the children.

2. Use the oversized teeth and toothbrush to demonstrate correct brushing methods. Show children how to direct the bristles at a 45-degree angle where the teeth and gums meet. Use a circular scrubbing motion.

3. Hand each child a toothbrush and have them copy your technique, using dry brushes.

4. Follow a systematic routine. Brush the top teeth outside surfaces first, and work from left to right. Follow the same system for the inside surfaces. Then brush the chewing surfaces. Repeat the same procedure for the bottom teeth, stressing the importance of following a consistent pattern rather than brushing haphazardly.

5. Label each of the toothbrushes with the child's name and store each one by poking the handle through the bottom of an overturned Styrofoam egg carton. (See Illustration 6.1.)

6. After children have practiced brushing with dry brushes, have them chew half of a disclosing tablet and then rinse their mouths. Explain that the red spots left on their teeth show where germs remain. Let them look in the mirror to see the red spots. (**Caution:** Be sure to check with parents before this exercise to see if any children are allergic to red dye. Also, let parents know that the child's tongue will be red for a day.)

7. Then have the children brush their teeth the way you showed

---

[3]Contact the American Dental Association, Bureau of Audiovisual Service, 211 East Chicago Ave., Chicago, IL 60611. Also available from this address is a large, colorfully illustrated flip chart, published by the American Society of Dentistry for Children and titled "Tooth Talk: A Teacher's Guide—Flip Chart for Use with Grades K–3."

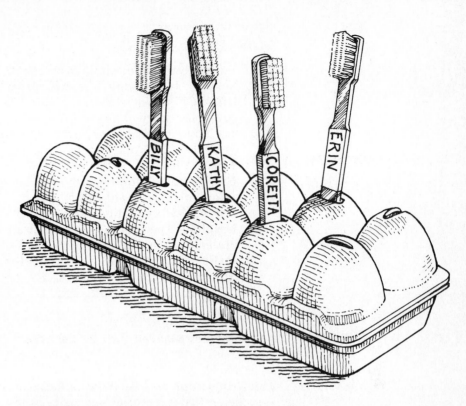

Illustration 6.1   **Labeled holder for children's toothbrushes**

them using a small amount of toothpaste until all the red color is gone.

8. Have them brush their tongues as well (the red dye will remain to some extent, however).

9. Suggest that after the children have brushed their teeth at home, they should ask their parents to brush them again.

10. Share this teaching activity with parents and ask their assistance in reinforcing dental hygiene habits at home. It is especially important that children brush before bedtime because bacteria is more active when the mouth is quiet.

HELPFUL HINTS

1. The use of disclosing tablets enables children to see in vivid detail where bacteria reside in their mouths.

2. Use correct terms, such as *plaque* and *bacteria*. (*Plaque* is the by-product of bacteria feeding on food in the mouth.)

3. Teaching how to floss the teeth may not be a practical activity for the preschool. However, this essential part of cleaning the teeth can be taught to parents in a parent education meeting.

4. Invite a local dentist to visit the children at school and to talk to parents during a parent meeting.

HELPFUL HINTS

1. Supply medical equipment in the dramatic play area.
2. Refer to the annotated bibliography under "Books About Other Childhood Experiences" in Part Four, "Language Arts," for storybooks about medical situations.
3. Try some of the books from the *Open Family Series,* published by Walker and Company, 720 Fifth Ave., New York, NY 10019. Titles include *Making Babies, That New Baby, About Handicaps, About Dying, On Divorce, The Adopted One, About Phobias* and *A Hospital Story.* (*A Hospital Story* is illustrated with photos about a child's hospital experience, and is written to be read by parents and children together.)
4. Invite a medical worker to visit the school and talk to the children about the work they do.

▶ **PURPOSE** **To understand the need for medical care**

MATERIALS — Large doll
— Medical equipment, such as stethoscope, tongue depressors, thermometer, hypodermic syringe without the needle, small flashlight, and doctor's coat

Illustration 6.2 **Using a doll is a good way to help children better understand medical care.**

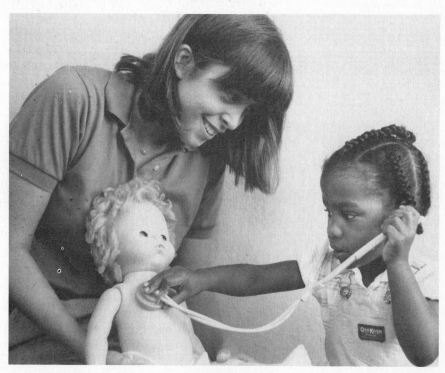

PROCEDURE
1. Dramatize a situation in which the doll is not feeling well.
2. Say:
   My doll (or some name for the doll) **is sick. Do you know what it means to be sick?**
3. Let children volunteer information from their own experiences.
4. Use their information to describe symptoms of illnesses (headache, sleepiness, fever, stomach ache, sore throat, and so on).
5. Ask them to help you decide what to do with your sick doll.
6. Emphasize that the doll should describe to the adult (parent, teacher, or medical worker) the physical symptoms, showing where the body aches.
7. Encourage the children to be aware of physical discomfort and praise their ability to describe it. (See Illustration 6.2 for a representation of this activity.)

Safety Activities

▶ **PURPOSE**   **To identify poisonous materials**

MATERIALS   — Empty, clean containers of poisonous items commonly found in the household, such as cleaners, polishes, perfumes, paint, bug sprays, aspirin, and medicines
            — Posters and stickers from a poison control center[4]

PROCEDURE   1. Show each of the containers to the children and ask if they know what is in it.
            2. Talk about how the contents of each container are used.
            3. Ask the children if they should put the contents in their mouths.
            4. Talk about poisons and what poisons can do.
            5. Talk about ways of reminding everyone that something is poisonous.
            6. Show stickers such as the one pictured in Illustration 6.3, and tell children that the "beeware" sticker means contents are poisonous.
            7. Put a sticker on each of the containers.
            8. Stress that contents of containers without the sticker can also be poisonous.

HELPFUL HINT

Keep Syrup of Ipecac handy (but out of children's reach). Syrup of Ipecac can be purchased at any pharmacy without a prescription and is a safe way to induce vomiting when recommended by a doctor or the poison control center.

Illustration 6.3   **The "Beeware" sticker indicates contents are poisonous.**

---

[4]There is a nationwide network of regional poison control centers. Look in the phone book under "Poison Control Center" for the office nearest you.

▶ **PURPOSE**   **To understand the importance of using a safety car seat**

MATERIALS   — Child's safety car seat
— Large building blocks
— Discarded seat belts or canvas straps

PROCEDURE   **1.** Build a car with the blocks.
2. Attach the safety seat to one of the blocks to make a back seat.
3. Have children take turns riding in the child's safety seat.
4. Make seat belts for the driver with canvas straps or used seat belts.
5. Let the children help each other into the safety seat.
6. Talk about the importance of safety car seats.
7. Ask what can happen if the car has to stop suddenly.
8. Display posters showing children in safety car seats and adults wearing seat belts.

HELPFUL HINTS

1. Information about car seat loan programs is available from state and regional offices of the National Child Passenger Safety Association.
2. Use the song "Buckle Your Seat Belt" from Hap Palmer's record, *Learning Basic Skills Through Music— Health and Safety, Vol. III* (AR 526). Available from Educational Activities, Inc., P.O. Box 392, Freeport, NY 11520.

▶ **PURPOSE**   **To learn how to use the telephone to call for help**

MATERIALS   — Telephone with push-button numbers
— Brightly colored adhesive tape
— Adhesive labels with small pictures of animals familiar to children, such as dogs and cats[5]

PROCEDURE   **1.** Color-code the "operator" button of the telephone with a piece of adhesive tape labeled "O."
2. Fasten one dog label next to the "9" button.
3. Put two kitten labels next to the "1" button. (See Illustration 6.4 for Steps 2, 3, and 8.)
4. Talk to the children about emergency situations, such as a fire, illness, or physical injury. Allow time for each child to share personal experiences.
5. Talk about the importance of calling for help when there is an emergency.
6. Show the children the telephone with color-coded labels.

---

[5] Children who cannot identify numbers can recognize and name animals. Stress "911" as children become more familiar with the location of the numbers on the phone.

Illustration 6.4 "911" identified with dog and cat labels

7. Explain that if they need to call for help, it is important to know who to call and what to say.

8. Teaching the use of the telephone is most effective when working with small groups of children at the same level of ability. Very young children can learn to push the "O" button; older preschoolers (ages four and five) will be able to learn to call "911" by pushing "doggy, kitty-kitty."

9. Ask each child to push either "O" or "911" and pretend that he or she is calling for help. The teacher or another adult can play the role of the operator.

10. Have each child practice giving his or her name, the address (especially the city), and the nature of the emergency. (See "To learn to say names, addresses, and phone numbers" on page 149.)

11. Very young children can practice pushing "O," saying "help," and leaving the phone off the hook.

12. As children become more familiar with the procedure, have them role-play in emergency situations. Pretend, for example, that a babysitter has fallen and is unconscious, a parent is too sick to get help, a sibling has swallowed too many pills, and so on.

13. Explain to children that they should run to a neighbor's house for help if there is a fire in the house.

14. Repeat role-playing frequently. When children are familiar with the routine of calling for help, remove the labels from the buttons of the telephone and have them practice pushing "0" or "911" without the aids. Remind the children they are not to practice on a phone that is operational because operators, police, ambulance drivers, and firemen cannot help people who really need them if they receive a call that is not a real emergency.

15. Enlist the help of parents to reinforce learning to phone for help

from home. (Although dialing is more difficult for little fingers, this activity can be adapted for use with a rotary telephone dial.)

COMMENTS   The emergency number "911" will be in effect nationwide beginning in 1984. If possible, children should learn to call "911" rather than "0" because "911" will immediately place the phone line on hold with ring-back capabilities if the caller should hang up. The address of the caller will flash on the screen of the operator's terminal, enabling the operator to dispatch help.

    If the child dials "0," the computerized capabilities of the "911" code are not functional, so it is important that the child learn to ask for help, give the address — especially the city, and leave the phone off the hook so the operator can trace the location.

▶ **PURPOSE**   **To be aware of appropriate ways to use play equipment**

MATERIALS   — Collection of unsafe toys with sharp or jagged edges; small toys and toys with small parts; stuffed toys with poorly constructed seams; loud noise-making toys; toys with sharp points, pins, staples, and wires; and toys that propel objects (such as dart guns and bows and arrows)

PROCEDURE   **1.** Read a story emphasizing toy safety to the children.
    2. Talk about safety, encouraging the children to share their experiences.
    3. Show unsafe toys one at a time and ask the children to help explain why each toy is unsafe.
    4. Discuss what children can do to help identify, call attention to, and avoid unsafe toys.

COMMENTS   Write U.S. Consumer Product Safety Commission, TOYS, Washington, D.C. 20207, or call toll-free 800-638-2666 for information on toy safety.

▶ **PURPOSE**   **To learn proper use of swings, slides, and climbing apparatus**

MATERIALS   — A series of sketches, photographs, or slides showing staged sequences of proper and improper ways to play on swings, slides, and climbing apparatus

PROCEDURE   **1.** Make a series of sketches, photographs, or slides as described above. Use the following guidelines:[6]

Swings

— Sit in the center of the swing; never stand or kneel.
— Hold on with both hands.

[6]From *"Play Happy, Play Safely" Playground Equipment Guide* (U.S. Consumer Product Safety Commission, Washington, D.C. 20207).

— Stop the swing before getting off.

— Walk way around a moving swing — not too close to the front or the back.

— Never push anyone else in the swing or allow others to push them.

— Have only one person in one swing at a time.

— Never swing empty swings or twist swing chains.

— Avoid putting head and feet through exercise rings on the swing sets.

Slides

— Hold on with both hands as they go up the steps of the slide, taking one step at a time; never go up the sliding surface or the frame. Keep at least one arm's length between children.

— Slide down feet first, always sitting up, one at a time.

— Be sure no one is in front of the slide before sliding down.

— Be patient, not to push or shove, and to wait their turn.

— Leave the front of the slide after they have taken their turn.

— Never use a metal slide that has been sitting out in the sun.

Climbing apparatus

Geodesic domes or arches and jungle gyms:

— Use the correct grip; use fingers and thumbs ("lock grip") for climbing and holding; use both hands.

— Watch carefully when climbing down and avoid those climbing up.

— Avoid having too many people using the equipment at once.

Horizontal ladders and bars:

— All start at the same end of the equipment and, using the "lock grip," move in the same direction.

— Stay well behind the person in front and avoid swinging feet.

— Never use equipment when it is wet.

— Avoid speed contests or trying to cover too large a distance in one move.

— Drop from the bars with knees slightly bent and land on both feet.

2. Show a picture of the improper way to use a swing (for example, standing up or not holding on with both hands).

3. Ask the children if this is the right way to use the swing. Identify what is wrong and describe what should be done instead.

4. Show a picture of the correct way to use the swings.

5. Do the same for other areas of the playground, following each example of incorrect use of equipment with a picture of correct use.

▶ **PURPOSE**   **To learn to listen and look for cars**

MATERIALS   — Tape recorder

PROCEDURE   1. Tape-record sounds of cars approaching and driving by on the street. Include silent pauses between each car or group of cars.

2. Talk to the children about listening for cars in the street. Tell them they can sometimes hear a car before they see it.

3. Take them into the playground and mark a path so they can pretend they are crossing the street.
4. Have them stand at the "curb" and listen while you play the tape recorder from behind them, varying the directions from which the sounds emanate.
5. Have each child point and look in the direction of the sound.
6. Talk about the fact that sounds are softer when the cars are farther away and louder as the cars get closer.
7. Have the children practice listening and looking for cars on the street.

COMMENTS The teacher can use other opportunities to teach safety on the streets. Taking short walks in the neighborhood or going on field trips are times to practice what the children have learned in school.

The American Automobile Association publishes an excellent series of booklets designed for adults who work with preschool children. Titles include "Preschool Children in Traffic," "When I Go Outside," "I Listen and Look for Cars Coming," "How I Cross a Street," and "Traffic Signal Lights." Contact your local AAA for ordering information.

▶ PURPOSE **To learn to avoid strangers**

MATERIALS — The storybook *Never Talk to Strangers* by Irma Joyce (New York: Western Publishing, 1967); see "Comments" below

PROCEDURE
1. Read the story or make up a flannelboard story with the theme of saying "no" to strangers.
2. Talk about the meaning of *stranger*.
3. Have children give examples of strangers.
4. Ask a series of "what if" questions appropriate to the ages of the children, such as:
   What if a stranger (someone you don't know) says, "Come here and have some candy"? What do you say?
   Other situations might include a stranger offering to take a child to his or her sick parent; an invitation to enter a car or house to see some kittens; or a plea for help.

COMMENTS *Never Talk to Strangers* is a simply written and colorfully illustrated book that was featured on a network TV documentary depicting animals in humorous situations to make the point of not talking to strangers. Reading the story is a good way to lead into a discussion or "what if" situations about interacting with strangers.

Using puppets is another way to teach assertiveness and strategies for dealing with strangers. Young children often relate more comfortably to puppets than adults when testing out their own verbal skills.

Another excellent resource is the book *Dinosaurs, Beware* by Marc Brown and Stephen Krensky (Boston: Little, Brown and Company, 1982). This safety guide, illustrated with dinosaurs in a humorous style, discusses common situations both in the home and away from it. Sixty safety tips show what to do in case of emergency, how to keep emergencies from happening, what to do when a stranger comes to the door, how to react to a fire, the importance of wearing a seat belt, and so on.

Teaching young children about potential sexual abuse and abduction is most effectively done by parents in the home. The school can help by providing workshops, referral agencies, and published materials for parents. Refer to the Bibliography of Resources for some excellent resources.

Bibliography of Resources

Adams, Caren, and Jennifer Fay. *No More Secrets.* San Luis Obispo, Calif.: Impact Publishers, 1981. An excellent book designed primarily to help parents protect their children from sexual assault. Chapters cover strategies for teaching children what to do and say to protect themselves, how to listen and watch for behavior signals, and games to teach prevention of assault. Community action suggestions and a list of resources make this a valuable book for parent education.

Chinn, Peggy L. *Child Health Maintenance.* St. Louis: C. V. Mosby, 1979. A lengthy, detailed text covering health care from birth through adolescence. Topics include common illnesses, social and learning problems, and death and dying during childhood and adolescence. A good book to have in the school reference library.

Dayee, Frances S. *Private Zone.* Edmonds, Wash.: Charles Franklin Press, 1982. A well-illustrated, nonthreatening book written in language simple enough for children three to nine years old. The purpose of this "read aloud" book is to create an atmosphere of open discussion about a delicate subject in a nonfrightening way; to give children tools to use as preventive measures against sexual assault and aid in recognizing trouble signs; to offer ways of guarding against repeated assaults; and to teach children recognition and reporting skills if sexual assault situations occur.

King County Rape Relief. *"He Told Me Not to Tell."* Renton, Wash.: King County Rape Relief, 1979. A collection of suggestions for parents or teachers when talking to children about sexual assault. The booklet includes suggestions for teaching prevention and reporting.

Lorin, Martin I. *The Parent's Book of Physical Fitness for Children: From Infancy Through Adolescence.* New York: Atheneum, 1978. A pediatrician explains exercises, nutrition, and health-promoting programs geared to different developmental stages.

Newman, Susan. *Ice Cream Isn't Always Good!* New York: Project Two, 1971. A small pamphlet with photos and story about an elementary-school girl who accepts the offer of ice cream from a stranger and how she uses the phone to call for help.

Norwood, Christopher. *At Highest Risk.* New York: Penguin Books, 1980. A well-researched book with information about chemicals hazardous to unborn and young children.

Pringle, Sheila M., and Brenda E. Ramsey. *Promoting the Health of Children.* St. Louis: C. V. Mosby, 1982. An excellent guide for child-care workers and health-care professionals to the health of children from infancy to adolescence. Health maintenance and health problems of each age group are covered in detail.

Prudden, Bonnie. *How to Keep Your Child Fit from Birth to Six.* New York: Doubleday, 1983. A series of illustrated exercises adults can use with young children.

Reinisch, Edith H., and Ralph E. Minear, Jr. *Health of the Preschool Child.* New York: John Wiley & Sons, 1978. Covers topics dealing with nutrition, infections, behavioral problems, first aid, and accident prevention and gives an overview of the preschool health program with sample forms for the teacher to use with parents.

Samuels, Mike, and Nancy Samuels. *The Well Child Book: Your Child from Four to Twelve.* New York: Summit Books, 1982. Illustrated manual with information on development, diseases, choosing a doctor, common accidents, anatomy, physiology, nutrition, and exercise.

Schiller, Jack G. *Childhood Illness: A Common Sense Approach.* New York: Stein and Day, 1974. A doctor discusses childhood health problems from diaper rash to flat feet.

Siffert, Robert S. *How Your Child's Body Grows.* New York: Grosset and Dunlap, 1980. An orthopedic surgeon explains simply and clearly how the body grows and develops. Includes a section on the young athlete.

Stowell, Jo, and Mary Dietzel. *My Very Own Book About Me.* Spokane, Wash.: Spokane Rape Crisis Center, 1980. A coloring book/workbook for children using the concepts of the body's private parts and "ok/not ok touch." Written text provides information to help a child establish personal rights.

Williams, Joy. *Red Flag, Green Flag People.* Fargo, N. Dak.: Rape and Abuse Crisis Center, 1980. A coloring book for young children focusing on the dangerous stranger.

Winick, Myron. *Growing Up Healthy.* New York: Morrow, 1982. A guide to nutrition covering such topics as what to eat during pregnancy, how to breast-feed a baby, obesity, hyperactivity diets, and fast foods. A good referral guide for parents.

WHERE TO WRITE FOR MORE INFORMATION

American Academy of Pediatrics, 1125 A St., San Rafael, CA 94901. Publishes "Guidelines for the Management of Infectious Diseases in Day Care for California" (1983).

American Automobile Association, 8111 Gate House Rd., Falls Church, VA 22042. Provides an excellent series of booklets designed for parents and teachers to use with young children. Each booklet is illustrated and written in story form to be shared with the child. Titles include "I Listen and Look for Cars Coming," "Traffic Signal Lights," "When I Go Outside," "How I Cross the Street," and "Preschool Children in Traffic: Parents' Guide for Action."

Analeka Industries, P.O. Box 141, West Linn, OR 97068. Supplies anatomically correct dolls, developed by Roi Hokinson and Brenda Watson, that can be used to help teachers, parents, police and counselors talk with young children about abuse prevention.

Child Care Information Exchange, C-44, Redmond, WA 98052. Publishes "Infection and Day Care" (March/April 1983) and "Health Policies and Procedures" (September/October 1983).

Child Protective Services. Every state has at least one agency that receives and investigates complaints about child abuse and neglect. Look in the phone book under Juvenile Probation, Department of Protective Services, or Social Services, or simply call the police for information about the protective service in your state. Teachers and child-care workers are required by law to report suspected cases of child abuse. Protective services can provide the child-care center and parents with brochures and other resources on the topic of child neglect and abuse. The school should have phone numbers and names of contacts on hand at all times.

Kemper Insurance Company, Long Grove, IL 60049. This company publishes an excellent series of colorfully illustrated booklets for teachers and parents to read to young children. Topics include safety lessons about playing with matches, keeping trash cleaned up, electrical plugs, flying kites, playing in the street, and riding bikes.

National Child Identification Center, P. O. Box 5839, Fresno, CA 93755. This organization provides parents with suggestions on how to help keep children from becoming victims of abduction. Children's identifications are kept on file by this nonprofit organization and, in the event of emergencies, computers and other electronic equipment assist in searching for the lost child. Bumper stickers and window decals are also available.

Rape Crisis Center of Syracuse, 423 W. Onondaga St., Syracuse, NY 13203. Send $3.00 to order *Sometimes I Need to Say No!* by Lisa W. Strick, a series of short skits designed for children using songs and humor. The concepts are based on a privacy continuum moving from general to specific issues of sexual assault. Included are supplemental activities for teachers, parents, and children.

U.S. Consumer Product Safety Commission, Division of Consumer Response and Information, 5401 Westbard Ave., Bethesda, MD 20207. Write for a free copy of *Listing of Education Materials for Use by Schools.* The agency will provide up to ten free copies of any of the materials listed in the booklet. Some of the educational materials deal with bicycle safety, child and infant safety, consumer products, fire, kitchen safety, playground safety, poison prevention, and toy safety. An excellent source of well-designed materials for the school and for parent workshops.

PART SEVEN

Cooking and Nutrition

Introduction

Cooking in the preschool is a versatile activity that can be used to reach several, quite different objectives. It is an intrinsically exciting experience, as children love to do things they see adults doing, and cooking offers an opportunity for them to do something "real." It provides a way for youngsters to feel important and to achieve a sense of accomplishment.

But cooking can be more than fun. With the proper selection of recipes and use of materials, cooking provides many opportunities for cognitive, social, and cultural learning as well.

You can use cooking to expose children to a variety of sensory and cognitive experiences. Let the children *see* how the food can change before their eyes. They can observe how brittle noodles become soft and slippery after boiling or how an egg becomes hard when it is cooked. Let them *smell* the aroma of foods — bread baking, apples simmering, pancakes browning. Provide many opportunities for them to *feel* the different textures of food, like the squishiness of bread dough oozing through their fingers and the roughness of nut shells. You can call their attention to *hearing* the different sounds of foods, such as corn popping or the crunch of celery when it is chewed. Note the colors, shapes, and sizes of foods — the black, shiny seeds of the papaya next to the bright orange of the fruit; the white of the coconut meat and the rough, hairy brown shell surrounding it.

With guidance and encouragement, the children begin to learn about units of weights and measures[1] (one teaspoon of oil, two cups of milk, a half pound of flour, three drops of vanilla) and how these units relate to one another (three teaspoons equal one tablespoon, one cup equals half a pint, sixteen ounces equal one pound). They learn to use the right tools to achieve the best results — measuring cups for liquids, spoons for powders and for solids such as shortening. They also learn meanings of new words: *dice* the carrots, *fold in* the egg whites, *grate* the lemon rind.

The children learn why liquid must be added gradually and why greens must be dry for salad. They can watch physical and chemical

---

[1] For metric measures, see page 282.

changes take place when bread rises, whipping cream solidifies into butter, and when peanuts are ground into peanut butter. They become aware of the need to learn about time: mixing for two minutes, waiting for the timer to ring, looking at the clock to see when the muffins will be ready.

There are also social gains. Through cooking activities, the child learns and feels the importance of sharing in a group project and realizes the need for cooperation. Planning the project, taking turns at stirring and pouring, and talking about the ingredients all require individual contributions to a group effort.

Foods and cooking illustrate cultural differences among ethnic groups, and some of the recipes in this section have been selected to emphasize these contrasts: sushi from Japan, Chinese won tons, Mexican tortillas. Food is generally a topic of interest to all the parents in a school, and many adults may be very eager to contribute their own favorite ethnic recipes. This kind of involvement on the part of parents allows them to contribute something unique and worthwhile to the program and exposes the children to a wider array of food tastes and flavors from a variety of cultural and ethnic backgrounds. Stories and songs can be tied in with the preparation and serving of certain foods to celebrate customs or holidays. Dishes should be planned and selected to fit into a schedule that allows plenty of time for preparation and consumption. Elaborate dishes that require a great deal of adult preparation and much waiting by the children should be discouraged.

Good nutrition should be a key objective of any preschool curriculum. Children need to be educated about food — what it is for, how it is related to health and well-being, and how it is produced and consumed. Perhaps more than any other age group, preschoolers are most susceptible to television commercials touting highly sugared foods such as cereals, candy bars, fruit-flavored drinks, and so on. Very young children have no way of knowing that the animated cartoons on the television screen are attempts to sell products and are not necessarily factual. Even adults are misled by commercials advertising "all natural" ingredients or the addition of vitamins and minerals to products that are low in fiber and high in salt, sugar, saturated fat, modified starches, and fillers.

The attempt to teach young children concepts of good nutrition and to be wise consumers is not an easy task. It requires them to make difficult distinctions and judgments about when to trust others and when to be skeptical. And while concepts of good nutrition are definitely worth teaching, they do not necessarily alter behavior.

The preschool teacher has a unique opportunity to involve youngsters in learning about nutrition and foods and to expose children and parents to healthy foods and good eating habits. Avoid recipes that call for salt, refined sugars and flour, and ingredients with little food value. Instead, use recipes that require whole grains, honey instead of sugar, carob instead of chocolate, molasses and wheat germ, fresh or dried fruits, and nuts and seeds — all of which are tasty and healthful. Remember too that if the teacher conveys enthusiasm for preparing and eating healthy foods, children are more likely to do the same. The positive experiences can help reinforce the teacher's comments about selectivity and skepticism in buying foods. Teachers are among the most important adults in a young child's life, and your attitudes about food and nutrition can be a strong influence on a child's thinking and behavior.

Because young children learn best when they participate in an activity, the recipes in this section were chosen to allow children to discover and learn through involvement. Most recipes can be prepared by a group of children and are good activities for teaching cooperation and teamwork. However, there will be times when you may want to encourage children to work individually so they can practice following directions and measuring and having the feeling of doing something all by themselves. Several recipes have been adapted to accommodate individual portions (Pancakes, Raggedy Ann Salad, Deviled Eggs, Muffin Pizzas, Baked Apple); in other recipes, the number of servings indicated are child-size portions, and these recipes can be adapted for single servings as needed. Some teachers like to use prepared mixes for foods such as gingerbread, pancakes, and muffins in order to simplify the individual cooking procedures. (For example, the teacher can make illustrated directions, like those on page 288 using gingerbread mix, to measure out three tablespoons mix into a cup, add one tablespoon water, stir, and bake in an electric frypan for fifteen minutes.) Ideally, however, the child should be learning good nutrition and preparing healthful foods while learning to cook by himself or herself. Thus, the use of prepared mixes should be kept to a minimum.

As much as possible, projects should be planned and presented so that the children may do the measuring, pouring, sifting, cracking of eggs, cutting, peeling, kneading, and mixing. This means preplanning and anticipating the needs of the children on the part of the teacher. If possible, try recipes at home before using them in the classroom. You may find it most useful to measure the dry ingredients in advance and to place only the amount needed in front of the children. You may also find it less distracting to limit the number of children for certain kinds of activities, selecting those who are more independent to help those who are less experienced. Cleanup should be part of the planning. Children enjoy wiping, sweeping, and washing, and they will participate in these activities as readily as in the cooking if you provide for their involvement by having small brooms, sponges, and aprons handy and by putting soapy water in a sink or basin that the children can reach. Other helpful suggestions to keep in mind are:

1. Preplan the steps of a cooking project and discuss the plans with the children before beginning. They should be clear about what they are expected to do, and what the adults will do, before the cooking materials are made available to them.
2. Identify children with food allergies. Post a list of the names of children who are allergic, along with the foods they cannot eat. Some of the more common substances to which preschoolers are allergic are milk and milk products, juices with high acid content (such as orange and grapefruit), chocolate, eggs, nuts, food additives, wheat, and food coloring.

3. Never let children stand on chairs to reach the top of the stove. Adults should do the cooking over burners. Turn pot handles away from the stove edge. Whenever possible, use electric fry pans or pots on a table at the child's level, so he or she can help with the cooking. Be sure to remind children that these utensils are hot. (See Illustration 7.1.)
4. Limit the number of children to avoid crowding and to allow for adequate participation by each child.
5. Use low work tables and chairs.
6. Use unbreakable equipment whenever possible.
7. Have enough tools and utensils for the children.
8. Have only the necessary tools, utensils, and ingredients at the work table. Remove all other materials as soon as they are no longer needed.
9. Have the children use blunt knives or serrated plastic knives for

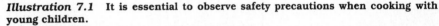

Illustration 7.1 **It is essential to observe safety precautions when cooking with young children.**

Dear Parents:
DID YOU KNOW THAT . . .

1. almost 90 percent of the mothers in a survey reported that they let their five- to seven-year-old children select the breakfast cereal?
2. television program content can have a negative effect on children's behavior?
3. watching aggressive and violent programs tends to increase aggressive behavior in young children?
4. as many as two-thirds of the commercials associated with children's TV programs are for sugared snacks?

HOW CAN WE IMMUNIZE OUR CHILDREN AGAINST TV COMMERCIALS?

What we plan to do at school:

1. The teachers are going to help the children identify commercials on TV.
2. We are going to talk about commercials and why the cereal and snack food companies show them.
3. We are going to let children test the claims that some TV ads make about certain products.
4. We will present our own "commercials" for nutritious foods — fresh fruits, vegetables, dairy products.

What you can do at home:

1. Watch TV with your children. See if they can tell the difference between a commercial and the program.
2. Show them that what they see is not always what they get.
3. Teach them what is good for their teeth and what is bad for their teeth.
4. Reinforce what we are doing at school and *share your good ideas with us.*

Illustration 7.2   A sample note you can send home to parents

cutting cooked eggs, potatoes, bananas, and so on. Use vegetable peelers only after demonstrating and supervise the children carefully.

10. Allow plenty of time for discussing, looking at, touching, tasting, and comparing. Use every step in the cooking project as an opportunity for the children to expand their learning.
11. Long hair should be pulled back and fastened. Floppy clothing and cumbersome jackets should be removed. Aprons, although not essential, are helpful.
12. Hands should be washed before children begin on the project.
13. Inexperienced children should begin with simple recipes that involve little cooking.
14. Be very cautious when serving or preparing foods that might cause choking, especially nuts, raw carrots, celery, and popcorn. Children should always sit down to eat. Remind them to chew food thoroughly.

Healthful Foods

▶ **PURPOSE** **To learn what the body needs to be healthy**

MATERIALS — Flannelboard
— Pictures of fruits, vegetables, and whole grains
— Pictures of processed foods that are high in sugar, salt, and fats
— Pictures of dairy products, such as milk, eggs, cheese, and yogurt

PROCEDURE
1. Talk about healthful foods such as fresh fruits, fresh vegetables, and grains.
2. Talk about how the body needs these foods to stay healthy and to grow.
3. Show milk products and explain that these foods supply calcium for strong bones and healthy teeth. Point out that some children cannot eat milk products because they are allergic, so they have to get calcium from other foods like leafy green vegetables.
4. Show pictures of processed foods, such as candy, sodas, potato chips, fried potatoes, and hot dogs.
5. Explain that these foods do not help the body to grow and be healthy.
6. Divide the flannel board to display healthful foods on one side and processed foods on the other. (See Illustration 7.3.)

Illustration 7.3   **Flannelboard with food illustrations**

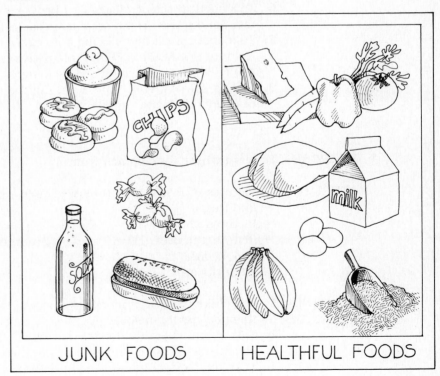

JUNK FOODS   HEALTHFUL FOODS

7. Hold one picture up at a time and ask:
Does your body need this to be healthy?
Let volunteers place each picture on the proper side of the board.
8. Ask children to cut out and bring other pictures to share.

DISCUSSION   Explain that eating too much sugar can hurt the teeth and make a person unhealthy. Eating too much salt and fried or fatty foods is harmful to the heart. People should eat foods that help keep them healthy and not eat if they are not hungry. The body and heart have to work extra hard when a person eats more than he or she needs.

▶ **PURPOSE**   **To identify fresh foods**

MATERIALS   — Variety of fresh fruits and vegetables, such as an orange, apple, pear, zucchini, squash, potato, lettuce, broccoli
— Canned and frozen foods, such as frozen orange juice, frozen vegetables, and canned fruits

PROCEDURE   **1.** Show each food item and ask the children to identify it.
2. Give children time to talk about the foods they eat.
3. Talk about fresh foods and how they grow.
4. Show one item at a time and ask if that food is fresh. Ask how they know (it is not wrapped in a package or in a can).
5. Explain that fresh foods have to be washed carefully before they are cooked or eaten because they have been sprayed with chemicals that kill bugs.
6. Talk about processed foods and how they have to be handled much more and often need more chemicals in them to preserve them.
7. Talk about fresh foods being better for their bodies.
8. Hold up one fresh food and one processed food in each hand and ask children to tell you which is better to eat.
9. Visit a grocery store and have children identify fresh and processed foods.

▶ **PURPOSE**   **To learn where food comes from**

MATERIALS   — Pictures of foods, including vegetables, meat, fish, seeds, grains, and fruits
— Pictures showing how these foods grow in their natural habitat (fish in the ocean, fruit trees in an orchard, animals on a farm, and so on)
— Flannelboard

PROCEDURE   **1.** Ask children to identify the pictures of various foods as you place them on the flannelboard.
2. Talk about where the foods come from.
3. Match the foods up with pictures of their natural habitat.
4. Take the children on a field trip to an orchard or a farm.
5. Grow some of the foods from seeds.

DISCUSSION   Talk about the amount of time, labor, water, and energy required to produce foods. Discuss waste and how children might help avoid throwing food away.

Read these books and talk about them with the children:

— *The Carrot Seed* by Ruth Krauss (New York: Harper & Row, 1945)
— *More Potatoes* by Millicent Selsam (New York: Harper & Row, 1972)
— *Apples* by Nonny Hogrogian (New York: Macmillan, 1972)

▶ **PURPOSE   To learn about vegetables and how to grow them**

MATERIALS   Select one or more from the following:

— root foods (potatoes, carrots, beets, onions, radishes, turnips)
— stem foods (asparagus, celery, rhubarb)
— leafy foods (lettuce, spinach, cabbage)
— flowers (broccoli, cauliflower, artichokes)

PROCEDURE   **1.** Show one food at a time from each group.
2. Talk about each food and how the children like to eat them (raw, cooked in dishes).
3. Let children select one or two vegetables from each group and buy seeds to plant them.
4. Discuss how the seeds will grow and what they need to grow (water, plant food, removal of weeds, protection from bugs).
5. Ask children to tell what they think the plant will look like, and whether it will grow above or below the ground.
6. As each plant grows and is ready for harvesting, have children examine the vegetable, tell how it grows, and name the part that they eat (the root, stem, leaves or flowers).
7. Remind children that there are many poisonous leaves and flowers and they should not eat plants without permission.

HELPFUL HINTS

1. Children will take a more active interest in this project if each child is assigned to a particular plant. Put the child's picture on a post next to the plant.
2. Let children help prepare their vegetable to eat after harvesting.

▶ **PURPOSE   To learn about seeds**

MATERIALS   — Seeds: pumpkin, poppy, sesame, sunflower, corn, fresh string beans, peas in the pod, and peanuts in the shell

PROCEDURE   **1.** Show a variety of seeds.
2. Let the children examine them, name them, and eat them.
3. Read a story such as *The Carrot Seed* by Ruth Krauss (New York:

Harper & Row, 1945) and talk about how new plants come from seeds.

4. Plant some of the seeds and watch them grow.

DISCUSSION Seeds are very nutritious. They contain many important vitamins, minerals, and protein to help bodies grow strong and healthy.

HELPFUL HINT

Make peanut butter, toast pumpkin seeds, and make sesame sticks (see "Cooking Activities").

Cooking Activities

Table of Equivalent Measures

1 teaspoon	= 60 drops
1 tablespoon	= 3 teaspoons
⅛ cup	= 2 tablespoons
¼ cup	= 4 tablespoons
⅓ cup	= 5⅓ tablespoons
½ cup	= 8 tablespoons
1 cup	= 16 tablespoons
1 lb. margarine/butter (4 sticks)	= 2 cups
	2 sticks = 1 cup = 16 tablespoons
	1 stick = ½ cup = 8 tablespoons
1 medium egg	= 4 tablespoons (for easier measuring, add 1 teaspoon water and mix well)

Metric Conversion

1 teaspoon	= 5 ml	¼ cup	= 60 ml
⅛ teaspoon	= .6 ml	⅓ cup	= 80 ml
¼ teaspoon	= 1.2 ml	½ cup	= 120 ml
½ teaspoon	= 2.5 ml	¾ cup	= 180 ml
1 tablespoon	= 15 ml	⅔ cup	= 160 ml
½ tablespoon	= 7.5 ml	1 cup	= 240 ml

QUICK BREADS

Play Dough Biscuits

2 cups whole wheat pastry flour, sifted
3¾ teaspoons baking powder

1 teaspoon salt
⅓ cup oil
¾ cup milk

Let children measure and sift dry ingredients. Stir in liquids gradually, and mix lightly. Using as little flour as possible on the table top, let children knead and roll out dough about ¼" thick. Cut to any desired size or shape. Cook in lightly greased electric fry pan on top of table on low heat. Let biscuits brown and rise. Turn and cook on other side. (Packaged refrigerated biscuits also cook up nicely.) Children tend to over-handle the dough at first, but soon learn to knead lightly. Makes about 20 small biscuits.

Quick Bread

3¾ cups whole wheat flour
¼ cup wheat germ
1 cup molasses
2 cups buttermilk or plain yogurt

2 teaspoons soda
pinch of salt
raisins and chopped dates (optional)

Preheat oven to 375°. Mix all ingredients together. Bake in one large or several small greased loaf pans for 30–40 minutes.

HELPFUL HINT

Use cookie cutters to cut bread into different shapes (hearts on Valentine's Day, for example). Spread with butter, mayonnaise, peanut butter, or egg salad. Supply the children with small containers of raisins, alfalfa sprouts, shredded carrots, and so on, to create eyes, nose, hair, and mouth for their sandwiches.

Brown Bread

¾ cup flour
1¼ teaspoons soda
¾ teaspoon salt
1 cup graham cracker crumbs, finely crushed
3 tablespoons shortening
1 egg

1 cup buttermilk (or 1 cup milk to which 1 teaspoon vinegar or lemon juice has been added)
½ cup molasses
½ cup raisins

Preheat oven to 400°. Sift flour, soda, and salt. Add graham cracker crumbs. Blend in shortening until texture is like meal. In a separate bowl mix remaining ingredients; combine with dry mixture. Spoon into two well-greased #303 cans. Bake for 35 minutes. Test for doneness with knife blade. Cool in cans for about 10 minutes before slicing. Serve with cream cheese.

Steamed Monk's Bread

1 cup corn meal or corn flour	2 tablespoons wheat germ
1 cup whole wheat flour	1 teaspoon baking powder
¼ cup soy flour	1 egg
¼ cup bran (moistened with water)	1 tablespoon honey
	1 cup buttermilk

Mix all dry ingredients together. Mix egg, honey, and milk together and add to dry mixture. Stir until well-blended. Shape into a round loaf. Line the bottom of a steamer with wax paper or banana leaves. Steam loaf over high flame for 20 minutes. Serve warm.

Note: This is an excellent recipe for making bread without an oven. Children can participate in every part of the preparation.

Graham Crackers

1 cup graham flour	¼ cup vegetable oil
1 cup whole wheat flour	1 banana, sliced
½ teaspoon baking soda	1 teaspoon vanilla
¼ cup apple juice concentrate (unsweetened)	1 teaspoon cinnamon

Stir the graham flour, whole wheat flour, and baking soda together in a large bowl. Blend the remaining ingredients in a blender (or beat thoroughly with an egg beater). Add to the dry ingredients and mix well. Divide the dough in half and let the children roll each half out with a rolling pin on a floured surface. Roll to the thickness of a cracker. Poke the dough with a fork and cut into 2″ squares. Bake on a nonstick cookie sheet at 350° for 6–8 minutes. Makes 3 dozen.

Tortillas

⅔ cup warm water	1 cup Masa Harina (corn flour)

Gradually stir water into Masa Harina until the dough can be worked into a smooth ball. Let children take a small handful of mix, form into a ball, and roll into a circle with a rolling pin or by hand (or use a tortilla press). Bake about 2 minutes on a hot griddle, turning frequently. Eat with butter and a little salt. These tortillas are also delicious with grated cheese.

Muffins

2 cups whole wheat flour, sifted	¼ cup molasses
¼ cup wheat germ	1 cup milk
1 tablespoon baking powder	1 egg, beaten
½ teaspoon salt	¼ cup melted shortening

Preheat oven to 400°. Combine dry ingredients. Combine milk and egg. Stir into dry ingredients. Add shortening and stir lightly. Batter should still have lumps. Fill greased muffin tins about ¾ full. Bake 10–15 minutes. Makes 2 dozen small muffins or 1 dozen regular size.

HELPFUL HINTS

1. Wash hands before and after a cooking project.
2. Keep all cooking utensils clean.
3. Children and teachers with colds should not help with food preparation.

Popovers

4 eggs
2 cups milk
2 tablespoons oil (or melted butter)

2 cups flour
1 teaspoon salt

Preheat oven to 475°. Beat eggs well with egg beater or wire whisk. Add milk and oil; mix well. Sift dry ingredients together; add liquid mixture gradually. Beat until smooth. Fill well-greased muffin tins ⅓ full. Bake for 15 minutes. Reduce heat to 350° and continue baking for 20–25 minutes. Makes approximately 24 popovers. Serve with butter or honey.

Note: An oven with a glass door allows children to watch the batter rise.

HELPFUL HINTS

Substituting foods:

1. Remove 2 tablespoons of coarse ground flour for every cup of white flour. Omit sifting.
2. ¾ cup of honey = 1 cup sugar; reduce liquid in recipe by ¼ cup for every cup of honey used.
3. In recipes that call for no liquid and where crispness is important, add 4 tablespoons additional flour for every cup of honey.
4. When using honey, reduce baking temperature by 25°.
5. Three tablespoons of carob powder plus 2 tablespoons of water or milk = one square of chocolate.

French Toast

2 eggs
¼ cup milk
½ teaspoon vanilla
1 teaspoon grated orange or lemon rind (optional)

1 tablespoon butter
4 slices bread

Beat eggs, milk, vanilla, and rind together. Heat butter in frying pan (an electric fry pan at the table works well). Have egg mixture in a shallow flat dish. Cut bread in half, soak in mixture, and brown on both sides. Serve with butter or a little warm applesauce.

Pancakes

**2 cups whole wheat or un-
  bleached white flour**
3 teaspoons baking powder
¼ cup toasted wheat germ

2 eggs
1¼ cups milk
¼ cup melted shortening

Let children measure and sift together flour and baking powder. Stir in wheat germ. Beat eggs; stir in milk. Combine with dry ingredients. Mix until smooth, but do not overmix. Add melted shortening. Grease and heat electric fry pan at the table. Drop batter by spoonful on hot pan (medium high heat). When bubbles appear on the surface, the pancake is ready to be turned. Serve hot with melted butter and syrup or honey. Makes 3 dozen small pancakes.

Note: Let children vary the recipe by selecting other ingredients to add to the batter, such as blueberries, chopped nuts, diced apples, or raisins. This is also a good opportunity to introduce children to different toppings. Suggest that they put a dab of sour cream and brown sugar on a bite of pancake, or try fresh fruit with yogurt. In this way children learn that certain foods do not always have to be prepared in exactly the same way. They can experiment with different tastes in small portions and discover the fun of creating their own recipes.

A good storybook to read before this cooking project is *Pancakes, Pancakes!* by Eric Carle (New York: Alfred A. Knopf, 1970). Bright collage-type illustrations show where the flour, eggs, milk, and butter come from; text explains how to cook pancakes.

Pancakes — Cup Cooking or Individual Portions

1. Wash hands.
2. Take one bowl.
3. Measure 10 tablespoons flour into bowl.
4. Measure 1 teaspoon baking powder into bowl.
5. Measure 1 tablespoon wheat germ into bowl.
6. Stir and mix all the dry ingredients well.
7. Add 3 tablespoons egg.
8. Add ⅓ cup milk.
9. Add 1 tablespoon melted butter.
10. Mix until smooth.
11. Ask the teacher to help drop batter into hot fry pan.

Note to teacher: In "cup cooking," or individual portion cooking, each step is illustrated on a separate card, and the card is placed next to the appropriate materials or ingredients. Cards and accompanying materials and ingredients are arranged in numbered sequence, and the child is instructed to follow each in turn, matching what he or she is doing to the picture on the card.

Illustrations 7.4 and 7.5 depict this procedure. Illustration 7.4 shows an example of the actual cards that would be used; Illustration 7.5 represents a child following all the steps to make a chef's salad. Although chef's salad is shown here, the kind of cards used and the process shown apply equally well to the pancakes recipe above or to any of a number of other recipes.

Refer to the Table of Equivalent Measures at the beginning of this section to prepare ingredients for individual measurements.

SPREADS

Butter

whipping cream   salt

Shake cream in jars or beat with egg beater until butter forms. Rinse with water and press out excess milk with spoon. Serve sweet or add salt to taste. Serve with sour dough French bread or soda crackers.

Peanut Butter

2 cups roasted peanuts, in the   2 tablespoons salad oil
   shell

Let children shell the peanuts (be sure there are enough extra for them to eat). Put peanuts through a grinder or blender. If a hand-style meat grinder is used, you may want to put the peanuts through twice. Add oil.

HELPFUL HINTS

1. Cut out pictures of healthful foods — fresh fruits, vegetables, dairy products, meat, fish, and poultry — and post them for the children to see.
2. Invite community workers, such as the doctor, nutritionist, and dentist, to visit the school and talk about proper diet.
3. Plan parent meetings with speakers from the consumer protection agency. Discuss sensible food purchasing and meal planning.
4. Avoid prepackaged convenience foods; use recipes that call for natural, unrefined ingredients.
5. Try substituting honey for sugar and whole grains for refined flour.
6. Read books on good nutrition.

Illustration 7.4 **Individual portion cooking cards**

Honey Butter Spread

two parts butter   **dash of cinnamon** (optional)
one part honey

Stir until well mixed. Serve with hot biscuits.

SALADS

Fruit Salad

Invite parents to contribute whatever fresh local fruits are available that children can bring to school. In addition, have on hand fruits such as bananas, apples, oranges, fresh pineapple, peaches, pears, melons, strawberries, mangoes, papayas, seedless grapes, and tangerines. Whenever possible, try to introduce some less common varieties of fruits along with the familiar ones. In season, use a variety of melons and berries for a colorful and delicious mixture.

Illustration 7.5 **Child following individual portion cooking cards to make a chef's salad**

Let children help peel bananas and oranges, wash grapes, and cut the fruit with blunt or serrated knives. A mixture of plain or flavored yogurt with a tablespoon or two of honey makes a delicious topping. Some children may prefer to eat the fruit salad without topping.

Preparation of a "community" fruit salad is an excellent social occasion for adults as well as children. This should be an unhurried, relaxed project with plenty of time for discussion about colors, contrasts, taste, and how different fruits grow. Some of the adults might be responsible for looking up information about the various fruits (such as how and where they grow) before the salad preparation. Learning can be reinforced by collecting and posting pictures of the fruit and letting the children identify and talk about them.

Carrot-Apple-Pineapple Salad

½ lb. celery
6 medium carrots
juice of 2 lemons
2 apples, peeled or unpeeled
1 large orange
2 pineapple rings, cut up, or ¾
    cup pineapple bits

⅓ cup raisins
½ cup chopped nuts (walnuts,
    pecans, or almonds)
½ cup whipping cream
1 tablespoon honey

Wash and scrape celery and carrots. Shred finely. Shred or dice the apples and sprinkle with lemon juice. Peel and dice the orange. Add pineapple, raisins, and nuts. Whip the cream, fold in honey, and stir into salad mixture.

This is a good opportunity for children to practice shredding. Be careful that they do not get their fingers too close to the shredder. Adults should finish the shredding while children cut the fruit and prepare the dressing. Makes 12–14 small servings.

HELPFUL HINTS

1. Give each child a serving of cottage cheese or yogurt. Supply containers of fresh fruit, such as small pieces of pineapple, banana, grapes, pears, oranges, and apples. Let each child select fruits of his or her choice to stir into the cottage cheese.
2. Avoid foods that spoil rapidly. Keep sauces, meats, and dairy products refrigerated.
3. Serve cheese, raw vegetables, and fresh fruits for snacks.
4. Save pumpkin seeds from your jack-o'-lantern. Soak them in salt water, then toast in oven.

COOKING ACTIVITIES · Salads

COOKING ACTIVITIES · Salads   291

Carrot Salad

4 medium carrots
⅓ cup raisins
½ cup pineapple bits
sunflower or sesame seeds (optional)

6 tablespoons plain yogurt
2 teaspoons honey
juice of ½ lemon

Wash and scrape carrots. Shred finely with a grater. Add raisins, pineapple, and seeds. Stir honey and lemon juice into the yogurt. Mix thoroughly with carrots. Makes 8 servings.

Sprouts

alfalfa seeds
mung beans
soy beans

large glass jar
cheesecloth

Soak about one teaspoonful of alfalfa seeds or small handful of soy or mung beans overnight in a jar of warm water. Drain. Cover top of jar with cheesecloth and secure with a rubber band. Put the jar on its side in a dark place or inside an open paper bag. Rinse and drain well three times a day for three days. On the fourth day, place the jar in direct sunlight to develop chlorophyll (sprouts will turn green). When sprouts are green, wash and eat with sandwiches and salads.

Note: Mung and soy beans will take two or three days longer to sprout. Sprouting kits are available from Sprouts Are Good, 226 Hamilton Ave., Palo Alto, CA 94301.

Sprout Salad

4 cups mixed sprouts (mung bean, alfalfa, soy)
2 small carrots, shredded
1 apple, pared, cored, and shredded

½ cup sunflower seeds
½ cup raisins
½ cup plain yogurt
1 tablespoon honey
juice of ½ lemon

Combine sprouts, carrots, apple, seeds, and raisins in a salad bowl. Mix yogurt, honey, and lemon juice together. Toss with salad. Makes 12 servings.

Cinco de Mayo Salad

1 head lettuce
1 lb. cheddar cheese
2 tomatoes
1 red onion
1 package corn chips (6–8 oz.)
1 lb. lean hamburger

1 small package of taco seasoning mix (1¼ oz.)
1 large can red kidney beans, rinsed and drained
1 bottle creamy thousand island dressing (12 oz.)

Shred lettuce, grate cheese, cut up tomatoes, chop onion, and crumble the corn chips. Sauté hamburger together with taco seasoning. Mix all ingredients in a large salad bowl and toss with dressing. Avocados, mushrooms, and a dash of hot sauce can also be added if desired. Serves 25–30. (This was voted the favorite salad by parents and children at a Cinco de Mayo potluck supper.)

HELPFUL HINTS

1. In selecting a cooking project, list all the possibilities it provides children for learning concepts through active involvement (washing, scrubbing, peeling, cutting, comparing, learning about shapes, textures, colors). (See Illustration 7.6.)
2. Keep cooking projects simple. Shelling peas, shucking corn, and washing vegetables are educational and fun activities.
3. Help children plant a vegetable garden to provide food for cooking projects.
4. Very young children can help wash vegetables, scrub potatoes, tear lettuce, and shell peas.
5. Older children can help grate, measure, beat, and grind.
6. Adults should do the sharp cutting and the more difficult peeling.
7. Make vegetable kabobs by cutting a variety of vegetables into squares, triangles, and circles.
8. Serve fresh orange sections with green leafy vegetables. Vitamin C from the fruit helps increase iron absorption.

Raggedy Ann Salad

peach or pear halves, fresh or canned	**pimento**
	cheese
celery or carrot sticks	**carrots or red cabbage shredded**
cottage cheese	**lettuce leaves**
raisins or prunes	

Give each child a peach or pear half and a scoop of cottage cheese. Set out the other ingredients on the table in muffin tins, so children can create their own Raggedy Ann salad. (The body is the fruit half, with cottage cheese scoop for the head. Arms and legs are celery or carrot sticks; raisins or prunes make the eyes, nose, shoes, and buttons. Use the shredded cheese, carrots, or cabbage for the hair and the lettuce leaf for the skirt.)

Illustration 7.6 **Ask children to use vegetable peelers only after you have demonstrated—and supervise the children carefully.**

Chinese Workingman's Salad[2]

4 cups bean sprouts (about ½ pound)
2 cups cooked chicken, shredded
3 cups lettuce, shredded
½ cup coriander, chopped (Chinese parsley)
⅓ cup toasted sesame seeds

¼ cup sesame oil
4½ tablespoons vinegar
2 tablespoons soy sauce
½ teaspoon salt
¼ teaspoon five fragrant spices (available in Oriental food stores)

Combine the first five ingredients in a salad bowl. Mix the remaining ingredients and pour over the salad. Toss lightly and serve. Serves 25–30.

Note: Five fragrant spices is a cocoa-colored powder consisting of a blend of star anise, cloves, fennel, anise pepper, and cinnamon. Let the children sniff the fragrant spices and experience a new taste when it is mixed with the salad.

[2]From Karen Croft, *Good for Me Cookbook* (Palo Alto, Calif.: R & E Research, 1971). The author says: "My mother developed this recipe from a dream she had. In her dream she was eating a delicious salad and its name, oddly enough, was Chinese Workingman's Salad. Luckily she remembered the ingredients and we've enjoyed the salad ever since." Reprinted by permission.

Cottage Cheese

1 quart milk
2 tablespoons vinegar

sour cream (optional)
fruit

Heat milk until bubbles begin to form (it should feel hot to the touch). Remove from heat and stir in vinegar, continuing to stir while mixture cools and curd forms. Hold a strainer over a glass bowl and separate the curds from the liquid (whey). Gently press the curds with a wooden spoon to further squeeze out the whey. Add a little sour cream for smoothness. Serve the curds (cottage cheese) with fresh fruit.

HELPFUL HINT

To hard-cook eggs for easier peeling, put the eggs in cold water and add a pinch of salt. Bring water to a boil, then reduce heat and simmer for 15 minutes. Immediately immerse the eggs in cold water. To make peeling easier, crack the eggs all over and roll each egg gently between palms of hands to loosen the shell.

Potato Salad

4–6 medium sized potatoes, boiled
2 hard-cooked eggs

1 can pitted olives
½ cup mayonnaise
salt and pepper to taste (optional)

Let children peel and dice the potatoes and eggs. Cut olives into small pieces. Mix all ingredients together. (Other ingredients, such as green pepper, tuna, celery, and onions, can be added.) Makes 12–15 small servings.

Note: This is a good recipe for beginners because the ingredients are easy to peel and cut. Serrated knives work well in this project. Children who have never been allowed to cut with knives enjoy the success they have with cutting potatoes. The salad is made fairly quickly and the children can taste the results without having to wait.

Macaroni Salad

2 cups macaroni, uncooked
3–4 hard-cooked eggs
½ cup celery, diced
½ cup pitted olives
1½ cups cheddar cheese, shredded

6 radishes
small bunch of parsley
½ cup mayonnaise
salt and pepper to taste (optional)

Cook and drain macaroni according to directions on package. Let children peel and cut the eggs, dice the celery and olives, and shred the cheese. Adults can slice radishes and chop parsley. Mix all ingredients with mayonnaise. Season with salt and pepper to taste. Makes 15–20 small servings.

EGGS

Scrambled Eggs

6 eggs
⅓ cup milk

½ teaspoon salt (optional)
2 tablespoons butter

Break eggs into large bowl. Beat with egg beater; add milk and salt. Melt butter in an electric fry pan placed on the table so children can help with the cooking. Set temperature of pan at low so eggs will cook slowly. Pour mixture into the pan and use wooden spoons or spatula to pull cooked egg away from the sides of the pan. Have the children stir and move the mixture around so the uncooked portions get cooked. Eat immediately. Makes 10 small servings.

HELPFUL HINTS

1. Provide a variety of other ingredients for children to add to their eggs, such as shrimp, mushrooms, onions, cheese.
2. Children who are experienced in cracking eggs can use this activity to practice separating the yolk from the white since making a mistake won't matter.
3. Discuss other ways eggs are cooked — poaching, baking, hard and soft cooking, frying sunny side up, and so on — and what happens to the whites and yolks. What is an egg? What can it grow into?

Deviled Eggs

6 hard-cooked eggs
3 tablespoons mayonnaise

1 teaspoon prepared mustard
celery salt

Peel and cut eggs in half lengthwise. Let children remove yolks and mash with mayonnaise, mustard, and celery salt to taste. Let children stuff the whites with small spoons or forks or with cake decorators. Eggs can be decorated with sprigs of parsley, stuffed olives, or paprika.

Egg Foo Yung

⅓ cup raw carrots, finely cut
⅓ cup celery, finely cut
⅓ cup fresh garden peas
4 eggs

¼ cup diced scallions or green onions
½ teaspoon salt (optional)
oil for cooking

Combine and cook carrots, celery, and peas in the smallest amount of water necessary (about ⅓ cup water in a covered pan for about 5 minutes or less). Drain. Break eggs into a bowl and beat with an egg beater. Add scallions, salt, and cooked vegetables. Pour enough cooking oil into electric fry pan just to coat. Turn heat to medium. Spoon in egg mixture to make small pancake-sized egg foo yung. Cook until top is nearly firm. Turn with a spatula and cook on other side for another minute or two. Makes 16 small pancakes.

Note: This recipe can be varied to suit the needs of the teacher and children. Cooked diced ham, chicken, or shrimp can be added; bean sprouts or diced bell peppers can also be substituted in order to let the children taste new foods.

RICE AND GRAINS

Steamed Rice

2 cups brown rice   **3 cups water**

Put rice into a large pot and add water. Cover pan with tight-fitting lid. Cook rice on high heat until most of the water is cooked away. Turn heat down as low as possible and steam the rice for about 25 minutes. Fluff rice with a fork before serving. Children like rice with butter and salt. Makes 20 servings.

Note: Wheat berries cooked along with the rice adds a delicious contrasting texture. Use about ¼ cup.

HELPFUL HINTS

1. Sit down and eat with the children. Show them that you enjoy food.
2. Talk about different kinds of foods.
3. Notice whether young children are influenced in their eating habits by TV commercials.
4. Offer new foods more than once.
5. Send notes home about good nutrition and the new foods each child has helped prepare in school.
6. Invite parents to share their recipes with the school.

Fried Rice

2 eggs
2 green onions (scallions)
½ cup cooked meat such as pork, beef, chicken

4 cups cooked rice (leftover day-old rice is best)
2–3 tablespoons soy sauce

Scramble two eggs and set aside. Clean and dice green onions, stems and all. Add to diced cooked meat and stir-fry meat and onions until heated through. Set aside. Heat two tablespoons oil in fry pan and add cooked rice. Stir and cook until rice is heated through. If rice is very dry, you may need to add a little water and cover the pan in order to thoroughly heat the rice. Add all other ingredients, including soy sauce. Stir until meat, onions, and eggs are evenly distributed. Serve with extra soy sauce. Makes 10–12 servings.

Chicken Soup with Rice

2 cups chicken stock   **tofu** (optional)
½ cup cooked brown rice

Bring chicken stock to boil; add ½ cup rice (more or less as desired). A good way to introduce tofu is to cut a small piece of tofu into tiny squares and simmer along with the rice for 5 minutes. Makes 4 small servings.

HELPFUL HINT

Read Maurice Sendak's *Chicken Soup with Rice* (New York: Harper & Row, 1962) to the children.

Osushi

2 cups short grain rice   **½ teaspoon salt**
2 cups water   **grated carrot, peas, mushrooms**
¼ cup white vinegar   (optional)
2 tablespoons sugar

Wash and cook rice as in Steamed Rice recipe. Meanwhile, make sushi su (vinegar) by boiling together vinegar, sugar, and salt. When rice is cooked, pour it into a flat pan and spread it out. Pour sushi su over the rice. Cool immediately by fanning. Let children form the rice into balls about the size of an egg. Bits of grated carrot, peas, mushrooms, or other vegetables can be added for color and variety. Makes 24 small servings.

Oatmeal

1 cup water   **⅛ teaspoon ground ginger**
1 cup unsweetened apple juice   **1 cup oatmeal or other whole**
½ teaspoon cinnamon   **grain cereal**

Combine water, apple juice, and spices. Bring to a boil. Stir in cereal. Cook for one minute, continuing to stir. Reduce heat and stir occasionally until liquid is absorbed. (If desired, add raisins, bananas, dates, or chopped fruits in season.) Makes 6 small servings.

Note: Different types of cereals require different cooking times. Follow directions on the package.

Muesli

1½ cups rolled oats (uncooked)
1½ cups fruit juice
2 tablespoons wheat germ
½ cup dried fruits, chopped fine
   (apricots, raisins, peaches,
   pears, apples, prunes)

½ cup chopped toasted almonds
   (optional)
1 tablespoon honey
2 tart apples, peeled, cored, and
   shredded

Combine oats and juice in a large bowl. Cover and refrigerate 8 hours or more. Before serving, add wheat germ, fruits, nuts, and honey. Stir well. Top with freshly shredded apples and serve with milk or cream if desired. Makes 8–10 servings.

Note: Children can help with most of the preparation.

MEATS

Meatballs

1 lb. ground beef
½ cup bread crumbs
½ cup canned milk
1 egg

¼ cup wheat germ and powdered
   milk (optional)
seasonings to taste

Mix all ingredients together and form into small balls. Cook in a lightly greased electric fry pan at the table, browning meatballs on all sides. Serve plain or with hot noodles and a simple tomato sauce with Italian seasoning. Makes about 2 dozen small meatballs.

Pasties

1 lb. raw turkey, ground (ground
   chicken or beef can be substituted; or use cooked,
   ground-up leftover meats)
1 cup onions, finely chopped
   (combine with a few green
   onions for color)
½ cup wheat germ (plain or
   toasted)
3–4 cloves garlic, crushed
1 teaspoon salt
½ teaspoon pepper

1 teaspoon oregano
4 packages refrigerator biscuits
   (8 oz. each)
grated cheese (sharp cheddar
   and parmesan work well)
grated carrots, chopped eggs,
   mushrooms, cooked potatoes, chopped parsley (optional)
1 egg
1 teaspoon water

Preheat oven to 375°. Mix together first seven ingredients and stir-fry over high to medium heat until cooked through. (Drain off grease if you substitute beef or other fatty meat.) Let cool. Prepare plates of cheese and other optional ingredients. Let children roll out or flatten individual biscuits (use a little flour if necessary). Each child can spoon a small amount of meat (about 1 teaspoon) onto a biscuit and add optional ingredients as desired. Moisten edges of biscuit dough with water and pinch together with fingers or tines of fork into crescent shapes. When ready to bake, place pasties on a lightly greased cookie sheet and brush each with a mixture of 1 egg beaten with 1 teaspoon water. Perforate with fork. Bake for 10–12 minutes. Cool slightly before eating. Makes 48 small pasties.

Teriyaki Meatballs

1 lb. ground beef
½ cup bread crumbs or cooked rice
½ teaspoon garlic puree

¼ cup soy sauce
¼ teaspoon powdered ginger
¼ cup water
1 tablespoon honey

Mix all ingredients together and form into small balls. Cook in a lightly greased electric fry pan at the table, browning meatballs on all sides. Serve with rice and soy sauce. Makes about 2 dozen small meatballs.

Won Ton

½ lb. lean pork, ground (raw turkey or chicken can be substituted)
2 green onions
¼ lb. raw shrimp
6–8 water chestnuts
1 tablespoon light soy sauce

¼ teaspoon ground ginger
2 teaspoons cornstarch
1 tablespoon water
1 package won ton skins
chicken broth (½ cup per serving)

Place pork in mixing bowl. Clean and finely chop green onions, including the green stems. Clean, devein, and finely chop raw shrimp. Chop water chestnuts. Add everything to the pork except the won ton skins and broth. Blend well. Place 1 teaspoon of meat mixture in the center of each won ton skin. To fold, bring up two sides of the skin to fold won ton in half. Dampen the edges with a little water to make the skin stick together. Pinch around the meat to seal it. Pull the two bottom edges together and pinch firmly to seal, using a little water if necessary. (See Illustration 7.7.) Cover won ton with a damp cloth to keep them from drying out. While children are wrapping the won ton, bring several quarts of water to boil in a large pot. Add the won ton. When water returns to a boil, add half a cup of cold water and let come to a boil again. The won ton are cooked when they float to the top. Heat chicken broth in a pot. To serve, place cooked won ton in a bowl and ladle broth over them. Chopped eggs and bits of cooked meat can be used for garnish. Makes about 50 won ton.

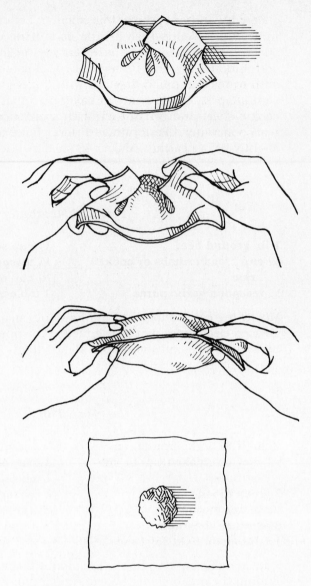

Illustration 7.7 **Folding and forming won ton**

Muffin Pizzas

1 teaspoon garlic salt	mozzarella cheese, ground beef,
1 teaspoon Italian seasoning	sausage, salami, onions, ol-
1 can tomato sauce (15 oz.)	ives, green pepper, mush-
8 English muffins (16 halves)	rooms

Preheat oven to 450°. Add garlic salt and Italian seasoning to tomato sauce and heat through. Toast muffins lightly. Spread sauce on each half and let children select ingredients to put on each pizza. Bake in hot (450°) oven until meat is cooked, or place under broiler for a few minutes.

VEGETABLES AND DIPS

Vegetable Soup

**variety of chopped vegetables:
carrots, potatoes, celery, tomatoes, onions, peas, beans
soup stock made with meat
bones or instant soup base
and water**[3]

alphabet noodles or rice (optional)
seasonings to taste

Plant a garden outdoors and have the children harvest the vegetables, or invite children to bring vegetables from home. Talk about colors, textures, and tastes while children help to wash, scrape, and peel the vegetables.

Make soup stock in pressure cooker or electric pan. Let children add their vegetables. Add a handful of alphabet noodles or rice if desired. Season with salt, oregano, herbs, and other spices to taste.

Glazed Carrots

**4 carrots
1 tablespoon butter
1 tablespoon brown sugar or
honey**

¼ cup water

Scrape and slice carrots into thin strips. Place in a large electric fry pan. Add mixture of butter, sugar or honey, and water. Cover and cook slowly, stirring occasionally until tender. Makes 6–8 servings.

Raw Vegetable Platter

Provide a variety of raw vegetables, such as carrots, tomatoes, bell peppers, radishes, celery, cauliflower, and cucumbers. Wash and cut into bite-size pieces. Arrange attractively on a platter at each lunch or juice table.

Introduce new foods such as fresh peeled water chestnuts, Jerusalem artichokes, and jicama.

Dilled Yogurt Dip

**1 cup low-fat yogurt
2 tablespoons vinegar
½ small yellow onion**

**½ teaspoon dill seeds
¼ teaspoon dry mustard
¼ teaspoon minced garlic**

Mix all ingredients and use as dip for fresh vegetables.

Talk about the different odors of the various ingredients. Discuss

---

[3] Another simple soup base can be made by browning lean hamburger with minced onion and adding tomato sauce, bouillon cubes, and water.

what each ingredient tastes like by itself and when mixed together. Ask the children if they can still detect the taste of the individual ingredients after they have been combined.

Buttermilk Dip

½ cup dry low-fat cottage cheese (sometimes known as Farmer's cheese)
4 cups shredded cheddar cheese
½ teaspoons nutmeg

2 cups buttermilk
1 clove crushed garlic
3 tablespoons cornstarch

Let children help shred the cheese. Mix the cottage cheese and cheddar cheese with cornstarch and nutmeg. Heat buttermilk with garlic over low heat until just hot to the touch. Add cheese mixture, stirring constantly until cheeses are melted. Serve warm as a dip for fresh vegetables or bite-size pieces of sour dough bread.

Latkes (Potato Pancakes)

2 medium potatoes
1 egg

¼ cup flour
1 teaspoon salt

Peel and grate the potatoes coarsely. Mix with lightly beaten egg, flour, and salt. Fry tablespoonful-size pancakes in hot vegetable oil. Brown on both sides. Serve with sour cream or applesauce. Makes 10–12 small latkes.

DESSERTS AND SNACKS

Coconut Apricot Candy

1 cup dried apricots (or pears)
½ cup nuts
½ teaspoon vanilla

1 cup shredded coconut
½ teaspoon grated orange rind
1 tablespoon lemon juice

Let children help wash the dried fruit. Steam the fruit for 5 minutes. Put apricots, coconut, and nuts through a food chopper. Add grated orange rind and lemon juice. Knead the mixture until well blended. Add small amounts of orange juice to moisten as necessary. Makes one dozen small candy balls.

Note: Be very certain children's hands and nails are scrubbed clean before they help with this project.

Natural Finger Jello

3 cups fruit juice (do not use pineapple)

4 packets plain gelatin

Pour half the fruit juice (1 ½) cups) into a medium-size bowl. Sprinkle gelatin over the juice. Let stand for 1 minute. Heat remainder of juice to boiling and add to first mixture, stirring until gelatin is completely dissolved. Pour into 9″ square baking pan and chill until firm. Cut into 1″ squares. This gelatin is firm enough for children to pick up the squares with their fingers.

Toasted Pumpkin Seeds

Save the seeds from the jack-o'-lantern pumpkin. Dip them in a solution of salt water (1 tablespoon salt in 1 ½ cups water). Drain and spread the seeds on an ungreased cookie sheet. Bake in a 350° oven. Stir to dry out and toast lightly on all sides. Show the children how to crack and eat the toasted seeds.

Mashed Pumpkin

Steam or bake pieces of the pumpkin until tender. Mash the cooked pumpkin and use for cookies.

Pumpkin Cookies

½ cup (1 stick) butter or margarine	½ teaspoon ginger
1 ¼ cups brown sugar	½ teaspoon cinnamon
2 eggs	½ teaspoon nutmeg
1 ½ cups cooked mashed pumpkin	2 ¼ cups flour, sifted
	4 teaspoons baking powder
½ teaspoon salt	1 cup raisins
	1 cup walnuts (optional)
	1 teaspoon vanilla extract

Preheat oven to 375°. Cream together butter and sugar. Add eggs, pumpkin, and seasonings. Mix well. Sift flour and baking powder together; stir in raisins and nuts. Add flour mixture slowly to creamed mixture and blend well. Stir in vanilla. Drop by the teaspoonful onto greased cookie sheets. Bake about 15 minutes or until lightly browned. Makes about 3 dozen cookies.

Puddle Cake

1 ½ cups unbleached white or whole wheat pastry flour, sifted	1 cup brown sugar
	1 teaspoon soda
	6 tablespoons salad oil
3 tablespoons cocoa (or carob powder)	1 teaspoon vanilla
	1 tablespoon vinegar
½ teaspoon salt	1 cup cold water

Preheat oven to 350°. Sift all dry ingredients into an ungreased 8″ x 8″ x 2″ pan. With a mixing spoon, make a well in the center of the pan. Make a puddle in the well by pouring the liquid ingredients into it. Stir with a spoon until the mixture is smooth. Bake 35–40 minutes. Serves 12–15.

Vegetable Cookies

2 cups flour
1½ teaspoons baking powder
¾ teaspoon salt
1½ teaspoons cinnamon
¼ teaspoon nutmeg
1 cup wheat germ
¾ cup butter or margarine
1 cup dark brown sugar, firmly
   packed

1 large egg
1 teaspoon vanilla
¾ cup milk
1 cup zucchini, finely grated, or
   1 cup carrots, grated
½ cup raisins

Preheat oven to 375°. Stir together all the dry ingredients. Cream butter and sugar; beat in egg and vanilla. Add flour mixture alternately with milk. Stir in vegetables and raisins. Drop by the teaspoonful onto lightly greased cookie sheets. Bake 12–14 minutes. Makes about 50 small cookies.

Melon Finger Food

1 ripe melon (cantaloupe, honeydew, or casaba)

Cut melon in half and remove all seeds. Cut halves into eighths and remove peel. Cut the meat into slices, sticks, or chunks. (A small melon scoop may be used to make melon balls.) Serves 8–10.

Applesauce

6 tart apples
1¼ cups water

3–4 tablespoons honey
cinnamon

Let children help peel, core, and slice the apples. Cover and cook in water until tender (approximately 20–30 minutes). Add honey and cinnamon to taste. Makes 12 small servings.

Baked Apple

one small apple for each child
variety of nuts

variety of dried fruits
honey

Remove apple cores to within ½ inch of the bottom of the apple. Let children select nuts and dried fruits to fill the hollow apples. Moisten with a small amount of honey and place the apples in a baking dish. Add water or fruit juice to a depth of ½″ to prevent sticking and promote steaming. Cover with foil and bake at 375° for 40 minutes or until tender. Serve warm or chilled.

Fruity Yogurt Pops

**1 cup fresh fruit, finely chopped
or crushed (strawberries,
raspberries, bananas,
peaches, or pineapple), or
1 can frozen orange juice
concentrate (12 oz.)**

**4 cups plain yogurt
honey** (optional)

Blend fruit with yogurt. (If fruit is tart, add honey to taste.) Pour into 3-oz. paper cups. Place popsicle stick in the center of each cup and freeze. Serves 15.

Yogurt Creamsicles

**6 ounces orange juice concen-
trate
1 cup plain yogurt
1 tablespoon honey**

**6 ounces water
1 tablespoon vanilla**

Blend all ingredients. Pour mixture into ice trays. When partially frozen, insert popsicle sticks and complete the freezing.

Celery Crunch

**1 stalk of celery
1 cup crunchy peanut butter
¼ cup coconut**

**⅓ cup Grape Nuts cereal
¼ cup wheat germ
dash nutmeg** (optional)

Trim and wash celery. Let children mix remaining ingredients, stuff the celery, and cut into bite-size pieces. This snack has a delicious, nutty flavor.

Apple Honey Nutters

**6 apples
½ cup crunchy peanut butter
¼ cup wheat germ**

**¼ cup nonfat dry milk
2 tablespoons honey**

Wash and core apples. Combine the remaining ingredients and stuff into the center of the apples. Slice into round pieces 1″ thick. Serves 12–18.

Sesame Sticks

**1 cup cornmeal
¼ cup wheat germ
4 tablespoons sesame seeds (the
brown seeds with hulls are
more nutritious than the
white)
2 teaspoons sea salt**

**3 teaspoons vegetable herb sea-
soning
3 tablespoons safflower oil
1 tablespoon sesame oil
4 oz. plain low-fat yogurt
2 sheets waxed paper, 12″ x 15″**

Preheat oven to 375°. Let children measure dry ingredients into mixing bowl. Stir safflower and sesame oil into yogurt until well blended. Add yogurt mixture to dry ingredients. Mix well. Divide the dough into three balls. Place one ball at a time on a sheet of waxed paper. Cover with second sheet and roll dough with rolling pin to make a 12″ x 15″ rectangle. Remove top paper and let children help cut the dough into 1″ x 2″ strips. Invert onto a nonstick cookie sheet. Remove paper. Bake 15–20 minutes. Cool. Serves 10–12.

Note: Vegetable herb seasonings are available at most health food stores. A mixture of onion, garlic, and celery powders can be substituted.

Strawberry Yogurt

1 cup strawberries	**1 cup yogurt (plain or straw-**
⅓ cup powdered milk	**berry flavored)**

Mash strawberries. Beat in powdered milk; add yogurt. Serve in small cups. (Bananas or other fresh fruit can be substituted.) Makes 6–8 small servings.

Banana–Wheat Germ Snacks

bananas	**honey**
milk	**toasted wheat germ**

Let children peel and cut bananas into bite-size pieces. Dip each piece into a mixture of half milk and half honey. Drop pieces of banana into a plastic bag filled with wheat germ and shake until well coated. Serve on a tray with colored toothpicks.

Honey Custard

3 eggs	**1 teaspoon vanilla**
⅓ cup honey	**nutmeg**
2 cups scalded milk	

Preheat oven to 325°. Place eggs in mixing bowl and beat well. Mix in all remaining ingredients except nutmeg. Pour into one-quart casserole or four custard cups. Sprinkle with nutmeg. Place in a baking pan holding ½″ hot water. Bake for 35 minutes or until a knife inserted in the center comes out clean. Cool, then refrigerate until serving time. Serves 6–8.

Note: The custard will take longer to cook when placed in a casserole (about 50 minutes).

Indian Custard Pudding

1 quart milk	2 tablespoons sugar
¼ cup water	½ teaspoon salt
½ cup molasses	¼ teaspoon each nutmeg, ginger, and cinnamon
½ cup stone-ground cornmeal	
1 tablespoon butter	1 egg

Preheat oven to 325°. Scald the milk. Mix water, molasses, and cornmeal. Blend into milk and bring to a boil. Remove from the heat; add butter, sugar, salt, nutmeg, ginger, and cinnamon. Cool. Beat the egg and add to the other ingredients. Pour into a buttered casserole and bake for 1 hour. Serves 12.

Crunchy Snacks

3 cups old-fashioned oats	½ cup blanched almonds, chopped
1 cup unsweetened coconut	½ cup honey
1 cup wheat germ (toasted or untoasted)	2 tablespoons water
	¼ cup oil or melted butter

Preheat oven to 250°. Combine first four ingredients in a bowl. Warm the remaining ingredients in a saucepan and pour them over the oat mixture. Mix so all particles are coated. Spread in a thin layer (no thicker than ½″) on a cookie sheet and toast for about 20 minutes in the oven. Stir occasionally to toast evenly. Serve as a snack.

Cheese Crispies

2 cups (about ½ lb.) sharp cheddar cheese, grated	1 cup flour, sifted
½ cup (one stick) butter, softened	¼ teaspoon salt

Preheat oven to 375°. Let children combine all the ingredients with their hands or with a pastry blender until thoroughly mixed. Form into small balls and place an inch apart on cookie sheet. Bake for about 12 minutes.

Popcorn

corn for popping	salt
¼ cup (approximately) oil	melted butter (optional)

Pour enough oil to just cover the bottom of an electric popcorn popper (preferably the kind with a clear top so children can watch). Add popcorn to cover. Have bowls or baskets handy so children can salt small amounts of popcorn to share.

HELPFUL HINTS

1. Let children examine the kernels of corn before popping. Explain that this is a special kind of corn grown just for popping and that it is different from the kind we eat off the cob. Each kernel of popcorn has moisture ("a drop of water") inside of it, and when the popcorn gets hot, the moisture turns into steam and causes the kernel to explode.
2. Place an electric popper without the top on a large sheet spread on the floor. Have children sit back and watch how far the corn can pop.
3. Play "Popcorn" by Hot Butter (Stereo MS3242 — Musicor Records, A Division of Talmadge Productions, Inc., 240 W. 55th St., New York, NY 10019).

Egg Nog

4 eggs
⅓ cup honey
4 cups milk

1 teaspoon vanilla
nutmeg (optional)

Beat eggs and honey with rotary beater. Then beat in milk and vanilla. Sprinkle with nutmeg if desired. Serves 8–10.

Fruit Shake

2 cups cold juice (orange, pineapple, or grape)

½ cup powdered milk
1 drop vanilla

Combine all ingredients in a one-quart plastic container. Add crushed ice and shake until mixed. Serves 4–6.

Frothy Fruit Drink

2 oranges, peeled
2 bananas, peeled
2 cups apple juice

½ teaspoon cinnamon
2 cups crushed ice

Blend first three ingredients in blender until frothy. Gradually add crushed ice while still blending. Serve with a sprinkle of cinnamon on top. Makes 15 small servings.

Fruit Sorbet

1 cup fresh strawberries
1 banana

¼ cup unsweetened apple juice

Wash and hull strawberries. Cut into halves. Slice the banana. Place the fruit in an airtight container and freeze. When frozen (or partially frozen), place fruit and juice in blender and blend until mixture is the consistency of ice sorbet. Add more juice if needed. Makes 4–6 small servings.

ICE CREAM

Every child should experience the fun and excitement of making homemade ice cream. The following recipes are for the old-fashioned hand-crank freezer.

Honey Ice Cream

3 eggs	**3 tablespoons vanilla**
1 cup honey	**½ teaspoon salt**
1 quart milk or half and half	**2 bags crushed ice**
2 pints whipping cream	**2 cups rock salt**
1 can evaporated milk	

Let children crack eggs into a large bowl; beat with rotary beater. Stir in honey (you may need to help, since the mixture gets quite sticky). Gradually add milk, stirring until honey is well mixed. Add remaining ingredients. Mix thoroughly, using rotary beater if necessary.

Pour mixture into a five-quart ice cream freezer can and chill for 30 minutes. The can should not be more than ⅔ full to allow for expansion.

When chilled, place freezer can of ice cream mix in tub of ice cream maker. Put top and crank in place. Alternately add 1 cup of crushed ice and ¼ cup rock salt until ice and salt mixture comes to the lid of the freezer can (approximately 8 lbs. of ice and 1¼ cups of rock salt). Let children take turns turning the crank slowly until the ice cream is so thick that the handle can no longer be turned (about 30–40 minutes).

Drain excess water from tub, remove dasher from the can; and plug the hole in the can lid. Leave can of ice cream in tub of ice and salt. Cover entire freezer with a towel or some heavy material and allow to chill for 30 minutes or more. Serves 24.

Fresh Strawberry Ice Cream

2–3 pint baskets strawberries	**1 quart milk**
3 cups sugar	**1 (13 oz.) can evaporated milk**
juice of 5 lemons	**1 pint whipping cream**

Hull and mash the strawberries with sugar. Add juice of lemons and let mixture stand at room temperature for 1 hour. Add milk and cream and pour into ice cream freezer. Follow instructions for Honey Ice Cream.

Bibliography of Resources

The following books will be especially helpful to teachers who want to adapt recipes using natural foods and for those who want to learn more about nutrition.

Albright, Nancy. *The Rodale Cookbook.* New York: Ballantine Books, 1982. A comprehensive book of recipes using natural foods. Includes useful listing of natural food stores in the U.S., nutritional content of many foods, food substitution table, cost table, and a section of cooking hints.

Bershad, Carol, and Deborah Bernick. *Bodyworks: The Kids' Guide to Food and Physical Fitness.* New York: Random House, 1979. Biology, physical fitness, and food and nutrition presented in story format. For children who can read.

Brody, Jane. *Jane Brody's Nutrition Book.* Des Plaines, Ill.: Bantam Books, 1981. The *New York Times* columnist's well-written and well-researched book with general information on all aspects of nutrition from abortion to zinc.

Cadwallader, Sharon. *Cooking Adventures for Kids.* Boston: Houghton Mifflin, 1974. Nutritious recipes for cooks, ages eight to fourteen. Includes helpful suggestions on kitchen safety, conservation, information about herbs, cooking techniques, and metric conversion.

Cadwallader, Sharon, and Judi Ohr. *Whole Earth Cook Book.* Boston: Houghton Mifflin, 1972. Many excellent and simple recipes using natural foods.

Endres, Jeannette Brakhane, and Robert E. Rockwell. *Food, Nutrition, and the Young Child.* St. Louis: C. V. Mosby, 1980. A useful text for students who wish to learn about nutrition for young children. Discusses children's food needs from infancy through age five. Includes food service management for day-care settings.

Feingold, Ben F., and Helene S. Feingold. *The Feingold Cookbook for Hyperactive Children.* New York: Random House, 1979. A doctor proposes the theory that hyperactivity and other behavior problems are related to food allergies. Includes recipes.

Gooch, Sandy. *If You Love Me Don't Feed Me Junk.* Reston, Va.: Reston Publishing Co., 1983. Personal accounts and stories of eating with children. Includes recipes.

Goodwin, Mary T., and Gerry Pollen. *Creative Food Experiences for Children.* Washington, D.C.: Center for Science in the Public Interest, 1980. A comprehensive book of food experiences designed to teach young children how the food they eat affects their growth and development. Useful information is provided with each recipe to educate children to make good food selections. Many excellent ideas for the teacher to incorporate into the curriculum.

Gross, Joy. *The Vegetarian Child.* Secaucus, N.J.: Lyle Stuart, Inc., 1983. The vegetarian alternative and how to make it healthy. Recipes included.

Hunter, Beatrice Trum. *The Natural Food Cookbook.* New York: Pyramid, 1969. Over two thousand recipes using whole grains and natural foods such as nutritional yeast, wheat germ, soy flour, and so on. Includes a check-list of basic natural foods and sources of supply. Baking powder, baking soda, and refined sugar are not used in these recipes.

Johnson, Barbara, and Betty Plemons. *Cup Cooking.* Lake Alfred, Fla.: Early Educators Press, 1983. Single-portion recipes that young children can use to learn how to measure, mix, count, and cook.

Kamen, Betty, and Si Kamen. *Kids Are What They Eat: What Every Parent Needs to Know About Nutrition.* New York: Arco Publishing, 1983. Advice on coping in the supermarket, planning menus, and maintaining health. Includes bibliography of books, organizations, and filmstrips.

Lambert-Lagace, Louise. *Feeding Your Child (from Infancy to Six Years Old).* New York: Beaufort Books, 1982. Breast-feeding, baby foods, and young children's diets are discussed by the author, a Canadian mother and nutrition consultant. Recipes are in metric system.

McEntire, Patricia. *Mommy I'm Hungry.* Sacramento, Calif.: Cougar Books, 1982. How to instill good eating habits, from infancy on. Recipes included.

McWilliams, Margaret. *Nutrition for the Growing Years.* New York: John Wiley, 1980. Basic nutrition text, easily understood, that contains chapters on preschool children's nutritional needs.

Marbach, Ellen S., Martha Plass, and Lily Hsu O'Connell. *Nutrition in a Changing World.* Provo, Utah: Brigham Young University Press, 1979. This preschool curriculum guide stresses the importance of nutrition education for young children. Written for teachers with little or no training in nutrition. The guide offers preschoolers many opportunities to experience a wide variety of foods through sight, sound, taste, smell, and touch.

Minear, Ralph E. *The Brain Food Diet for Children.* Indianapolis, Ind.: Bobbs-Merrill, 1983. The doctor's research at Harvard proposes a diet for the full development of the child's intellect. His diet included with menus.

Parents' Nursery School. *Kids Are Natural Cooks.* Boston: Houghton Mifflin, 1974. A cookbook of recipes compiled by the parents of children in a nursery school. The text explains why things are done and leaves some choices to the discretion and creativity of the cooks. Directions include how to improvise a churn to make butter, how to make cottage cheese, and how to grow healthful foods.

Peck, Judith. *Leap To the Sun. (Learning Through Dramatic Play).* Englewood Cliffs, N.J.: Prentice-Hall, 1979. Creative movement to promote self-expression and self-confidence for ages three to eleven. Illustrated.

Prudden, Bonnie. *How to Keep Your Child Fit From Birth to Six.* New York: Dial Press, 1983. Exercises and homemade equipment for developing a young child's awareness of physical fitness. Over three hundred photos. Prudden is director of the Institute of Physical Fitness in New York City.

Randell, Jill, and Christine Olson. *Educator's Guide: Food Experiences for Young Children.* Ithaca, N.Y.: Cornell University, 1981. This book presents in detail materials and experiences to help children develop healthy food habits through food and nutrition activities.

Richert, Barbara. *Getting Your Kids to Eat Right.* New York: Simon & Schuster, 1981. Practical planning, with recipes, from a mother. Information on additives, reading labels, analyzing nutrient needs, and combining foods for complete proteins.

Smith, Lendon. *Feed Your Kids Right.* New York: Dell, 1980. A pediatrician approaches total health, including both mental and physical aspects. He explains how problems can be treated with good eating and vitamins.

————. *Improving Your Child's Behavior Chemistry.* New York: Pocket Books, 1976. Hyperactivity, disobedience, nightmares, bedwetting, and allergies may be related to poor diet and body chemistry; all are discussed in this book.

Tassajara Bread Book. Berkeley, Calif.: Shambala Publications, 1970. A very well-designed booklet written by the chief priest of the Zen Center in San Francisco. Recipes are prepared with whole grains. Sections devoted to yeasted and unyeasted breads, quick breads, and some interesting background information about Tassajara, the Zen monastery in the hills of Monterey County, California, where the students of Zen meditate and exist on a simple diet of vegetables and grains.

Warren, Jean. *Super Snacks/Sugarless.* Everett, Wash.: Warren Publishing House, 1982. Written for parents and teachers of young children who want to offer alternatives to sugary foods. Suggestions and recipes for special-occasion foods containing no sugar, honey, or artificial sweeteners.

Wishik, Cindy S. *Kids Dish It up Sugar-free.* Port Angeles, Wash.: Peninsular Publishing, 1982. Beginner cooks learn their way around the kitchen and about nutrition, arithmetic, planning, cooperation, timing, and the satisfaction of creating a product for others to enjoy.

PART EIGHT

Computers for Preschoolers

Introduction

Jenny's parents bought a computer for their own use only to find that once their daughter discovered how to press the keys and make things happen on the screen, she wanted equal time on the computer. When they realized that Jenny could turn on the machine, load a disk, and recognize key commands, they began to buy educational software programs so that she could play games on the computer. Jenny is four years old.

Stories like these of children's involvement with computers are reported in the media with increasing frequency, along with statements from parents and teachers — many of them former skeptics — praising the impressive learning experiences offered by the computer. Children with learning disabilities or short attention spans are reported to be highly attentive to computer programs. Bright children appear to learn faster when working with a computer than even their parents expected. The computer has been lauded for its infinite patience, and, because it is nonjudgmental, teachers point out that a child need not fear being ridiculed for making an error. In addition are the many claims that our children will have to be computer literate if they are to succeed in the adult world. It is not surprising that, in light of such claims, many teachers wonder if the preschool should include a computer center.

What are the advantages for children, and what harm, if any, can result from an early introduction to this new technology? To date, little research has been conducted on the effects of computers on young children, but a few studies report some positive results.

One project completed in 1983 reported significant improvement in reading readiness among preschoolers exposed to the computer.[1] The subjects of the study were a group of twenty nonreading preschoolers (ten boys and ten girls, ranging in age from three to five years old). The children were first tested on standardized prereading tests, then half of them were introduced to the computer. For three to four weeks; each child was tutored by a computer on listening skills,

---

[1] This study was conducted by the publisher of computer software programs for children: Program Design, Inc., 95 E. Putnam Ave., Greenwich, Conn. 06830.

following directions, fine motor skills, eye-hand coordination, and the concepts of *same* and *different*. Prereading test scores of the computer group improved 47.4 percent from initial to final testing one month later. The scores of the control group with no computer training improved only 13.5 percent.

Another study carried out at the Institute of Child Development at the University of Minnesota sought to determine the extent of children's interactions with a computer. The purpose of the study was to find out whether the intellectual and social development of preschoolers allowed them to make meaningful use of the computer.[2] Some of the questions asked were: Can preschool children use a standard keyboard? Will children at the computer require too much teacher attention? Can preschoolers work together cooperatively at the computer? Will the computer disrupt social interaction in the classroom because children will prefer to play with the computer rather than with each other?

Chosen for the study was a class of four- and five-year-olds at the University Child Care Center. After the children received an initial orientation, the computer was made available in the classroom during playtime along with all the other activities usually available. Use of the computer was limited to groups of two at a time with no restriction on how long the group could stay at the computer. (The researchers found that children stayed an average of twenty minutes.) Teachers let the children work independently unless help was sought or seemed to be needed.

Researchers found that the standard keyboard was not too difficult for the child to manage; that children shared use of the computer and helped each other pick correct keys to punch; and that the computer did not disrupt normal social activity in the classroom. Children appeared to prefer working at the computer with someone rather than alone. The findings indicate that, if provided with age-appropriate software, preschoolers are capable of interacting with a computer and of working cooperatively with peers with minimal teacher supervision.

Another study, conducted at Stanford University, compared the effectiveness of television and the computer in teaching basic relational concepts to preschoolers.[3] The children, ages two-and-a-half to four years, were given pretests to determine their basic knowledge of concepts such as *above, below, over,* and *under*. The children were then divided into three groups: the *control* group (which would receive no further training or information), the *television* group, and the *computer* group. Each child in the television group spent eight minutes watching an animated cartoon developed by the makers of "Sesame Street." Each child in the computer group played for a maximum of eight minutes with a game from JUGGLES' RAINBOW, de-

[2] Alexandra Muller, "Preschoolers at the Computer," *Commodore: The Microcomputer Magazine,* 25 (August/September 1983), 86–89.

[3] Jennifer Brawer, "The Effectiveness of the Computer and Television in Teaching Basic Relational Concepts: A Comparative Study" (Paper presented at the International Communication Association Conference, San Francisco, Calif., May 27, 1984).

Illustration 8.1   **From all indications, computers are neither monsters depriving children of valuable playtime, nor are they miracle workers replacing classroom teachers.**

veloped by The Learning Company. Post-tests were given to all three groups immediately following the instruction periods.

Post-test scores of the television group improved by 23 percent; the computer group's scores improved by 27 percent; and there was no significant improvement in scores of the control group. A second post-test administered three to five days later showed that the children had retained the knowledge they had gained.

This study is significant in that it shows that preschool children can learn relational concepts with the use of a computer, and that the computer appears to be as effective in teaching these concepts as "Sesame Street," a program research has already shown to be successful in teaching concepts to young children.

Although positive results like these are encouraging, computers in preschools are still too novel for teachers to draw definitive conclusions from current research. This means that, for the present, teachers must use their own good judgment in recommending whether or not a computer is a worthwhile investment for the preschool.

Some teachers are concerned not only about the cost of computer equipment, but also that pressure for computer literacy is diverting attention from accepted teaching and learning practices based on Piagetian principles of child development (see the Introduction to Part Three, "Math Experiences"). These teachers argue that, since most preschoolers are preoperational, children should learn concepts by interacting with real materials in a spontaneous manner, not by being exposed to a computer with programs that control their activities. It is only through active, physical participation that youngsters can integrate cognitive skills. Such learning, these teachers say, cannot be replicated by a computer.

But from all indications, computers are neither monsters depriving children of valuable playtime, nor are they miracle workers replacing classroom teachers. True, some programs direct children to respond in a drill-like fashion. Other programs, however, are designed to respond to the child's "instructions." One example is LOGO, a computer language designed by Seymour Papert, a mathematician and student of Piaget. Through the use of a small cursor on the screen, called a *turtle*, the child can *see* how a computer program works by creating graphics. (See the glossary at the end of this part for definitions of computer terms.) Unlike software programs where children must respond to preprogrammed situations, learning and using LOGO enables children to make the computer respond to and remember their commands.[4] The potential is real for using LOGO as a device for teaching children *how* to think rather than *whai* to think.

Programming in LOGO is most successful with children ages six and older who are sufficiently competent with the keyboard to be able to type commands. Most younger children are not able to program in this manner without a great deal of adult assistance.

The activities in this part are designed for teachers and preschoolers who have had little or no experience using a computer. The tasks are presented in order of difficulty, beginning with some simple preprogrammed packages that teachers who are unfamiliar with computers will find easy to teach and supervise. We suggest beginning with software similar to The Learning Company's Butterfly Game (in JUGGLES' RAINBOW) because input is simple (the children can press any key) and the results on screen are colorful, engaging, and immediate. Introduction to preprogramming experiences like these during the early years will help children be more comfortable with computers in elementary school.

Later on in this part, we introduce an activity using a simple form of LOGO that is sometimes referred to as *instant key* LOGO. Teachers may find workshops in teaching LOGO helpful if they wish to provide more sophisticated activities for older children.

The software programs used in our activities are intended to be examples, not endorsements. Teachers should preview the many programs available (preferably with the children) before making selections. (See the next section, "Guide to Selecting Software," for guidelines.) In fact, selecting software to satisfy the needs of the classroom should precede the purchase of a computer. The "Preschool Educational Software Buyer's Guide" at the end of this section lists many of the publishers and titles of programs designed for young children, and includes the computer systems with which they are compatible. Although we use the Apple IIe to illustrate our activities, the suggestions for teacher-child interactions remain essentially the same regardless of the system you may choose for your classroom.

Dialogue for the instructions is intended to help children learn the mechanics of each game. We have found that after the children become familiar with the procedures there is much latitude for spon-

---

[4]See Seymour Papert, *Mindstorms, Children, Computers and Powerful Ideas* (New York: Basic Books, 1980).

taneity. At that point, children enjoy working together while the teacher functions as a resource.

For those teachers who remain skeptical about computers for preschoolers, we suggest that you keep an open mind and take a look at some of the available programs. You may come to appreciate the computer as a worthwhile teaching tool that greatly enhances your curriculum.

Guide to Selecting Software

Selecting good quality, age-appropriate software is a time-consuming task. Many stores do not carry a large selection of preschool software programs, and salespeople are not knowledgeable enough about child development to make good recommendations. A software program may be advertised as an award winner but prove to be a disappointment in actual use. Or a teacher may be impressed with a program only to find that children do not respond as expected. Ideally, the program should be previewed with the children before it is purchased. The teacher should always practice using each program before introducing it to the children.

Remember too that each computer has its own specific operating system. When buying software, be sure the program is designed to operate on your particular computer.

Software programs frequently have several games on one disk. Like phonograph records on which you find some songs that are more appropriate than others, games on a disk will vary in quality and usefulness.

Software that is best-suited for preschool children has the following characteristics:

1. Has a clear objective; does what it is supposed to do.
2. Uses colorful, playful graphics; is fun for the child to use.
3. Uses a patient, try-again approach; the child controls the pace.
4. Does not have violence.
5. Does not use loud buzzers or negative graphics.
6. Is interactive with the child.
7. Requires thinking; is challenging for the child.
8. Has "staying power"— that is, it holds the child's attention with a minimum of adult assistance.
9. Relates content to the child's culture and level of understanding.
10. Is easy for both adult and child to use.

The rating sheets shown in Illustrations 8.2 and 8.3 are based on this list of criteria. You can use the first sheet when evaluating software on your own; the second sheet can be used when you preview a program with a child. Both rating sheets can be adapted as necessary to suit your own priorities for evaluating software.

EVALUATING SOFTWARE FOR PRESCHOOL CHILDREN

Evaluator _____ Date _____

Name of Disk _____

Name of Company _____

Name of Game _____

The evaluator may want to assign a letter or number to a rating scale.

	Rating	Comments
1. Clear objective		
2. Colorful graphics		
3. Positive reinforcers		
4. Absence of violence		
5. Patient approach		
6. Pace determined by child		
7. Some repetition		
8. Interactive style		
9. Lets child make decisions		
10. Requires thinking; challenging		
11. Staying power		
12. Easy to use		
13. Standard commands		
14. Appropriate content		
15. Fun to use		

Illustration 8.2 **Software rating sheet**

Setting up a Computer Center in the Classroom

The following suggestions are designed to help the teacher set up a computer center in the classroom:

1. Find the electrical outlets in the classroom. Select a location where the computer is protected from direct sunlight and extreme hot or cold temperatures.
2. Tape down electrical cords so that children won't trip on them.
3. The computer should be placed where it can be supervised easily. The teacher should be able to keep an eye on it from any location in the classroom.

EVALUATING SOFTWARE WITH PRESCHOOL CHILDREN

Evaluator _____   Date _____

Name of Disk _____

Name of Company _____

Name of Game _____

The evaluator may want to assign a letter or number to a rating scale.

	Rating	*Comments*
1. Is it easy for the child to use?		
2. Are the commands understandable by the child?		
3. Is the feedback appropriate and effective?		
4. Is it patient?		
5. Is the pace determined by the child?		
6. Is it interactive?		
7. Does it let the child make decisions?		
8. Is it challenging?		
9. Does it hold the child's attention?		
10. Is it fun for the child to use?		

Illustration 8.3   **Software rating sheet**

4. Put the computer near an activity area that requires minimum supervision, but do not isolate it from other activities.
5. The computer should be positioned so that the teacher can scan the rest of the class while supervising computer activities. (The computer should not be facing a wall.)
6. Position the monitor in such a way that glare and reflection are minimized.
7. Place the computer on a table large enough for two children to sit side by side facing the keyboard with room for the teacher to sit beside them.
8. Be sure the table is at a height that puts the keyboard at a comfortable level for the children.
9. Place the disk drive and the disk storage container on the same side of the table as the teacher's chair.
10. Read the user's manual and follow directions for care of the computer.

HELPFUL HINTS

1. Have charts hanging on a nearby wall listing the procedures to follow when operating the computer system. The charts will be helpful to adult volunteers and others who may not be familiar with the procedures. (See Illustration 8.4.)
2. Keep an "experience log" in a binder where you can record each child's reactions and progress.
3. Put a sign-up sheet on a clipboard so that children can sign or print their names and be assigned a turn at the computer.

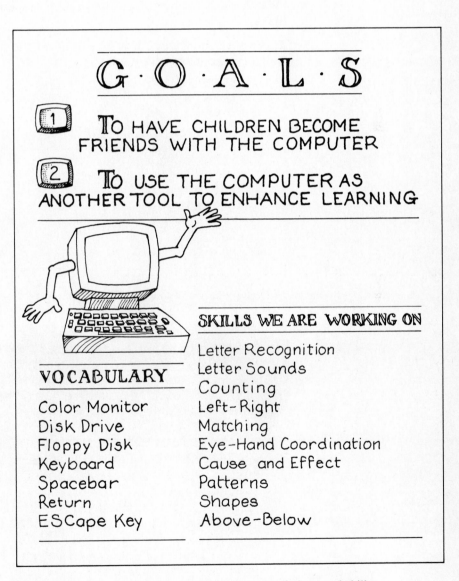

G·O·A·L·S

1 TO HAVE CHILDREN BECOME FRIENDS WITH THE COMPUTER

2 TO USE THE COMPUTER AS ANOTHER TOOL TO ENHANCE LEARNING

VOCABULARY

Color Monitor
Disk Drive
Floppy Disk
Keyboard
Spacebar
Return
ESCape Key

SKILLS WE ARE WORKING ON

Letter Recognition
Letter Sounds
Counting
Left-Right
Matching
Eye-Hand Coordination
Cause and Effect
Patterns
Shapes
Above-Below

Illustration 8.4 **Wall chart presenting goals, vocabulary, and skills**

OPERATING THE COMPUTER ("BOOTING" THE DISK)

"Cold Start" (when the computer is off):

1. Open the disk-drive door.
2. Hold the disk with your thumb on the label.
3. Insert the disk with the label facing up. (See Illustration 8.5.)
4. Close the disk-drive door.
5. Turn on the computer and the monitor (or TV).
6. The in-use light will go on and the drive will whir.
7. *Wait.*
8. When the in-use light is off (and the whirring stops), the computer is ready for you to use.

"Warm Start" (when the computer is on and you want to change disks):

1. Be sure the "busy" or in-use light on the disk drive is off.
2. Open the disk-drive door.

Illustration 8.5   **Demonstration for children of "booting the disk"**

3. Hold the disk with your thumb on the label.
4. Remove the disk and insert new disk with the label facing up.
5. Close the disk-drive door.
6. Press special loading keys (on the Apple IIe, press CONTROL, OPEN APPLE, then RESET).
7. In-use light will go on and the drive will whir.
8. *Wait.*
9. When the in-use light is off (and the whirring stops), the computer is ready for you to use.

Activities[5]

INTRODUCTORY ACTIVITIES

▶ **PURPOSE**   **To reinforce concepts helpful in using the computer**

MATERIALS   Selected activities from Part Four, "Language Arts":

— "To learn relational concepts," page 157 (adapt to teach concepts of up, down, next to, top, and bottom)
— "To learn concepts of right and left," page 158
— "To learn to listen and follow directions," page 162
— "To recognize right and left hands," page 168

PROCEDURE

1. Give children experiences with the activities listed above before introducing them to the computer.
2. The same activities can be adapted so that they are specifically related to the computer, such as following directions in the use of a make-believe computer made of cardboard.
3. Offer activities teaching the above concepts in other areas of the curriculum while the children are learning to use the computer.
4. Provide many physical experiences teaching directionality, sequencing, and so on so that children can experience these concepts with the whole body.
5. A related activity is to have children jump on a numbered pattern, while the teacher stresses "first," "next," and "last."

---

[5]Note that in this chapter many activities have multiple purposes listed. This has been done to better acquaint the teacher unfamiliar with the computer to its varied uses and possibilities. Note also that in this chapter only one activity is presented on a page. This should permit greater ease of use while the teacher is seated with students at the computer terminal.

▶ **PURPOSE**   **To learn the meaning of *menu***

MATERIALS — Restaurant menus
— Magazine pictures of food
— Tables and chairs
— Eating utensils
— Napkins
— Small pads and pencils for taking orders
— Make-believe food (optional)

PROCEDURE 1. Set up the dramatic play area like a restaurant.
2. Talk with the children about their experiences in restaurants to determine if they are familiar with ordering food and the work of a waiter or waitress.
3. Make a menu, using pictures of food.
4. Have some children play the role of waiter or waitress, explaining that they are to take orders for food.
5. Have some children be the customers at the restaurant and order from the menu.
6. Let the waiter or waitress pretend to write down the orders from the picture menu.
7. Talk about the menu and its purpose.
8. Mention that there are all kinds of menus, including the kind the children may see posted on the walls in fast-food restaurants.
9. Point out that another kind of menu is the one the computer shows us so that we can select a game of our choice.
10. You may want to show the children an example of a computer menu at this time.

▶ **PURPOSE**   **To introduce children to the computer**

MATERIALS   — Computer
              — Computer cover
              — Monitor
              — Disk drive

PROCEDURE   **1.** Gather a group of children (or the entire class) in front of the computer.
              2. Say:
              This is a [specific name] computer. It is a machine we can use to help us learn. We use it in a special way. I will show you how to have fun with it.
              When we are not using the computer, we will have this cover over it. We keep our hands off the computer when the cover is on. When the cover is off, you may use it.
              First you need to learn how to use it, so I will teach you one at a time.
              3. Let children go to other areas of the room to work on other activities while you work with one child at a time on the computer.
              4. Use the next activity and a simple software program like the one described there to introduce individual children to the computer.

              Note: Set aside a large block of time allowing at least five minutes for each child. Interest will be high and children will all want a turn.

▶ **PURPOSE**   **To let the child experience the three-fold connection of the body, the keyboard, and the screen**

To explain the main parts of the computer and how they work

To give the child an opportunity to operate the computer

To follow pictorial instructions

MATERIALS   — Computer, color monitor, disk drive
— Washable felt-tip pen or blue paper bracelet
— Butterfly game from JUGGLES' RAINBOW program (The Learning Company)

INTRODUCTORY
COMMENTS   This game is appropriate for ages two through six. A strip of paper divides the keyboard to separate right and left sides. Juggles the clown asks the child to press keys on the left and right sides of the keyboard. When the correct keys are pressed, colorful shapes and graphics appear accompanied by sound effects. The child does not have to recognize letters; pressing any key on the correct side of the keyboard will activate the program. In this activity the game is primarily used to emphasize the connection between the child's body, the keyboard, and the screen. Reinforcing *right* and *left* is only incidental.

PROCEDURE   1. Have the computer turned off.
2. Invite the child to sit down facing the center of the keyboard and monitor.
3. Point out and identify the computer's name, the keyboard, the monitor, the disk drive, and the floppy disk.
4. Encourage the child to say each word.
5. Demonstrate how to load the disk (load JUGGLES' RAINBOW) and turn on the computer.
6. Tell the child that only the teacher touches the disk drive and floppy disk.[6]
7. Say:
Hear the whirring sound? It is now loading our game into the computer.
8. When the picture menu appears on the monitor, say:
This is the picture menu. We use it to choose the game we want. Do you see the butterfly? Let's choose that game.
Pointing to number 2, ask:
What number is Butterfly?
When child responds correctly, say:
That's right! So we are going to press key number 2. Can you find it and press it?
Assist by saying:
It is somewhere in this row, (run finger along row of numbers).
After child presses key, say:
Hear the whirring sound? It is loading the Butterfly game into the computer.

---

[6]Children who have computers at home may already be familiar with loading the disk, but it is probably best to establish some general rules for all children until everyone is familiar with the equipment. You can acknowledge that the child knows how to load the disk, but explain that he or she may not do so at school until all the children learn how to work with the computer.

9. When Juggles appears say:
There's Juggles the clown on the left side (point) **and on the right side** (point).
10. When the blue strip appears, say:
Now let's make our keyboard look like the screen. Can you do that with this blue paper?
If necessary, help the child attach the strip of paper that comes with the game to the keyboard.
11. Say:
Now show me your right hand.
Use washable felt-tip pen to write *R* on the child's right hand (or attach a blue paper bracelet), explaining that it is to help the child remember.
12. Touch the child's right arm, then right hand, then the keyboard, then the monitor, explaining that everything on that side of the blue strip is the right side. Say:
Run your hand back and forth along the right side of the keyboard.
13. Repeat the same procedure for the left side.
14. Explain that in this game, keys on the right side are pressed with the right hand. Keys on the left side are pressed with the left hand. If children cross over, place both their hands on the lower ledge of the keyboard and repeat your explanation.
15. Assist the child in the practice sequences by reading the words on the screen. Later on, when the child becomes acquainted with the game, the teacher will not have to read the instructions.
16. Continue to stress the physical connection between the child and equipment by running your hand along the child's arm and hand and the keyboard and monitor as the child plays the game.
17. When the red picture clue (divided red bar) appears, point and say:
Do you see that? It means press a key on that side.
18. When the Butterfly section of the game appears, no instructions are needed. Allow the child freedom to explore independently. Some typical comments from children are:
Oh, look what happened!
Look what I did!
I wonder what it will be.
Look, I made a butterfly!
I did it again!
Hey, it's the same!
19. Record each child's reactions and progress in the log book.
20. After everyone has had a turn with this game, allow second turns about five minutes long.
21. As children become familiar with the game, encourage them to play it with a friend.
22. To return to menu, press SHIFT and ?.

Note: The reason for marking only one hand in this exercise is that very young children who are concentrating on experiencing the connection between the body and the computer are more likely to become distracted and confused if both hands are marked.

USING THE COMPUTER

▶ **PURPOSE**

To reinforce concepts of above and below

To experience matching colors

To watch patterns develop

To follow pictorial instructions

To recognize shapes

To have experiences in eye-tracking, cause-and-effect relationships, spatial awareness, and relating horizontal to vertical planes

MATERIALS

— Computer, color monitor, disk drive

— Rainbow game from JUGGLES' RAINBOW program (The Learning Company)

INTRODUCTORY COMMENTS

This game is appropriate for prereaders through age six. A strip of paper divides the keyboard to identify *above* and *below*. When the correct keys are pressed, colorful shapes and graphics appear accompanied by sound effects.

PROCEDURE

1. Load JUGGLES' RAINBOW.
2. When picture menu appears, say:
   This is the picture menu. We use it to choose a game. Do you see the rainbow? Let's choose that game.
   Pointing to number 1, ask:
   What number is Rainbow?
   When child responds correctly, say:
   That's right. So we are going to press key number 1. Can you find it and press it?
   If necessary, help by saying:
   It is somewhere in this row (run finger along row of numbers).
3. When child presses key, say:
   Do you hear the whirring sound? It is loading the Rainbow game into the computer.
4. When Juggles appears, say:
   There's Juggles the clown, above (point) **and below** (point).
5. When the blue strip appears, say:
   Now let's make our keyboard look like the screen. Can you do that with the blue paper?
   If necessary, help the child attach the strip of paper that comes with the game to the keyboard.
6. Then say:
   Can you show me the part of the keyboard above the blue strip? Can you show me the part of the screen above the blue strip? Can you show me the part of the keyboard below the blue strip? Can you show me the part of the screen below the blue strip? Now press any key.
7. Help child play the game by reading the words on the screen.
8. When the picture clue (small red square in a box) appears, point and say:

See that? It means press a key above (or **below**).

9. When the Rainbow section of the game appears, no instructions are needed. Allow the child to explore independently.

10. Some comments the teacher might make include:
    What happens when you keep pressing the keys?
    Can you make the colors of the rain match the rainbow?

11. Record each child's reactions and progress in the log book.

12. Encourage two children to play the game together.

13. Allow exploration with pressing the spacebar, which advances the game to the next section.

14. To return to menu, press SHIFT and ?.

Note: In addition to Butterfly and Rainbow, the third game, Windmill, reinforces concepts of left, right, above, and below. Windmill should be introduced after the child is familiar with Butterfly and Rainbow.

▶ **PURPOSE**   **To provide experience in letter recognition, letter matching, and letter sounds**
To provide keyboard familiarity

MATERIALS   — Computer, color monitor, disk drive
— CHARLIE BROWN'S ABC's program (Random House, Inc.)

INTRODUCTORY   This game is suitable for ages three through six. Large upper- and
COMMENTS   lower-case letters are presented along with colorful graphics and sound effects. First, any letter key may be pressed and a large picture of an object beginning with that letter appears on the screen. That same letter key, when pressed again, puts the object into animated graphics. (Some helpful precomputer activities emphasizing upper- and lower-case letters can be found in Part Four, "Language Arts.")

PROCEDURE   1. Load CHARLIE BROWN'S ABC's. Say:
This is a game about letters and the way we sound them. Press any letter key.
2. Assume that the child presses the L key. When picture appears, say:
What letter is that?
Child responds: **L.**
3. Say:
Yes! Pointing to picture of lipstick, ask: **What is that?**
Child responds: **Lipstick.**
4. Say:
Yes. What letter does lipstick begin with?
Child responds: **L.**
5. Say:
That's right.
Have child make "L" sound and say "lipstick," noting the "L" sound.
6. Say:
What happens if you press L again?
(Child presses L key and Lucy puts on her lipstick. When key is pressed again, Lucy puts on her lipstick again.)
7. Typical comments from children are:
Watch! Watch this! I'm going to do it again!
See? Do you want to do it again?
Look! Let's take the lipstick off and put it on again!
8. Allow children to press letters at random and name the letter and corresponding picture they see on the screen.
9. Record reactions, progress, and language development in log.

Note: PEANUTS MAZE MARATHON is another colorful game from the same publisher. A joystick is used to move an object through the maze from one picture to another. This game is good for developing eye-hand coordination, directionality, and eye-tracking.

► **PURPOSE**   **To develop visual memory**

To provide experiences in matching objects

To provide opportunities for language development and taking turns when played with a friend

MATERIALS
— Computer, color monitor, disk drive
— READER RABBIT AND THE FABULOUS WORD FACTORY program (The Learning Company)

INTRODUCTORY COMMENTS

This game is appropriate for ages three and up. Colorful pictures are hidden under boxes. The arrow keys are used to move the cursor to the box the child wants to look under. The child presses the space bar to reveal the object under the box. The purpose of the game is to match pairs of like pictures. Some reinforcing precomputer activities include the board game "Concentration" and playing "What's Missing?" by presenting several objects, removing one, and having the child recall the missing object.

PROCEDURE

1. Load program.
2. When the picture menu appears, say:
There is a picture matching game on this program that is a lot of fun. If we press the letter A and then the number 4, we will get that game.
Can you press A4?
3. As the disk drive loads the program, say:
Listen, now it's loading the picture matching game.
4. When objects appear on the screen, say:
These are the things we are going to see in our game.
Let child study the objects.
5. Say:
It says "Press SPACEBAR." Can you do that?
6. After spacebar is pressed, say:
All the things we just saw are hiding under here (point to boxes) **and we are going to find them.**
7. **See this cursor?** (point to cursor on screen)
We can move it around with our arrow keys.
8. Invite child to experiment with the arrow keys for awhile. Then say:
We can look under the box where the cursor is by pressing the spacebar.
9. Invite child to press the spacebar. When picture appears, say:
Now there is another one just like it under one of the other boxes. Can you find it?
Where would you like to look?
10. Assist child in noting which direction the cursor needs to go and which arrow keys will get it there, with comments such as:
Yes, you want the cursor to move down. Which arrow key points that way?
11. Play the rest of the game with the child, showing your enthusiasm and excitement over each accomplished match.

▶ **PURPOSE**   **To provide experiences in shape matching, letter matching, number recognition, and counting**
To provide experiences in eye-hand coordination
To provide experiences in visual discrimination
To provide experiences in decision making

MATERIALS   — Computer, color monitor, disk drive
— Joystick
— Matchbox game from ELECTRONIC PLAYGROUND program (Software Entertainment Company)

INTRODUCTORY
COMMENTS   This program is appropriate for ages three through six. Matchbox itself has three different matching games: Shape Match, Letter Match, and Number Match. All three games are played in the same manner using the same format. A joystick is used to move a friendly character some children have called "Walkie" to select matching shapes and letters. In the number game, the children count objects and then select the correct number. Smiling faces appear when correct choices are made. (Some related activities can be found in Part Four.)

PROCEDURE   1. Load ELECTRONIC PLAYGROUND.
2. When picture menu appears, say:
(Pointing to screen) **That says Electronic Playground.**
(Pointing to "Walkie") **We will call this little character "Walkie."**
Let's play the first (point) **game. It is called Matchbox.**
3. Give child the joystick and say:
Let's move "Walkie" to the first game and push the joystick button to choose the first game.
4. Child moves "Walkie" to the first game with the joystick and pushes button to select game.
5. When Matchbox menu appears, point and say:
Would you like to play with shapes, letters, or numbers?
6. In this example, assume the child selects shapes. Say:
Where do we need to move "Walkie"?
7. Child points to shape game. Say: **That's right!**
Let child move "Walkie" and push button to select game.
8. When game appears, point and say:
See this shape? Where is the one that matches it?
9. When child points to matching shape, say:
That's right. Now let's move "Walkie" to that shape and press the button.
10. Each time a correct answer is given, smiling faces appear.
11. Some typical comments from children are:
He needs to go this way if we want a happy face.
Go up, "Walkie."
Come on, "Walkie."
Go to the right place, "Walkie."
12. When an incorrect answer is chosen causing the shape to disappear, ask: **Why did the shape disappear?**
When it disappears that means "Try again."
13. Record and log reactions of children.
14. When children become familiar with the game, encourage them to play it with a friend, taking turns after each correct answer.

▶ **PURPOSE**   **To reinforce letter matching**

To provide experiences in eye-hand coordination, visual discrimination, cause-and-effect relationships, and directionality

MATERIALS   — Computer, color monitor, disk drive
— Joystick (or keyboard, optionally)
— The "E" game, one of six games on THE LEARNING LINE program (Eric Software Publishing)

INTRODUCTORY COMMENTS   This program is appropriate for ages four through seven. The "E" game is a colorful, animated letter-matching game. There is a clothesline hanging between two palm trees. Letters hang from the clothesline. When a letter appears at the top of the screen, a joystick is used to move a monkey to the matching letter on the clothesline. There are five other matching games on this program played in the same manner using the same format. (See "To match identical letters," page 170, and "To learn names of letters," page 171.)

PROCEDURE   1. Load THE LEARNING LINE.
2. When the picture menu appears (a clothesline hanging between two palm trees, with six items pinned to the clothesline), say: **This is the picture menu. We use it to choose the game we want. Which game would you like to play?**
3. Assume the child picks the letter game. Say: **Can you show me a letter on the clothesline?** (Run finger along the line.)
4. Child points to the letter E.
5. Say: **Yes. We are going to use the joystick to move the monkey up to the letter E.**
6. Child moves monkey to the letter E selecting letter match game.
7. When game appears, say: **See this letter?** (Point to the letter which appears at the top of the screen.) **Can you find the same letter on the clothesline?**
8. Have child point to the letter on the clothesline. Say: **Yes! Now can you move the monkey to that letter?**
9. When a correct response is made, the letter comes down off the line with the monkey and the monkey pushes it away.
10. Some typical children's comments are: **Oh, I can find that one! Let's make him push the letter. Oh, I can do that! I'm going to get them all!**
11. Record and log reactions.

Note: Other games on THE LEARNING LINE program are:

— Shirt game: matching articles of clothing
— Cat game: word matching with picture clues
— Face game: matching details on faces
— Ten game: number matching
— Bouquet game: classifying objects

Related activities for each of these games can be found in Part Four.

▶ **PURPOSE**   **To provide counting experiences**

To reinforce number recognition

To provide experiences in eye-hand coordination and directionality

MATERIALS — Computer, color monitor, disk drive
— Joystick (or keyboard, optionally)
— Jelly Beans, one of three games on the SWEET SHOPPE program (Eric Software Publishing)

INTRODUCTORY COMMENTS   This game is appropriate for ages four through seven. Children count jelly beans falling from a jar. Next, from a row of numbered balloons, they select the number that tells how many jelly beans fell. Then a joystick is used to move a friendly character to the correctly numbered balloon. A happy face made of jelly beans appears with each correct answer. This game provides colorful and entertaining experiences in counting, number recognition, and directionality. (See pages 113–115 for activities using cardinal numbers to reinforce number recognition.)

PROCEDURE
1. Load SWEET SHOPPE program.
2. When picture menu appears, say:
   This is the picture menu. We use it to choose the game we want to play. Let's play Jelly Beans. It's a counting game. Do you see the jelly beans?
3. Pointing to friendly character, say:
   Let's use the joystick to move this character, Mr. Jelly Bean, to the jelly beans to pick our game.
4. Child uses joystick to select game.
5. When game appears, a jar full of jelly beans tips over, spilling some of the jelly beans. Say:
   How many jelly beans fell from the jar?
6. Child counts jelly beans, using finger to point if necessary.
7. Say:
   Yes. Now can you find that number up here? (Run finger along row of numbers on screen.)
8. Have child point to the number.
9. Say:
   Yes. Now can you use the joystick to move Mr. Jelly Bean to that number?
10. Record and log reactions. Children enjoy watching the jar tip over, spilling the jelly beans.
11. To return to menu, press ESC.

Note: The other two games on this program are played in a similar manner, but the graphics and concepts differ. The Ice Cream game provides colorful experiences with simple subtraction. The Popcorn game is an experience with simple addition.

   THE GRABIT FACTORY, a program by the same company, also has number matching and simple addition and subtraction with colorful animated graphics and sound effects. It is suitable for ages five through eight.

INTRODUCING CHILDREN TO LOGO

LOGO is a computer language designed by Seymour Papert, a mathematician and student of Piaget. Papert contends that the most beneficial learning is "learning without being taught."[7] Through the use of LOGO, children can create computer graphics and see how programming a computer works. Papert suggests that computers can make the abstract concrete, thus helping children learn better by making their thinking processes conscious. That is, computers can teach children *how*, rather than *what*, to think.

In LOGO, a small triangular shaped cursor called a *turtle* moves about on the monitor display screen in response to commands typed into the computer. (See glossary at the end of this part for definition of computer terms). The turtle leaves a visible track enabling the programmer to see a graphic display of his or her commands. This is an excellent way for children to develop an understanding of how programming works.

A variety of LOGO programs are available for various computers. One of these is ZOOM, a simplified version of Apple LOGO. ZOOM makes it possible for preschoolers to create their own graphic designs by using an *instant key* input system. For example, pressing the F key causes the turtle to draw a line as it moves *forward* a fixed distance. Pressing the R key causes a fifteen-degree turn to the *right*. A single key-stroke is all that is needed, rather than an entire command that requires more complex procedures.

Children can store their programs simply by pressing P and then typing a name for it. Pressing I and then the name recalls (invokes) the program.

If children are not clear about the concepts of *forward*, *backward*, *right*, and *left* as depicted on the screen, there may be some confusion. The turtle moving to its right or left on the screen is not the same as the child's right or left as he or she sits facing the screen. We suggest children use the R and L keys simply to "make the turtle turn," rather than to teach concepts of right and left. As the children become more competent, the teacher might want to play a game in which he or she is the turtle facing the class and the children "program" the turtle to move to its right or left and forward or backward. Then let each child take turns being the turtle.

The turtle head may be difficult to see on some monitors when the ZOOM program is used. Try the blue background first. If children have trouble seeing the cursor, you may want to modify the monitor's background color as suggested in the appendix activity. The user's manual accompanying your computer may provide similar instructions.

We recommend that LOGO be used by children four-and-a-half to five years old who have had some previous experience with the computer keyboard.

[7] Seymour Papert. *Mindstorms, Children, Computers and Powerful Ideas.* New York: Basic Books, 1980.

▶ **PURPOSE**   **To prepare the keyboard for LOGO using ZOOM**

MATERIALS   — Apple IIe computer, black-and-white or color monitor, disk drive
— Apple LOGO disk
— ZOOM from the Apple LOGO TOOL KIT disk
— Green, blue, yellow, and orange adhesive dots

INTRODUCTORY   Color-coding the keys helps children locate the letters of the keyboard
COMMENTS   with ease. Codes also identify various functions or commands. For
example, green keys (marked with F, B, R, and L) make the turtle go
forward or backward and turn to its right or left. The yellow key stores
or saves the design or program. The blue key brings the design back
from storage or memory. The orange key returns the turtle to "home"
position. (See Illustration 8.6 of the Apple IIe keyboard.)

PROCEDURE   1. Label green dots with the letters R, L, F, and B and place them on
the corresponding letters of the keyboard.
2. Label the P key with a yellow dot marked P.
3. Label the I key with a blue dot labeled I.
4. Label the H key with an orange dot labeled H.
5. As children become familiar with these commands, the teacher
can identify and label other keys as listed in the instructions that
appear on the screen.

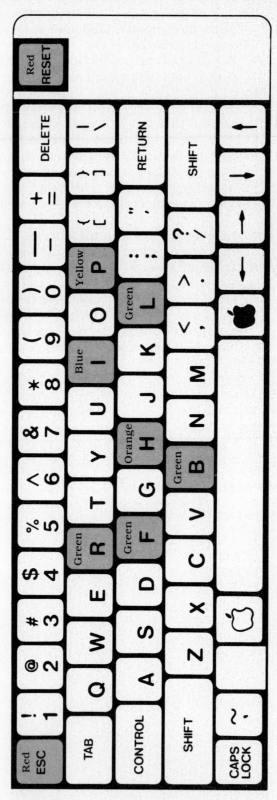

Illustration 8.6   Apple IIe keyboard.   Reprinted with the permission of Apple Computer, Inc.

R, L, F, B = Green = makes turtles go

P = Yellow = stores program

I = Blue = invokes procedure

ESC and RESET = Red

H = Orange = moves turtle "home" to middle of screen

▶ **PURPOSE**   **To experience the functions of a computer by giving commands, storing procedures, and invoking procedures**

To experience the computer in ways other than responding to preprogrammed software

MATERIALS — Apple IIe computer, color monitor, disk drive
— Apple LOGO disk
— ZOOM from the Apple LOGO TOOL KIT disk

PROCEDURE   1. Color-code the keyboard (see previous activity).
2. Modify the background color of the monitor if necessary (see appendix activity).
3. Load Apple LOGO disk. The screen will display the following:
IF YOU HAVE YOUR OWN FILE DISKETTE,
INSERT IT NOW, THEN PRESS RETURN
4. Remove Apple LOGO disk.
5. Insert TOOL KIT disk. Press RETURN. The screen will display:
WELCOME TO LOGO
6. Type: LOAD "ZOOM
Press RETURN and wait. You will see the turtle cursor and the instructions:
PRESS SPACEBAR AND START ZOOMING!
7. Encourage the child to make the turtle move by pressing any of the green keys.
8. Let the child experiment with the keys for a while.
9. Explain that the R and L keys turn the turtle, while the F key moves the turtle forward and the B key moves it back. The H key brings the turtle "home" when it has gone off the screen.
10. When the child has made a design on the screen show him or her how to save the design:
Press yellow P.
Type a name for the design (child's name works well).
Press RETURN key.
The design will disappear from the screen, but will be saved or stored in the computer's memory.
11. To bring the design back:
Press blue I (to invoke procedure).
Type the name of the design.
Press RETURN key.
The computer will put the design back on the screen.

Note: Use paper and pencil to list the name of each design made and stored so that children can easily bring back their designs from the computer memory.

If your computer has a printer hooked up to it, you can print out the graphic designs made by the children by using a graphics screen printing program (such as ZOOM GRAFIX). It is very rewarding and gratifying to the child to have a printed copy of his or her design.

If keys are inadvertantly pressed that cause the turtle to stop, press RETURN; type ZOOM; and press RETURN.

To invoke (bring up) instructions on the screen, hold down the SHIFT key and press ?.

▶ PURPOSE   **To create graphics with the Koala Pad**

              To provide experiences in sequential procedures, eye-hand coordination, directionality, decision making, fine motor skills, and visual discrimination and tracking

MATERIALS   — Apple IIe computer, color monitor, disk drive
              — Koala Pad Touch Tablet
              — MICRO ILLUSTRATOR program (supplied with the Koala Pad) (See Illustration 8.7.)

INTRODUCTORY This activity is appropriate for ages three and up. The Koala Pad
COMMENTS   Touch Tablet is a 5″ x 9″ touch-sensitive pad with two buttons at the top. Graphics and some game commands are controlled on the monitor by moving a finger or stylus across the surface of the Koala Pad. It takes some practice for children to master the mechanics involved in operating the Koala Pad. Free-form drawing (using the DRAW option) is easiest for preschoolers. Give them plenty of time to practice. Children may be most successful if they master the use of one button at a time. Starting with the use of the left button, explain how the cursor will leave a line if they hold the left button down, but if they do not want to leave a mark on the screen, they must release the button.

              After mastering the use of the DRAW option and the left button, children can learn to use the FILL option. The FILL option enables the child to select a color to fill in any of the spaces with the cursor. If your computer has a printer hooked up to it, you may print out the graphics designs created by the children.

PROCEDURE   1. Load MICRO ILLUSTRATOR.
              2. When title page appears, push the left button on Koala Pad.
              3. When the picture menu appears, say:
                 This is the picture menu. We use it to choose what we want to make and the color we want to use.
                 Today we are going to draw (point to "draw" option).
              4. Give these instructions:
                 Use your stylus to put the cursor on "draw."
              5. **While your stylus is on "draw," press the left button.**
              6. **With the stylus, put the cursor on the color you want.**
              7. **Now press the left button.**
              8. **Lift the stylus up.**
              9. **Push the button** (to get to the screen).
              10. **Place the stylus on the pad.**
              11. **Hold the button down while you move the cursor. Now you are drawing!**
              12. **If you want to move the cursor without drawing, do not push the button.**
              13. To return to the menu, lift the stylus and push the button.
              14. To erase graphics, return to the menu, use stylus to choose "Erase," and follow erase instructions.

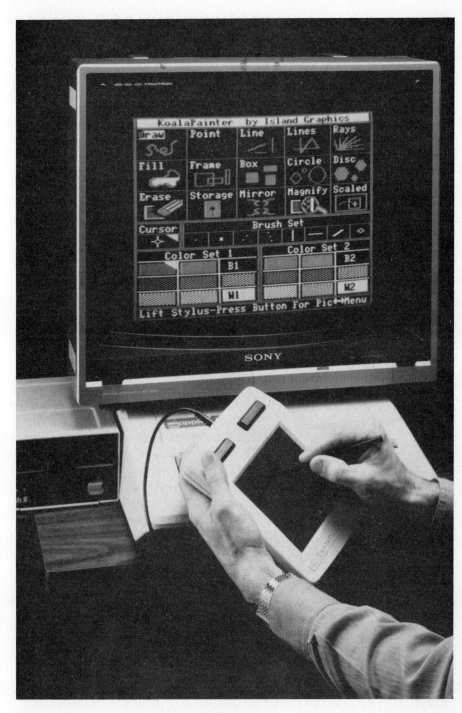

Illustration 8.7 **Koala MICRO ILLUSTRATOR.** Used by permission of Koala Technologies Corporation.

Bibliography of Resources

SOURCES FOR ACTIVITIES

Software for our activities came from the following companies:

The Learning Company, 545 Middlefield Rd., Suite 170, Menlo Park, CA 94025.

Eric Software Publishing, 1713 Tulare, Fresno, CA 93721.

Random House, Inc., 201 E. 50th St., New York, NY 10022.

Software Entertainment Company, 541 Willamette, Eugene, OR 97401.

Koala Technologies Corporation, 3100 Patrick Henry Dr., Santa Clara, CA 95050.

ADDITIONAL RESOURCES

New documents and journal articles are being published daily in the field of computer education. To keep up with the latest information, the teacher can refer to the following:

ERIC (Educational Resources Information Center) provides monthly indexes of documents and journal articles pertaining to computers and young children. ERIC documents are abstracted and indexed in *Resources in Education (RIE)* and may be read on microfiche at libraries housing ERIC materials. Further information may be obtained by writing ERIC/EECE Clearinghouse, University of Illinois, 805 W. Pennsylvania Ave., Urbana, IL 61801-4897.

Journal articles are annotated and indexed in *Current Index to Journals in Education (CIJE)* and may be found in libraries. Article reprints may be obtained from University Microfilms International, Article Reprint Department, 300 N. Zeeb Rd., Ann Arbor, MI 48106.

PRESCHOOL EDUCATIONAL SOFTWARE BUYER'S GUIDE [8]

Preschool Software Companies

ARTWORX
150 N. Main St.
Fairport, NY 14450
(800) 828-6573

ATARI PROGRAM
EXCHANGE
P.O. Box 3705
Santa Clara, CA 95055
(408) 942-6790

AVANT-GARDE
P.O. Box 30161
Eugene, OR 97403
(503) 345-3043

BECI (BOSTON
EDUCATIONAL
COMPUTING INC.)
78 Dartmouth St.
Boston, MA 02116
(617) 536-5116

CHILDREN'S
COMPUTER
WORKSHOP
1 Lincoln Plaza
New York, NY 10023
(212) 595-3456

CLASSIC FAMILY S/W
2357 Southway Dr.
P.O. Box 21341
Columbus, OH 43221
(614) 486-3563

COMPU-TATIONS
P.O. Box 502
Troy, MI 48099
(313) 524-2317

COMPUTER LEARNING
CENTER 4 CHILDREN
1775 E. Tropicana Ave.
Liberace #8 Las Vegas,
NV 89109
(702) 798-3085

COUNTERPOINT
SOFTWARE INC.
Suite 140
Shelard Plaza N.
Minneapolis, MN 55426
(800) 328-1223

CURSOR
Box 550
Goleta, CA 93116
(805) 683-1585

DENIS
P.O. Box 274
Midland Park, NJ 07432

DYNACOMP INC.
1427 Monroe Ave.
Rochester, NY 14618
(716) 442-8960

EDUSOFT
P.O. Box 2560
Berkeley, CA 94702
(415) 548-2304;
(800) 227-2778

EDU-WARE SERVICES
INC.
P.O. Box 22222
Aguora, CA 91301
(213) 706-0661

HARTLEY
COURSEWARE INC.
P.O. Box 431
Dimondale, MI 48821
(616) 942-8987

HAYDEN SOFTWARE
CO.
600 Suffolk St.
Lowell, MA 01853
(800) 343-1218
(617) 937-0200

HUNTINGTON
COMPUTING
P.O. Box 1297
Corcoran, CA 93212
(800) 344-5106
(800) 692-4146

IDEATECH
P.O. Box 62451
Sunnyvale, CA 94088
(408) 985-7591

KANGAROO INC.
332 S. Michigan Ave.
Suite 700
Chicago, IL 60604
(312) 987-9050

LAUREATE LEARNING
SYSTEMS INC.
1 Mill St.
Burlington, VT 05401
(802) 862-7355

MERRY BEE
815 Crest Dr.
Omaha, NE 68046
(402) 592-3479

MICROCOMPUTERS IN
EDUCATION
Robbinsdale Area Schools
4148 Winnetka Ave. N.
Minneapolis, MN 55427
(612) 533-2781

MICRO-ED INC.
P.O. Box 444005
8108 Eden Rd.
Eden Prairie, MN 55304
(800) 642-7633

MICRO SCHOOL
PROGRAMS-BERTAMAX
INC.
3647 Stone Way North
Seattle, WA 98103
(206) 282-6249

MINNESOTA
EDUCATIONAL
COMPUTING CONSORTIUM
2520 Broadway Dr.
St. Paul, MN 55113
(612) 638-0638

NTS SOFTWARE
211 S. Orange Ave.
Nialto, CA 92376
(714) 875-2968

ORANGE CHERRY MEDIA
7 Delano Dr.
Bedford Hills, NY 10507
(914) 666-8434

PDI (PROGRAM DESIGN
INC.)
95 East Putnam Ave.
Greenwich, CT 06830
(203) 661-8799

PROGRAMS BY MR. BOB
P.O. Box 94
Montrose, CA 91020
(213) 952-3001

RADIO SHACK EDUCATION
DIVISION
One Tandy Center
Fort Worth, TX 76102
(800) 433-5682
(800) 772-8938

RANDOM HOUSE
SYSTEMS
7307 S. Yale
Tulsa, OK 74136
(918) 492-5644

RIGHT ON PROGRAMS
(DIV. OF COMPUTCOM
INC.)
P.O. Box 977
Huntington, NY 11743
(516) 271-3177

SCOTT, FORESMAN AND
COMPANY
1900 East Lake Ave.
Glenview, IL 60025
(312) 729-3000

SIERRA ON-LINE
Sierra On-Line Bldg.
Coarsehold, CA 93614
(209) 683-6858

SOFTWARE
PRODUCTIONS INC.
2357 Southway Dr.
P.O. Box 21341
Columbus, OH 43221
(614) 486-3563

SOUTHWEST EDPSYCH
SERVICES
P.O. Box 1870
Phoenix, AZ 85001
(602) 253-6528

SPINNAKER SOFTWARE
CORP.
215 First St.
Cambridge, MA 02142
(617) 868-4700

TEXAS INSTRUMENTS
P.O. Box 53
Lubbock, TX 79408
(800) 858-4075

THE LEARNING
COMPANY
545 Middlefield Rd.,
Suite 170
Menlo Park, CA 94025
(415) 328-5410

XEROX EDUCATION
PUBLICATIONS/WEEKLY
READER
245 Long Hill Rd.
Middletown, CT 06457
(203) 347-7251

[8]Reprinted with permission from *Personal Software*, November 1983, pages 43, 45, 47, 49, 51, 53, 185. Copyright, 1983. Hayden Publishing Company.

Software for Preschoolers

PACKAGE/COMPANY	SYSTEMS	PRICE	GRAPHICS	SOUND EFFECTS	DESCRIPTION
Language Arts Skills					
TEACHER'S PET Artworx	APL II, II+, IIe; TRS; COM VIC 20, 64	$14.95 tape; $18.95 disk R/M	C	Y	Teaches children to recognize letters in the alphabet
HODGE PODGE Artworx	APL II, II+, IIe; ATA 400, 800, 1200; COM VIC 20	$19.95 R/M	C	Y	Teaches children to recognize letters in the alphabet
MY SPELLING EASEL Atari	ATA 400, 800	$29.95 M	C	Y	Teaches spelling skills
MY FIRST ALPHABET Atari	ATA 800	$34.95 M	C	Y	Teaches children to recognize letters in the alphabet
ALPHA-BECI Beci	COM VIC 20, 64; ATA	$16.95 R/M	C	Y	Teaches matching; upper- and lowercase letters
ALPHA BEAM WITH ERNIE Children's Computer Workshop	ATA 2600	$29.95 R/M	C	Y	Reinforces letter matching; directions
COOKIE MONSTER'S LETTER CRUNCH Children's Computer Workshop	TRS-C	$19.95 R/M	C	Y	Reinforces letter recognition
COOKIE MONSTER'S MUNCH Children's Computer Workshop	ATA 2600	$29.95 R/M	C	Y	Reinforces prereading and prewriting skills
EARLY ELEMENTARY I and II (ALPHA DRILL, ALPHABET LINE, INSIDE OUT) Compu-tations	APL II, IIe	$29.95 M	C	Y	Teaches children to recognize letters in the alphabet
LET'S ALPHABETIZE Computer Learning Center	APL, II, II+, IIe; ATA 400, 800, 1200	$10.95 R/M	B/W	Y	Teaches alphabet skills
LETTERS Computer Learning Center	APL II, II+, IIe; ATA 400, 800, 1200	$9.95 R/M	B/W	Y	Teaches children to recognize letters in the alphabet
WHAT DIFFERENCE? Computer Learning Center	TRS, I, III	$12.95 R/M	B/W	Y	Teaches children to differentiate between groups of words
EARLY GAMES FOR YOUNG CHILDREN Counterpoint	APL II, II+, IIe; ATA 400, 800, 1200; IBM PC; COM VIC 20, 64; TRS I, III; TRS-C	$29.95 M	C	Y	Teaches letter recognition, alphabet sequence; typing skills

APPLE-APL (II, II+, IIe)   TRS-80-TRS (I, II, III, 4)   NORTH STAR-NS   COMPUSTAR-CS   R-RETAIL   CP/M SYSTEMS-
ATARI-ATA (400, 800, 1200)   IBM-IBM   H(orizon)   HEATH/ZENITH-H/Z   M-MAIL ORDER   CP/M
COMPAQ-CPQ   TI-TI (99/4, 99/4A)   A(dvantage)   SUPERBRAIN-SB   Programs on
COMMODORE-COM (64, PET,   RADIO SHACK COLOR-   NEC PC 8000-NEC   OSBORNE-OSB   disk unless
VIC 20)   TRS-C   CANON AS 100-CAN   specified

Software for Preschoolers (cont.)

PACKAGE/COMPANY	SYSTEMS	PRICE	GRAPHICS	SOUND EFFECTS	DESCRIPTION
Language Arts Skills					
CHOMP Denis	COM PET	M	B/W	N	Teaches word recognition; vowel and consonant sounds
HODGE PODGE; HODGE PODGE II Dynacomp	APL II, II+, IIe; TRS I, III	$14.95 tape; $18.95 disk R/M	C	Y	Teaches children to recognize letters in the alphabet
ALPHABET SONG Edusoft	APL II, II+, IIe	$24.95 M	C	Y	Teaches children to recognize letters in the alphabet
SPELLING & READING PRIMER Edu-ware	APL II, II+, IIe; ATA 400, 800, 1200	$39.95 M	C	N	Teaches reading and spelling skills
SPELLING BEE GAMES Edu-ware	APL II, II+, IIe; ATA 400, 800, 1200	$39.95 M	C	Y	Teaches spelling skills
LETTER RECOGNITION Hartley	APL IIe	$26.95 M	C	N	Teaches letter recognition
VOWELS Hartley	APL IIe	$79 M	C	Y	Teaches vowel sounds
ALPHABET JMH	COM VIC 20	$9.95 M	C	Y	Teaches children to recognize letters in the alphabet
FIRST WORDS Laureate	APL II, IIe	$185 M	C	Y	Teaches prereading skills
NURSERY TIME Merry Bee	APL II+, IIe	$29.95 M	C	Y	Children can create own story or rhyme
ABOVE OR BELOW Micro-Ed	COM 64	$14.95 R/M	C	Y	Matches letters to line spaces
MATCHING SMALL WITH CAPITAL LETTERS Micro-Ed	COM 64	$7.95 R/M	C	Y	Teaches upper- and lower-case matching skills
MATCHING WORDS Micro-Ed	COM 64	$7.95 R/M	C	Y	Teaches word matching skills
MATCHIT Micro School Programs	ATA 400, 800, 1200; TRS	$24.85 tape; $29.50 disk R/M	C	N	Teaches upper- and lower-case matching skills
ELEMENTARY VOLUME 7, PREREADING Minnesota Educational Computing Consortium	APL II	$38 M	C	Y	Teaches prereading and memory skills
PREREADING Minnesota Educational Computing Consortium	ATA 400, 800	$38 M	C	Y	Teaches prereading and memory skills

APPLE-APL (II, II+, IIe)
ATARI-ATA (400, 800, 1200)
COMPAQ-CPQ
COMMODORE-COM (64, PET, VIC 20)
TRS-80-TRS (I, II, III, 4)
IBM-IBM
TI-TI (99/4, 99/4A)
RADIO SHACK COLOR-TRS-C
NORTH STAR-NS
H(orizon)
A(dvantage)
NEC PC 8000-NEC
CANON AS 100-CAN
COMPUSTAR-CS
HEATH/ZENITH-H/Z
SUPERBRAIN-SB
OSBORNE-OSB
R-RETAIL
M-MAIL ORDER
Programs on disk unless specified
CP/M SYSTEMS-CP/M

Software for Preschoolers (cont.)

PACKAGE/COMPANY	SYSTEMS	PRICE	GRAPHICS	SOUND EFFECTS	DESCRIPTION
Language Arts Skills					
WORKING WITH THE ALPHABET (ALPHABET SOUP, ALPHABETICAL ORDER) Orange Cherry Media	ATA 400, 800, 1200; TRS; APL II, II+, IIe; COM PET	$28 tape; $34 disk R/M	C	N	Teaches children to recognize letters in the alphabet
PRESCHOOL SOFTWARE IQ BUILDER I, II PDI	APL II, II+, IIe; ATA 400, 800, 1200	$18.95 tape; $23.95 disk R/M	C	Y	Teaches matching; letter and word recognition
PRESCHOOL Programs by Mr. Bob	TRS I, III	$14.95 M	C	Y	Teaches antonyms
ALPHAKEY Radio Shack	TRS I, III, 4	$39.95 R	B/W	N	Teaches alphabet skills
ALPHABET KEYBOARD Random House	APL II, IIe, II+; TRS	$24 tape; $34 disk M	B/W	N	Teaches keyboard familiarity
ALPHABET SEQUENCE Random House	APL II, II+, IIe; TRS	$24 tape; $45 disk M	B/W	N	Teaches children to recognize letters in the aphabet
EARLY READING Scott, Foresman and Co.	TI 99/4A; APL II, II+, IIe; ATA 400, 800, 1200	$58.95 R/M	C	Y	Teaches word identification and classification
LEARNING WITH LEEPER Sierra On-Line	APL II, IIe	$34.95 disk R	C	Y	Teaches counting, matching, and creativity skills
MICRO MOTHER GOOSE Software Productions	APL II	$39.95 R/M	C	Y	Teaches keyboard familiarity
ALPHABET BEASTS/CREATURE FEATURES Software Productions	APL II	$29.95 R/M	C	Y	Teaches letter and number recognition
THE READING MACHINE Southwest Edpsych Services	APL II	$59.95 M	C	Y	Teaches reading skills
HEY DIDDLE DIDDLE Spinnaker	APL II, II+, IIe; ATA 400, 800, 1200; IBM PC; COM 64	$29.95 ($39.95 in ROM) R/M	C	Y	Teaches Mother Goose rhymes; reading skills
KINDERCOMP Spinnaker	APL II, II+, IIe; ATA 400, 800, 1200; IBM PC; COM 64	$29.95 ($39.95 in ROM) R/M	C	Y	Teaches drawing, scribbling, naming, sequencing, matching, and lettering skills
ALPHABET ZOO Spinnaker	APL II, II+, IIe; ATA 400, 800, 1200; IBM PC; COM 64	$29.95 ($39.95 in ROM) R/M	C	Y	Teaches children to recognize letters in the alphabet

APPLE-APL (II, II+, IIe)
ATARI-ATA (400, 800, 1200)
COMPAQ-CPQ
COMMODORE-COM (64, PET, VIC 20)

TRS-80-TRS (I, II, III, 4)
IBM-IBM
TI-TI (99/4, 99/4A)
RADIO SHACK COLOR-TRS-C

NORTH STAR-NS
H(orizon)
    A(dvantage)
NEC PC 8000-NEC
CANON AS 100-CAN

COMPUSTAR-CS
HEATH/ZENITH-H/Z
SUPERBRAIN-SB
OSBORNE-OSB

R-RETAIL
M-MAIL ORDER
Programs on disk unless specified

CP/M SYSTEMS-CP/M

Software for Preschoolers (cont.)

PACKAGE/COMPANY	SYSTEMS	PRICE	GRAPHICS	SOUND EFFECTS	DESCRIPTION
Language Arts Skills					
EARLY LEARNING FUN Texas Instruments	TI 99/4A	$29.95 R/M	C	Y	Teaches letter recognition
JUGGLES' RAINBOW The Learning Company	APL II, II+, IIe; ATA 400, 800, 1200	$29.95 R/M	C	Y	Teaches reading skills
STICKYBEAR ABC's Xerox	APL II, II+, IIe	$39.95 R/M	C	Y	Teaches children to recognize letters in the alphabet
Perception Skills					
ERNIE'S MAGIC SHAPES Children's Computer Workshop	TRS-C	$19.95 R/M	C	Y	Teaches shape differentiation
BIG BIRD'S EGG CATCH Children's Computer Workshop	ATA 2600	$29.95 R/M	C	Y	Reinforces directions, left and right; strategy
BIG BIRD'S SPECIAL DELIVERY Children's Computer Workshop	TRS-C	$19.95 R/M	C	Y	Teaches cognitive skills
EARLY GAMES FOR YOUNG CHILDREN Counterpoint	TRS I, III; APL II, II+, IIe; ATA 400, 800, 1200; IBM PC; COM VIC 20, 64; TRS-C	$29.95 M	C	Y	Teaches shape discrimination
MAXIT; RESCUE; SKEET; ETC. Cursor	COM PET, CBM	$5.95 cassette M	B/W	Y	Teaches logic, strategy, arcade games, precision
HODGE PODGE; HODGE PODGE II Dynacomp	APL II, II+, IIe; TRS I, III	$14.95 cassette; $18.95 disk R/M	C	Y	Teaches letter recognition
CHILDREN'S CAROUSEL Dynacomp	APL II, II+, IIe	$19.95 disk R/M	C	Y	Teaches counting; shape and number recognition
CHILD'S PLAY Huntington Computing	APL II, II+, IIe	$19.99 R/M	C	Y	Teaches object and size differentiation; eye-hand coordination
STARS Microcomputers in Education	COM PET	$9.95 M	B/W	N	Teaches size differentiation; logic
MATCHING SHAPES Micro-Ed	COM 64	$14.95 R/M	C	Y	Teaches shape recognition

APPLE-APL (II, II+, IIe)   TRS-80-TRS (I, II, III, 4)   NORTH STAR-NS   COMPUSTAR-CS   R-RETAIL   CP/M SYSTEMS-CP/M
ATARI-ATA (400, 800, 1200)   IBM-IBM   H(orizon)   HEATH/ZENITH-H/Z   M-MAIL ORDER
COMPAQ-CPQ   TI-TI (99/4, 99/4A)   A(dvantage)   SUPERBRAIN-SB   Programs on
COMMODORE-COM (64, PET, VIC 20)   RADIO SHACK COLOR-TRS-C   NEC PC 8000-NEC   OSBORNE-OSB   disk unless
CANON AS 100-CAN   specified

Software for Preschoolers (cont.)

PACKAGE/COMPANY	SYSTEMS	PRICE	GRAPHICS	SOUND EFFECTS	DESCRIPTION
Perception Skills					
SAMMY THE SEA SER-PENT; ADVENTURES OF OS-WALD PDI	ATA 400, 800, 1200	$18.95 cassette; $23.95 disk R/M	C	Y	Teaches listening and directional skills
TEDDY'S MAGIC BAL-LOON PDI	ATA 400, 800, 1200	$34.95 cassette; $36.95 disk R/M	C	Y	Teaches discrimination skills; directionality
PRESCHOOL Programs by Mr. Bob	TRS I, III	$14.95 M	C	Y	Teaches memory skills
EARLY LEARNING FUN Texas Instruments	TI 99/4A	$29.95 R/M	C	Y	Teaches shape discrimination; sorting
GERTRUDE'S SECRETS The Learning Company	APL II+, IIe	$44.95 R/M	C	N	Teaches order and sequence, shape and color discrimination; recognizing patterns; logical thinking
Number Skills					
TEACHER'S PET Artworx	APL II, II+, IIe; ATA 400, 800, 1200; TRS; COM VIC 20, 64	$14.95 cassette; $18.95 disk R/M	C	Y	Teaches beginning math skills
MONKEY ON A TREE Atari	ATA 800	$22.95 M	C	Y	Teaches beginning math skills
NUMBER-BECI Beci	COM VIC 20, 64; ATA 400, 800, 1200	$16.95 R/M	C	Y	Teaches number recognition, counting, grouping by shape and color
ADD/SUB Beci	COM VIC 20, 64; ATA 400, 800, 1200	$16.95 R/M	C	Y	Teaches addition and subtraction
GROVER'S NUMBER ROVER Children's Computer Workshop	TRS-C	$19.95 R/M	C	Y	Reinforces addition and subtraction skills
EARLY ELEMENTARY I AND II Compu-tations	APL II, IIe	$29.95 M	C	Y	Teaches introductory number skills
SCRAMBLE (WEEKDAYS AND NUMBERS) Computer Learning Center	TRS-I, III	$10.95 R/M	B/W	Y	Teaches matching and number skills

APPLE-APL (II, II+, IIe)	TRS-80-TRS (I, II, III, 4)	NORTH STAR-NS	COMPUSTAR-CS	R-RETAIL	CP/M SYSTEMS-
ATARI-ATA (400, 800, 1200)	IBM-IBM	H(orizon)	HEATH/ZENITH-H/Z	M-MAIL ORDER	CP/M
COMPAQ-CPQ	TI-TI (99/4, 99/4A)	A(dvantage)	SUPERBRAIN-SB	Programs on	
COMMODORE-COM (64, PET, VIC 20)	RADIO SHACK COLOR-TRS-C	NEC PC 8000-NEC CANON AS 100-CAN	OSBORNE-OSB	disk unless specified	

Software for Preschoolers (cont.)

PACKAGE/COMPANY	SYSTEMS	PRICE	GRAPHICS	SOUND EFFECTS	DESCRIPTION
Number Skills					
EARLY GAMES FOR YOUNG CHILDREN Counterpoint	APL II, II+, IIe; ATA 400, 800, 1200; IBM PC; COM 64, VIC 20; TRS I, III, TRS-C	$29.95 M	C	Y	Teaches number recognition and counting
COUNT: ADDITION/SUBTRACTION; MULTIPLICATION/DIVISION Denis	COM PET	$8 M	B/W	N	Teaches counting from 0 to 25
MATH WHIZ QUIZ Dynacomp	ATA 400, 800, 1200	$13.95 tape; $17.95 disk R/M	C	Y	Teaches counting and number skills
COUNT AND ADD Edusoft	APL II, II+, IIe	$24.95 M	C	N	Teaches basics of addition; numbers, pictures, shapes
COUNTING BEE Edu-ware	APL II, II+, IIe	$39.95 M	C	Y	Teaches counting, weights, measures, basic math skills
MICROMATH (INCL. MICROADDITION, MICROSUBTRACTION, MICRODIVISION, MICRO-MULTIPLICATION) Hayden	APL II; ATA 400, 800	$29.95 R/M	C	Y	Teaches math skills
MUSICAL MATH Hayden	APL II; ATA 400, 800	$34.95 R/M	C	Y	Teaches math skills
CHILD'S PLAY Huntington Computing	APL II, II+, IIe	$19.99 R/M	C	Y	Teaches counting and number skills
COUNTING JMH	COM VIC 20, 64, PET; ATA 400, 800	$9.95 M	C	Y	Teaches counting skills
STARS Microcomputers in Education	COM PET	$9.95 M	B/W	N	Teaches number skills
NUMBER WORDS MATCH Microcomputers in Education	COM PET	$9.95 M	B/W	N	Teaches number skills
NUMBER MATCH Micro School Programs	ATA 800; TRS-C, TRS III	$24.95 tape; $29.50 disk R/M	C	N	Teaches number skills and matching
COUNTING Minnesota Educational Computing Consortium	ATA 400, 800	$34 M	C	Y	Teaches counting skills

APPLE-APL (II, II+, IIe)	TRS-80-TRS (I, II, III, 4)	NORTH STAR-NS	COMPUSTAR-CS	R-RETAIL	CP/M SYSTEMS-
ATARI-ATA (400, 800, 1200)	IBM-IBM	H(orizon)	HEATH/ZENITH-H/Z	M-MAIL ORDER	CP/M
COMPAQ-CPQ	TI-TI (99/4, 99/4A)	A(dvantage)	SUPERBRAIN-SB	Programs on	
COMMODORE-COM (64, PET, VIC 20)	RADIO SHACK COLOR-TRS-C	NEC PC 8000-NEC CANON AS 100-CAN	OSBORNE-OSB	disk unless specified	

Software for Preschoolers (cont.)

PACKAGE/COMPANY	SYSTEMS	PRICE	GRAPHICS	SOUND EFFECTS	DESCRIPTION
Number Skills					
STARTING OUT (INCLUDES HOW MANY? COUNTING, SEQUENCES, DICE DOMINOS) NTS	APL II+; TRS I, III	$129 M	C (APL)	Y (TRS)	Teaches number skills
PRESCHOOL Programs by Mr. Bob	TRS I, II	$14.95 M	C	Y	Teaches number concepts from one to nine
MATHEMATICS ACTION GAMES, MODULE A (INCLUDES FROG JUMP, SPACE JOURNEY, PICTURE PARTS PACKAGE) Scott Foresman and Co.	TI 99/4A	$75 each R/M	C	Y	Teaches number skills
LEARNING WITH LEEPER Sierra On-Line	APL II, IIe	$34.95 disk R	C	Y	Teaches math skills
EARLY LEARNING FUN Texas Instruments	TI 99/4A	$29.95 R/M	C	Y	Teaches counting and number reecognition
BUMBLE GAMES The Learning Company	APL II+, IIe	$39.95 R/M	C	Y	Teaches counting, number pairing, and spatial awareness
STICKYBEAR NUMBERS Xerox	APL II, II+, IIe	$39.95 R/M	C	Y	Teaches introductory number skills
Miscellaneous Skills					
ESCAPE TO EQUATUS Atari	ATA 800	$24.95 M	C	Y	Teaches problem-solving skills
MAGIC MELODY Atari	ATA 400, 800	$17 M	C	Y	Reinforces creativity; plays music based on pattern child creates
I'M DIFFERENT Atari	ATA 800	$24.95 M	C	Y	Teaches matching and differentiation skills
SCRAMBLE (SUPERHEROES AND FARM ANIMALS) Computer Learning Center	TRS I, III	$10.95 tape R/M	B/W	Y	Teaches animal recognition
DOODLE DRAW Dynacomp	ATA 400, 800, 1200	$14.95 tape; $28.95 disk R/M	C	N	Reinforces drawing skills
COLOR GUESS Ideatech	APL II, II+, IIe	$12.95 ($1.50 shipping) R/M	C	N	Reinforces reading and spelling of color words

APPLE-APL (II, II+, IIe)	TRS-80-TRS (I, II, III, 4)	NORTH STAR-NS	COMPUSTAR-CS	R-RETAIL	CP/M SYSTEMS-
ATARI-ATA (400, 800, 1200)	IBM-IBM	H(orizon)	HEATH/ZENITH-H/Z	M-MAIL ORDER	CP/M
COMPAQ-CPQ	TI-TI (99/4, 99/4A)	A(dvantage)	SUPERBRAIN-SB	Programs on	
COMMODORE-COM (64, PET, VIC 20)	RADIO SHACK COLOR-TRS-C	NEC PC 8000-NEC CANON AS 100-CAN	OSBORNE-OSB	disk unless specified	

Software for Preschoolers (cont.)

PACKAGE/COMPANY	SYSTEMS	PRICE	GRAPHICS	SOUND EFFECTS	DESCRIPTION
Miscellaneous Skills					
JEEPERS CREATURES Kangaroo	APL II, II+, IIe; ATA 800, 1200	$35 R/M	C	Y	Teaches animal recognition
LOGO Radio Shack	TRS-C	$49.95 R	C	N	Introduces computer concepts
TELLING TIME Random House	APL II, II+, IIe	$45 tape; $57 disk M	B/W	N	Teaches children how to tell time
FARM LIFE Right On Programs	APL II+, IIe; COM PET, 64	$18 M	C	N	Teaches basic concepts of farming and farm production
LEARNING WITH LEE-PER Sierra On-Line	APL II, IIe	$34.95 R	C	Y	Teaches counting, matching, creativity skills
DELTA DRAWING Spinnaker	APL II+, IIe; ATA 400, 800, 1200; IBM PC; COM 64	$39.95 cartridge; $49.95 disk R/M	C	N	Reinforces drawing skills
FACEMAKER Spinnaker	APL II+, IIe; ATA 400, 800, 1200; IBM PC; COM 64	$34.95; $39.95 (ROM) R/M	C	Y	Reinforces memory and concentration skills

APPLE-APL (II, II+, IIe)
ATARI-ATA (400, 800, 1200)
COMPAQ-CPQ
COMMODORE-COM (64, PET, VIC 20)

TRS-80-TRS (I, II, III, 4)
IBM-IBM
TI-TI (99/4, 99/4A)
RADIO SHACK COLOR-TRS-C

NORTH STAR-NS
H(orizon)
A(dvantage)
NEC PC 8000-NEC
CANON AS 100-CAN

COMPUSTAR-CS
HEATH/ZENITH-H/Z
SUPERBRAIN-SB
OSBORNE-OSB

R-RETAIL
M-MAIL ORDER
Programs on
disk unless
specified

CP/M SYSTEMS-CP/M

Glossary of Computer Terms

Boot　To start up a computer by loading a program into memory from an external storage medium such as a disk. Often accomplished by loading a small program whose purpose is to read the larger program into memory. The program is said to "pull itself in by its own bootstraps," hence the term *bootstrapping* or *booting*.

Chip　The small piece of semiconducting material (usually silicon) on which an integrated circuit is fabricated. The word *chip* refers to the piece of silicon itself, but is often used for an integrated circuit.

Cold start　The process of starting up the computer when the power is first turned on by loading the operating system into memory. (Compare with *Warm start*.)

Command　A communication (usually typed on the keyboard) from the user to a computer system directing it to perform some action.

Computer　An electronic device for performing predefined (programmed) computations.

Computer system　A computer and its associated hardware and software.

Connector　A physical device, such as a plug, socket, or jack, used to connect one hardware component of a system to another.

Control character　A character that controls or modifies the way information is printed or displayed. Some commands require the user to hold down the CONTROL key while typing some other character.

Crash　To cease operating unexpectedly, possibly damaging or destroying information in the process.

Cursor　A marker or symbol displayed on the screen that marks where the user's next action will take effect or where the next character typed from the keyboard will appear. (In LOGO, the cursor is called a *turtle*.)

Digit　One of the characters 0 to 9, used to express numbers in text form.

Disk　An information storage medium consisting of a flat, circular magnetic surface on which information can be recorded in the form of small magnetized spots, similar to the way sounds are recorded on tape. Some disks are hard disks; flexible disks are called *floppy disks*.

Disk drive　A peripheral device that writes and reads information on the surface of a magnetic disk.

Diskette　A term sometimes used for the small (5¼-inch) flexible (*floppy*) disks.

Disk operating system (DOS)　A software system that enables the computer to control and communicate with one or more disk drives.

Display 1. Information exhibited visually, especially on the screen of a display device. 2. To exhibit information visually. 3. A display device.

Display device A device, such as a television set or video monitor, that exhibits information visually.

Display screen The glass or plastic panel on the front of a display device on which images are displayed.

Escape mode A state of the computer entered by pressing the ESC key, in which certain keys on the keyboard take on special meanings for positioning the cursor and controlling the display of text on the screen.

Execute To perform or carry out a specified action or sequence of actions, such as those described by a program.

Graphics 1. Information presented in the form of pictures or images. 2. The display of pictures or images on a computer's display screen.

Hardware Those components of a computer system consisting of physical (electronic or mechanical) devices. (Compare with *Software*).

Keyboard The set of keys built into the computer, similar to a typewriter keyboard, for typing information to the computer.

Load To transfer information from a peripheral storage medium (such as a disk) into main memory for use; for example, to transfer a program into memory for execution.

Logo A programming language designed to teach programming to children, making use of the computer's graphic display capabilities.

Memory A hardware component of a computer system that can store information for later retrieval.

Menu A selection of choices on the display screen.

Modem A device enabling the computer to transmit and receive information over a telephone line.

Operating system A software system that organizes the computer's resources and capabilities and makes them available to the user or to application programs running on the computer.

Output 1. Information transferred from a computer to some external destination, such as the display screen, a disk drive, a printer, or a modem. 2. The act of transferring such information.

Peripheral device A device, such as a video monitor, disk drive, printer, or modem, used in conjunction with a computer. Often physically separate from the computer and connected to it by wires, cables, or some other form of interface, typically by means of a peripheral card.

Program A set of instructions conforming to the rules and conventions of a particular programming language, describing actions for a computer to perform in order to accomplish some task.

Prompt To remind or signal the user that some action is expected, typically by displaying a distinctive symbol, a reminder message, or a menu of choices on the display screen.

Software   Those components of a computer system consisting of programs that determine or control the behavior of the computer (Compare with *Hardware.*)

Startup disk   A disk containing software recorded in the proper form to be loaded into the computer's memory to set the system into operation. Sometimes called a *boot disk.*

User   The person operating or controlling a computer system.

Video monitor   A display device capable of receiving video signals by direct connection only and which cannot receive broadcast signals such as commercial television waves.

Warm start   The process of restarting the computer after the power is already on without reloading the operating system into main memory and often without losing the program of information already in main memory. (Compare with *Cold start.*)

Appendix Activity

▶ **PURPOSE**   **To change the background color on the monitor from blue to black**

MATERIALS   — Apple IIe computer, color monitor, disk drive
— Apple LOGO disk
— ZOOM from the Apple LOGO TOOL KIT disk

INTRODUCTORY   If the head of the turtle cursor is difficult to see against the color
COMMENTS   background of the monitor, use the following procedure to change the
background color from blue to black.

PROCEDURE
1. Load Apple LOGO disk. The screen will display the following:
   IF YOU HAVE YOUR OWN FILE DISKETTE,
   INSERT IT NOW, THEN PRESS RETURN
2. Remove Apple LOGO disk.
3. Insert TOOL KIT disk. Press RETURN as instructed on the screen.
   The screen will now say
   WELCOME TO LOGO
4. Type: LOAD "ZOOM
   Press RETURN and wait.
   When instructions appear on the screen, press space bar for turtle to appear.
5. Press period to exit. The screen will display
   YOU ARE ON YOUR OWN NOW
6. Type: EDIT "ZOOMSETUP
   Press RETURN.
7. Use right arrow key to move the cursor down to the line that says
   SETBG 5.
8. Move right arrow just beyond 5.
9. Use left arrow key to backspace over 5, then type 0 (the number
   0, not the letter).
10. Hold down CONTROL and then press C *at the same time.* The
    screen will say
    ZOOMSETUP defined
    A blinking cursor will appear.
11. Type: ZOOM
    Press RETURN.
12. The following instructions will appear on the screen:
    PRESS SPACEBAR TO START ZOOMING!

PART NINE

Themes

Introduction

Themes provide direction and structure around which to plan the curriculum. When classroom activities such as art, music, stories, cooking, and woodworking are planned around a theme, concepts can be more easily reinforced. Children relate to the continuity and cohesiveness of a theme. Teachers also find planning easier if there is a focus for the various activities.

This section suggests a number of themes that can be developed over a five-day week. Some schools and centers have different groups of children attending on different days and at different times. If one group comes to school on Tuesday and Thursday, and another group comes on Monday, Wednesday, and Friday, you may want to plan your weekly themes to accommodate both groups using these suggestions:

1. Present the most important activities when the largest number of children are in class.
2. Adapt one activity to suit different needs and ages.
3. Repeat tasks so some of the children can experience the same activity more than once.

With these suggestions in mind, the five-day plan might be condensed to three lesson plans: repeat Monday's lesson on Tuesday; use a new lesson on Wednesday and again on Thursday; and teach the third lesson on Friday. Or, some portions of a plan might be repeated while others would be different each day.

The first theme, "Summer and the Sun," is presented in chart form in Illustration 9.1 to show how the week might be organized. Coordinating all the elements into one day (in this plan, for example, all the rainbow activities are planned for Thursday) helps to reinforce the concept. Suggested projects and lists of books and music do not have to be used in the sequence offered. They are merely suggestions to remind you of other related ideas. Add your own resources as you develop your lesson plans.

In some child-care centers, the luncheon menu is posted for the week. Try posting the theme with the menu. If parents know about your weekly theme, they can reinforce the child's interests and activities at home.

We hope this very general pattern of themes will help you design

	Art Projects	Stories	Music	Indoor Activities	Outdoor Activities
MONDAY	paint yellow circles	*Sun Up*	"Good Morning to You" "All Night, All Day"	make ice cream	temperature and thermometers
TUESDAY	make sun-dried objects	*Sunlight*	repeat songs from Monday	plants need sunlight experiment	walking and balance board exercises
WEDNESDAY	make sun prints	*The Shadow Book*	"Rose, Rose and Up She Rises" "My Shadow"	globe and flashlight experiment	sun dials shadow tag
THURSDAY	paint rainbows	*A Rainbow of My Very Own*	repeat songs from Wednesday	prisms	hose rainbows
FRIDAY	tie-dye cloth	*Let's Find out About the Sun*	review all songs of the week	mirror "flashlight" experiments	solar cooking

Illustration 9.1 Theme: Summer and the Sun

many more for your particular school. Feel free to alter, depart from, or embellish the suggestions offered here to suit the needs and interests of your children.

Summer and the Sun

ART PROJECTS

1. Make sun-dried objects (see "Modeling 'Goop'," page 16). Have children observe the drying process outdoors.
2. Finger-paint with yellow paint on precut circles. Discuss the color and shape of the sun. Does it always look the same?
3. Make sun prints (see "To make finger etchings," page 25).
4. Paint rainbows.
5. Tie dye cloth (see "To tie dye a piece of cloth," page 31).
6. Make sun tea by placing two herbal tea bags and one quart of water in a large covered glass jar. Set in the sun for two–three hours. Serve chilled with lemon.

STORIES

Cartwright, Sally. *Sunlight.* New York: Coward, McCann and Geoghegan, 1974.

de Regniers, Beatrice Schenk. *The Shadow Book.* New York: Harcourt, Brace & World, 1960.

Freeman, Don. *A Rainbow of My Very Own.* New York: Viking, 1966.

Shapp, Martha, and Charles Shapp. *Let's Find out About the Sun.* New York: Franklin Watts, 1975.

Tresselt, Alvin. *Sun Up.* New York: Lothrop, 1949.

MUSIC

"All Night, All Day" in *Making Music Your Own* by Mary Tinnin Jaye. Morristown, N.J.: Silver Burdett, 1966.

"Good Morning to You" and "Rose, Rose and Up She Rises" in *The Fireside Book of Children's Songs* by Marie Winn. New York: Simon & Schuster, 1966.

"My Shadow" in *Exploring Music 1* by Eunice Boardman and Beth Landis. New York: Holt, 1966.

INDOOR ACTIVITIES

1. Make ice cream (see page 309).
2. Display two plants that are alike. Place one in a dark corner and one in a window to demonstrate that plants need sunlight.
3. Discuss how we can use sunlight to measure time. Use a globe and flashlight to illustrate how the sun lights only part of the earth at any one time.
4. Display prisms and let the children make rainbows. Although the concept of refracted light is too complicated for young children, they can understand that sunlight through a prism (or through water, as in a true rainbow) causes the rainbow to appear. Ask them to identify all seven colors in the rainbow.
5. Use small hand mirrors to reflect light onto the wall. Discuss how important the sun is to us as our major light source.

OUTDOOR ACTIVITIES

1. Display real thermometers and discuss the sun's importance as a heat source.
2. Do walking or balance board exercises (see activities under "Balance," page 95).
3. Display a sun dial, either a real one or one made of cardboard.
4. Play shadow tag.
5. Make hose rainbows (see "To learn about a rainbow," page 223).

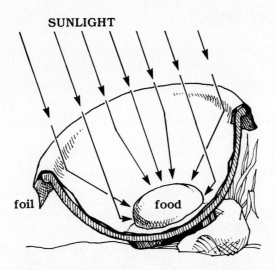

Illustration 9.2 **Using sunlight for cooking**

6. Solar Cooking:
Position a bowl lined with heavy foil so the sun rays are focused on the cooking surface. (The more sunlight that reflects off the foil to the food, the better the results!) Children can melt cheese or peanut butter spread on crackers. (See Illustration 9.2.)

Black History

ART PROJECTS

1. Collect *Ebony* and *Ebony, Jr.* magazines.
2. Cut and paste pictures of black children and families.
3. Have children use felt-tip pens and paint to illustrate poems and stories about blacks (see bibliography of multi-ethnic books, page 187).

STORIES

Adoff, Arnold. *My Black Me: A Beginning Book of Black Poetry.* New York: Dutton, 1975.

Giovanni, Nikki. *Spin a Soft Black Song: Poems for Children.* New York: Hill and Wang, 1971.

Greenfield, Eloise. *Me and Nessie.* New York: Crowell, 1975.

McGovern, Ann. *Black Is Beautiful.* New York: Four Winds, 1972.

Stone, Elberta. *I'm Glad I'm Me.* New York: Putnam's, 1971.

MUSIC

"African Noel" in *Making Music Your Own* (75180). Silver Burdett Company, 250 James Street, Morristown, NJ 07960.

African Songs and Rhythms for Children (FC 7844) by Ella Jenkins. Folkways Records, 632 Broadway, New York, NY 10012.

Call-and-Response Rhythmic Group Singing (SC 7638) by Ella Jenkins. Folkways Records.

Jambo and Other Call-and-Response Songs and Chants (FC 7661) by Ella Jenkins. Folkways Records.

Rhythms of Childhood (FC 7563) by Ella Jenkins. Folkways Records.

Sing Children Sing: Songs of the Congo (TC 1644). Caedmon, 1995 Broadway, New York, NY 10023.

Step It Down: Games for Children by Bessie Jones (8004). Rounder Records, 186 Willow Ave., Somerville, MA 02114. Includes a book of song games.

INDOOR ACTIVITIES

1. Some black families celebrate *Kwanza* from December 26 to January 1 in recognition of traditional African harvest festivals. *Kwanza* means "fresh fruits." The holiday stresses unity of the family. Share this information with the children.
2. Make pecan pralines, molasses peanut brittle, molasses bread, or some recipe using fresh fruits (see "Cooking Activities"). Wrap them to give for *Kwanza*.
3. Display posters such as "Black ABC's: Picture Story Prints," distributed by Society for Visual Education, 1345 Diversey Pkwy., Chicago, IL 60614. Available from the same distributor is "Children Around the World" (a set of six posters, one of which is "Children of Africa").
4. Write to Dial/Delacorte, School and Library Services, 750 Third Ave., New York, NY 10017 for free posters and bookmarks illustrating black culture.
5. Celebrate Martin Luther King's birthday on January 15. Display his picture with his famous quotation: "I have a dream that my four little children will one day live in a nation where they will not be judged by the color of their skin but by the content of their character."

OUTDOOR ACTIVITIES

1. Plan a field trip to a museum displaying African art.
2. Write Institute for Positive Education, 7528 Cottage Grove Ave., Chicago, IL 60619 for further information about *Kwanza* and activities suitable for preschool children.
3. Have a *Kwanza* party outdoors with African foods such as fresh fruits, corn, and molasses bread.

4. Invite African dancers and people wearing native costumes to visit the school.

Body Awareness

ART PROJECTS

1. Make life-size tracings (see "To learn parts of the body, left and right side," page 148).
2. Paper Bag Puppets:
   Set out construction-paper eyes, ears, noses, mouths, eyebrows, and so on. Children can choose what they need for a face and paste them on the bag.
3. Draw or paint self-portraits.
4. Finger-paint.
5. Make spackle handprints (see "To use spackle to make imprints," page 34).
6. Trace hands and draw in fingernails, rings, wristwatches, and so on.

STORIES

Aliki. *My Hands.* New York: Crowell, 1962.

Brenner, Barbara. *Faces.* New York: Dutton, 1970.

Green, Mary McBurney. *Is It Hard? Is It Easy?* New York: Young Scott Books, 1960.

Kraus, Robert. *Leo, the Late Bloomer.* New York: Windmill, 1976.

MUSIC

"Anatomical Song" in *Songs to Grow On* by Beatrice Landeck. New York: Edward B. Marks Music Corp., 1950.

"Hokey Pokey" in *Singing Games for Little People.* Long Branch, N.J.: Kimbo Educational Records, 1975.

"If You're Happy" in *Musical Games for Children of All Ages* by Esther L. Nelson. New York: Sterling, 1976.

"Looby Loo" in *Sally Go Round the Sun* by Edith Fowke. New York: Doubleday, 1969.

"Put Your Hands up in the Air" in *Learning Basic Skills Through Music, Volume I* by Hap Palmer. Freeport, N.Y.: Educational Activities, Inc.

"Ten Fingers" in *Eye Winker, Tom Tinker, Chin Chopper* by Tom Glazer. New York: Doubleday, 1973.

INDOOR ACTIVITIES

1. Have full-length mirrors at children's level.
2. Cut magazine faces into jig-saw puzzles.
3. Mark each child's right hand with a red *R* and left hand with a blue *L*. Play "Simple Simon" using left and right directions.
4. Have mittens, gloves, shoes, and boots marked with *R* and *L* symbols for children to sort, match, and try on.

OUTDOOR ACTIVITIES

1. Set up an obstacle course that will require children to jump, crawl, climb, and stretch.
2. Have a follow-the-leader parade. Ask the children to swing their left arms, touch their cheeks, and so on.
3. Play elbow tag, knee tag, ear tag.
4. Take photographs.

Chanukah

ART PROJECTS

1. Make the Star of David by cutting out two triangles and inverting one over the other to form a six-pointed star.
2. Make a clay menorah to hold eight candles with a raised spot to hold the *shamash*, a ninth candle used to light the others.
3. Make dreidels out of cardboard or oaktag and dowels. (See Illustration 9.3.)
4. Sponge-paint holiday shapes; use white, royal blue, and orange colors.

STORIES

Adler, David. *A Picture Book of Hanukkah.* New York: Holiday House, 1982.

Simon, Norma. *Hanukkah in My House.* New York: United Synagogue Book Service, 1960.

See also "Chanukah Stories," page 192.

MUSIC

"Hanukkah" in *Holiday Songs and Rhythms* by Hap Palmer. Freeport, N.Y.: Educational Activities, Inc.

"Hanukkah Song" in *Singing Bee* by Jane Hart. New York: Lothrop, Lee and Shepard, 1967.

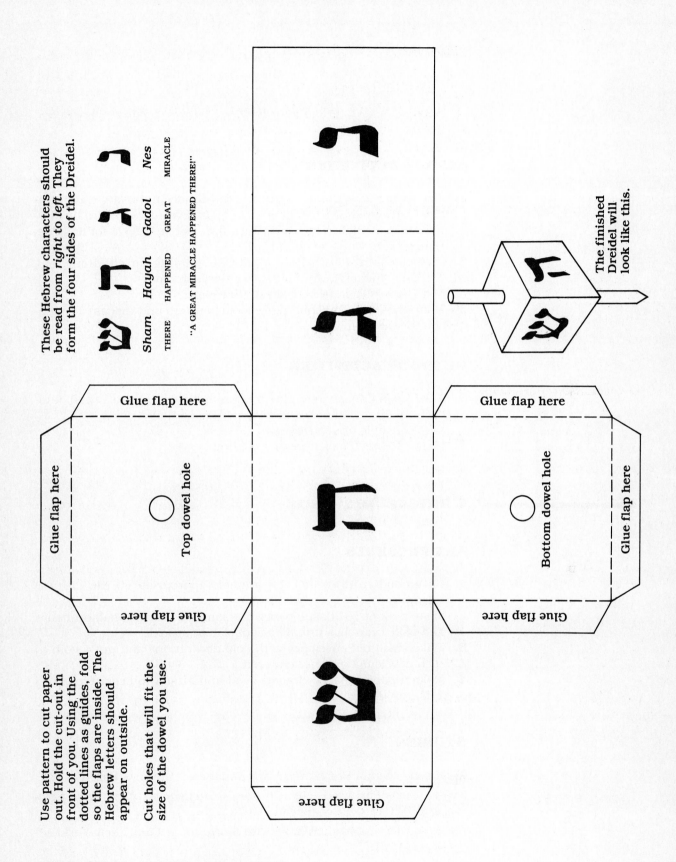

These Hebrew characters should be read from *right* to *left*. They form the four sides of the Dreidel.

Sham   *Hayah*   *Gadol*   *Nes*
THERE   HAPPENED   GREAT   MIRACLE

"A GREAT MIRACLE HAPPENED THERE!"

The finished Dreidel will look like this.

Glue flap here

Glue flap here

Top dowel hole

Glue flap here

Glue flap here

Glue flap here

Bottom dowel hole

Glue flap here

Glue flap here

Use pattern to cut paper out. Hold the cut-out in front of you. Using the dotted lines as guides, fold so the flaps are inside. The Hebrew letters should appear on outside.

Cut holes that will fit the size of the dowel you use.

Illustration 9.3   **Pattern for making a dreidel**

Israeli Children's Songs by Ben-Ezra. New York: Folkways Records.

"My Dreidel" in *Discovering Music Together* by Robert Smith. Chicago: Follett, 1968.

"O Hanukkah" in *Folk Songs of Israel*. Glendale, Calif.: Bowmar Records.

INDOOR ACTIVITIES

1. Play the dreidel game by spinning the dreidel and using nuts, candies, and small toys for tokens. See *The Hanukkah Story* by Morrison David Bial (New York: Behrman House, 1952) for instructions.
2. Invite a parent to tell the story of Chanukah to the children.
3. Display a menorah and light a candle each day.
4. Make *latkes* (potato pancakes). (See page 302.)
5. Make cookies with Chanukah cookie cutters and discuss the reason for the shapes.

OUTDOOR ACTIVITIES

1. Take small gifts such as the dreidels and paintings to Jewish children in a hospital or to elderly people.
2. Visit a temple or synagogue.
3. Visit a Hebrew bookstore or gift shop.

Chinese New Year

ART PROJECTS

1. Have children draw or color animals appropriate to the Chinese calendar.
2. Make pink or red tissue-paper blossoms; attach to small branches and poke branches into a base of clay or spackle.
3. Make small red envelopes with gold decorations and put a coin in each envelope to give to children.
4. Make a papier-mâché dragon head and attach to bedsheets to do a dragon dance.

STORIES

Anderson, Juanita B. *Charley Yee's New Year*. Chicago: Follett, 1970.

Evans, Doris Portwood. *Mr. Charley's Chopsticks*. New York: Coward, McCann & Geoghegan, 1972.

Flack, Marjorie, and K. Weise. *The Story About Ping*. New York: Viking, 1961.

Lewis, Thomas P. *The Dragon Kite*. New York: Holt, Rinehart, and Winston, 1974.

MUSIC

1. Write General Learning Corporation/Silver Burdett, 250 James St., Morristown, NJ 07960 for records of Chinese children's music. This company distributes *Making Music Your Own*, a six-record album with multi-ethnic music.
2. Write China Books and Periodicals, 125 Fifth Ave., New York, NY 10003 for children's records.
3. Contact local Chinese to help locate people who can perform Chinese music.

INDOOR ACTIVITIES

1. Make rice cakes with puffed rice or crispy rice baked with honey.
2. See "Cooking Activities" for ideas for Chinese foods. Learn to use chopsticks.
3. Do a dragon dance through the school letting some of the children be the inside of the dragon while other children play gongs, drums, and other percussion instruments.
4. Invite adults to help with origami (paper folding) to decorate the school. Use red paper (symbol of good fortune). Refer to *The Art of Paper Folding: For Young and Old* by Maying Soong (New York: Harcourt Brace Jovanovich, 1948).
5. Show a film such as *Tikki Tikki Tembo*, available in 16 mm from Weston Woods Studios, Weston, CT 06883. Book by Arlene Mosel (New York: Holt, Rinehart, and Winston, 1968).
6. Write School Products Division, 850 N. Grove Ave., Elgin, IL 60120 for *Mainland China — Today*, a set of sixteen large pictures with teacher's manual (order no. 68528).

OUTDOOR ACTIVITIES

1. Parade outside the school with the dragon and drums.
2. Take a field trip to a nearby Chinatown if possible.
3. Contact local Chinese groups to help plan celebrations appropriate to the children's ages.
4. Invite adult Chinese to dress in native clothing or bring Chinese costumes to display at the school.
5. Visit a museum displaying Chinese artifacts.

Christmas

ART PROJECTS

1. Make Christmas-tree decorations with construction paper, Styrofoam, scraps of foil, and tinsel.
2. Collect small pine cones and glue on glitter.

3. Make red and green play dough; use Christmas-shape cookie cutters.
4. Have children make Christmas cards and send them to friends and family.
5. Make children's handprints on good quality construction paper or in plaster of Paris for gifts.

STORIES

Aichinger, Helga. *The Shepherd.* New York: Crowell, 1967.

Duvoisin, Roger. *Petunia's Christmas.* New York: Knopf, 1952.

Jackson, Kathryn. *The Story of Christmas with Its Own Advent Calendar.* New York: Harcourt Brace Jovanovich, 1962.

Kraus, Robert. *How Spider Saved Christmas.* New York: Simon and Schuster, 1970.

Moore, Clement C. *The Night Before Christmas.* New York: Random House, 1961.

———. *A Visit from St. Nicholas.* New York: Simon and Schuster, 1971.

See "Christmas Stories," page 190, for more books.

MUSIC

"Christmas is Coming" in *More Songs to Grow On* by Beatrice Landeck. New York: Sloane, 1954.

"Pack up the Sleigh" in *Songs for Learning Through Music and Movement* by Hap Palmer. Sherman Oaks, Calif.: Alfred Publ., 1981.

"The Twelve Days of Christmas" in *The Fireside Song Book of Birds and Beasts* by Jane Yolen. New York: Simon and Schuster, 1972.

"We Wish You a Merry Christmas" in *190 Children's Songs* by David Nelson. New York: Robbins Music Co., 1967.

INDOOR ACTIVITIES

1. Decorate a Christmas tree (be sure it has been treated with a flame retardant).
2. Frost windows by spraying Glass Wax on stencils of snowflakes and other Christmas patterns.
3. Make and decorate Christmas cookies.
4. Exchange small, wrapped gifts that children have made in art activities.

OUTDOOR ACTIVITIES

1. Go Christmas-caroling in the neighborhood.
2. Visit a hospital or retirement home and bring small gifts or decorations made by the children.

3. Visit a store with a large Christmas display and a Santa.
4. Invite one of the parents to dress up as a Santa and visit the school.
5. Visit a tree farm to select a tree for the school.

Cinco de Mayo

ART PROJECTS

1. Make a *piñata* by inflating a large balloon and taping on rolls of paper to fashion a head, arms, legs, wing, and so on. Cover with papier-mâché (see "To make tissue collages," page 24). Leave a small hole at the bottom to insert toys and candy. Cover with several layers of tissue paper or newspaper strips. Let dry thoroughly and paint with bright colors. Decorations such as feathers, sequins, and bows can be added. Stuff toys and candies through the opening (pop the balloon) and tape shut.
2. Make maracas by placing rice or beans inside plastic egg-shaped containers and poking a hole to insert a wooden dowel. Paint the maracas.
3. Make clay pots and paint colorfully.
4. Make *cascarones* (decorated egg shells). Poke a hole in the pointed ends of eggs and empty them out. Rinse, dry, and paint with bright colors. Fill the shells halfway with confetti and cover the ends with colorful paper.

STORIES

Anderson, Eloise, A. *Carlos Goes to School.* New York: Frederick Warne, 1973.

Hampton, Doris. *Just for Manuel.* Austin, Tex.: Steck-Vaughn, 1971.

Hancock, Sibyl. *Mario's Mystery Machine.* New York: Putnam's, 1972.

Lexau, Joan. *Maria.* New York: Dial, 1964.

MUSIC

1. Play "Cinco de Mayo" from the record *Holiday Songs and Rhythms* by Hap Palmer. Available from Educational Activities, Inc., P. O. Box 392, Freeport, NY 11520.
2. Use the maracas made in Art Projects to dance.
3. Locate some families who may be able to help find *mariachi* band members to play at the school.
4. Write to Bowmar Records, 622 Rodier Dr., Glendale, CA 91201 for *Mexican Folk Songs,* a children's recording.
5. Play "La Raspa" sung by Ella Jenkins on the record titled *Little Johnny Brown* (SC7631), produced by Folkways Records. Good for creative movement.

INDOOR ACTIVITIES

1. Contact travel agencies and Mexican airlines for posters to decorate the classroom.
2. Display a Mexican flag and have children make copies.
3. Make tortillas (see page 284).
4. Make guacamole, using mashed ripe avocados, lemon juice, and a dash of hot sauce, for a dip with vegetables.
5. Blindfold one child at a time and let him or her try to break the *piñata* with a stick. Have the children take turns until toys and candies fall out for everyone to share.
6. Invite parents to bring Mexican artifacts and clothing to display.
7. Make "Cinco de Mayo Salad" (see page 291).

OUTDOOR ACTIVITIES

1. Have a procession outdoors with lanterns and Mexican flags.
2. Hide the *cascarones* (eggs filled with confetti) and let the children go on an egg hunt.
3. Let the children break the eggs over each other's heads.
4. Make adobe bricks with clay, water, and bits of straw. Mix well to dough-like consistency. Shape into flat bricks and let dry in the sun.

Easter

ART PROJECTS

1. Decorate eggs by dyeing, using crayon resist, painting, or gluing on decorations. Be sure the eggs are hardboiled. See "To use onion skin for dyeing a design," page 32.
2. Make an egg tree by decorating blown-out eggs and hanging them on a branch that has been secured in a can of plaster of Paris.
3. Make Easter bonnets with cardboard, ribbons, lace, and flowers.
4. Make bunny puppets out of white paper bags, using thin strips of black construction paper for whiskers, cotton for tails, and pink and black paper for eyes and ears.
5. Make collages with broken egg-shells.

STORIES

Adams, Adrienne. *The Easter Egg Artists.* New York: Scribner's, 1976.

Carrick, C. *A Rabbit for Easter.* New York: Greenwillow Books, 1979.

See "Easter Stories," page 191, for other books.

MUSIC

"The Easter Bunny" in *Singing Bee* by Jane Hart. New York: Lothrop, Lee and Shepard, 1982.

"Easter Rabbit" in *The Small Singer* by McLaughlin and Wood. Chicago: Follett, 1963.

"Easter Time Is Here Again" in *Songs for Learning Through Music and Movement* by Hap Palmer. Sherman Oaks, Calif.: Alfred Publ., 1981.

"Old Mister Rabbit" in *American Folk Songs for Children* by Ruth Seeger. Boston: Ginn and Co., 1961.

INDOOR ACTIVITIES

1. Cook egg recipes (see "Cooking Activities").
2. Hatch eggs in an incubator.
3. Make a spring mural with paintings and collages of blossoms, bunnies, and eggs.
4. Decorate the school with tye-dyed materials.

OUTDOOR ACTIVITIES

1. Have an Easter egg hunt.
2. Learn to care for a bunny.
3. Pick blossoms and flowers for a display in the school.
4. Plant seeds and talk about spring bulbs.

Families

ART PROJECTS

1. Display pictures of different kinds of animal families in the art area and have children draw or paint pictures depicting their own families.
2. Do body tracings of family members on large sheets of butcher paper. Cut out and display on the wall.
3. Ask parents, grandparents, brothers, sisters, and other family members to make a handprint with paint and let each child make a poster of his or her family's prints.

STORIES

Refer to Bibliography of Resources in Part Four, "Language Arts," and select books to read that cover such topics as animal families, families from other cultures, working mothers, and divorced and single-parent families.

MUSIC

1. Hap Palmer's *Learning Basic Skills Through Music* (Freeport, N.Y.: Educational Activities, Inc.) offers songs that are suited to the topic of children and families, such as "Growing" in Volume I.
2. Use "Birds in the Nest" from the album *Cloud Journeys* (B/B 111) by Barlin and Berman. Available from Learning Through Movement, 5757 Ranchito, Van Nuys, CA 91401.
3. Try these songs from *Mister Rogers' Songbook* (New York: Random House, 1970): "You Are Special," "When a Baby Comes," and "I'd Like to Be Mom/Dad."

INDOOR ACTIVITIES

1. Display posters showing families around the world.
2. Invite children from other cultures to bring pictures from home showing how families live in other countries.
3. Take pictures of the animal families in the school and display them.
4. Ask parents to share pictures of their children from the time they were babies. Make time-line posters labeling the ages of the children.
5. Set up family activities in the dramatic play areas of the school and let children act out what families do.

OUTDOOR ACTIVITIES

1. Invite family members to visit the school and plan some cooperative family games.
2. Have each family bring some fruit and make a fruit salad to share.
3. Take a field trip to a nearby zoo or animal sanctuary where the children can see animal families.

The Forest in Fall

ART PROJECTS

1. Torn-Paper Tree:
   Have children draw or paint a tree trunk. Provide scraps of red, brown, yellow, and orange paper to be torn into small bits and glued on the tree and ground as leaves.

2. Spatter paint over leaves (see "To make spatter paintings," page 21).
3. Bear Cave Diorama:
   Use a small cardboard box or a Styrofoam meat tray as a base. The cave can be made by stapling a crumpled brown paper bag in place. Children can add bits of pine needles, twigs, moss, sawdust, straw, and rocks. A tiny scrap of furry cloth tucked in the cave to represent the bear is the final touch.
4. Finger-paint in fall colors. Dry paintings may be cut into leaf shapes.

STORIES

Brown, Margaret Wise. *Fox Eyes.* New York: Pantheon, 1977.

Rockwell, Harlow. *The Compost Heap.* New York: Doubleday, 1974.

Spier, Peter. *The Fox Went out on a Chilly Night.* New York: Doubleday, 1961.

Tresselt, Alvin. *Johnny Maple-Leaf.* New York: Lothrop, 1948.

———. *Under the Trees and Through the Grass.* New York: Lothrop, 1962.

Udry, Janice May. *A Tree Is Nice.* New York: Harper & Row, 1956.

MUSIC

"A-Hunting We Will Go" in *Jim Along, Josie* by Mary Langstaff and John Langstaff. New York: Harcourt Brace Jovanovich, 1970.

"The Bear Went over the Mountain" in *Eye Winker, Tom Tinker, Chin Chopper* by Tom Glazer. New York: Doubleday, 1973.

"Let Us Chase the Squirrel" in *Making Music Your Own* by Mary Tinnin Jaye. Morristown, N.J.: Silver Burdett, 1966.

"Little Cabin in the Wood" in *Exploring Music 1.* New York: Holt, 1966.

Sivulich, Sandra Stroner. *I'm Going on a Bear Hunt.* New York: Dutton, 1973. (This can be chanted with body percussion, such as slapping thighs.)

INDOOR ACTIVITIES

1. Make applesauce (page 304).
2. Provide an assortment of fall leaves. The children could sort, match, classify, and so on (see pairing, matching, sorting, and classifying activities in Math and Language Arts sections).
3. Display a collection of tree products, such as nuts, acorns, seed pods, pine cones, and bark. Children can examine them with a magnifying glass.

Illustration 9.4   **A nature walk can be used as an opportunity for children to learn about the seasons and about growing things.**

OUTDOOR ACTIVITIES

1. Go for a nature walk and look for signs of fall. (See Illustration 9.4.)
2. Provide rakes and baskets for raking leaves.
3. Hide several walnuts around the yard. The children can play "squirrels."
4. Start a compost pile (see "To see how organic materials can be returned to the earth to be used again," page 243).

Friendship and Cooperation

ART PROJECTS

1. Make a "sharing collage" by having children bring fabric scraps, Styrofoam pieces, paper scraps, and similar materials from home. Place all materials on a lazy susan or trays to be passed around and shared in making a collage.
2. Make a cooperative mural by covering a table top with butcher paper and letting children draw with felt-tip pens to make a mural. The mural can be displayed or used as a background for other matted artwork.
3. Make a "friendship" book of pictures. Ask children, "What is a friend?"
4. Make friendship cards. Visit a senior citizens center. Let the

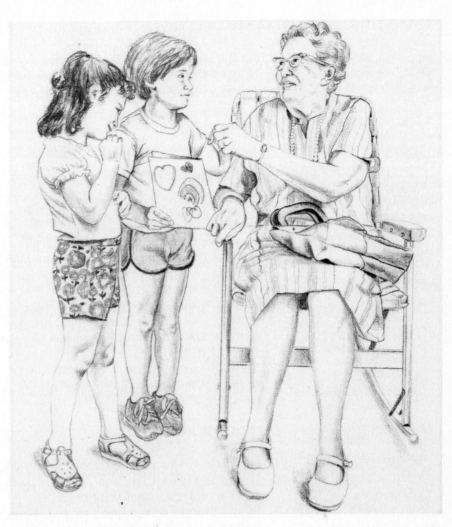

Illustration 9.5 **These children are sharing a friendship card, which they have made, with an elderly friend.**

children present their friendship cards to an elderly person. (See Illustration 9.5.)

5. Plan a mutual exchange project with another school, such as exchanging art work, cooking something special together, or planning and presenting a puppet show.

STORIES

Brenner, Barbara. *Mr. Tall and Mr. Small.* New York: Young Scott Books, 1966.

Brown, Marcia. *Stone Soup: An Old Tale.* New York: Scribner, 1947.

Cohen, Miriam. *Will I Have a Friend?* New York: Macmillan, 1971.

Freeman, Don. *Corduroy.* New York: Viking, 1968.

Tolstoi, Alexei. *The Great Big Enormous Turnip.* New York: Franklyn Watts, 1969.

MUSIC

"I Roll the Ball" and "The More We Are Together" in *Eye Winker, Tom Tinker, Chin Chopper* by Tom Glazer. New York: Doubleday, 1973.

"Move Over for Marty" by Malvina Reynolds. Amadeo Music, 1962.

Have a rhythm band and discuss how everyone makes the music together.

INDOOR ACTIVITIES

1. Prepare vegetable soup (page 301). Have each child bring a vegetable from home.
2. At appropriate times, such as cleanup, setting the juice tables, or feeding the animals, discuss the benefit of everyone helping one another. (No one person has to do all the work, the work is finished faster, and so forth.)
3. Display and discuss pictures of people working and playing together. Take pictures of the children working together.
4. Act out *The Great Big Enormous Turnip* and discuss the importance of helping one another.
5. Form discussion groups and conduct problem-solving sessions to evaluate the day's activities and concerns.

OUTDOOR ACTIVITIES

1. Have relay races and talk about group cooperation.
2. Play group games, such as "Farmer in the Dell," "Little Sally Saucer," or "Ring Around the Rosy."
3. Plan a group work project, such as planting and caring for a garden or cleaning the playhouse.
4. Do group exercises.
5. Form a committee to be responsible for necessary tasks such as care of animals, cleaning wash basins, wiping tables, and putting toys away.
6. Invite senior citizens to share in an outdoor planting project.
7. Carry paper bags and take a walk around the neighborhood to help pick up litter.
8. Assign an older child to teach a younger child a new skill.

Halloween

ART PROJECTS

1. Make masks with paper plates by drawing and cutting out eyes, nose, and mouth. Punch holes in each side to tie yarn or elastic.

Let children color and decorate masks with crayons, cloth scraps, feathers, and other costume decorations.

2. Make trick-or-treat bags by decorating grocery bags with paper cutouts, scraps of cloth, and felt-tip markers. Attach sturdy construction material handles.

3. Make costumes with large grocery bags, old sheets, or pillowcases.

STORIES

Balian, Lorna. *Humbug Witch.* Nashville, Tenn: Abingdon Press, 1965.

Battles, Edith. *The Terrible Trick or Treat.* Reading, Mass.: Young Scott, 1970.

Bridwell, Norman. *Clifford's Halloween.* New York: Four Winds Press, 1967.

Kroll, Steven. *Amanda and the Giggling Ghost.* New York: Holiday House, 1980.

Slobodkin, Louis. *Trick or Treat.* New York: Macmillan, 1972.

See "Halloween Stories," page 191, for additional books.

MUSIC

"Halloween Sounds," "I'm a Witch," and "Three Black Cats" from *The Small Singer*, Bowmar Records.

"March of the Ghosts" from *The Small Player*, Bowmar Records.

Bowmar also has excellent records for other holidays. Write or order from Bowmar Records, 622 Rodier Dr., Glendale, CA 91201.

INDOOR ACTIVITIES

1. Carve small jack-o'-lanterns, insert candles, and light them during snack time.

2. Make other jack-o'-lanterns by using toothpicks to attach eyes, ears, nose, and mouth made out of radishes, carrots, bell peppers, or yarn.

3. Wash and dry seeds scooped out of pumpkins; bake them and eat during snack time. Seeds can also be used for collages.

4. Bake pumpkin goodies (see "Thanksgiving" theme and "Cooking Activities").

OUTDOOR ACTIVITIES

1. Have a Halloween parade through the school.

2. Hide small pumpkins and have a pumpkin hunt.

3. Visit a pumpkin patch.

Healthy Bodies

ART PROJECTS

1. Have children lie down on butcher paper; outline their bodies.
2. Help children identify parts of their bodies on the outline and label the parts.
3. Draw and color fruits and vegetables, milk products, and other healthful foods.
4. Place posters of healthy foods around the school.
5. Make mobiles of the children's healthy foods art.
6. Use cut-up potatoes and apples to make art prints (see "To use paint to make prints," page 21).

STORIES

Castle, Sue. *Face Talk, Hand Talk, Body Talk.* New York: Doubleday, 1977.

Craig, Marjorie. *Miss Craig's Growing up Exercises.* New York: Random House, 1973.

Diskin, Eve. *Yoga for Children.* New York: Arco Publishing, 1977.

Dobrin, Arnold. *Peter Rabbit's Natural Foods Cookbook.* New York: Frederick Warne, 1977.

Goodbody, Slim. *The Healthy Habits Handbook.* New York: Coward-McCann, 1983.

Marshall, James. *Yummers!* Boston: Houghton Mifflin, 1972.

Musicant, Elke, and Ted Musicant. *The Night Vegetable Eater.* New York: Dodd, Mead & Co., 1981.

Richards, Ruth, and Joy Abrams. *Let's Do Yoga.* New York: Holt, Rinehart, and Winston, 1975.

Sharmat, Mitchell. *Gregory, the Terrible Eater.* New York: Four Winds Press, 1980.

Showers, Paul. *You Can't Make a Move Without Your Muscles.* New York: Thomas Y. Crowell, 1982.

MUSIC

1. Play restful music as a background for yoga. Refer to *Let's Do Yoga* by Richards and Abrams, listed above, for some simple yoga positions for preschoolers.
2. Use Slim Goodbody's recording "Inside-Out" (Caedmon, TC1712) along with his book, *The Healthy Habits Handbook*, for ideas about exercising to music.
3. Play Hap Palmer's "Posture Exercises" and "Exercise Every Day"

from his record *Learning Basic Skills Through Music, Volume III* (Freeport, N.Y.: Educational Activities, Inc.).

INDOOR ACTIVITIES

1. Display posters and art work of healthy foods.
2. Display pictures of children exercising, such as the illustrations in the books listed above.
3. Prepare well-balanced snacks with healthful foods and discuss foods that are good for children.
4. Read *Gregory the Terrible Eater* by Mitchell Sharmat and talk about junk foods and healthy foods.
5. Read *Yummers!* by James Marshall and talk about overeating and why that is unhealthy.
6. Set up dental and health check-up stations with appropriate equipment for dramatic play.
7. Invite community health-workers to visit.

OUTDOOR ACTIVITIES

1. Refer to some of the exercise books listed above and do exercises with the children.
2. Plant vegetables and discuss the importance of sunshine, water, and food for the plants and how that relates to the children's well-being.
3. Attach adhesive-backed paper (sticky side out) to 3 x 5 cards. Let each child carry one of the cards and bring back small samples of growing things that require sunshine and water, such as blades of grass, weeds, and so on.
4. Talk about athletics and how athletes train their bodies; take a field trip to a nearby high school or college to let the children see how older people build strong bodies.

Insects

ART PROJECTS

1. Egg Carton Insect:
   Have children paint two sections of an egg carton. They can then add waxed-paper wings and pipe-cleaner legs and antennae.
2. Folded Butterfly:
   Fold paper cut into butterfly shape in half. Make one for each child. Have the children drip paint inside the fold, then refold and press. Black paper with white and orange paint gives a dramatic monarch butterfly result.

3. Make an ecosystem (see "To appreciate the balance and harmony of nature," page 242).

STORIES

Carle, Eric. *The Very Hungry Caterpillar.* New York: World, 1971.

Friskey, Margaret. *Johnny and the Monarch.* Chicago: Children's Press, 1900.

Mari, Iela, and Enzo Mari. *The Apple and the Moth.* New York: Dial, 1970.

Milne, A. A. *Winnie-the-Pooh.* New York: Dutton, 1926.

MUSIC

"Bringing Home a Baby Bumblebee," in *Sally Go Round the Sun* by Edith Fowke. New York: Doubleday, 1969.

"Five Little Ants," and "Grasshoppers" in *Let's Do Fingerplays* by Marion F. Crayson. Washington, D.C.: Robert B. Luce, 1962.

"Here Is a Beehive" in *The Kindergarten Book* by Lilla Belle Pitts. Boston: Ginn and Co., 1957.

"Little Arabella Miller" in *Eye Winker, Tom Tinker, Chin Chopper* by Tom Glazer. New York: Doubleday, 1973.

Zeitlin, Patty, and Marcia Berman. *Spin, Spider, Spin.* Freeport, N.Y.: Educational Activities Records, 1974.

INDOOR ACTIVITIES

1. Display honeycomb.
2. Use honey in cooking or just for tasting.
3. Have a local beekeeper come to visit. Discuss the fact that bees sting only when angry or frightened. Many children think bees are "bad" and want to hit or squash them.
4. Display live insects in a terrarium. Provide food, sticks for climbing, water, and other things necessary for insect life.
5. Use sequence cards to show the life cycle of a butterfly.

OUTDOOR ACTIVITIES

1. Go on an insect hunt. Identify the insects that are found.
2. Have a grasshopper race. Ask who can hop like a grasshopper? (Children may want to move like other insects as well.)

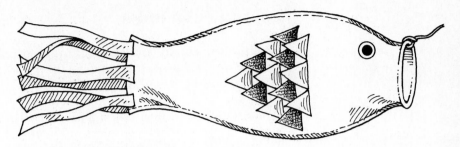

Illustration 9.6 **Carp kite**

Japanese Cherry Blossom Festival

ART PROJECTS

1. Make cherry blossoms with pink tissue attached to twigs.
2. Make carp kites:
   Cut two matching fish shapes from light-weight paper. Glue shapes together along the outside edges. Glue some wire or pipecleaner around the mouth and attach streamers to the tail. Attach kite string to the mouth so that when the kite is pulled, wind will pass through the fish. (See Illustration 9.6.)
3. Make a mural for the classroom with cherry trees in blossom. Paint trees and let children decorate the limbs with tissue blossoms.
4. Do origami (paper folding). (See "Chinese New Year," page 366.)

STORIES

Anno, Mitsumasa. *Anno's Alphabet: An Adventure in Imagination.* New York: Crowell, 1975.

Yashima, Taro. *Umbrella.* New York: Viking, 1969.

———. *The Village Tree.* New York: Viking, 1953.

———. *Youngest One.* New York: Viking, 1962.

MUSIC

"Japanese Rain Song" with Roberta McLaughlin in *Making Music Your Own.* (Six-record album produced by Silver Burdett and distributed by General Learning Corp., 250 James St., Morristown, NJ 07960. Album #75180.)

Write Bowmar Records, 622 Rodier Dr., Glendale, CA 91201 and Folkways Records, 906 Sylvan Ave., Englewood Cliffs, NJ 07632 for catalogs listing Japanese music suitable for young children.

INDOOR ACTIVITIES

1. Show the film *Festival in Japan*, produced by Sakura Motion Picture Co. and distributed by Japan National Tourist Organization, 1420 Commerce St., Dallas, TX 75201. (The main office is located at 45 Rockefeller Plaza, New York, NY 10020 if you wish to write for additional information and materials.)
2. Display posters and pictures of Japanese people.
3. Invite Japanese families to share artifacts, eating and cooking utensils, materials, kimonos, and kites.
4. Have a display of Japanese dolls commemorating *Hina Matsuri*, the Japanese doll festival, which begins March 3. Priceless heirloom dolls are arranged in an elaborate display (not to be played with).
5. Cook osushi (page 297). Serve in tea ceremony.
6. Play Japanese musical recordings.

OUTDOOR ACTIVITIES

1. Invite local Japanese to visit and perform festival dances.
2. Plant some blossoming trees and shrubs.
3. Take a field trip to a park or area where the children can see blossoms.
4. Visit a Japanese restaurant, grocery store, or kite store.
5. Shop in an Asian import store for display items.

Native Americans [1]

ART PROJECTS

1. Make Indian necklaces with colored macaroni.
2. Make sand paintings (see "To make colored sand paintings," page 25).
3. Make totem poles by cutting egg cartons in half lengthwise. Decorate with colorful paints and attach construction paper for the crossarms. Corks, spools, and Styrofoam can also be used.
4. See *Indian Crafts and Lore* by Ben W. Hunt (New York: Western Publishing, 1976).
5. Other Indian ornaments include rattles, belts, headbands, armbands, masks, and hair ornaments.

---

[1] American Indian Day is celebrated in many states on the fourth Friday in September.

STORIES

Aliki. *Corn Is Maize.* New York: Crowell, 1976.

Bauer, Helen. *California Indian Days.* New York: Doubleday, 1963.

Baylor, Byrd. *They Put on Masks.* New York: Scribner's, 1975.

Brindze, Ruth. *The Story of the Totem Pole.* New York: Vanguard, 1951.

Perrine, Mary. *Salt Boy.* Boston: Houghton Mifflin, 1968.

Talaswaima, Terrance. *Hopi Bride at the Home Dance: A Hopi Indian Story.* Oraibi, Ariz.: Hopi Publishers, 1974.

MUSIC

1. Refer to *Indian Music Makers* (New York: Morrow, 1967) by Robert Hofsinde (Gray Wolf). The book gives simple directions for making Indian musical instruments.
2. Write to Canyon Records, 4143 No. 16th St., Phoenix, AZ 85016 for a catalog of records, cassettes, slides, posters, and bibliographies about Native Americans.
3. Have children play tom-toms and dance to *Indian Songs of the Southwest* (Thunderbird Records 1943B).
4. Another record is *Sounds of Indian America: Plains and Southwest,* distributed by Indian House, Box 472, Taos, NM 87571.

INDOOR ACTIVITIES

1. Have an exhibition of Indian art, pottery, jewelry, Kachina dolls, small totem poles, and other artifacts.
2. Make the school into an Indian village with tepees, rugs, clothing, pottery, and posters.
3. Write Navajo Film and Media Commission, The Navajo Tribe, Window Rock, AZ 86515 and request a list of films for young children.
4. Refer to *Southwestern Indian Recipe Book: Apache, Papago, Pima, Pueblo, Navajo* by Zora G. Hesse (Palmer Lake, Colo.: Filter Press, 1973). Includes recipes for bread, stews, vegetables, and other traditional foods.
5. Make Indian custard pudding (page 307).

OUTDOOR ACTIVITIES

1. Make pottery using the "coil" method:
   Flatten out a ball of clay or baker's dough for the base. Then roll out more dough into a "snake" and coil it around the base, building up the sides by winding it around and up. Smooth inside of pot with damp fingers. The pot can be painted when dry.
2. Build an Indian tepee village.
3. Make a large totem pole.
4. Make sand paintings.

Outer Space

ART PROJECTS

1. Make a class project of building a space missile (see some of the stories listed for ideas).
2. Make posters showing the earth, the moon, and the sun. Do not expect the children to understand the complexities of the solar system. Let them see the comparative sizes of the sun, moon, and the earth. Help them practice identifying and pointing to the sun, moon, and the earth.
3. Make space suits.
4. Use play dough to make replicas of the sun, moon, and earth.

STORIES

Becklake, John. *Man and the Moon.* Morristown, N.J.: Silver Burdett, 1981.

Branley, Franklyn M. *A Book of Astronauts For You.* New York: Thomas Y. Crowell, 1963. (This author has written other books on astronomy, such as *Moon Rockets, Planets,* and *Satellites.*)

———. *The Moon Seems to Change.* New York: Thomas Y. Crowell, 1960.

Kerrod, Robin. *A Space Station.* New York: Warwick Press, 1978.

Minarik, Else H. *Little Bear* ("Little Bear Goes to the Moon"). New York: Harper & Row, 1957.

Moché, Dinah L. *The Astronauts.* New York: Random House, 1978.

Moncure, Jane Belk. *Magic Monsters Learn About Space.* Chicago: Childrens Press, 1980.

Seevers, James A. *Space.* Milwaukee: Raintree Children's Books, 1978.

Wheat, Janis Knudsen. *Let's Go to the Moon.* Washington, D.C.: National Geographic Society, 1977.

MUSIC

1. Use the recording "Science Fiction Sound Effects" (Folkways Records, FX 6250) for background music during dramatic play.
2. Use "March like a Robot" from *Rhythm Band Time* (MH-41) available from Melody House Recordings, 819 N.W. 92nd St., Oklahoma City, OK 73114.
3. *Come and See the Peppermint Tree* (Dean Records, 2735 Macomb St., N.W., Washington, D.C. 20008) has two bands relating to outer space: "Riding on a Star" and "Moon in the Yard".

INDOOR ACTIVITIES

1. In addition to the Art Projects, build a space-ship panel using Branley's *A Book of Astronauts for You* that shows the Mercury capsule instrument panel.
2. Use cardboard cartons to make helmets.
3. Place a star chart on the ceiling.
4. Place luminous stickers on a star chart and attach to the top of a large carton or crate that the children can crawl into.
5. Make cookies in the shapes of moons, stars, sun, and rockets.

OUTDOOR ACTIVITIES

1. Demonstrate with a ball how rockets go up and come back down. (See page 12 of *Rockets and Satellites* by Franklyn Branley. New York: Thomas Y. Crowell, 1970.)
2. Play with a small parachute (see "To combine movements using a parachute," page 101).
3. Talk about how a rocket works and demonstrate how a jet of air pushes the rocket up by inflating a balloon and letting go of it. (See page 10 of *Space* by James A. Seevers.)
4. Build an outdoor space station. (See *A Space Station* by Robin Kerrod.)

The Seashore

ART PROJECTS

1. Sand-painted starfish:
   Give the children a starfish shape to trace and cut out. Have them paint their starfish with white glue. They can shake sand over the glue and let dry.
2. Let children paint a fish-shape paper cutout with water colors.
3. Sponge-paint with pieces of real sponge.
4. Make collages with seashells, pebbles, and driftwood.
5. Have children paint a seashore wall mural.

STORIES

Garelich, May. *Down to the Beach.* New York: Four Winds, 1973.

Lionni, Leo. *On My Beach There Are Many Pebbles.* New York: Ivan Obolensky, 1961.

———. *Swimmy.* New York: Pantheon, 1968.

Tresselt, Alvin. *I Saw the Sea Come In.* New York: Lothrop, 1954.

Zion, Gene. *Harry by the Sea.* New York: Harper & Row, 1965.

MUSIC

"Mary Ann" in *Wake Up and Sing!* by Beatrice Landeck and Elizabeth Crook. Edward B. Marks, 1969.

"She Sells Sea Shells" in *Cock-a-Doodle-Doo! Cock-a-Doodle-Dandy!* by Paul Kapp. New York: Harper & Row, 1966.

"There's a Hole at the Bottom of the Sea" in *Eye Winker, Tom Tinker, Chin Chopper* by Tom Glazer. New York: Doubleday, 1973.

INDOOR ACTIVITIES

1. Display hermit crabs and fish and large, colorful pictures of sea life.
2. Provide trays of seashells for children to handle and examine.
3. Use seafood, such as tuna or shrimp, in cooking.
4. Salt water versus fresh water experiment:
   Have two glasses of water and a raw egg. Add two tablespoons of salt to one glass and stir. The egg will float in salt water and sink in fresh water.

OUTDOOR ACTIVITIES

1. Fishing pole (see "To name and describe single and plural objects," page 146).
2. Sand casting (see "To make sand castings," page 35).
3. Take a field trip to the beach or to a tropical fish store.
4. Have children form a circle. Inside the circle, children can take turns being sea animals, such as a crab, octopus, whale, or shark. Encourage them to think about how each animal moves through the water.
5. Drip sand castles:
   Very wet sand in dish pans can be dripped into fanciful castle shapes.

Seeds and Growing Things

ART PROJECTS

1. Make a seed collage.
2. Make prints with fruits and vegetables. (See "To use paint to make prints," page 21).
3. Sunflower:
   Cut colored-paper petals to paste on paper plate to make a sunflower. Use paper-punch dots for seeds or let the children draw them with a felt-tip pen.

STORIES

Galdone, Paul. *The Little Red Hen.* New York: Seabury, 1973. (Can be done as flannelboard story.)
Hutchins, Pat. *Titch.* New York: Macmillan, 1971.
Krauss, Ruth. *The Carrot Seed.* New York: Harper, 1945.

MUSIC

"The Garden Song" by David Mallett. Old Road Music, 1977.

"Growing" in *Learning Basic Skills Through Music, Volume 1,* by Hap Palmer. Freeport, N.Y.: Educational Activities, Inc.

"Oats, Peas, Beans and Barley Grow" in *Jim Along, Josie* by Nancy Langstaff and John Langstaff. New York: Harcourt Brace Jovanovich, 1970.

INDOOR ACTIVITIES

1. Plant seeds in a glass jar (see "Learning About Living Things," pages 224–232).
2. Grow sprouts (page 291).
3. Have sequence cards showing the development from seed to plant.
4. Using magazine pictures or real fruits and vegetables, discuss whether we eat the root (carrot), leaf (spinach), stalk (celery), or some other part.
5. Make peanut butter (page 287).

OUTDOOR ACTIVITIES

1. Prepare ground and plant a garden.
2. Plant grass in small containers for children to take home after it sprouts. Measure growth daily. Discuss a plant's need for sun, water, and soil.

Spring Around the World

All countries and cultures celebrate the coming of spring. Use all the following suggestions for an international theme or concentrate on one that will have meaning for your group.

ART PROJECTS

1. Japanese Cherry Blossom Festival (see page 381):
   Straw-blow branches and use pointer finger dipped in pink paint to finger-dot blossoms.

2. *Cinco de Mayo* — Mexican Independence Day (see page 369):
   Paint in bright red and blue a piece of paper cut in the shape of a fish. Attach string for kite.
3. Paper Bag *Piñata:*
   Papier-mâché an inflated balloon with several layers of newspaper. Last layer can be tissue paper. When *piñata* is dry, use a pin to pop balloon. Small trinkets can be taped on before the *piñata* is hung outdoors.
4. Foil Ornaments:
   Use aluminum foil pie tins or circles of foil wrap. Children can punch holes with dull pencils. Hang ornaments in windows or over lights.
5. *Holi* — Hindu Spring Festival:
   Using cut potatoes or felt shapes glued to wood blocks, print typical Indian motifs (fish, elephant, paisley, and others). Use traditional *Holi* colors of red and yellow.

STORIES

Ets, Marie Hall. *Gilberto and the Wind.* New York: Viking, 1963. (Mexico)

Joslin, Sesyle. *La Fiesta.* New York: Harcourt, Brace & World, 1967. (Mexico)

Keats, Ezra Jack. *My Dog Is Lost!* New York: Crowell, 1960. (Mexico)

Matsuno, Masako. *A Pair of Red Clogs.* Cleveland, Ohio: William Collins & World, 1960. (Japan)

Price, Christine. *The Valiant Chatee-Maker.* New York: Frederick Warne, 1965. (India)

Yashima, Taro. *Umbrella.* New York: Viking, 1962. (Japan)

MUSIC

"Dulce, Dulce" in *You'll Sing a Song and I'll Sing a Song* by Ella Jenkins. Folkway Records, 1966. (Mexico)

"He's Got the Whole World in His Hands" and "It's a Small World" in *88 Standard Children's Songs* by Charles Hansen. Educational Music and Books.

"Mexican Hand Clapping Chant" in *Little Johnny Brown* by Ella Jenkins. Scholastic Records, 1972. (Mexico)

"Purim" in *Music in Our Country* by James L. Mursell. California State Series, 1958. (Israel)

"Sakura [Cherry Blossom]" in *Songs that Children Sing* by Eleanor Chroman. New York: Oak Publications, 1970.

"Shalom Havarim" and "Zum Gali Gali" in *Songs that Children Sing* by Eleanor Chroman. New York: Oak Publications, 1970. (Israel)

INDOOR ACTIVITIES

1. With a globe or world map, discuss places where particular customs are celebrated.
2. Display typical clothing of various countries.
3. Ask a community member who celebrates the holiday you are discussing to visit and discuss its cultural meaning with the children.
4. Fold paper fans.
5. Discuss a typical cherry blossom parade. Display real cherry blossoms.
6. Make tortillas (page 284).
7. Discuss the fireworks and parades of *Cinco de Mayo*.
8. Explain that children in Israel dress in Biblical costumes for their spring festival.
9. Make *latkes* (potato pancakes). (See page 302.)
10. Show pictures of Indian children celebrating *Holi*, the spring festival that occurs just before monsoon season. The children shower each other with water or with powder that has been colored red and yellow.
11. Prepare a small assortment of spices that come from India: curry, cinnamon, dill, and coriander, for example. Let children smell them.

OUTDOOR ACTIVITIES

1. Have an international costume parade.
2. Fly fish kites (Japan).
3. Hang a *piñata* and let children try to break it with a broom (Mexico). Small trinkets that fall out will cause a scramble; be prepared to hand out extras!

Thanksgiving

ART PROJECTS

1. Make turkeys using stuffed paper bags for the body and attaching cutouts for the head, wings, tail feathers, and legs.
2. Make Indian headbands with cloth or construction paper.
3. Make Indian necklaces with colored macaroni.
4. Make collages with dried seeds, grasses, and paper scraps.
5. Make a mural showing the pilgrims' first Thanksgiving, or of the Mayflower crossing the ocean from England to Plymouth Rock.

STORIES

Baker, Betty. *Little Runner of the Long House.* New York: Harper and Row, 1962.

Balian, Lorna. *Sometimes It's Turkey — Sometimes It's Feathers.* Nashville, Tenn.: Abingdon Press, 1973.

Brustlein, Janice. *Little Bear's Thanksgiving.* New York: Lothrop, Lee and Shepard, 1967.

Dalgliesh, Alice. *The Thanksgiving Story.* New York: Scribner's 1954.

Kroll, Steven. *One Tough Turkey.* New York: Holiday House, 1982.

Williams, Barbara. *Chester Chipmunk's Thanksgiving.* New York: Dutton, 1978.

MUSIC

"The Landing of the Pilgrims" by Felicia Hemans in *190 Children's Songs* by David Nelson. New York: Robbins Music Co., 1967.

"A Song of Thanksgiving" from *Autumn.* Bowmar Records.

"Thanksgiving" in *Holiday Rhythms* by Lucille Wood and Ruth Tarner. Bowmar Records.

"Thanksgiving at Grandma's" by F. F. Churchill in *Growing with Music* by Harry R. Wilson. Englewood Cliffs, N.J.: Prentice-Hall, 1966.

INDOOR ACTIVITIES

1. Use a cornucopia filled with dried gourds, fruits, and vegetables as a large centerpiece for a display table.
2. Make popcorn, cook pumpkin, make a pumpkin pie or pumpkin cookies, make cornbread (see "Cooking Activities").
3. Grind up cranberries and oranges to make relish: one orange (wash and remove seeds, do not peel) to four cups cranberries, with one cup sugar or its equivalent in honey. Pack in small scalded baby-food jars as gifts.
4. Plan a Thanksgiving feast and invite friends and parents to participate.

OUTDOOR ACTIVITIES

1. Plant corn seeds.
2. Collect autumn leaves and discuss the colors and textures.
3. Visit a turkey farm.
4. Visit a junior museum or a center featuring Indian artifacts.
5. See "Native Americans" theme for additional ideas.

Transportation

ART PROJECTS

1. Print with spools to make a wheel picture.
2. Make boats by hammering or gluing wood scraps.

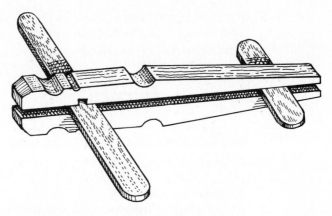

Illustration 9.7 **Clothespin toy airplane**

3. Clothespin Airplanes:
Use 1 spring-type clothespin and 1½ popsicle sticks for each airplane. Remove the wire spring and have children glue the popsicle sticks on the flat side of one clothespin half to make the wings and tail. The other clothespin half is then glued in place so that the two flat sides are matched. Let the airplanes dry thoroughly, overnight if possible, before children paint them. (See Illustration 9.7.)

STORIES

Alexander, Anne. *ABC of Cars and Trucks.* New York: Doubleday, 1956.

Burton, Virginia. *Mike Mulligan and His Steam Shovel.* Boston: Houghton Mifflin, 1943.

Lenski, Lois. *The Little Airplane.* New York: Henry Z. Walck, 1965.

———. *The Little Sailboat.* New York: Henry Z. Walck, 1965.

———. *The Little Train.* New York: Henry Z. Walck, 1965.

Rockwell, Anne, and Harlow Rockwell. *Thruway.* New York: Macmillan, 1972.

MUSIC

"The Bus Song," "Down by the Station," and "This Train" in *Eye Winker, Tom Tinker, Chin Chopper* by Tom Glazer. New York: Doubleday, 1973.

"Row, Row, Row Your Boat" in *Treasury of Folk Songs for the Family* by Tom Glazer. New York: Grosset & Dunlop, 1964.

INDOOR ACTIVITIES

1. Enlarge or change area for playing with wheel toys to encourage conversation and cooperative group play.

2. Display pulleys, gears, and wheels so that children can experiment with them. Discuss how principles on which they operate are used in machinery.

OUTDOOR ACTIVITIES

1. Set out a "train" of cardboard boxes and let children sell tickets and act as engineer, passengers, conductor, and so on.
2. Have children try to move a heavy box by pushing. Then put the box on a wagon and let them try again. Discuss the use of wheels to make it easier to move objects.
3. Go on a wheel hunt: How many wheels can you find in the yard? How are they used?
4. Fly paper airplanes.
5. Float milk carton boats in pans of water.

Valentine's Day

ART PROJECTS

1. Make valentines with red construction paper, fabric and paper scraps, doilies, lace, and other trim.
2. Make a valentine box.
3. Make a valentine mobile to hang in the school.
4. Make heart-shaped folders for each child's valentines.

STORIES

Anglund, Joan Walsh. *A Friend Is Someone Who Likes You.* New York: Harcourt Brace Jovanovich, 1958.

——. *Love Is a Special Way of Feeling.* New York: Harcourt Brace Jovanovich, 1960.

Cohen, Miriam. *Be My Valentine.* New York: Greenwillow Books, 1978.

Modell, Frank. *One Zillion Valentines.* New York: Greenwillow Books, 1981.

Schulz, Charles. *Be My Valentine, Charlie Brown.* New York: Random House, 1976.

MUSIC

"I Got a Letter This Morning" in *American Folk Songs for Children* by Ruth Seeger. Boston: Ginn and Co., 1961.

"Love Somebody" in *The Small Singer* by McLaughlin and Wood. Chicago: Follett, 1963.

"Valentine's Song" in *Songs for Learning Through Music and Movement* by Hap Palmer. Sherman Oaks, Calif.: Alfred Publ., 1981.

"Will You Be My Valentine?" by Betty Ruth Baker in *Piggy Back Songs* by Jean Warren. Everett, Wash.: Warren Publishing House, 1983.

INDOOR ACTIVITIES

1. Make a loving branch:
   Hang heart-shaped ornaments such as construction-paper hearts, Styrofoam with valentine decorations attached, Baker's clay hearts, and doilies on a small branch that has been painted white.
2. Distribute valentines from the box made in Art Projects.
3. Talk about the meaning of *Valentine* and who the children might want to remember on this holiday.
4. Make a large valentine to give to elderly or sick people in a local hospital or retirement home.
5. Make valentine cookies.

OUTDOOR ACTIVITIES

1. Paste hearts on windows. Spray edges with Glass Wax.
2. Use heart stencils to spray Glass Wax on windows.
3. Have children deliver valentines around the school yard on their tricycles.
4. Finger-paint outdoors with red paint on large sheets of white butcher paper attached to a wall or walk.

Winter Weather

ART PROJECTS

1. Make a snowman (see "To make soap snow," page 33).
2. Weather Wheel:
   Give children cardboard circles scored into sections. Have children draw or paste an umbrella, sun, clouds, kite, snowman — whatever seems appropriate for local weather. Attach pointer in center with a brad. Observe weather and move pointer to appropriate section each day. (See Illustration 9.8.)
3. Make blotter paper umbrellas (see "To make blotter art," page 25).
4. Paint a snow picture with white paint on blue paper.
5. Make bird feeders:
   a. Spread peanut butter on pine cones and hang outdoors.
   b. Fill scooped-out orange rind with bread and bird seed. Hang with cord sling.

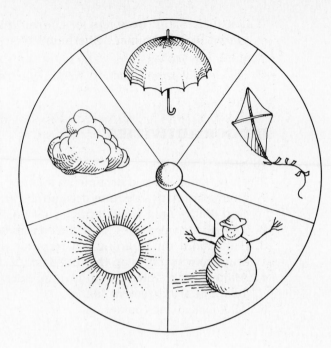

Illustration 9.8   **Weather wheel**

STORIES

Burton, Virginia. *Katy and the Big Snow.* Boston: Houghton Mifflin, 1943.

Keats, Ezra Jack. *The Snowy Day.* New York: Viking, 1962.

Shaw, Charles G. *It Looks like Spilt Milk.* New York: Harper & Row, 1947. (Good flannelboard story.)

Tresselt, Alvin. *Rain Drop Splash.* New York: Lothrop, 1946.

Welber, Robert. *The Winter Picnic.* New York: Pantheon, 1970.

MUSIC

"The Big Snowman" in *Creative Movement for the Developing Child* by Clare Cherry. Belmont, Calif.: Fearon, 1968.

"Little April Shower" by Larry Morey. Walt Disney Productions, 1942.

"Sky Bears" and "What Shall We Do?" in *Making Music Your Own* by Mary Tinnin Jaye. Morristown, N.J.: Silver Burdett, 1966.

INDOOR ACTIVITIES

1. Place a slightly dampened baking sheet in a freezer overnight. Remove from freezer and let children observe the crystals under a magnifying glass.
2. Crystals:
   Put ½ teaspoon alum and ¼ cup hot water in a glass and insert a

pipe cleaner. Crystals will climb the pipe cleaner over night. Provide a magnifying glass to observe the crystals.
3. Cut paper snowflakes.
4. Have a set of flannelboard figures with a selection of clothing appropriate for winter weather.
5. Rain Puddle Game:
Cut different sizes and shapes of rain puddles out of newspaper. Have each child take a turn walking around, jumping over, stomping through, and playing in them.

OUTDOOR ACTIVITIES

1. If there is snow, play in it! If not, provide cardboard sleds and skis for pretending.
2. After rain, look for signs of how plants, insects, and birds are affected by rain.

Complete List of Activities and Resources

Part Two   Music, Drama, and Movement

Part Three   *Math Experiences*

Part Four   *Language Arts*

Part Five   *The Physical World*

Part Six   Health and Safety

Part Seven   Cooking and Nutrition

Part Eight   *Computers for Preschoolers*

Part Nine   *Themes*

Student Response Form

We would appreciate hearing a little about your background and having your reactions to this fourth edition of AN ACTIVITIES HANDBOOK FOR TEACHERS OF YOUNG CHILDREN. Your comments and suggestions will help us to respond to the needs of users of future editions. Please complete this questionnaire and return it to

College Marketing
Houghton Mifflin Company
One Beacon Street
Boston, MA 02108

1. Do you like the format (large pages, spiral binding) of the *Handbook?*

   YES_____   NO_____

2. What material and features did you find most useful? _____
   _____
   _____

3. Which material or features were least useful? Why? _____
   _____
   _____

4. Are there too many or too few activities in each of the sections? Should new activities be added in the next edition?

	Too many activities	Too few activities	New activities needed (yes/no)
1 Art and Woodworking	_____	_____	_____
2 Music, Drama, and Movement	_____	_____	_____
3 Math	_____	_____	_____
4 Language	_____	_____	_____
5 The Physical World	_____	_____	_____
6 Health and Safety	_____	_____	_____
7 Cooking	_____	_____	_____
8 Computers	_____	_____	_____
9 Themes	_____	_____	_____

5. Did you find the directions for activities clear and easy to understand? _____

6. Did the bibliographies meet your needs? _____
   If not, what is lacking in these lists? _____
   _____

7. How could the book be improved? _____
   _____
   _____
   _____

8. What was the title of the course in which you used this *Handbook?* _____

9. Was this book used as a supplement to another text? _____
   If so, what was the name of that text and by whom was it written and published? _____

   _____

10. What other courses have you already taken in early childhood education? _____

    _____

11. Are you an undergraduate (if so, what year) or a graduate student (if so, have you done any teaching yet)? _____

12. Do you intend to keep this book to use in your teaching of young children? _____

    _____